Sir Sayyid Ahmad Khan and Muslim Modernization in India and Pakistan

Studies in Oriental Culture, Number 15
Columbia University

Sir Sayyid Ahmad Khan and Muslim Modernization in India and Pakistan

Hafeez Malik

Columbia University Press New York
1980

About the Author

HAFEEZ MALIK is Professor of Political Science at Villanova University in Pennsylvania. From 1961 to 1963, and from 1966 to 1980, he was Visiting Lecturer at the Foreign Service Institute of the U.S. State Department. His publications include *Muslim Nationalism in India and Pakistan* (Washington, D.C.: Public Affairs Press, 1963), *Iqbal: Poet-Philosopher of Pakistan* (New York: Columbia University Press, 1971), *Sir Sayyid's History of the Bijnore Rebellion* (East Lansing: Michigan State University, 1967).

From 1971 to 1974, he was President of the Pakistan Council of the Asia Society, New York. Also, he is Director of the American Institute of Pakistan Studies, the President of the Pakistan-American Foundation. Since 1977, he has been the Editor of the *Journal of South Asian and Middle Eastern Studies*.

Library of Congress Cataloging in Publication Data

Malik, Hafeez.
 Sir Sayyid Ahmad Khan and Muslim modernization in India and Pakistan.

 Bibliography: p.
 Includes index.
  1. Ahmad Khan, Syed, Sir, 1817–1898.
 2. Muslims—India—History. 3. India—History—
19th century. 4. Muslims—India—Biography.
 I. Title.
 DS475.2.A5M26   954.03′092′4 [B] 80-13905
 ISBN 0-231-04970-6

Columbia University Press
New York   Guildford, Surrey

With love to my son,
  Dean H. Malik,
  who inherits the noble traditions of
  the East and the West

Studies in Oriental Culture
Edited at Columbia University

Contents

Preface   ix

Introduction   1

  1. The Framework of Modernity   21

  2. Sir Sayyid's Political Socialization and Orientations   59

  3. Perceptions of 1857 and the Theory of Participatory Rule   103

  4. Muslim Reaction to Modern Education   125

  5. Mobilization of National Will for Modern Education   173

  6. Theory of Muslim Nationalism   229

  7. Religious Modernism   255

Epilogue   281

Appendixes   297

Notes   301

Bibliography   325

Index   333

Preface

IN THE DAYS of Islamic militancy, when the embassies of the United States are burned, and American diplomats become hostages, and the most sacred shrine of Islam in Mecca is occupied by the fundamentalists, a book on Muslim modernization is bound to raise eyebrows. Despite historical contacts between the west and the Muslim world, very little appreciation of Islam or the Muslim societies exists in the west. Precisely for this reason, when the political movements rock the world of Islam, the west is bewildered. In this book, I have endeavored to analyze the west's creative impact on the Muslims of South Asia. Muslims' response to the West has not always been hostile; they have made attempts to learn from the west and develop a symbiotic relationship. It is the arrogance of the west, and its uncontrolled passion for political domination which brings out hostile responses.

The structure of western domination, which lasted until 1945, has crumbled, and in its place a politically conscious new world has appeared to which the Muslims belong. In each Muslim society different kinds of revolutions erupt, which often pass under the rubric of Islam. The picture is indeed complex. One such revolution in "Muslim India" was that of modernization, whose fires were stoked by Sir Sayyid Ahmad Khan. In the long run, this revolution would prove to be creative and decisively shape the Muslim societies in India and Pakistan, and indeed in the larger world of Islam.

To complete this study I invested at least fifteen years, and for many more I have been comtemplating the dynamics of Muslim societies in the Middle East and Southwest Asia. Central Asian Muslims, whose ancestors in large numbers settled in contemporary Pakistan and northern India, have always fascinated me from a comparative perspective. Consequently, I have been able to examine the Indic Muslims' struggle for modernization in the larger framework of the Muslim world. This study, however, is not a descriptive history, but an integrative interdisciplinary investigation, employing the conceptual tools of the social sciences, including sociology, anthropology, and political science, that attempts to put in relief the profile of modern liberal Islam.

During the course of my research, I received cooperation from the British Museum and the India Office Library in London. I am fortunate to have friends here and abroad who generously helped me to collect Sir Sayyid's rare works. I am grateful to Professor Peter Hardy of the School of Oriental and African Studies in London who managed to get duplicate copies of Bader-ud-Din Tayabji's papers; and to Professor Azad-ud-Din Khan in India, who ransacked for me the bazaars of Aligarh, Lucknow, and Old Delhi to purchase at "any" price Sir Sayyid's published works or manuscripts. I am also grateful to Lynda P. Malik, my wife, for her expertise in sociology and the role of Islam as a cultural force in the modern world.

I would like to acknowledge the friendly help of Professor Stanley Wolpert, who read the entire manuscript and offered valuable suggestions to improve it. At Villanova University, I have always received generous assistance and cooperation from Fr. John M. Driscoll, President, and Dr. James Cleary, Vice-President. In a truly ecumenical spirit, Villanova University has played a pioneering role in promoting Pakistan and Islamic studies by supporting the American Institute of Pakistan Studies and the *Journal of South Asian and Middle Eastern Studies*.

Other friends and colleagues, particularly Dr. Justice Javid Iqbal, Sharif al-Majahid, Fred Khouri, Isma'il al-Faruqi, Jack Schrems, Robert W. Langran, Susan Hausman, Nadia H. Barsoum, and the late Dr. Hameed-ud-Din, gave me valuable assistance and encouragement. Many of the ideas contained in this study were sharpened as a result of challenging views expressed by American diplomats and government officials who attended my lectures at the Foreign Service Institute of the U.S. State Department during the last two decades. Many thanks to all of them.

HAFEEZ MALIK

Sir Sayyid Ahmad Khan and Muslim Modernization in India and Pakistan

Introduction

THERE ARE APPROXIMATELY two hundred and fifty million Muslims in South Asia. They are far more numerous than the total Arab population or the Muslim populations in Southeast Asia or the Soviet Union. Islam was introduced to Southwest and South Asia by the Umayyad Caliphate (661–750). In the year 700, Kabul, Afghanistan's present-day capital, was subdued. Four years later Khurasan was annexed as a province of the Caliphate. In the following years Turkistan and other adjoining areas were reduced. Centers of Buddhist learning and culture, including Bukhara, Balkh, and Samarqand, accepted Islam and became citadels of Islamic civilization. Through Baluchistan, in 710, the Umayyad power brought the Indus valley up to the borders of Kashmir into *dar al-Islam,* the land of Islam. In 1947, this area gave birth to the state of Pakistan.

I

Muslim power spread in India, from the eleventh-century invasions of Sultan Mahmūd (1014–1030) of Ghazni to the consolidation of the Mughal Empire in the sixteenth century. During this period, central Asian Muslims settled in various parts of India, and the Sufis won over the population of Bengal to Islam. With Hindu converts accepting Islam and joining the Muslim culture, there developed an Indic Islamic community, which is now split into the three independent states of Pakistan, India, and Bangladesh.

With the decline of the Mughal power in India during the eighteenth century, the British started to conquer the empire in 1756, when they took over the province of Bengal. From then on, as in other Muslim lands in the world, humbled Muslims in South Asia confronted the brave new world of western Christendom. Historically, the two worlds had acted and reacted with each other since the inception of Islam in the seventh century. However, in the perception of the west a confrontation had existed with the east from time immemorial. In the dawn of history it was represented by the contest between the Greeks and the Persians, and later it centered on the duel between the Romans and the great Hellenistic monarchies. In the Middle Ages the confrontation was represented by the struggle between the dynamic forces of Islam and those of Christianity. Currently, a relentless struggle for dominance continues between the forces of democracy and communism.

In the Middle Ages Islam took the initiative to pressure the west. From the conquest of Jerusalem in 638, under the leadership of Caliph 'Umar ibn al-Khattāb (634–644), Islam was on the march toward the west. In the eleventh century a Muslim state was established in Byzantine territory within striking distance of Constantinople, another in Sicily whose incursions reached Rome, and a more powerful one in Spain, from which Muslims conducted raids into France for nearly two centuries. From the ninth through the twelfth centuries Islam had also absorbed the main features of Persian, Semitic, and Hellenistic civilizations. Muslim scholars, including Arabs, Persians, and central Asians, not only translated Greek and Indian sciences into Arabic, but enriched them with their own original contributions and then transmitted them to Europe via Spain. This historical process eventually helped to bring about the Renaissance in Europe.

In the eleventh century, the west endeavored to reverse the political tide of Islam. Pope Urban took the initiative in 1095 to launch the first crusade against Islam. In a public meeting at Clermont in France the Pope exhorted his fellow Christians:

Let western Christendom march to the rescue of the east. Rich and poor alike should go. They should leave off slaying each other and fight instead a righteous war, doing the work of God, and God would lead them. For those that died in battle there would be absolution and the remission of sins. Life is miserable and evil here, with men wearing themselves out to the ruin of their bodies, and their souls. Here they are poor and unhappy; there they would be joyful and prosperous and true friends of God. There must be no delay. Let them be ready to set out when the summer had come, with God to be their guide.[1]

This was probably the most powerful speech ever delivered in medieval times, which presented a doctrine of counter-*jihād*. The motives which inspired the crusades were curiously mixed, blending the hunger for territorial acquisition, commercial expansion, romantic adventure, and salvation through penance.

The crusades lasted from the eleventh to the fourteenth century. Before their inception the center of civilization was considered to be in the lands of Islam; after the crusades faded out, hegemony in science and culture began to pass to the west. Starting with the sixteenth century, the Caliphate of Islam passed to the Ottoman Turks, when Sultan Salim I conquered Egypt in 1517 and received the caliphal title of *Amīr al-Momenīn* (leader of the faithful) from Motawakil al-Hakim, the last descendant of the Abbasid caliphs. For nearly two and a half centuries the Ottomans had been what the European historians called "the scourge of Christendom." However, at the gates of Vienna in 1683, with the timely help of the Polish king, John Sobieski, the west stopped the onward march of the Ottomans. Subsequently, the Habsburgs and the Czars inflicted a series of defeats upon the Turks. The Treaty of Azov, dictated by Russia in 1707, offered conclusive evidence that the political tide had turned against the lands of Islam. Finally, the powerless "sick man of Europe" was allowed in the European diplomatic framework by the Congress of Paris in 1856.

The Ottoman power, at its zenith, especially in southeastern Europe, blocked the expansion of western power and trade in the east. Consequently, the west discovered a new route to the east when in 1498 Vasco da Gama opened a sea route to India skirting the Cape of Good Hope. This route was successively dominated by the Portuguese, the Dutch, and the English. However, by the nineteenth century the Ottomans could no longer stop the expansion of western imperialism.

What were the motivations for imperialism? Justifications for empires and imperialism were many and varied, including: racism, duty toward "backward people," missionary zeal, fortune-seeking, adventure and the lure of the exotic, a sense of pride, a lust for power and territorial acquisition, and commerce. Lenin offered his now classic explanation of imperialism

as a special stage of capitalism in which the domination of monopolies and finance capital has taken shape; in which the export of capital has acquired pronounced importance; in which the division of the world by the international trusts has begun, and in which the partition of all the territory of the earth by the greatest capitalist countries has been completed.[2]

Writing in 1879, one year after the Congress of Berlin had very nearly eliminated Turkish power from Europe, the 84-year-old German historian, Leopold von Ranke, described the imperial triumph of the west over the east:

The Ottoman Empire has been mastered and penetrated in all directions by the spirit of Christianity. If we talk of the spirit of Christianity we do not only have in mind religion. The words "culture" and "civilization" also would express it very incompletely. It is the genius of the Occident. It is the spirit that transforms peoples into organized armies, builds roads, digs canals, covers the oceans with navies and transforms them into possessions and fills the distant continents with colonies. It explores the depths of nature through exact research, takes possession of all fields of knowledge, and continually renews them by fresh efforts without losing sight of the eternal truth which administers order and law among men in spite of the variety of their passions. We see this spirit in a state of extraordinary progress. It has won America from the rough forces of nature and intractable peoples. It pushes into the most remote Asia. China is hardly closed any longer and Africa is surrounded on all her shores. Irresistibly, in many guises, unassailably, armed with weapons and science, the spirit of the Occident subdues the world.[3]

II

How did the Muslims respond in the nineteenth century to the triumphant march of western civilization? Theoretically independent, but in reality subdued by the west, the Ottoman empire (including the Arab provinces) and Iran responded positively to western modernity. At the peak of their political power the Ottoman elites believed their institutions to be superior to those of the west. However, after 1832 the Turkish elites adopted two principles of reform: (1) that modern European society, based on science and technology, was superior to that of the Ottomans; therefore, its new institutions and methods should be adopted; and (2) the old Ottoman institutions should be destroyed as they were replaced. Consequently, the Tanzīmāt (Reorganization) reforms of 1839 were initiated to usher in modernization, secularism, and the breakdown of the traditional way of life.[4] In Egypt, Khedive Isma'īl (1863–1879), "an enlightened despot striving to make his country part of Europe," created the first Egyptian "parliament" in 1866, promulgated the Primary School Law in 1868, and in July 1871 established the House of Sciences in Cairo, where Egyptian and European scholars delivered public lectures on Qur'ānic exegesis, Islamic law, and Arabic literature, but also on botany, physics, astronomy, mechanics, architecture, and the railways.[5]

Like Ottoman Turkey, and Egypt, the ruling elites in Iran, in cooperation with their Shah, selectively adopted western technical, cultural, and political institutions. During the nineteenth century modernization was primarily the work of Mirza Taqi Khan Amīr-i Kabīr (during 1848–1851), Shah Nasir-ud-Din (during 1848–1896), and Mirza Husain Khan Sipahsalar (during 1870–1873). Amīr-i Kabīr, who became Chief Minister (1848) of 16-year-old Shah Nasir-ud-Din, established in 1851 the Polytechnic College in Tehran. The college contained departments of medicine, mining, engineering, and military sciences. Mirza Husain Khan had spent many years as a diplomat to India, Russia, and Turkey, and was eagerly receptive to modern progressive ideas. As Prime Minister he established the cabinet system, reorganized the army, and restructured the provincial administration. In 1873 he persuaded the Shah to undertake the first of his three journeys to Europe "for the purpose of observing the European way of life in order that His Majesty may introduce more benefits for the people of Persia." [6] After each of these visits a number of western innovations appeared in Iran.

One by one, central Asian Muslim states were absorbed into the Russian empire: Tashkent was taken in 1865, Bukhara in 1868, Khiva in 1873, Geok-Tepe in 1881, and Merv in 1884. Two streams of thought spread rather widely among the Muslims of the Russian empire: Islamic modernism, and socialism. During the course of his stay in Russia from 1886 to 1889, the well-known pan-Islamic leader, Sayyid Jamal-al-Din Al-Afghani (1838–1897) not only obtained the Czar's permission to have the Qur'ān and other Islamic books published in the Russian empire, but also inspired many "Russian" Muslims to actively participate in jadīd (modern) Islam, which endeavored to reconcile scientific and industrial progress with religion. [7] Six "Russian" Muslims, including five Tatar and one Uzbek—Shihab-ud-Din Marjani (1818–1899), Isma'īl Bey Gasprinski (1851–1914), Mūsā Jarallah Bigi (1875–1949), Abdullah Bubi, Abdur Rashid Ibrahimov, and Abdur Rauf Fitrat—became the leading figures in the progressive and liberal national movement. The Imam of the St. Petersburg mosque, Bigi, believed that Communism was compatible with Islam, and could be absorbed philosophically in Islam. [8]

Like the modernists who learned to exercise liberal ijtihād

(the right of interpreting the Qur'ān and the *sunna* or of forming a new opinion by applying analogy), and rejected *taqlīd* (submission to traditional authority), socialist Muslims tended to cast socialist ideas in the light of their own national conditions. This approach evolved, after the Bolshevik Revolution, into the doctrine of national Communism. Central to this doctrine, as developed by the Volga Tatar Muslim, Mīr Saʿīd Sultan Galiev (1880–1939), was the concept of "proletarian nations," as opposed to the proletarian class. With this socialist *ijtihād,* Sultan Galiev and his associates, notably Burhan Mansurov (d.1937), and Mulla-Nur Vahitov (1885–1918), attempted to integrate "Marxist nationalism" with Islam and to devise an "eastern strategy" whereby the national revolution was to spread.[9] Tolerated temporarily, these doctrines and their exponents were eventually crushed by the Soviet Union. Muslim republics in Central Asia were not modernized until the 1930s, when the Soviet development plans began to industrialize them.

North Africa came under French domination, and the British extended their influence to the Sudan. In the Sudan the Mehdiyya movement (1881–1899), being the ideological nucleus of a fundamentalist universal Islamic state, was opposed to modernization, which had been introduced earlier in Egypt and later in the Sudan by the British. In 1899 the British and Egyptian governments established a condominium government over the Sudan. During the first thirty years of the condominium more than 170 military expeditions were sent to crush Mehdist uprisings, most of which were messianic in nature. The memory of the Mehdi of Sudan inspired new mehdis to appear in Nigeria and Somalia, where they fought the British well into the twentieth century.[10]

South and Southeast Asia were incorporated into the British and Dutch empires, where their imperialism was fiercely resisted. In Indonesia, the Dutch exploited Muslim sectarian conflicts to extend their rule. In Sumatra the returning Muslim pilgrims popularized *wahhabism,* which had already established fundamentalist Islam in Arabia in collaboration with the House of Ibn al-Saud. Opposing customary laws in order to establish the

Shari'a, the Indonesian wahbabi purists touched off the *padri* wars in the Minangkabau area of Sumatra during 1785–1838. The Dutch policy was designed to give customary law precedence over Islamic laws, and it restricted contacts between Indonesians and the larger Muslim world. This divisive policy inadvertently enabled Islam to associate with Indonesian national culture as a focal point of revolt against the Dutch.[11] This association continued through the various Indonesian revolts and uprisings of the Dutch period until freedom was won in 1950.

In South Asia, where the British started the process of conquest in 1756, Muslim reaction graduated from hostility to enthusiastic cooperation with the forces of modernity, especially after 1857, when India was finally conquered. In early nineteenth century Shah 'Abdūl 'Azīz (d.1823), the son of the savant of Delhi, Shah Walīy Allah (1703–1762), declared India *Dar-al-Harb* (the land of war) for the Muslims. In response to this declaration, Muslims, under the leadership of Sayyid Ahmad Shahīd (1786–1831) and Isma'īl Shahīd (1779–1831), started a war of liberation in the borderlands of India. In 1830 they established an Islamic state, which included parts of Afghanistan and the Northwest Frontier Province of contemporary Pakistan. There the *Shari'a* was enforced as the law of the land, and the people followed Sayyid Ahmad Shahīd as "the promised messiah."[12] The Sikhs, who had established themselves in the Punjab on the ruins of the Mughal power, destroyed this Islamic state, but Shahīd's followers continued the resistance even against the British, who had defeated the Sikhs in 1849.

Firmly committed to cooperation with the British, Sir Sayyid Ahmad Khan (1817–1898) emerged after 1857 as a modernizing leader, at a time when the British believed that Muslims in India were bound by conscience to spurn British authority and western civilization. Like the Muslim modernists in Central Asia and the Ottoman empire, Sir Sayyid espoused the causes of: (1) rationalism in Islam, which established a new orientation—that religion existed as an aid to man's progress, and man did not exist just for religion; (2) social reforms patterned after western culture; (3) modern education through English, and (4)

Muslim nationalism. Sir Sayyid's thesis emphasized also that (5) civilizations do not belong to nations, but to man. Consequently, progress and prejudice could not mix. To achieve the goals of his normative values, Sir Sayyid endeavored to establish Muslim-British rapproachment in India.

This orientation pitted Sir Sayyid against Jamal-al-Din Al-Afghani, an inveterate foe of British imperialism. Both were modernists, but with a difference. A true Muslim internationalist, who had risen above the bonds of nationalism—to this day a controversy rages whether Afghani was born in Iran or Afghanistan—Afghani urged Muslim states to adopt western science and technology, and to unify under one Caliphate (Ottoman or otherwise) in order to resist western imperialism. Sir Sayyid would have no part of the Caliphate, especially Ottoman, and he espoused science and technology, not as weapons against the west, but as benefits to be integrated into Muslim culture.

How the Muslims could modernize themselves without being identified in any degree with western civilization was a dilemma that Afghani and his followers had failed to resolve or even recognize. Afghani's ideology galvanized the Muslims in Central Asia, the Middle East, and Indonesia. Even in India, Muslims responded fervently to Afghani's call of pan-Islamism. Sir Sayyid remained a Muslim nationalist, deprecating his fellow Muslims' involvement in the extraterritorial romance of pan-Islamism. Cooperation with British imperialism was an historical necessity to Sir Sayyid, which an "outsider" like Afghani could not appreciate.

III

In contemplating the political landscape of the Muslim world, one can conclude that by the end of the nineteenth century modernist Islam and fundamentalist Islam had firmly established their orientations. In the twentieth century secularism emerged, first in Turkey, and then in some Arab states. The political processes in the contemporary Muslim states can be classified in light of

this tripartite typology. It might be well for policy-makers in the
west and elsewhere to appreciate the profile of each in order to
design appropriate instrumentalities of understanding and interaction.

For the secularists, especially in Turkey, the ideological
transformation was not easy. However, once the Rubicon was
crossed, the secular orientation was easy to defend. The Islamic
state became defunct, and pragmatism was elevated to the status
of ideology. Recognizing ethnic, linguistic, and geographical distance between Muslim states, the secularists abandoned the ideal
of pan-Islamism. Some secularists believed that Islam could
adopt selectively some features of western democracy and of
Marxism/socialism, and reconcile them with its own tenets.[13] At
this point in time (1980), Syria and Iraq under the Ba'th parties
seem to partially fill this description, while Turkey continues to
style itself as secular.

Indian Islam in the 1930s and 1940s presented an extraordinary dilemma in as much as most of the fundamentalist parties
and Islamic seminaries, including Jami'at'ulamā'-i Hind, Majlis
Ahrār (in the Punjab), and Dar al-'ulūm Deoband, preferred
Indian secularism to Islamic Pakistan. Jama't-i Islami actively
campaigned against the creation of Pakistan, arguing that an Islamic state would "jail" Islam in a limited territory, and that
modernist Muslims would not be able to create a "truly Islamic
state." After 1947, Jama't-i Islami became the leading exponent
of the Islamic state in Pakistan.

In the recreation of an Islamic state, the fundamentalists, like
an American School of judicial review, invoke the doctrine of
"original intention." The original paradigm of an Islamic state,
in the eyes of Sunni Muslims, was established by the Prophet
Muhammad (571–632), and by his four "rightly guided" successors from 633 to 661. This paradigm existed concretely over a
span of 50 years, since the Prophet Muhammad was called to
prophecy in 611 at age 40. Successor Caliphates, Umayyad
(661–749), Abbasid (749–1258), and Ottoman (1517–1920), are
generally viewed as monarchies, deceptively labelling themselves
as Islamic states in order to acquire legitimacy. Consequently,

the fundamentalists extrapolate from the paradigm of this 50-year period, seeking literal truth in the Qur'ān and the *Sunna*. In the interpretation of both, they seek the original intention of the Prophet and his four successors.

In the nineteenth and twentieth centuries the fundamentalist leaders produced a prodigious amount of literature. On the extreme right of the political spectrum are the works of Muhammad 'Abd al-Wahhāb (1703–1787) in Saudi Arabia; Sayyid Ahmad Shahīd and Isma'īl Shahī in India; and Muhammad Ahmad (1844–1885), the founder of the mehdiyya movement in the Sudan. To them any compromise with modernity amounted to mixing "good" with "evil." More moderate fundamentalists, recognizing the need to change, included in their ranks Abul Kalam Azad (1888–1958) at least until 1920; the founder of Jama't-i Islami, Abul A'la Maudūdi (1903–1979) in India and Pakistan; Hasan al-Bannā' (1906–1949), the Egyptian founder of Ikhwan al-Muslimīn (Muslim Brotherhood), and his followers, Sayyid Qutb in Egypt, and Shaikh Mustafa al-Siba'ī in Syria.[14] A profile of their paradigm can be sketched.

The Islamic state must be headed by an elected Caliph, either for life or a specified term. He should appoint ministers to conduct public administration, delegate his judicial power to an independent judiciary, and organize the armed forces under the guidance of a professional general. However, the Caliph himself remains the final arbiter of all state power. The *Shari'a* becomes the supreme law of the land, rigidly enforcing the Qur'ānic laws: (1) family laws (inheritance, divorce, and custody of children), (2) welfare laws (*zakā, 'usher,* and *jizya,* the latter to be levied on non-Muslim citizens in lieu of their exemption from military service), (3) penal laws (involving amputation of hand for theft, and capital punishment for adultery), (4) financial laws (right to own property, and interestless banking). In guaranteeing the right to private ownership of the means of production, distribution, and exchange, this paradigm (perhaps unwittingly) projects capitalism as an Islamic economy. Laws not specifically defined in the Qur'ān can be legislated by an elected assembly of Islamic experts. In the fundamentalists' eyes they alone are the experts;

others would only corrupt the Islamic state. Consequently, state-craft becomes the exclusive preserve of the *'ulamā'*, the fundamentalist scholars.

In the fundamentalist orientation the Qur'ān appointed the Muslims as guardians over humanity, and granted them "the right of suzerainty and dominion over the world" in order to enforce "goodness" in all societies. Describing the western civilization as "materialistic," the fundamentalists project Islamic civilization as "spiritual," which morally justifies Muslims' hegemony over others. Scientific education, which is recognized as the base of power for western civilization, is heartily encouraged. The fundamentalists believe that for the modern sciences of meteorology, astronomy, botany, geology, and biology, there are appropriate allusions in the Qur'ān. The scientific view is not necessarily to be integrated into the culture, but science is to be an instrument for establishing Islamic superiority.

No contemporary Muslim state can fit into this fundamentalist paradigm. Saudi Arabia, often described as a fundamentalist state, is only a monarchy—not entirely an Islamic state—even though it is committed to the application of the *Sharī'a* while the state's economy is being modernized by the technocrats. In Pakistan, the pious façade of an Islamic state conceals the reality of the unpopular and by definition unrepresentative character of the military regime since July 1977. Actually, the only state which comes close to the fundamentalist paradigm is Iran, which has adopted a new constitution reflecting a Shi'ite interpretation of Islamic fundamentalism.

Shi'ite fundamentalism considers the first three caliphs—Abū Bakr (632–34), 'Umar (634–44), and 'Uthmān (644–56)—as "usurpers" and views the fourth caliph, Ali ibn Abi Tālib (656–61) and his descendants from Fatima, the Prophet's daughter, as the only legitimate *imams* (the Shi'ite term for caliphs). The Shi'ite paradigm thus shrinks to a lesser span of time, since the 12 *imams,* the lineal descendants of Ali, never ruled over any state, but provided spiritual guidance from their retreats. The principal subdivisions among the Shi'ites are the so-called "twelvers" and "seveners." This division took place after the death of the sixth *imam*, Ja'fer al-Sādiq (d.765); the "twelvers" acknowledged his younger son, Mūsa al-Kāzim, and the "seveners" supported the claim of the elder brother Isma'īl. The minority followed Isma'īl, whose descendants established the Fatimid Caliphate in Egypt (969–1171 A.D.). These Isma'īlīs now live in India, Pakistan, Soviet Central Asia, Syria, the Persian Gulf, and East Africa. The majority (the "twelvers") are located in Iran.

The twelfth *imam*, Muhammad Hujjat Allah, surnamed al-Mehdi (the guide) disappeared at age 5. No *imam* has been elected since 879 because the disappearance of al-Mehdi, his absence (*ghayba*), did not mean that he had perished. The doctrine of the *ghayba*, and of his final return as the *mehdi* (guide), to dispense justice and righteousness in a world now full of sins, forms the basis of the "twelvers" creed. During the *imam*'s absence, the creed and the law are interpreted by the *mujtahids* (scholars, i.e. the ayatollahs), who act as the *imam*'s agents. Currently, there are in Iran 12 ayatollahs—6 being the grand ayatollahs. Ayatollah Khomeini is one of the most eminent ayatollahs.

The Iranian constitution (1979) has established the "twelvers" Shi'ite Islam as the state religion, and recognized "Ayatollah al-'Ozma Imam Khomeini," the Leader (*Rahbar*) in the absence of Imam Muhammad Hujjat Allah. Theologically, Khomeini is an *imam* surrogate since the line of *imams* cannot continue in the "hidden presence" of al-Mehdi. Also, the Constitution established three branches of government: (1) judiciary; (2) the 270-member legislature (with members to be elected by citizens for 4-year terms), containing a 12-member Council of Guardians, who would make sure that laws repugnant to the Qur'ān and the "twelvers" creed are not enacted; (3) executive, containing the (a) president, and (b) prime minister and his cabinet. Constitutionally responsible for coordinating the functions of the three branches of the government, the president is neither head of the Iranian state nor head of the government. Elected for life, the fountainhead of Iran's sovereign power is the *Rahbar*, who legally represents the hidden *imam*'s will. Politically, the *Rahbar* Khomeini exercises this power by virtue of his charisma,

which, according to article 5 of the Constitution, includes the
qualities "of a just and God-relient *faqīh* (jurist par excellence),
bravery, tact, and sagacity that the overwhelming majority of
people have recognized in his leadership." In the event of the
Rahbar's death, his sovereign authority devolves upon a 3- or 5-
member council of leadership (*shura-i Rahbari*). Again a Leader
would emerge, once having achieved recognition of the leadership qualities defined in chapter I of the Constitution.[15] In theological terms such a leader would function, like his predecessor,
in the name of the "hidden" *Imam*.

The extent to which the Iranian fundamentalist paradigm
achieves success, will depend upon whether the fundamentalists
can establish their credentials as leaders capable of manipulating
modern geopolitical problems diplomatically, and the social and
economic problems of their state pragmatically. They have succeeded as revolutionaries; whether they succeed as builders of a
stable and progressive Islamic Iran remains to be seen.

Overawed by the political and scientific superiority of the
west in the nineteenth century, the modernists were anxious to
learn from the west. The modernists in the Ottoman empire and
in "Muslim India" came to look upon Western civilization as
genuinely superior to their own. Their approach emphasized reason as against futile endeavors to recreate the past, and the concept of national progress, guided by science and technology, became the main preoccupation of all modernists. In Central Asia,
the modernists used the same mode of thought to reconcile socialism with Islam.

In the twentieth century the modernists developed a "love/
hate" orientation toward the west. The love reflected the conviction of some modernists that "the representative institutions
evolved in the west a practical method by which Islamic democracy can find concrete form in the large populations of today."[16]
Hate for the west, shared with the fundamentalists, developed
because of imperialist domination. In most Muslim countries
anti-Soviet and antiwest sentiments run very deep; that is why
the world movement of nonaligned nations contains practically
every Muslim state. In the Middle East the advent and expansion

of Israel, attributed entirely to the power of the west, further
sharpens antiwestern attitudes, from which the Soviet Union
benefits. Since 1973 the skyrocketing price of oil has reflected, to
a large extent, a mood of economic warfare against the West.
The Muslim modernists, like the fundamentalists, are thus committed to freeing "the Islamic spirit of the East, and to breaking
the shackles imposed by the West." In this psychological milieu
the modernists are making an ideological attempt to reestablish
Islamic identity vis-à-vis capitalist bourgeois democracy and the
dictatorship of the proletariat in the Communist societies.

Since the end of the world imperialist system in 1945 the
modernists (who generally inherited power from the imperialist
powers) have grappled with the problems of political development. Nowhere have they succeeded in establishing a viable Islamic system, while they have practiced "functional secularism."
Pre-1978 Iran, Egypt, Afghanistan, and Pakistan are the prime
examples. Most modernist Muslim states, and most noticeably
Pakistan, share four problems of political development:

(1) *Political Instability and the Search for Legitimacy:* They have
not developed institutions for the peaceful transfer of political
power. Military or one-party dictatorships have prevailed, causing serious problems of legitimacy. In Weberian formulation, legitimacy transforms naked power into authority, which is accepted and obeyed without resort to coercion. Without
legitimacy no polity can develop a meaningful capability for conflict resolution, and govern without resistance. Thus, the creation
of legitimate order is considered to be the essence of political development in modern times.

To cope with the problems of political instability and the
usurpation of power by the military *juntas,* Muslim scholars as
well as judges have relied upon the doctrine of necessity. An "Islamic" version of it was developed by Ibn Tamiya (1263–1328),
and Ibn Khaldun (1332–1406) stating that any Muslim government, no matter how it attained power, was legitimate as long as
it ruled according to the *Shari'a,* and consulted the *'ulamā',* the
recognized interpreters of the Canon Law. A more modern and
western variation was adopted from Hans Kelsen's doctrine of

"revolutionary legality." In the judgments[17] of the Supreme
Court of Pakistan, Kelsen's doctrine (twisted and tortured according to some) figured prominently, while one could also detect muted undertones of Ibn Tamiya's and Ibn Khaldun's formulations.

In 1954 an autocratic governor-general of Pakistan, Ghulam
Muhammad, dissolved the constituent assembly by proclamation, "because it had become unrepresentative." In reality, the
Assembly was about to adopt a constitution of which he disapproved. To resolve this deadlock, the Supreme Court established
the doctrine of necessity, validating Ghulam Muhammad's action. However, the minority judgment maintained that the law
of necessity applied only "in times of war or other national disas-
ter."

Again in 1958 an autocratic president, Iskander Mirza,
abrogated the 1956 constitution. Chief Justice Muhammad Munir
once again invoked the doctrine of necessity. Calling the coup
d'etat a revolution, he stated, "if the revolution is victorious in
the sense that the persons assuming power under the change can
successfully require the inhabitants of the country to conform to
the new regime," then the successful new regime becomes a
valid "law-creating fact."[18] This formulation could have easily
invoked Ibn Tamiya and Ibn Khaldun.

A similar scenario was reconstructed in July 1977, when the
Chief of the Army Staff, General Zia-ul-Haq removed Prime
Minister Z. A. Bhutto from office and imposed Martial Law on
Pakistan. Pakistan's Supreme Court heard the petitioner's attor-
ney, Yahya Bakhtiar, contend that General Zia's action
"amounted to treason under Article 6 of the 1973 constitution."
Defending General Zia, Pakistan's eminent lawyer, A. K. Brohi,
brought a Kelsenian flourish to his argument. He described the
coup d'etat of July 5 as a *"new grundnorm"* and an "extraconstitu-
tional fact which attracted the doctrine of revolutionary legality."
Supporting Brohi, Pakistan's Attorney-General Sharifuddin Pirzada relied upon the doctrine of necessity, and assured the Supreme Court that General Zia was "to remain in power for a
limited period in order to prepare the ground for the holding of

open and fair national and provincial elections for the establish-ment of a democratic, civilian government." Describing this coup d'etat as "a phase of constitutional deviation,"[19] the Su-preme Court once again upheld the doctrine of necessity. Sub-sequently, General Zia reneged twice on his promises to hold elections, in October 1977 and in November 1979, t'us calling into question the legitimacy of his Martial Law regime.

Obviously, armed forces in Pakistan and in other Muslim countries do not realize that frequent recourse to military rule has a debilitating impact upon the growth of representative govern-ments. Also, it encourages dissident and minority parties to seek military support when they refuse to solve political problems by political means. In achieving short-term stability at the expense of legitimate and stable representative institutions, the generals delude themselves into thinking that they make any contribution to the political development of their societies. The judges are remiss in legitimizing every usurpation of power by ambitious bonapartes. The doctrine of necessity has earned no credit for the modernists.

(2) *Lack of Distributive Justice and Economic Underdevelopment:* They have not been able to develop economically or industrially to cope with the population growth. Granted that in some of the modernist states scarcity of natural resources has hampered their annual rate of growth; however, mismanagement, lack of mass participation, as well as lack of the peoples' representation in the decision-making, have been equally important factors. And the capitalist mode of economy has generated uneven distribution of national wealth. A philosophical view of industrialization has also developed among the modernists. To them, industrialization as a technique of production is ideologically neutral. It would yield results impartially in democratic, autocratic, or Communist politics. This approach provides an additional justification to the modernists for one-party rule, which is visible in Syria, Iraq, Egypt, and Iran under the Shah.

(3) *Ethnic Tensions and Lack of Political Participation:* There is a lack of national identity in some of the modernizing states' provinces and citizens, who do not feel that they have equitable

participation in the collective life of their states. This negative orientation is disrupting the national fabrics of Pakistan, Iran, Afghanistan, and Iraq. Each state is multi-ethnic, and each one confronts periodically an ethnic revolution repudiating territorial nationalism, which is officially fostered, and the concept of Islamic solidarity, which is encouraged to cement ethnic cohesion. None of these states has evolved any pragmatic policy to ensure parity of participation, and parity of esteem for their ethnic or regional communities. Consequently, cessationist movements have flourished, which are exploited by the foreign powers for their own geopolitical aims. Also, these states share their ethnic minorities with the Soviet Union (see table). This situation also shows a relative deprivation, both cultural and material, which the ethnic groups endure across the boundary lines.

ETHNIC DISPERSION AMONG SOME MUSLIM STATES AND THE SOVIET UNION

Ethnic Community	USSR	Iraq	Iran	Afghanistan	Pakistan	Divided Among States
Pashtun				x	x	2
Baluch		x		x	x	3
Nuristani (i.e., Kalash)				x	x	2
Kurd	x	x	x			4 (including Turkey)
Tajik	x			x		2
Kurghis	x			x		2
Turkoman	x	x	x	x		4
Uzbek	x			x		2
Aimak				x	x	2
Hazara				x		1
Qashqais			x			1
Arabs		x	x	x		3
Bakhtiaris			x			1
Lurs			x			1
Azerbaijanis	x		x			2
Punjabi (Muslim)					x	1
Sindhi (Muslim)					x	1
Kashmiri (Muslim)					x	2 (including India)
Total 18	6	3	9	10	6	36

In other words, a total of 18 ethnic groups are divided 36 times among 5 states. This calls for the development of innovative constitutional and economic arrangements between Iran, Afghanistan, and Pakistan, where ethnic groups would comingle to develop new transnational orientations.

(4) *Lack of Civil Rights and Ideological Identity:* There is a marked failure in defining the citizens' rights and privileges vis-à-vis the state, and in presenting a clear ideological image to the world. Despite an ideological emphasis on egalitarianism, all Muslim societies are vertically oriented, with power and privilege reserved for the classes on top of the social pyramid. Power is adored, and the equality of opportunity is rarely assured, except in the *nouveau riche* oil states, where opportunity is doled out to ensure dynastic interests.

IV

A bit of future gazing might be in order. Which particular orientation of Islam—fundamentalist or modernist—will decisively shape the future of the Muslim world? At present, the fundamentalist orientation seems to have the lead. But this will prove to be a short-lived phenomenon. Tracing the original intent of the Prophet and that of his associate(s) is beyond human capability, despite the *'ulamā's* claims to the contrary. Undoubtedly, the fundamentalist *'ulamā'* represent class interests, and at some point in time, they will be judged accordingly. The modern age demands more complex technical, as well as intellectual, capabilities, which cannot be acquired through traditional Islamic education. Consequently, the Iranian or Saudi fundamentalists must fall back upon the skills of modern technocrats. Equipped with modern technology, the armed forces cannot function in light of the fundamentalist ethos; their organizational structure and orientations reflect the modern west rather than the Islamic past. Despite Islamic injunctions the fundamentalists have not been able to establish interestless banking, or evolve an Islamic fiscal system. The fundamentalist paradigms of the Islamic state have yet to stand the crucible of success in the modern age.

The fundamentalists' fervent appeal to an idealized past attracts a large following. Also, they capitalize on the modernists' failures and accuse them of being secularists. In an emotionally charged Muslim world they generate militancy and draw a disproportionate amount of attention. But are they innovative and creative? Can they rethink and update Islamic orientations to cope with the future? Limited in their scope of *ijtihād,* the fundamentalists fail to recognize that the Muslim states are not a separate world unto themselves, but belong to that web of interdependence which the modern industrial and scientific age has evolved. The future will be shaped by the modernists, by men like Sir Sayyid, who conquered their prejudice and considered civilization the heritage of man. They alone can build bridges of understanding between Muslim and non-Muslim societies.

In the foreseeable future, the dialectical tensions between the fundamentalists and the modernists will accentuate, and their following will switch back and forth like a pendulum. Failure of either or both will strengthen secularist forces in the Muslim world, as happened in Turkey; but that is far off on the horizon.

I

The Framework of Modernity

THE BRITISH EAST INDIA COMPANY conquered Bengal in 1756, but it was not until after 1857 that the Muslims in India significantly responded to the cultural thrust of the West. Out of the internal dynamics of traditional Muslim society appeared Sir Sayyid Ahmad Khan (1817–1898) who realistically grasped the challenge of modernization which British rule had brought to India. He led the Muslims to enter the stream of modernization through four avenues of reform: political, educational, religious, and social. Like other pioneers of modernity in Asia and Africa, he used journalism to communicate with his fellow Muslims. His intellectual legacy is abiding, even though his tactics are no longer relevant. However, in order to appreciate his role it might be well to define modernization, its limitations and promises for Indic Muslim society.

With the liquidation of empires after World War II, scholars began probing the West's impact on Asia. Arnold Toynbee led the way in his phenomenal work, *A Study of History*. For Toynbee, modernity had begun toward the end of the fifteenth century when Western man "thanked not God but himself that he had outgrown his medieval, Christian discipline."[1] The development of a rational outlook is then the watershed between the traditional and modern eras of societal development, and it was marked in the West by the advent of science. Toynbee assigned to the middle classes the decisive role in evolving modern institutions from their medieval setting. However, during the sixteenth century the dynamic movement toward the understanding of nature was well under way. Consequently, Western societies coped with the challenge of modernity at a leisurely pace, over a period of several centuries.

In emphasizing the twin processes of commercialization and industrialization in modernization, David Apter highlights their social consequences in the following paradigmatic categories: "the growth of lending and fiscal devices, the need to support modern armies, the application of technologies in competitive market situations, and the influence of trade and voyages on the scientific spirit—all of which are evidence that modernity in the West attacked religion and superstition, family and Church, mercantilism and autocracy."[2]

In India the process of modernization was not initiated by any altruistic considerations. Commenting on the economic and communication infrastructure established by the British, William Wilson Hunter, a member of the Indian Civil Service and a younger contemporary of Sir Sayyid, wrote in 1862:

When the railway system is completed the efficiency of our English troops will be increased twenty-fold, and besides this, the growth of commerce and internal wealth which railways foster will be of itself a better security for the stability of our Indian Empire than all the legions of England and all her batteries of Lancaster guns. It is something for posterity to wonder at, our scheme of keeping India, not by the strength of our right hands, not by scourging with whips and scorpions, but by making the people who rebelled against us bless the day we conquered them."[3]

The moral of the story is that modernization often unleashes social and political forces which the initiators subsequently find impossible to control.

In a nutshell modernization is what Lucian W. Pye has defined as the world culture: "it is based on advanced technology and the spirit of science, on a rational view of life, a secular approach to social relations, a feeling for justice in public affairs, and above all else, on the acceptance in the political realm of the belief that the prime unit of the polity should be the nation-state."[4] An analysis of Sir Sayyid's approach to history and his view of the Muslims' social and political problems reveals that his life was devoted to the ideal of modernity. To him the nineteenth century was characterized by science, which had made possible the development of a superior technology in the West, facilitating the establishment of its hegemony over the East. For Sir Sayyid, Britain's political domination in India was not ensured merely by brute force. Rather, it reflected the triumph of modernity over tradition. Deploring traditionalism, he often defined it as Islamic obscurantism, that is, an attitude of mind which resisted the spirit of free inquiry and confined the Muslims within the narrow limits of a stultifying past, even when they knew that it hampered the growth of their culture and personality in India.

For the Muslims, Sir Sayyid believed, an encounter with science was not a new experience. During the period of the Abbasid Caliphate (750–1258) Islamic civilization had been enriched by Greek sciences; Muslims also made their own original contributions, and then via Spain transmitted this intellectual legacy to Europe, where it proved to be the catalyst for the Renaissance. Thus Sir Sayyid evolved a theory of cultural diffusion, which justified within an Islamic frame of reference the acceptance of modern sciences and national progress.

Sir Sayyid grasped the challenge of modernity slowly, and appreciated its possibilities for the Muslims after his visit to Britain in 1869. During his formative years (1817–1857), which were mostly spent in Delhi, he remained a traditional Muslim, largely seeking validation of his convictions and behavior by reference to generally established prescriptive Islamic norms. Most of his historical and religious treatises including particularly trivia on sufism, such as *Namīqā* (1864) and *Kalmāt al-Haq* (1850), and the biographical sketch of the Prophet Muhammad, *Jila'al-qulūb bi dhikr al-Mahbūb* (1842), reflected traditional views on mysticism, and the supernatural powers of the Prophet. Subsequently, most of these views disappeared under the scrutinizing glare of rationality. Sir Sayyid and the Muslim society in Delhi were exposed to modernity by virtue of their contact with the tiny British society and the modern Delhi College, which were established in Delhi with the advent of the British rule in 1803. The British rule not only introduced Delhi's citizens to a new subject culture, but also initiated a period of social mobilization which prepared the Indic Muslims, especially after 1857, to accept the process of change from traditional to modern ways of life. A glimpse of traditional Delhi confronting the carriers of modernity would shed light on the early environment of Sir Sayyid.

Traditional Muslim Society in Delhi

Delhi was built by the Mughal Emperor Shah Jahan (1628–1658) in 1648. The town with the Red Fort received the name of Shah-jahhan-Abad, and was built on the Jamna river to the north of Firozabad. Gradually the town became known simply as Delhi, and later, after the construction of the British Raj's New Delhi in 1911, as Old Delhi. A wall five and a half miles long with seven gates surrounded Old Delhi. The central axis was the Chandni Chawk, the legendary avenue of the silversmiths, 69 feet broad. It led from the Fort's entrance to the Fatahpuri Mosque, which was built by one of Shah Jahan's wives. In 1658 Shah Jahan constructed the beautiful Jamia Masjid, which became the focal point of Muslims' religion activities. Old Delhi, which Sir Sayyid knew, was (and still is to a certain extent) the town of colorful bazaars and craftsmen, the meeting place of the merchants, and had long and narrow alleys leading to the neighborhoods of the workers and the mansions of the rich.

Delhi was not a very populous city. When the British came in 1803 the population was estimated to be 150,000. It increased to 208,000 in 1901, only three years after Sir Sayyid's death. Before 1857 the Muslims had a numerical edge over the Hindus. The relationship between the two was harmonious, while both communities maintained their cultural identity. However the focal point of Hindu-Muslim cultural synthesis was the Red Fort, where the Mughal kings and princes liberally adopted secular Hindu mores and folkways, and the citizens of Delhi emulated the royalty. Describing the cultural patterns of Delhi's Muslims, Sir Sayyid's namesake, Sayyid Ahmad Dehlawi, (1846–1918) says: "All the customs of Muslim women, and because of them the customs of Muslim men, are almost all of Hindu origin. Some of the customs have been adopted without any change; for some, though original names have been retained, their styles have been changed. In some cases change is only in name; some have been integrated even in religious matters with only a slight change in the nomenclature."[5] On the occasions of birth, circumcision, engagement, marriage, and even death, according to the eyewitness accounts of pre-1857 Delhi Muslim culture, Hindu and Muslim women sang the same folk songs.

Intermarriages between the princes of the Red Fort and Hindu nobility were not uncommon. The royal precedent was established by Emperor Akbar (1556–1605), whose successor and son Jahangir was born in 1569 to his Hindu wife, the daughter of Raja Bihari Mal of Amber. Jahangir married Jodh Bai (whose maiden name was Jagat Goshaini and was also called Balmati), who became the mother of Emperor Shah Jahan (1592–1666). Even devout Aurangzeb married a Hindu lady and so did his successor and son Bahadur Shah I. This royal tradition was maintained by the father and grandfather of the last Mughal Emperor, Bahadur Shah II (1837–1857), whose mother's name was Lal Bai.[6] All of these Hindu ladies were converted to Islam, yet through them and their Hindu relatives, patterns of Hindu culture were diffused into the culture of the Red Fort. However, the Muslim culture also made inroads into the Hindus' cultural patterns. A majority of them adopted Urdu as their tongue, some learned Persian and Arabic, and a few even achieved recognition as accomplished poets of Urdu and Persian. Hindus also visited the tombs of the Muslim saints in order to seek their blessings and to make their offerings in homage. Some Hindus also adopted the Muslim dress, particularly the *achkan* (long fitted coat), and the *pajama* (loose trousers). Thus came into existence the unique phenomenon of Delhi—the Hindustani culture, which subsequently the nationalist school of Indian historians generalized to mean "the All-India composite culture," indicative of the Muslims' assimilation into the Hindu culture.

After 1803 Delhi was a parasitic city, and so was its population. The Muslim society was hierarchical, and the tradition of *noblesse oblige* was still alive. In fact within the Muslim society two cultures coexisted—the *Karkhanadar* (worker) culture, and the *Sharīf* (refined and superior) culture (see Figure 1.1). They interacted on the margins of economics and religion. The term *Karkhanadar* applied comprehensively to workers of all grades:

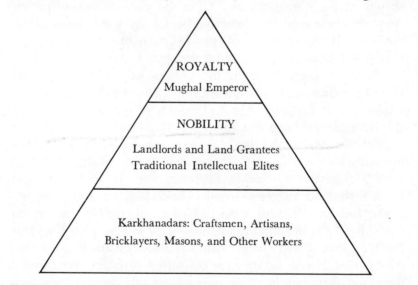

FIGURE 1.1 SOCIAL STRATIFICATION OF MUSLIM SOCIETY (DELHI: 1803–1857)

craftsmen, artisans, tailors, bricklayers and masons of all kinds, *tonga*-drivers, washermen, barbers, and domestic servants.[7]

Karkhanadars lived in separate neighborhoods, and had a subculture of their own. Unlike their Hindu counterparts, the *Karkhanadar* women observed pardah (seclusion from public gaze), and lived a very confined and humdrum existence. The monsoon rains pouring out of black clouds eased the oppressive heat of Delhi and often moved these women to find expression in folk poetry. Their reaction consisted of long-drawn-out verbal duals with neighbors, which started each morning when husbands departed for work, and terminated promptly at the end of the day, when husbands returned. Thus came into existence many intriguing and exquisitely abusive expressions, which are preserved in the corpus of folklore. Only the washerwomen were expected to move out of their homes to fetch soiled clothes from the *sharīf* families. They alone had access to the *zanana* (female quarters), where they delivered the laundered clothes and received wages. This contact improved the speech and manners of washerwomen, and created in them a measure of self-confidence and tact. Laundry was delivered after long intervals, providing an opportunity for the washerman's family to wear decent clothes. The *sharīf* families knew all about it, but what could they do? Reprimands and open threats of terminating the service were answered by a disarming adroitness on the part of the washer women. Regular losses of new and expensive clothes were written off for the loyal services.[8]

Karkhanadars' cockney Urdu was racy and spicy. They always rolled up several words into one, and had a difficult time pronouncing certain Arabic and Persian letters of the Urdu alphabet; *waqt* (time) in their pronunciation was always *wakhat;* *matlab* (meaning) was *matbal;* and *jaldi* (haste) was *zaldi*. Names were similarly corrupted and abbreviated; *shams ud-Din* was invariably *Shamū; Arshad* or *Irshad Husain* was simply *Shadū;* and *wazir-ud-Din* became *Wazīra*. They did have zest for life and after a day's hard work they enjoyed cock fights or flew kites or watched champion wrestlers' fights on the banks of the Jamna river. On Fridays (Muslim Sabbath) no one worked; after mid-

day congregational prayers the *Karkhanadars* enjoyed town gossip
on the steps of the Jamia Masjid or they drifted towards the
Chandni Chowk, strolling along the brightly lit avenue, where
they would buy a few inexpensive things or simply window
shop. Especially during the summer nights they seldom returned
home till long after midnight. Most of the *Karkhanadars* were
poor and lived strictly from hand to mouth. They married early,
aged quickly, and died early.

   Karkhanadar children hardly ever acquired any education,
and were left unattended to form a street corner society of their
own. They passed the time in horseplay and light-hearted banter,
occasionally engaging in gang wars. Their games varied from
season to season, but they were always loud and boisterous and
could never be confined to their own neighborhoods.[9] Consequently, the members of the *Sharīf* culture held them beneath
contempt. Poets despaired of their shrieks, piercing their peaceful
world, and the *Sharīf* parents dreaded the thought of their children ever mingling with the *Karkhanadar*—children who would
not only spoil their polite manners and morals, but corrupt the
chaste pronunciation of their Urdu. Like other children of the
Sharīf culture, Sir Sayyid learned to eschew their company early,
and retained the dread of "low-class servant boys" all his life.

Mughal Royalty

Pyramidal in shape, the *Sharīf* society consisted of three strata:
the royalty, the nobility, and the traditional intellectual elites.
The royalty was headed by the three kings, including Shah Alam
(1759–1806), Akbar Shah II (1806–1837), and Bahadur Shah II
(1837–1858), who succeeded each other during 1803–1857. The
royalty was housed in the Red Fort. Isolated from the surrounding world by its own wall of red sandstone 52 feet high, the Red
Fort (which still stands) was almost a thousand yards long and
half as wide. During the first decade of the nineteenth century
the fate of India was sealed there.

   The Marathas, whom Emperor Aurangzeb had described as

rebels and "mountain rats" and fought against for 27 years (1680–1707), had become the masters of Delhi and the Red Fort from 1785 onwards. Madho Rao Sindhia, the Maratha chief, who had actually been invited to Delhi by Emperor Shah Alam's ministers to help them, had established his hegemony by his appointment as Deputy Regent of the Empire. Emperor Shah Alam thus became a Maratha dependent, and a pensioner. Ghulam Qadir (Rohila), the grandson of legendary Najib-ud-Daulah, nurtured a deep resentment of Shah Alam, who had devastated his ancestral estate in alliance with the Marathas.[10] Ghalam Qadir had in fact been castrated by the Emperor's orders. Taking advantage of Sindhia's absence from Delhi, Qadir attacked Delhi in 1788, and on August 10 avenged his "honor" by blinding Shah Alam.[11]

Qadir also humiliated the imperial family by stripping the women naked, and then beating them. Some women threw themselves over the high walls of the Red Fort, and were drowned in the river Jamna below. The floors of the apartments were dug up, and all the articles were seized. Shah Alam was left without care, even without meals (except coarse bread and water) for seven days. Also, the old queens of Emperor Muhammad Shah were evicted from their apartments, and confined in one of the bastions for several days. Although Qadir was subsequently defeated and executed by the Marathas on March 3, 1789, Mughal royalty and prestige were damaged beyond repair.

The Marathas had alloted the blind Emperor, according to the British sources, Rs. 600,000 annually for his and that of his dependents' expenses. But soon complaints were heard that the Marathas not only defaulted in their assumed financial obligations, but also tightened the grip of their military rule over Delhi. Not knowing the rules of realpolitik, in utter naiveté prince Jawan Bakht addressed a letter[12] in 1787 (probably with the connivance of his father, Shah Alam) to King George III of Britain, saying:

We . . . casting our eyes towards future events, and the mercies of divine providence in this stormy ocean of our distress, rely on your

Majesty for the restoration of our authority; and if your Majesty, who adorns the throne of the universe, will graciously condescend to issue your high commands to the Governor-General to effect the restoration of the royal House in these kingdoms, punish our rebellious subjects, and re-establish the august house of Timoor [Mughal dynasty], such conduct will be perfectly consistent with the dictates of generosity and the usages of sovereign princes.[13]

This letter was never forwarded to Britain, but the British came to the Emperor's rescue in 1803, when the Maratha-British hostilities broke out. On September 7, 1803, Lord Lake advanced on Delhi and defeated the Maratha army, and on September 16 was admitted into the Emperor's audience. The East India Company deliberately established an ambiguous legal relationship with Shah Alam. The Company wanted "to secure the prestige of the Mughal name without any admission of its superior authority."[14] On July 27, 1803, Lord Wellesley, in a personal letter to Shah Alam, said:

If your Majesty should be disposed to accept the asylum which I have directed the Commander-in-Chief to offer . . . your Majesty may be assured that every demonstration of respect and every degree of attention which can contribute to the ease and comfort to your Majesty and the Royal Family will be manifested, and that adequate provision will be made on the part of the British Government for the support of your Majesty, your family and household.[15]

Lord Lake, the victorious Commander-in-Chief, however, wrote to Emperor Shah Alam promising "to render your Majesty every demonstration of my loyalty and attachment and I consider it to be a distinguished honor, as it is a peculiar privilege, to execute your Majesty's commands."[16] While the Governor-General sought to make the Emperor his protege and a vassal, the Commander-in-Chief of the British East India Company presented himself to be an instrument of the Mughal Emperor's sovereignty.

The British allotted Rs. 60,000 monthly for Emperor Shah Alam's personal expenses, and granted the total provision of eleven and a half lakhs [Rs. 1,600,000] a year. The so-called Assigned Territory, situated to the west of the Jamna river, was earmarked to raise this money. Its management was to be in the hands of the British Resident at the Court of Delhi. In Delhi two sets of courts were established: one revenue and another criminal, and in the latter *shari'a* (Islamic law) was administered. *Qadis* and *Muftis* were appointed to these courts. However, the capital punishment was to be confirmed by the Emperor.[17]

This legal arrangement inaugurated a new political era for Delhi's citizens, Political authority was polarized: while the *de facto* ruler was the Resident, the *de jure* ruler was the Mughal Emperor, who was sovereign only in the Red Fort, where he continued to reside. *Pax Britannia* brought peace and security not only to the citizens of Delhi, but also to the Royal family in the Red Fort. Thus came into existence the subject political culture, which lasted throughout the nineteenth and the first two decades of the twentieth century, when the British Government initiated constitutional reforms which involved the citizens in the political processes of India. Meanwhile the citizens developed an "affective orientation"[18] to the subject political culture, enjoying simultaneously the peace it established, while resenting the humiliation of a rule by a foreign power.

The residents of the Red Fort lived in a make-believe world and developed a social stratification of their own. The Emperor was a class unto himself; *Shah-zaday* (king's sons) and *Shah-zadiyāñ* (king's daughters) stood below him. Emperor Shah Alam had thirteen sons and fourteen daughters, while his successor, Akbar Shah II, had a total of fourteen sons and daughters. Bahadur Shah II, the last Emperor, had twelve sons. They constituted the upper class in the society of the Red Fort. They were allotted generous allowances and had the privilege of standing in rows on either side of the throne in the court. They were not men of sagacity or learning; they were pompous and vainglorious, and lived on the illusory grandeur of the past. Then came the descendents of former Emperors and princes, who were called *Salatīn*. In 1836 the number of *Salatīn* receiving pensions from the Emperor's allowance was 795. In 1848 their total number was 2,104. The Red Fort was thus overcrowded, since each member of the Royalty insisted on the privilege of living within the Fort. In 1856 only 45 out of 130 living sons and grandsons of the former Emperors lived outside the Red Fort.[19] Most of them received a very meager allowance from the Emperor, but they maintained the facade of imperial grandeur. Describing the *Salatīn's* ghetto in the Red Fort, Major George Cunningham wrote in an official dispatch that

within this are numerous mat huts in which these wretched objects live. When the gates were opened there was a rush of miserable, half-naked, starved beings who surrounded us. Some men apparently eighty years old almost in a state of nature, who from the earliest infancy had been shut up, others young men, some sons of kings whose mothers had died—others young children who had only the space within these walls to look forward to as their world.[20]

The brothers and uncles of the reigning Emperor were kept in confinement, but their economic condition was better than other *Salatīn,* since they received larger allowances. They were not allowed to attend the court. The *Salatīn's* quarters in the Red Fort were surrounded by a high wall so that no one could see its internal decay and misery; thus it was physically isolated from the Emperor's ápartments. *Salatīn* as a class were poorly educated, and lacked any technical or administrative ability or experience. Although they enjoyed prestige and sympathy in Delhi, the lower stratum of *Salatīn* was probably no better off than the skilled *Karkhanadars.* The Mughal Royalty's ineptitude and social uselessness was partly the product of the subject political culture, which was superimposed by the British rule. The Emperors had no administrative control in Delhi and the areas which were nominally under their jurisdiction. They had no share in the decision-making process during the East India Company's Residency in Delhi; and administration was vested in the Residents. In denying jobs or useful occupations to the Royalty the Company made the *Salatīn* social and economic parasites; lack of education and grace eventually discredited them in the eyes of the people.

The three last Emperors were generally considered to be men of letters, although Shah Alam was by far the best in his literary accomplishments and political skill. As pensioners of the Company they abdicated their political roles, except for Bahadur Shah II, who was willy nilly drawn into the whirlwind of 1857. Literary pursuits were the only occupations left to them, providing harmless outlets for their creativity. Consequently, Urdu poetry had a lush flowing in this age. Shah Alam was an accomplished poet in four languages—Urdu, Hindi, Punjabi and Persian. Mirza Muhammad Rafi Sawda, and Mirza Muhammad Fakher Makiyn, two contemporary masters of Urdu and Persian poetry, were known to have corrected Shah Alam's verses.[21] Shah Alam's Persian elegy composed on the loss of his eyes expresses personal anguish as well as vanished glory, and in literary terms is far more effective than Bahadur Shah's Urdu elegy composed in his lonely exile to Rangoon. A few verses from Shah Alam's elegy demonstrate his poetic talent:

> Lo, the dire tempest gathering from afar,
> In dreadful clouds has dimm'd the imperial star,
> Has to the winds, and broad expanse of heaven,
> My State, my royalty, and kingdom given;
> Time was, O King, when clothed in power supreme,
> Thy voice was heard, and nations hailed the theme;
> Now sad reverse, for sordid lust of gold,
> By traitorous wiles, thy throne and empire fold.[22]

Some of Shah Alam's poetical works and one prose work are extant: a copy of his *Persian Diwan* is preserved in the manuscript collection of the British Museum in London, and another is owned by Bihar Research Society in Patna. (To the best of this author's knowledge the *Persian Diwan* has not been published.) Azad has pointed out that Shah Alam composed four Urdu Diwans, but they are no longer available; nor is his poem, *Manzūwm-i Aqdas,* describing the story of a Chinese Emperor. *Nādirat-i Shahi,* which was edited and published by Imtiaz Ali Khan Arshiy in 1944, contains Shah Alam's Hindi and Punjabi verses both in Devanagri and Urdu scripts. Also, it is an invaluable source of information regarding the religious and secular ceremonies of the Hindus and the Muslims, which were integrated into the culture of the Red Fort.

Professional poets in residence at Shah Alam's court often cruelly exploited the blind monarch. Azad has described poet Insha Allah Khan's (died 1817) subtle "beggary," which invariable succeeded in emptying Shah Alam's pockets.[23] His son Akbar Shah was also known to have written poetry and had adopted *Shū'a* as his pen name. Though bearing the lofty name of his illustrious ancestor, Akbar Shah was a man of modest ability and composed occasionally modest poetry. His son Bahadur Shah, however, was not only an accomplished poet and an author of an Urdu Diwan, but was a patron and contemporary of the best masters of Urdu and Persian poetry including Ibrahīm Zawq, Asad Allah Khan Ghalib (1797–1869), Hakīm Momin Khan Momin (1800–1852), Nawab Ghulam Mustafa Khan Shaiftah, Mufti Sadr-ud-Din Azurdah, and Imam Bakhsh Sahbai'y. The period of the last three Emperors produced Urdu poets par excellence, and their works are collectively described today as the classical poetry of Urdu.

Not having the substance of power and grandeur, the Emperors dulled their sensitivity by punctiliously observing the imperial protocol; and to fill the abundance of leisure time, they celebrated at least 28 ceremonies, and religious and secular holidays annually. Four of these holidays—Dussehra, Diwali, Holliy, and Rakhri Bandhan—were strictly Hindu. The annual celebration of the Emperor's coronation lasted for forty days. Members of the *Sharīf* culture, both Hindu and Muslim, were invited to banquets in the Red Fort and elaborately feted. On the tenth day *Tawray Bandiy* took place, when trays containing from 2 to 22 varieties of food were sent to *Sharīf* families. Actually the prestige and rank of the *Sharīf* families determined the quantity and variety of food. On a *Ratjagah* (a sleepless night) the Emperor and the queen fried seven portions of *dal* (lentils) and distributed them among the invited guests, thus hoping to ward off the evil eye from the imperial family.

During the month of Muharram the Emperor turned himself into a *faqīr* (mendicant) in the name of Imam Husain, the grandson of the Prophet Muhammad, who was mercilessly martyred in Karbala in 680 A.D. Wearing a green dress, and a long chain of silver around his neck, the Emperor deemed it an honour to be dragged around by two Sayyids (the descendants of the Prophet). On the eighth of Muharram the Emperor played the role of a water carrier in the name of Abbas (an uncle of the Prophet Muhammad). Wearing a red *lungī* (loin cloth) of a coarse material, and carrying a *mashak* (water container made of leather) the Emperor roamed around the Red Fort distributing cold water to thirsty residents.[24]

The women of the Red Fort were utterly superstitious. For any natural or man-made problem the remedy in their eyes was to be sought in making offerings to the mausoleums of Muslim saints in Delhi and elsewhere. Out of this bent of mind came into existence a ceremony called *Phūl Walluñ Key Seyr* (a promenade of the flower gatherers) during the reign of Emperor Akbar Shah II. Mirza Jahangir, the favorite son of Akbar Shah, had picked a quarrel with the Resident, Mr. Seton. The quarrel developed into a battle, and Mirza did not surrender until Seton stormed the imperial palace with the British troops. Consequently, he was banished to Allahabad as a State prisoner. To obtain his release from the British prison, Mirza's mother, Nawab Mumtaz Mahal, vowed to place a cover of flowers with all the befitting pomp and show at the mausoleum of Khawja Qutb-ud-Din Bakhtiyar Kaki, which is located in the town of Qutb Sahib (Mehrolly), about ten miles from Delhi. Meanwhile, Mirza behaved well at Allahabad and was allowed to return to the Red Fort. In order to honor her vows, Akbar Shah accompanied Mumtaz Mahal to Qutb Sahib and distributed a large quantity of food to the poor. Hindu and Muslim citizens of Delhi also came to share the joy of the first family. Akbar Shah was pleased and announced that it would be an annual event henceforward. This secular fair was also celebrated annually by Bahadur Shah.[25] After 1857 it was all but forgotten, only to have reappeared most recently in the capital of the Republic of India.

Admittedly, the Emperors' lavish spending on these cere-

monies and holidays defied principles of prudence and economics; but the ceremonies served a social purpose. They maintained the Royalty's bonds of social solidarity with the citizens of
Delhi, who, regardless of their religious and cultural differences,
held the Emperors in esteem and affection. Also, contacts diffused intercultural values, which influenced the cultural patterns
of both Hindus and Muslims.

Muslim Nobility and the Elites

The nobility constituted the second stratum of *Sharīf* society. As
a class the nobility of this period included the descendents of
former Mughal *mansabdars*. The *mansabdars* were civil and judicial
administrators, and military commanders of varying ranks. For
their services they received temporary estates, which enabled
them to draw their salaries and defray other expenses. After 1803
mansabdari as an administrative institution virtually ceased to
exist; it was superseded by the British army and the covenanted
service, which came to be known as the Indian Civil Service
(I.C.S.) after 1857. Although the I.C.S. was largely patterned
after the *mansabdari* system, its personnel was exclusively British.
The East India Company in most cases recognized the land
grants of the *mansabdars'* descendants, and allowed fixed pensions
for some, especially if they had rendered military or political services. The *Umara,* as the members of the nobility were collectively called, were thus economically tied to the Company's rule.
    Although numerically small, the *Umara's* political role since
the death of Emperor Aurangzeb Alamgir in 1707 had been significantly responsible for the decaying fortunes of the Mughal
Empire. With the exception of a few *Umara,* most of them kept
personal interest ahead of that of the Empire. Until the rule of
Aurangzeb a majority of them were foreign born, and organized
themselves into a party vis-à-vis the Indian born. Like Sir
Sayyid's ancestors the *Umara* had come from Central Asia; re-
taining their central Asian culture they kept Persian as their
mother tongue and maintained their non-Indian character. However, during the reign of the last three Emperors the *Umara's* de-

scendants spoke Urdu and called themselves "the Muslims of India." Despite their decline and reduced fortune the Umara lived affluently; the best of them even lived grandly.

Delhi's 36 districts were named after illustrious nobles who had lived during the reigns of early Mughal kings. In the residential districts of the nobles many "splendid palaces" were seen by the British visitors, where the descendants of former mansabdars still lived. Among the big palaces were those of Qamer-ud-Din Khan, Minister of Emperor Muhammad Shah (1719–1748), Ali Mardan Khan, Nawab Ghazi-ud-Din Khan, Sa'dat Khan, and that of Dara Shukoh, the elder brother of Emperor Aurangzeb. These palaces were surrounded by high walls, and their entryways led through arched gateways of brick and stone. On the top were music galleries, attended by professional musicians. In front of the residential apartments were spacious courtyards for the elephants and horses, and the servants of the visitors. Female apartments were separated by a wall and had access through private corridors. All of them had gardens with fountains to adorn the center. Each palace was provided with a set of bathrooms, and a basement. Built of chaste marble, the bathrooms actually consisted of several rooms into which light filtered through "glazed windows at the top of the domes." The basements were built with marble to escape from the heat of Indian summers, and consisted of several apartments.

The Umara's houses were located in the area between the Jamia Masjid and the Red Fort. Two streets were especially prestigious, noted William Francklin, a British visitor in 1793–94:

the first leading from the palace gate through the city, to the Delhi gate, in a direction north and south. This street was broad and spacious, having handsome houses on each side of the way, and merchants' shops well furnished with a variety of richest articles. Shah Jahan caused an aqueduct of red stone to be made, which conveyed the water the whole length of the street. . . . The second grand street entered in the same manner, from the palace to the Lahore gate, lying east and west, it was equal in all respect to the former.[26]

The world of the Umara was secure, although intellectually sterile. Some of them indulged in poetry to pass the leisure time.

As a class they had failed to cope with the new political and cultural challenges, and certainly had no appreciation of the dynamic qualities of the Western culture which basically threatened their own Central Asian culture. A large number of the *Umara* were annihilated by the British as a retribution for their support of Bahadur Shah in 1857. Not satisfied with the *Umara*'s slaughter, the victorious soldiers of the Company took out their vengeance against the neighborhood, and demolished each lofty house. (Now that area is called *maydān* [the plain] in one corner of which is located the simple and graceful tomb of Maulana Abul Kalam Azad [1888–1958], the first Minister of Education in Jawaherlal Nehru's cabinet.) Only a tiny fraction of the *Umara* survived, including some of the relatives and chief minister of Bahdur Shah, who remained loyal to the British cause. Sir Sayyid belonged to this class, and despite his commitment to modernity his personality reflected both the virtues and vices of this class.

The intellectual elites, who constituted the third stratum of *Sharif* society, represented the ten well-known traditional professions. As a class they were economically dependent on the nobility and the royalty, and the latter leaned on them for intellectual nourishment and moral support. In the first edition of *Athar al-Sanadīd,* a pre-1857 archeological study of Delhi, Sir Sayyid included a chapter on the most successful and well-known of the traditional intellectual elites.[27] These obsolete elites, even in the period of decay and fall of Muslim power (1803–1857) in India, reflected the kinds of arts and scholarship most admired by Muslim society. They present a vivid contrast to the kind of modern Muslim elites Sir Sayyid and his Aligarh Movement subsequently helped to create in India (see Table 1.1).

Actually, since Aurangzeb's time the caliber of the intellectual elites was also declining; however, *Sharif* society not only thought well of itself, but also considered its intellectuals as the best. Sir Sayyid extravagantly complimented these elites, saying:

People of [this city] do not have their counterparts in any other lands; here every individual combines in him thousands of virtues and is a nosegay of innumerable arts; and one and all they are dedicated to

TABLE 1.1. TRADITIONAL MUSLIM INTELLECTUAL ELITES (DELHI: 1803–1853)

Categories in Order of Their Prestige	Relative Number	Source of Income
(1) *Mashaikh* (mystics living in Monasteries or Mosques)	18	Monthly stipends by the Mughal Emperor, princes; members of the nobility; public offerings
(2) *Rasūl Shahi* (mystics who renounced worldly connections and shaved hair from all parts of their body)	4	Public charity
(3) *Majzūb* (mystics in trance who have completely renounced worldly connections)	8	Public charity
(4) *'Ulamā'-i Kirām* (physicians)	12	Employed by the Mughal Emperor; princes; members of the nobility, landlords; fees for professional services
(5) *'Ulamā'-i Din* (religious scholars)	29	Stipends from the Mughal Emperor; princes; landlords; members of the nobility; land endowments for schools; offerings of the students; a few employed by the British East India Company
(6) *Qurrā wa Huffāz* (cantors and memorizers of the Qur'ān)	5	Stipends from the Mughal Emperor; princes; members of the nobility; landlords; public offerings
(7) Poets	17	Stipends from the Mughal Emperor; princes; members of the nobility; landlords; some stipends from the British East India Company
(8) Calligraphists	10 (+1 Hindu)	Fees for professional services
(9) Artists	4	Commissions for artistic works done for the royalty and nobility
(10) Musicians	7 (+2 Hindus)	Stipends by the Mughal Emperor; princes; royalty and public support on ceremonial occasions

scholarship and writing. Morality is instinctively ingrained in their character that if one were to comment on only one aspect of its thousands of books on ethics could be produced. Yet [these scholars] are modest and considerate; their regard for friendship is beyond description, and they are utterly without envy and they never nurse a grudge.[28]

This evaluation of, and enthusiasm for, the traditional elites changed fundamentally after Sir Sayyid's visit to Britain in April 1869, where he spent the next eighteen months. In Britain, Sir Sayyid observed the role of modern European elites, including scientists, engineers, and economists, who, instead of being a burden on their governments, were mainly responsible for Europe's industrial and economic prosperity, and consequently of its political hegemony. However, to the credit of the traditional elites (especially its fifth category, which Sir Sayyid described as 'ulamā'-i Dīn, traditional religious scholars) it must be pointed out that they showed the way to religious simplicity and rationality, and more significantly defined the framework of Muslim social reforms in the Indian environment, which Sir Sayyid adopted and subsequently amplified in the light of modernity. To their debit, it should be noted that in identifying modern education with Western political domination and the spread of Christianity, they failed to appreciate the significance of modernization, which had also shaken Christianity and the Western culture to its foundations during the previous three centuries. An understanding of their positive contributions to Sir Sayyid's conception of social reforms, and their negative attitude towards modern education, is essential.

The studies of modernization (particularly Ward's analysis of Japanese political culture) have developed a hypothesis that the traditional Japanese culture had within itself an indigenous potential for modernization. Commenting on Ward's hypothesis, Pye suggested "that a strong and effective traditional system may provide the ideal basis for subsequent development if they provide a people with a firm sense of identity, but the strength of the traditional order will impede development to the degree that it makes impossible the infusion of any new or modern elements of political culture."[29] I suggest that an analysis of the Indic Islamic culture, and the role of the 'ulamā (traditional religious scholars), would lend strength to Ward's hypothesis, and Pye's proposition.

Indic Islamic culture, despite some violent reactions against the infusion of certain modern elements within its fold, continuously accommodated itself to the introduction of modern education and a rational approach towards Islamic convictions and social reforms. Regarding the latter, however, the *'ulamā'* made their contributions within the framework of traditional Islam and were not at all influenced by Western rationalism. The movement for the Islamic reforms was undertaken by Shah Waliy Allah (1703–1762) and was developed by his followers, including Shah Abdul Aziz (1745–1823), Sayyid Ahmad Shahīd (1786–1831) and Mawlana Isma'īl Shahīd (1779–1831). Sir Sayyid, while he was deeply influenced by Shah Waliy Allah, knew intimately the last three, and adopted their rational approach to Islam, and particularly their view of the Muslim's social reforms.

Muslim Cultural Identity vs. Cultural Assimilation

Muslim leadership in India, traditional as well as modern, has always been called upon to define Islamic culture, and the limits of its interaction with the Hindu culture. While the Hindu culture has always been assimilative, and willing to synthesize with other religions, Islam in India had to face the problem of preserving its distinct identity, which closer cultural relations with the Hindu society would progressively erode. Striking a balance between the two processes (i.e., cultural identity vs. cultural assimilation) has not been easy; and despite the creation of Pakistan in 1947, the problem for the Indian Muslims has remained unsolved.

To Shah Waliy Allah and his followers, Islamic culture was described in a simple paradigm: *sunna* plus *shari'a* minus *bida'ā*. *Sunna* literally means "trodden path," and was understood by the pre-Islamic Arabs as the model behavior established by the founders of a tribe (*sunna al-ummā*). Also, the term was later applied to the normative conduct, which reflected some of the pre-Islamic customs and established the primary norm of the Islamic culture. *Shari'a,* literally the path to be followed, applied to

the Canon law of Islam—the totality of Allah's commandments—and embraced all individual as well as social actions.
Broadly speaking the *Shari'a* defined injunctions of five kinds.
"Those strictly enjoined are *fard,* and those strictly forbidden are
haram. Between them we have two middle categories, namely,
things which you are advised to do (*mandūb*), and things which
you are advised to refrain from (*makrūh*), and finally there are
things about which religion is indifferent (*ja'iz*). . . . Thus the
Shari'a is totalitarian; all human activity is embraced in its sovereign domain." *Bid'ā* or impious innovation "is that which contravenes the Prophetic model [*sunna*]."[30]

This paradigm of Islamic culture is essentially ideal; the
real culture of all Muslim societies including those of the Middle East falls considerably short of this ideal. Pre-Islamic cultural patterns have survived, although the traditional social reformers have attacked them as *bid'ā* and urged the Muslims
(both Arab and non-Arab) to discard them in favor of the *sunna.*
In the Indian environment *bid'ā* became a synonym for the Hindu
folkways and mores which were retained by the converts, and
because of them were diffused into the Indic Muslim society.
Consequently, for Shah Waliy Allah and his followers Muslim
social reforms led to the greater Islamization of the society. Islamization, as a sociological term, implied eschewing Hindu cultural patterns (the converse of which would lead to cultural assimilation with the Hindus) and adhering to those cultural values
of the Arabs which were accepted and exemplified by the
Prophet Muhammad as his *sunna.* Traditions and customs analogous to those of the Muslims in the Middle East were desired
and valued, while customs reflecting a Hindu coloring were positively discouraged and disdained. Islamization as a process of
Muslim social reform was always the obverse side of Muslim
politics in India.

In his well-known last testament, *Al-Maqalah al-Wadīya Fī
al-Nasihah Wa al-Wasiyā,* Shah Waliy Allah established the guidelines for the process of Islamization in the Hindu cultural milieu
of India. In the seventh precept, he said:

(a) Muslims should not "abandon the customs and mores of

the early Arabs, because they were the immediate followers of the Prophet Muhammad."   link to sak?

(b) Muslims "must not adopt the mores of the Hindus, or those of the people of *ajam*"[31]—countries beyond Arabia.

He also highlighted the Muslims' marriage and funeral customs, which come under the category of *bid'ā*. (1) "one of the reprehensible mores of the Hindus is their prohibition of a second marriage for widows. This was not a tradition among the Arabs, neither during the *jahiliyah* period nor after the advent of the Prophet Muhammad. May God bless him who would put an end to this [Hindu custom]." (2) Regarding the Muslim marriage, he stated: "one of the reprehensible habits of our people is that in the marriage contract an excessive dower is fixed. The Prophet Muhammad, on account of whom we are honored in religion and in this world, fixed for his spouses a dower, the value of which amounted to 500 dirhams." (3) "Another undesirable custom among our people is the incurring of unnecessary and exhorbitant expense on occasions of happiness. The Prophet fixed only two ceremonies [on the occasions of marriage and birth] that of *Walīyma*[32] and *'Aqīqah;*[33] only these two should be observed, and all others should be discarded."

Shah Waliy Allah also condemned Muslims' funeral ceremonies. (4) "We are also spendthrifts about funeral ceremonies. We have invented *Saywam* (third day), *chehlum* (fortieth day), *Shash Mahi* (six monthly), and then *Salanā* (annual) days of mourning, and the offering of prayers for the deceased. None of these customs existed among the ancient Arabs. The messages of condolence should be extended in the first three days and the family of the deceased should be treated to only three dinners. No other custom should be followed. After three days the women of the clan should get together and apply perfume to the garments of the female heirs of the deceased. If the widow is involved then she should observe mourning during the *idda* [i.e., the waiting period of four months and ten days, or if the widow is pregnant, till delivery, whichever is longer]; after this period she should wear mourning dress no more."

Shah Waliy Allah also extended the concept of *bid'ā* to the

mystical practices of the Indian Sufis (mystics). (5) "One should
not become a disciple of contemporary Sufis, because they are
engaged in varieties of bid'ā [impious innovations]." He described them as miracle-mongers, who preached "annihilation in
God" and considered the injunctions of Shari'a merely as a man's
confession of his inability "to pursue annihilation in and eternity
with God." This preoccupation of some Muslims "in the domains of annihilation and eternity, and the mystical practices"
appeared to Shah Waliy Allah as a deep malaise among the Indic
Muslims.[34]

Sayyid Ahmad Shahīd and his followers produced a prodigious amount of literature on Muslim social reforms both in
prose and verse. Their simple and direct style of Urdu prose
deviated for the first time in the history of Urdu literature from
the formal and verbose model of Abul Fadl's Persian prose. This
style was cultivated by Sir Sayyid, and it also became the accepted model of Urdu journalism during the nineteenth century.
The traditional social reformers' works can be divided into two
categories: (a) the works of Shahīd and his close associates, which
was designed mainly for the literate stratum of the Muslim society; and (b) the tracts which were written either in prose or verse
by Shahīd's itinerant preachers. They explained social reforms in
simplistic terms appealing more to emotions than to reason.
They attacked bid'ā which Muslims innovated themselves, and
the ones they adopted or retained from the Hindu culture. Some
of the more popular tracts were: Nasīyhat al-Muslimīyn (advice to
Muslims) by Khurram Ali; Hidayat al-Muminīyn wa sawalat
Asharat al-Muharram (guidance for believers and questions about
the ten days of Muharram) by Hasan Qanawji; Manajiy al-
Muslimīyn (deliverer of the Muslims) by Qadi Muhammad Husain; and Hujjat-i Qati'h (cutting proof) by Karamat Ali Jawnpuriy. Written primarily from 1854 to 1868, they were published
in Lahore, Delhi, Lucknow, and Calcutta.

Rigidly sectarian in their approach, the traditional social reformers attacked the Shi'ites' traditions as vehemently as they attacked the Hindu customs. To Hasan Qanawji, Islam was corrupted by bid'ā during the Umayyad Caliphate (661–749) because

the converts who secretly cherished their pre-Islamic customs diffused them into the Muslim society. This process ultimately weakened Islam, especially in India were "Muslims" "profess the faith, and also worship idols. They adore the tombs with Lingams upon them. Pirzadahs and Majawers (spiritual guides and tombs' custodians) while receiving offerings from their followers shout 'Gangaji key jay' or 'Rama Mahadev.' These 'Muslims' visit Mathura, Benares, Ajmer, and Makanpur as if they are on a pilgrimage [to Mecca]. They observe a thousand other idolatrous customs."

Also, shi'a ceremonies on Muharram celebrating the martyrdom of al-Husain (October 10, 680), the grandson of the Prophet Muhammad, were described as impious innovations. "When did God or the Prophet state that after Imam Husain was martyred a mourning procession should be taken out annually?" The usage, according to Qanawji was neither sanctioned by the Qur'ān nor by common sense; the Muharram passion play was merely a show, which often turned into sunni-shi'a riots, especially in Lucknow, and other cities of India. Khurram Ali, Qadi Muhammad Husain, and Karamat Ali Jawnpuriy covered much the same grounds with varying emphasis on different un-Islamic customs, while Jawnpuri lamented the fate of Islam in Bengal, where even books on Islam were not available except in large towns.

The poems on social reforms were simple and provocative, and equally offensive to the Shi'ites. Mazhar al-Haq, a Persian poem composed during Emperor Aurangzeb Alamgīr's reign (1658–1707) was popularized by Shahīd's itinerant reformers. Qadi Muhammad Husain published it as an appendix to his tract, Manajiy al-Muslimīyn, published in 1877 in Lahore with a prefatory remark that the poem was designed to expose superstitions and corrupt practices of the Muslims during Alamgīr's time, but they had survived and deserved to be condemned again:

> For their child parents become infidels;
> To preserve him from the small-pox they worship idols.
> Scholars too are profligate, encumbering weddings with expenses
>   and impious innovations.

The poem *Rah-i Sunnat* (the way of the sunna) by Mawlavi Awlad Hasan, first published in 1868 in Bombay, attacked the ceremonies on the Prophet's birthday and the mourning of al-Husain in Muharram, and condemned overt loyalty to the British Government. Consisting of 256 quatrains, and written diagonally in frames with a horizontal line under each, an Urdu poem *Haraq al-Ashrār* (burner of the wicked) delivered stern warnings of divine wrath against the worshippers of adorned sepulchres, the deceits of *pīrs,* and the adoption of Hindu cultural patterns. Finally, *Risalah Radd-i Shirk* (elimination of idolatry) and *Risalah Jihādiyah* (treatise on war) invoked Allah's aid against superstitious and deviant Muslims, whose "idolatry cannot be removed except by the sword," and called on the faithful to begin against the infidels a "sacred war":

> Jihad is mandatory for you, O! Muslims,
> Prepare at once for it if you have faith, O! Muslims.
> The warrior whose feet became dusty on the battlefield's sod,
> Escaped from hell, and became free from hell's fire.
> The warrior who fought briefly for Allah's truth,
> Won the adorned sepulchre of the Paradise.
>
> .   .   .   .   .
>
> Religion of Islam is on the decline,
> Domination of infidelity is ruining Islam.
> Had our forefathers not waged jihad,
> India would not have flourished with Islam.
> The power of sword ensured the domination of Islam,
> Had our forefathes been idle, what would have happened to
> Islam.

Shahīd did not write any book himself, but his epistles dealing with religious and social reforms were collected by Mawlana Isma'īl Shahīd, and Mawlana Abd al-Haiy in *Sirat al-Mustaqīym* (The Straight Path) and further amplified by Isma'īl Shahīd in *Taqwiyat al-Iman Wa Tadhkīyr al-Akhwan* (Strengthening of the Faith & Amonition to the Brothers). *Sirāt al-Mustaqīm* divided *bid'ā* into three categories: (a) The innovations which sprung from Muslims' association with the *mushrikīyn,* those who identify any animate or inanimate object with God, but appeared like genuine sufis; (b) those innovations which have developed by association with the Shi'ites; (c) and those corrupt and impious innovations which spread among the common people by virtue of their contacts with the Hindus. Under these categories Shahīd and his followers not only reiterated five kinds of impious innovations, which Shah Waliy Allah had enumerated, but added quite a few of their own determination. Shahīd's message was summed up in a comprehensive exhortation: "Follow the example of Muhammad of Arabia and relinquish all the customs of India, Iran, and Rome."[35]

Sir Sayyid had accepted Shah Waliy Allah, Sayyid Ahmad Shahīd and the latter's associates' framework of Muslim social reforms. However, he added a new dimension to the concept of bid'ā in urging Muslims that in secular matters where Islam was "indifferent," modern Western ways could be legitimately adopted. Meanwhile he continued to highlight the imperative of elminating Hindu customs from the Muslim culture. In his general approach to maintaining the Muslims' solidarity, Sir Sayyid deemphasized shi'a–sunni differences and appealed to both sects to reform their cultural patterns. While Shahīd's prolemics with the shi'aites sharpened antagonism, and weakened his movement considerably, Sir Sayyid's liberal approach forged cohesiveness among the shi'a and the sunni, making them effective partners in their political struggles for the creation of Pakistan in the twentieth century. In a nutshell, Sir Sayyid's conception of the Muslim social reforms included Islamization as well as modernization. The repercussions of this dynamic process are visible today in Pakistan as well as among the Muslims in India.

Social Mobilization of Muslims in Delhi

During 1803–1857 the city of Delhi also passed through a period of social mobilization—an overall process of change, which practically all Afro-Asian societies have experienced as the result of their contact with the West. Karl W. Deutsch has defined social

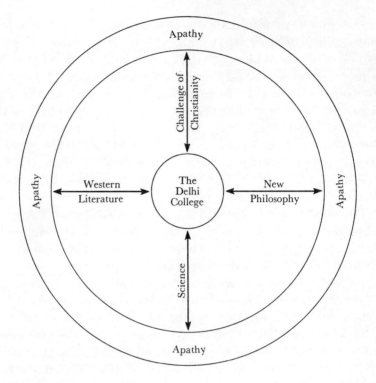

FIGURE 1.2 MUSLIM SOCIETY OF DELHI

mobilization as "the process in which major clusters of old social, economic, and psychological commitments are eroded or
broken and people become available for new patterns of socialization and behavior."[36] For want of statistical data, only some
indicators of Deutsch are highlighted, that is, the Muslims' "exposure to aspects of modern life" in Delhi. Modernity appeared
to the Delhi Muslims in the form of the British East India Company's beaurocratic installations, in the role of a small British
community, and most important of all the Muslims' exposure to
the science-oriented Delhi College.

   Originally called Madressah-i Ghazi-ud-Din and established
in 1972 by Nawab Ghazi-ud-Din Firuz Jang, the son of Nizam
al-Mulk, the founder of the State of Hyderabad, Deccan, the
Madressah was christened as the Delhi College in 1825 by the

British East India Company. On October 18, 1827, Sir Charles Metcalf, Resident at the Mughal Court in Delhi, recommended adding English classes to the Delhi College. In 1830 Itimad-ud-Daulah Sayyid Fadl Ali Khan, Minister of the King of Awadh, executed a will whereby he left Rs. 170,000 in trust with the British Government, stipulating that 5 percent interest on the Government-owned securities be spent "solely for the instruction of the sciences in Arabic and Persian," in the Delhi College.[37] Thus richly endowed, the Delhi College started teaching English and Western education through the medium of English in April 1834. While in 1835 English became the exclusive medium of instruction for higher education throughout India, the Delhi College retained the unique distinction of maintaining a dual educational system until its disappearance and final merger with the Government College at Lahore in April 1877.

This dual system at the Delhi College consisted of two academic departments: the Western Department, where modern Western education through the medium of English was given, and the Oriental Department, where in addition to teaching Arabic, Persian, and Sanskrit, modern education was provided through the medium of Urdu. Modern scientific education, however, became most popular among the students of both departments. How eagerly the lectures on scientific subjects were followed was described by Zaka Allah, an alumnus of the College, to Charles F. Andrews:

After each lecture, the notes used to be studied, over and over again, and copied out by many hands. It was like entering into a wholly undiscovered hemisphere of the human mind. The young students were allowed to try astonishing experiments with unknown chemical gases. They were invited to dip into the mysteries of magnetism, which was then coming to the front as a freshly discovered science. There was much yet to come; but these things formed actually for them a new world.

Also, this fascination with science extended into the students' homes within Delhi, where the new experiments were repeated in the presence of the parents. Commenting on the impact of

modern education on the minds of the young, Andrews observed
that it "did actually lead at first to a widespread unsettlement."
Consequently, the budding intelligentsia, in Andrews' observation, "demanded a life less bound by formal acts of prayer and
worship than that of conventional orthodox religion."

The spirit of free inquiry which was cultivated by Protes-
tantism lured some of the young Hindu students to Christianity;
none of the Muslim students converted to the religion of the conquerors, but some, including Zaka Allah and Nazir Ahmad,
were suspected to have appreciated the cultural impact of Christianity. This "intellectual unsettlement" which incidentally had
also occurred in Europe in the wake of scientific progress made
modern education suspect in the minds of the Delhi Muslims.

What intellectual impact did the modernized Delhi College
have on the traditional Muslim scholars of Delhi? Andrews, who
knew intimately several alumni of the College, has reproduced a
crucial passage from the memoirs of one:

The doctrines of ancient philosophy taught through the medium of Arabic were thus cast in the shade before the more reasonable and experimental theories of modern sciences. The old dogma, for instance, that
the earth is the fixed center of the Universe, was generally laughed at
by the higher students of the Oriental, as well as by those of the English Departments of the Delhi College. But the learned men, who
lived in the city, did not like this innovation on their much-loved
theories of ancient Greek philosophy, which had been cultivated among
them for many centuries past.[38]

Diffusion of Modernity: Delhi Muslims' Reaction 1803–1857

Behaviorally, the Delhi Muslims' reaction to modernity varied
from apathy to partial acceptance, from overt hostility to the
final acknowledgment of its superiority and the assiduous cultivation of modern education. In defining apathy, Lucian W. Pye
has stated that

frequent apathy hides deep resentments and frustrations over how the modern world has been communicated. Apathy can be a psychic device for covering humiliations and hostilities toward those who have damaged one's self-esteem by trying to push aside one's own world and replace it with a world that is foreign. Indeed, apathy can be only a short step removed from violent, aimless, and apparently spontaneous outbursts.[39]

Visiting Delhi in 1853, Altaf Husain Hali summed up the Muslims' "psychic device" for covering the inferiority of their decaying educational system:

In Panipat one could hardly hear a mention made of English education. People only thought of it as a means to acquiring British Government's employment rather than as a source of knowledge. On the contrary, our *'ulamā'* (scholars) called the English schools *majhlay* (abodes of ignorance). Also, in Delhi in the school in which I was enrolled, its teachers and students considered the graduates of the Delhi College merely ignoramuses. Consequently, not even in absent-mindedness did I ever desire of acquiring English education. I stayed in Delhi for one and a half years, but I never did once cast my glance at the College; nor did I have the opportunity to meet the students of the College, including Mawlavi Muhammad Husain Azad, Mawlavi Zaka Allah, and Mawlavi Nazir Ahmad.[40]

After 1857 Hali and the latter two became the ardent supporters of Sir Sayyid, and promoters of modern English education among the Muslims.

In keeping with the general tradition of Indic Muslim education, and to lure students to the Delhi College, a large number of scholarships were offered (as it is indicated in the figures below[41]) to students of middle- and lower-class families. The Mughal aristocracy generally ignored the College, and continued to educate their children at home, as was the case with Sir Sayyid, or sent them to the traditional schools for "higher" education (see Table 1.2).

In 1853 the Governor-General-in-Council adopted a resolution discouraging the award of scholarships to students in

TABLE 1.2.

Year	Scholarships	Nonscholarships	Total Number of Students
		Oriental Department	
1833	243	36	279
1834	230	18	248
1835	217	10	227
1836	164	34	198
1837	124	17	141
1838	89	34	123
		Western Department	
1833	134	18	152
1834	129	11	140
1835	127	61	188
1836	117	50	167
1837	68	40	108
1838	47	41	88

Government-run or subsidized institutions. This policy was mainly responsible for the decline of lower-middle-class students in the Delhi College in 1837–38. Encouraged by the relative popularity of modern Western education, the British administration attempted in 1846 to impose tuition fees according to the schedule in Table 1.3. Unable to make the financial sacrifice, a sizable number of parents withdrew their sons from the College. This general decline in the enrollment is reflected in the figures in Table 1.4. Another precipitous decline in the enrollment occurred in 1847–48 when two star students of the Western Department, including Ram Chandra and Chaman Lal, converted to Christianity. On the whole, however, the Delhi's middle and lower middle classes responded positively and steadily to modern education before 1857. The Hindus' response was certainly more

TABLE 1.3.

Parents' Income	Tuition Fee
Rs. 100 and above	Rs. 5 and above
Rs. 70–100	Rs. 3 and above
Rs. 35–70	Rs. ½ (8 annas)

TABLE 1.4.

Year	Total Number of Students	Students Paying Tuition	Amount of Tuition Paid
1835–36	365	—	—
1836–37	249	—	—
1837–38	211	—	—
1838–39	226	—	—
1839–40	189	—	—
1840–41	166	—	—
1841–42	326	—	—
1842–43	286	—	—
1843–44	305	—	—
1844–45	460	—	—
1845–46	375	—	—
1846–47	334	16	Rs. 192
1847–48	259	12	Rs. 321
1848–49	339	77	Rs. 622
1849–50	336	125	Rs. 958
1850–51	333	181	Rs. 1,358
—	—	—	
1852–53	315	230	Rs. 1,910
1853–54	233	239	Rs. 2,082
—	—	—	
1856–57	345	—	Rs. 2,405/1/3

positive than that of the Muslims', as is reflected in Table 1.5.[42]

Most of Sir Sayyid's educational ideas and experiments had their origins in the accomplishments of the Delhi College. Despite the fact that he was not a student of the Delhi College, he was an intimate friend and companion of Imam Bakhsh Sahbaiy, a well-known professor of Persian literature at the College. Sahbaiy helped him collect data for *Athar al-Sanadid,* and also edited the prose of the first edition. Moreover, especially after 1857, he found in Zaka Allah, and Nazir Ahmad, two alumni of the College, ardent supporters of his movement for modern education among the Muslims. Essentially this trio was the interpreter of modern education to Sir Sayyid until 1869, when he travelled to Europe.

The College blazed the trail in initiating a system of national education, which Macaulay's chauvinism destroyed in its in-

TABLE 1.5.

Year	Hindu	Muslim	Christian	English Education	Oriental Department		
					Persian	Arabic	Sanskrit
1835–36	201	158	5	166	81	61	56
1836–37	134	108	7	108	(141 in all 3 departments)		
1837–38	114	89	8	88	56	35	32
1838–39	140	80	6	123	39	35	29
1839–40	105	73	11	85	39	41	24
1840–41	93	70	3	84	34	28	82
1841–42	214	102	10	157	146	16	46
1842–43	146	128	12	124	75	40	36
1843–44	179	111	15	162	53	58	32
1844–45	299	146	15	245	109	75	31
1845–46	230	132	13	196	115	66	24
1846–47	209	107	18	198	58	65	24
1847–48	234	109	16	231	43	72	17
1848–49	222	105	12	226	47	56	17
1849–50	231	94	11	224	61	43	19
1850–51	206	105	22	222	56	39	18
—	—	—	—	—	—	—	—
1852–53	217	93	10	209	57	39	25
1853–54	206	112	15	211	57	38	27
1854–55	243	97	10	217	77	33	23
1855–56	158	83	4	—	—	—	—
Total	3,781	2,102	223	3,276	1,344	981	703

fancy. (It has not been completely reestablished in either India or
Pakistan after nearly 30 years of independent existence.) The English educators at the Delhi College decided to give modern scientific education in northern India through the medium of Urdu.
Overcoming the shortage of books, which were lugged from
Calcutta to Delhi, these dedicated scholars translated their lectures into Urdu, and then finally tackled the problem of translation on a scientific basis. In 1835, when the new British policy
veered away from the concept of modern education through the
Indian vernaculars, the Delhi College took another small but
bold step in the opposite direction. The Educational Committee
was created to translate in Urdu scientific books then taught in
European schools. In 1841 a subcommittee was created consisting of some well-known persons: James Princep, Sir Edward

Rylan, and Mr. Southerland. It was called upon to prepare a comprehensive plan of translation from English to Urdu. The subcommittee made the following recommendations: (1) books on grammar and syntax should be written; (2) from among the Indian scholars volunteers should be sought out, who should work under the supervision of the subcommittee, especially in translating the scientific works; (3) elementary textbooks for all scientific disciplines should be prepared; (4) finally, the subcommittee made a revolutionary proposal, which ran in many ways counter to the British imperial interest. It suggested that books on the governments and States' rise and fall should be written from the national viewpoint. In suggesting that the Educational Committee should consult with the Boards of Education of Bombay and Madras, the Governor-General-in-Council throttled the Committee.

Unnerved by the demise of their plans, the English faculty of the Delhi College, in cooperation with its Indian friends, launched "The Society for the Promotion of Knowledge in India through the Medium of Vernaculars," which subsequently came to be known as the Delhi College Vernacular Translation Society. The Executive Committee of the Society included local British officers and educators: T. Metcalf, C. Grant, E. C. Rewanshaw, W. Quintin, and Dawarka Nath Tagore, and Principal Bitrose as the Secretary. Among the members of the Society who made financial contributions, 52 were British and 116 were Indians. In addition to the Ruler of Awadh and his sons, from Hyderabad, sizable donations were sent by Sir Salar Jang, Siraj al-Mulk, and Raja Ram Bakhsh. The Society developed a comprehensive system of translation for scientific, agricultural, legal, and political terms. Though originally committed to translating scientific and other European works into Bengali, Hindi, and Urdu, it commissioned translations into Urdu only. By the end of 1847 the Society had at least 128 books from Arabic, Persian, and English translated into Urdu[43] (see Table 1.6).

Until 1868, Sir Sayyid remained committed to a policy of modern national education through the medium of Urdu. Needless to say that the educational experiment of the Delhi College

TABLE 1.6.

Science	Politics	History	Geography	Mathematics and Geometry	Law	Theology	Grammar	Total
(A) *Translations of English Books into Urdu*								
25	4	11	4	9	10	2	2	67
(B) *Translations of Arabic and Persian Books into Urdu*								
3	26	10	1	2	4	9	6	61
28	30	21	5	11	14	11	8	128

had illumined his thinking. Practical difficulties finally persuaded him to vote for English as the medium of instruction; however, for the development of a truly indigenous but modern educational system Sir Sayyid's retreat proved to be fatal.

The traditional Muslim elites, and some segments of the Mughal aristocracy, also took measured and calculated steps to meet the West in Delhi. Affecting European manners, one of the Mughal princes, Mirza Babur, the second son of Akbar Shah II, even "built an European-style house [behind the Diwan-i 'Am] whose Corinthian columns and stucco walls horrified admirers of Shah Jehan's architecture. He wore European clothes or, rather, uniforms and drove about the city in a coach with six horses."[44] Though unable to change his environment and the political circumstances in which the cruel hands of history had placed him, the last Mughal Emperor, Bahadur Shah, was always eager to know about England, "the Government, the manners of the Court, and the habits of the people."

Some instances of intermarriage between the Muslims and the English also occurred. A few Muslims who travelled to Britain married English women; one of them who was married to a Sayyid once had an audience with Bahadur Shah and his queen, and has left a vivid picture of their life in the Red Fort.[45] The mother of the famous Urdu poet, Nawab Mirza Khan Dagh (1831–1905), was supposedly married for a while to an Englishman before she married Prince Fath al-Mulk Mirza Ghulam Fakher-ud-Din (alias Mirza Fakhru), the third son of Bahadur Shah. Boston-born soldier of fortune, Sir David Ochterlony

(1758–1825), the first British Resident at Emperor Shah Alam's Court, even outraged his fellow-Britons by his outward "Islamization." Ochterlony's daughter, Husan Jahan Begum, born of his marriage with a Muslim lady, Mubarak Begum, was married to a nobleman and was readily accepted into the Muslim society without the stigma of being a half-breed attached to her.[46] The Yankee soldier, called Akhterlunīy by the Muslims, was always welcomed into respectable Muslim homes in Delhi, and was an intimate friend of Sir Sayyid's grandfather.

Among those Europeans who made India their home, Captain Alexander Haderly would also be remembered for having internalized the cultural values of Indic Islam. He composed Urdu poetry of some merit, and was a disciple of Zaiyn al-'Abidīyn 'Araf, one of the well-known disciples of Ghalib. Haderly learned Greco-Arabic medicine, called Tib-i yunaniy, and practiced it in Agra. At age 32 he died (1861) in Agra, although he was born and raised in Delhi. Posthumously, a collection of his poetry was published by Shawkat Ali Fatehpurīy and his brother Thomas Haderly.[47]

Among the traditional intellectuals, Shah 'Abdul Azīz (d. 1832) maintained cordial contacts with the British residents. Charles Seton (1806–1811), Skinner, and William Frazer (who was also a friend of poet Ghalib) often visited with Shah 'Abdul Azīz, and he was known to have returned Seton's social visits at the latter's residence. "Seton visited me at least three times," so was recorded in Shah 'Abdul Azīz's *Malfūzāt*, "but he is an ignoramus and flatterer. Once he accompanied me to the old city to see my place of birth and consequently he erected on the spot a memorial building, but it was hardly suitable."[48] Despite this, Shah 'Abdul Azīz described Seton a capable friend.

Asad Allah Khan Ghalib (1797–1869), the celebrated Persian and Urdu poet, had intuitively if not intellectually grasped the spirit of modernity, which he considered to be the secret of British power. A pensioner of the British East India Company, Ghalib travelled in October 1827 to the Company's capital Calcutta, and stayed there until November 29, 1829.[49] Abul Kalam Azad has speculated that, from about 1849, Ghalib's epistolary style, with its spontaneity, simplicity, and informality, reflected the Urdu prose style which had been popularized at the Fort William College (established in 1800) under Dr. John Gilchrist's auspices.[50] Thus Ghalib helped to bring into vogue a modern and secular Urdu prose style, the religious counterpart of which had been initiated by Shahīd's followers.

Ghalib also took exception in a *taqrīz* (review poem) to Sir Sayyid's editing and publishing (c. 1856) of Abul Fadl's *Ain-i Akbarī* (Institutes of Emperor Akbar), calling it a futile endeavor to extol the dead past, which ignored the scientific accomplishments of the British. A few verses from Ghalib's *taqrīyz*,[51] which Sir Sayyid indignantly returned to the poet, illustrate Ghalib's limited conception of modernity, and Sir Sayyid's general unawareness of it:

> Glad tidings to friends—this ancient *magnum opus,*
> Made another debut through Sayyid's endeavors.
> New light has been shed through great efforts,
> New appearance has covered this antique.
> [Sayyid's] opinion expressed in the new edition of *Āin*
> Hardly befits his high aims and aspirations.
> [Sayyid] tied his heart to a project, and entertained himself
> But wasted his time in a futile endeavor.
>
> . . . . .
>
> Put aside the *Āin,* and parley with me;
> Open thine eyes in this old world,
> And examine the [life] of the Englishmen,
> Their style, their manner, their trade, and their art.

2

Sir Sayyid's Political Socialization and Orientations

SIR SAYYID AHMAD KHAN'S forbears were Sayyids, the descendants of Fatimah and Ali, the daughter and the cousin respectively of the Prophet Muhammad. The followers of the Prophet hardly ever treated kindly the progeny of the Master. Al-Husain, the grandson of the Prophet, was martyred on October 10, 680, in the deserts of Karbala in Iraq. This was done by the order of Yazīd, the son of Mu 'āwiyah, who had established the Umayyad Caliphate (661–750) in Syria. Soon after the assassination of 'Ali (July 24, 661), the fourth Caliph of the Prophet, the Abbasids (750–1258), descendants of an uncle of the Prophet, Al-'Abbas ibn abd al-Muttalib, had overthrown the Umayyads as "defenders of the true faith," and champions" of the Prophet's house. Striking down all irreconcilable partisans of the Prophet's descendants, who considered the 'Abbasids as usurpers, the 'Abbasids also drove away "unsafe" Sayyids to distant lands. Fleeing from 'Abbasid persecution, Sir Sayyid's forebears drifted into

Iran, and then moved to Herat in Afghanistan. The founder of
the family in India was lured to Delhi by opportunities for a better life available in Shahjahan Abad, which the Mughal Emperor
Shah Jahan had built in 1648 near old Delhi.

Early Political Socialization

The Mughal Emperors, who welcomed the talents of Muslim
immigrants from abroad, utilized the members of this· Sayyid
family in the civil and judicial administration. Despite their residence in India for nearly 200 years, Sir Sayyid's family retained a
consciousness of their foreign origin. This extraterritorial consciousness basically determined Sir Sayyid's ancestors' and other
upper-class Muslims' *weltanschauung* in the Indian environment.
They viewed the culture and political problems of the Muslims
from this particular perspective, generally detaching themselves
from the Indian Muslim masses, but associating with them
closely in periods of crisis. In Sir Sayyid's family two spiritual
and intellectual traditions prevailed. The spiritual and mystic tradition, emphasizing "annihilation in God" and love of mankind,
was represented by his father, Sayyid Muhammad Muttaqīy.
Owing its origin to Hispano-Arab mystic Muhiy al-Din ibn al-
'Arabi's (1165–1202) innovated doctrine of *wahdat al-wujūd* (Unitarian monism), this mystic tradition degenerated in India, especially during the decline of the Mughal power, into a negative attitude of self-abnegation and escape from responsibility. The
other tradition was one of pragmatism. Sir Sayyid's maternal
grandfather, Farīd al-Din Ahmad (1747–1828) epitomized this
pragmatic and manipulative tradition, which was produced by a
class of professional administrators who lent their talents to the
powers that be and attached no allegiance to a particular sovereign. In the eyes of these Mughal professionals, a *de facto* sovereign very naturally deserved loyalty and service; the *de jure* capacity of the sovereign, however, was determined by his superior
power.
    During the seventeenth and eighteenth centuries this class

served Emperor Shah Jahan, Prince Dara Shukoh, and Emperor Aurangzeb 'Alamgīr with equal impartiality. After Aurangzeb, this class shifted its allegiance in quick succession from Bahadur Shah I to Jahandar Shah, Farrukhsīyar, and Muhammad Shah. After 1803, some members of this class also extended its cooperation and service to the British East India Company, and the Maratha rulers in the Deccan. While Khwajah Farīd al-Din served the British East India Company in Calcutta and Emperor Akbar Shah II in Delhi, his three younger brothers (out of seven) did the following: Khwajah Shahab al-Din served the British as a clerk; Khwajah Muhīy al-Din served as a chamberlain at the Mughal Court in Delhi, and Khwajah Nūr al-Din served as an officer in the Maratha army of Sindhia.[1]

Originally migrating from Hamadan in Iran, the Khwajah family settled in Kashmir and became merchants of Kashmiri silk and wool. Khwajah 'Abd al-Azīz, the grandfather of Khwajah Farīd, finally settled in Delhi, where the latter was born. Although respectable and affluent, the Khwajah family was not socially equal to the Sayyid family, with whom a relationship was established by virtue of the marriage between Khwajah Farīd's oldest daughter, 'Azīz al-Nisa, and Sayyid Muhammad Muttaqīy. While Khwajah Farīd's ancestors were merchants, the great grandfather of Sayyid Muttaqīy was a commanding officer in Emperor Aurangzeb's army. Emperor 'Alamgīr II (1754–1759) had bestowed the title of Jawād 'Ali Khan, and the rank of *yak-hazari* (commander of one thousand) on Sayyid Hadī, the father of Sayyid Muttaqīy.

The scion of military commanders and administrators, Sayyid Muttaqīy, for unexplainable reasons, rejected these ancestral professions and took to mystic flights involving frequent visits to Shah Ghulam 'Ali's Khanqah (monastery). He also took up swimming and archery—not as occupations but as pastimes. His income was derived from the agricultural land and the pension granted by the Mughal Court, which in those uncertain times was rather irregular, and frequently much less than the promised amount. At one time a lofty building, Mīr Muttaqīy's ancestral house, which was located near Jamia Masjid in a pres-

tigious northeast section of the city, had been repeatedly ransacked by Maratha freebooters, and was unfit and unsafe to dwell
in. Lacking both the will and the financial resources, Mir Muttaqīy prudently moved in with his father-in-law.[2] Khwajah
Farīd's *haveliy* (mansion), originally built by Mahdi Qulī Khan,
was a huge palatial building, befitting the status of a man who
was destined twice to serve Emperor Akbar Shah II as his prime
minister, and the British Government as its diplomat. Here in
this mansion—Haveliy Mehdi Quliy Khan—Sayyid Ahmad
Khan, the third child of his parents, was born on October 17,
1817.

Two traditions, in fact two distinct views of life, represented
by Sayyid Muttaqī and Khwajah Farīd, appeared before the eyes
of the young and impressionable Sayyid Ahmad. Dedicated to a
life of spirituality and personal freedom, and to a certain extent
fleeing from responsibility, Mīr Muttaqīy even turned down
Akbar Shah's proposal to confer upon him the ancestral titles,
with the addition of a new and highsounding one—Jawād al-
Daulah. Khwajah Farīd, an antithesis of his son-in-law, assiduously sought glory and titles, and built for himself an impos-
ing and successful career in the administration of the British East
India Company. Emulating his hero, his grandfather, Sayyid
Ahmad chose a life of activity and uphill endeavor, and eventually found his place in the glorious sun of the British Empire.

Very little is known about the first 34 years of Khwajah
Farīd's life in Delhi. In 1781 he went to Lucknow for three years
to study advanced mathematics under 'Allamā Taffadal Husain
Khan's care. Khan not only was a renowned scholar, but also had
served the Company as a *munshī* (tutor-cum-clerk), first of General Palmer and then of W. W. Hunter. On General Palmer's
suggestion, Nawab Asaf-al-Daulah, the ruler (1774–1797) of
Lucknow, appointed Khan as his envoy to Calcutta, where he
was already a known figure. In a letter to his wife written in
1862, Hunter poured contempt on "the animal called Moon-
shee," but said about 'Allamā Taffadal Husain Khan; "Our man
is the author of two or three popular works and a grammar; he is

likewise member of various learned societies, a good Mussalman, and a very handsome man of five-and-fifty. He believes in Genii, but admits that these are only to be met in parts of the world where no one has ever been. He is an educated man."[3] Not even the best scholar, by traditional Muslim standards, was quite an educated man in the eyes of the conquerors. Yet how proudly Sir Sayyid has stated: "Taffadal Husain Khan was known for his scholarship in all disciplines of learning, and particularly in mathematics. People gave him the title of *'allamā*, the most accomplished scholar. Khwajah Farīd al-Din studied the most advanced mathematical works under his instructions in Lucknow."[4] In addition to mathematical studies, Khan probably also introduced Khwajah Farīd to the Company's officials at the Lucknow Court.

In 1797, after 13 years in Delhi, Khwajah Farīd returned to Lucknow when Nawab Sa'dat 'Ali Khan became the ruler. This time Khwajah Farīd attained access to General Martin and other high-ranking British officials,[5] who recommended him to be the Superintendent of the Company's newly established Calcutta Madressah (Maddressah 'Aliyāh). In Calcutta, Lord Wellesley was impressed by his diplomatic skill and adroitness, and sent him to Iran in 1803 as an attaché of the British Embassy. The Mission's aim was to convince Emperor Fateh 'Ali Shah of Iran to send another ambassador to India in place of Ambassador Haji Muhammad Khalīl Khan, who had been killed "accidentally" on July 20, 1802, by the Company's soldiers. Muhammad Nabīy Khan, whom Khwajah Farīd assiduously cultivated in Shirez, finally became Iran's Ambassador to India. Recognizing his diplomatic success, the Company appointed him Political Officer at the Court of Ava in Burma. After a few months' stay in Burma, Khwajah Farīd returned to Calcutta. This time the Company appointed him Tehsildar (revenue officer) of the newly conquered territories in Bandiylkhand. "The position of Tehsiyladar in those days was exalted, and he could exercise a great deal of authority," commented Sir Sayyid. "He received no fixed salary, but received 10 percent of the total revenue collected by him."[6]

When the conquest was consolidated and permanent settlement was made, ordinary tehsiyldars were appointed. Consequently, Khwajah Farīd returned to Delhi in 1810 and was unemployed.

During his prolonged absence of almost 13 years the world of Delhi had changed. While he was still in Iran (1803) Lord Lake had conquered Delhi, and his friend and patron, General David Ochterlony, had become the Resident, and about 1806 was appointed a commander of the British garrison in Delhi and the Fortress of Allahabad. From 1810 to 1815 (when Khwajah Farīd was again in Calcutta), young Sayyid Ahmad saw General Ochterlony frequently visiting his grandfather at Haveliy Mahdi Quliy Khan, and he treasured the memories of those visits. One day, dazzled by the gold buttons on the General's coat and amused by the feathers in his hat, the 6-year-old Sayyid Ahmad asked the guest why he wore those colorful feathers. Unable to offer any suitable explanation, the General picked up the curious infant and affectionately placed him on his knee.

Sir Sayyid always cherished a painting of the General with his grandfather and Emperor Akbar Shah. In it, Khwajah Farīd as the prime minister and Ocheterlony as the commander were standing in front of the throne while leaning on their *jarībs* (staffs of honor) in the famous Diwan-i 'Aām (general audience hall) of the Red Fort.

How did Khwajah Farīd become Emperor Akbar Shah's prime minister? The circumstances leading to his elevation and his performance as a prime minister once more illustrate the contrasting ambitions, loyalties, and outlooks of Khwajah Farīd and his son-in-law Sayyid Muttaqīy. Probably in 1815, when Khwajah Farīd was in Calcutta, Akbar Shah offered Sayyid Muttaqīy the position of prime minister. Indifferent to the glamor of official status, and probably mindful of his administrative ineptitude, Sayyid Muttaqīy instead pressed the candidacy of his father-in-law. The king recognized the merits of this recommendation: Khwajah Farīd was a political and diplomatic success, and above all was trusted by the Company. Who could be more suitable to handle the delicate task of representing Akbar Shah's financial claims in the Company's councils. Akbar Shah believed not only that the royal pension was inadequate, but that the Company was also defaulting on her assumed obligations.[7] As a young lad, Sir Sayyid had also heard that the Mughal princes, in a desperate economic squeeze, would shout from their rooftops: *"Bhukay martay haiyñ, bhukay martay haiyñ"* (we die of starvation, we die of starvation).[8] Responding to Akbar Shah's invitation, Khwajah Farīd at once returned to Delhi in 1815, and was made the prime minister with the incredibly high sounding titles of *Dabīyr al-Mulk, Amīn al-Daulah, Maslah Jang.*

Khwajah Farīd was under pressure to solve the financial problems of Akbar Shah. To the king the obvious solution was to approach the Company for more money, but Khwajah Farīd decided to bring the royal expenses in harmony with the income, and hence to eliminate the need for negotiations with Calcutta. Allowances of Salatīn, who numbered almost 3,000, and the salaries of the employees, were slashed 10 percent. The two royal kitchens—one preparing *bara khasa,* food for high ranking employees, courtiers, and watchmen, and the other *chota khasa,* food for the people in the palace and those courtiers or physicians who were detained overnight in the Fort—were abolished. From the ceiling of the Diwan-i 'Aām (Hall of Audience), which had been devastated by the Marathas, Khwajah Farīd managed to extract gold, brass, and other metals. The metals were used to mint pennies, which were circulated in Delhi until 1857. Through this unregal but ingenious economic measure Khwajah Farīd paid off the royal debts, enforced regularity in the payment of allowances and salaries, and finally balanced Akbar Shah's budget.

The Red Fort's public opinion was one of outrage; people made uncharitable remarks about Khwajah Farīd's economic approach. Feeling uncomfortable and insecure in his position because of Akbar Shah's increasing display of unfriendliness, Khwajah Farīd resigned, and left Delhi for Calcutta. In his absence, Akbar Shah prepared a memorandum for the Company's Governor-General, asking for an increase in his pension. At this juncture Mīr Muttaqīy demonstrated an uncanny political sense in reminding the king that the Governor-General would certainly invite Khwajah Farīd's comments on his memorandum. What would he say? The budget had been balanced, and all the debts paid. Mir Muttaqīy reasoned that an increase in pension could not be negotiated without Khwajah Farīd's intervention. The humbled and friendless king capitulated, and agreed to reinstate Khwajah Farīd as his prime minister. In 1819, now exactly 72 years old, Khwajah Farīd once again returned to the Red Fort as the prime minister, and remained in that position for another period of three years. Once again Khwajah Farīd evaded, detoured, and ducked on the issue of the royal pension. Some said, what could be expected from the Company's collaborator? Annoyed and frustrated, Akbar Shah attempted to downgrade the Premiership by associating Nawab Mīr Khan, Raja Kaydar Nath, and Raja Sukh Ray with Khwajah Farīd. Maintaining his self-respect and dignity, Khwajah Farīd resigned his position for the second time in 1822 on the advice of an old friend, General David Ochterlony.[9] Six years later in 1828 Khwajah Farīd died; Sir Sayyid was then a little more than 11 years old.

Traditional Value System

Who exercised the dominant influence during the formative and most impressionable age of Sir Sayyid? Not the father, about whose life Sir Sayyid has made merely insignificant passing references in the scattered reminiscences of his early years. His grandfather was the hero who formed his personality, and his mother helped him develop his early value system, which was subsequently modified by experience and wider exposure to the West. Khwajah Farīd's life-long service to the British not only instilled respect for the British sovereignty in his family, but also made his descendants appreciate the extent of their dominions and power. Unlike the Maratha or the Mughal, the British power was not an illusion lacking substance or reality. It was based upon science and technology and an effective use of worldwide material resources. Even secluded and politically less informed women in Khwajah Farīd's family understood the significance of ubiquitous British power during the nineteenth century.

A few weeks after Khwajah Farīd's resignation, Maharaja Ranjit Singh, the ruler of the Punjab, sent a special envoy to Delhi to invite Khwajah Farīd to Lahore as his prime minister or political advisor. Ranjit Singh's envoy offered 30,000 rupees to Khwajah Farīd for his expenses, which were accepted. Should the old but ambitious Khwajah Farīd accept the new position? His friends recommended the acceptance of the offer; however, the issue became controversial in the family council. 'Azīz al-Nisā, Khwajah Farīd's oldest daughter and Sir Sayyid's mother, reasoned with her father against his friends' advice. "God has given you everything, father; you can live in any style and standard you like. Additional wealth would not add any more to your existing comforts." After this simple and common-sense explanation, 'Azīz al-Nisā argued in terms of power politics, which went straight home to the astute diplomat. "Your going to Lahore to administer Maharaja Ranjit Singh's kingdom, while we stay within the British possessions, is highly undiplomatic. Who knows what contingencies would develop, and what kind of revolutions would erupt." The implicit suggestion that Khwajah Farīd might be in a dilemma in Lahore should a conflict of interest develop between Maharaja Ranjit Singh and the British Government persuaded the veteran diplomat to reject the offer with thanks, and the 30,000 rupees were then returned. However, the episode reflected the fact that the family had learned to contemplate the contemporary political scene from the British viewpoint. This perspective, too, developed in Sir Sayyid early and remained forever with him.

While the family was exposed to western ideas, it was by no means completely westernized. Traditional values were preserved, and they too were internalized by Sir Sayyid and other grandchildren of Khwajah Farīd. Like a patriarch, Khwajah Farīd "presided over" the family luncheons. In the dining room, Persian carpets were covered by glistening white and narrow sheets. On both sides his sons and their wives, his daughters and their husbands, and all the grandchildren would sit to eat. While grown-ups took their own foods from the serving dishes, the grandfather asked each child his preference and then filled his empty plate. No one dared to let food drop out of the plates or produce any sound while chewing. Nor could they soil their fingers, although knives and forks were not used.

Khwajah Farīd also taught his grandchildren. After dinner, the children visited their grandfather in the brightly lit *diwan khanā* (sitting room), where the Persian carpets were covered by freshly laundered sheets. Each child, antiseptically clean and wearing immaculately clean clothes, was given a fresh lesson in Persian, Urdu, and mathematics. If a child even accidentally soiled the white sheet or appeared in an ink-stained dress, he was "chased out of the room like a dog." If the child returned with another set of new clothes, the grandfather would indignantly comment: "Were you dressed like the shoemakers that you had to change in order to appear again?" Taking their turns, the children repeated their previous lessons. Good students were rewarded and underachievers were castigated as *bay-pīr*, the guideless ones. Sir Sayyid learned the *Bostān*, by the celebrated Persian poet and writer, Sa'di Shirazi, from his grandfather. One day he was called upon to translate the verse:

Tam 'a ra sah harf-ast har sah tahīy
Wa-zan nīyst mar-matma añ ra bahīy

The word *tama 'a* (greed) consists of three letters, each one is empty, that is, each one is without a dot.

Translating the first half-verse, young Sayyid Ahmad omitted the verb *ast* (is), and stated: *"tama 'a,* three letters, three empty." Given a second and a third chance to correct himself, Sayyid Ahmad failed to notice his error. *"Bay-pīr,* you don't care to learn your lessons," thus rebuked the indignant grandfather, and tears rolled down the infant's rosy cheeks. The memory of this disapproval never faded from Sir Sayyid's mind.

To Khwajah Farīd, personal loyalty in friendship, regard for employees' sentiments and service, and above all disregard for religious bias were the most cherished values. Lala Malūk Chand, a Hindu *diwan* (manager) of Khwajah Farīd, served him faithfully all his working life. His loyalty was reciprocated by Khwajah Farīd's financial generosity and personal friendship. In his will, Khwajah Farīd apportioned absolutely equal amounts of money between Lala Malūk Ghand and his surviving younger brothers. Also, more like a brother than an employee, Lala Malūk Ghand could influence Khwajah Farīd's thinking and even ventured to offer unsolicited advice on sensitive issues. This religious tolerance was learned by Sir Sayyid early, and despite his later differences with the All-India National Congress and open espousal of the Muslims' cause in Indian politics, Sir Sayyid maintained warm and loyal relations with his Hindu friends.

Sir Sayyid's mother reinforced these traditional values, and after Khwajah Farīd's death she was his first teacher. Sa'dī's second well-known work, *Gulistān,* Sir Sayyid learned from his mother. Informal instruction, however, proved to be more powerful in building Sir Sayyid's character. She emphasized forgiveness, even for enemies, and tolerance for opponents. "A man who had benefitted from me," Sir Sayyid recorded, "did me some wrong. I obtained evidence of his culpability and could have gotten him convicted in a criminal proceeding. I was bent upon revenge, but my mother advised: 'forgive him, for nothing is more moral than forgiveness; if you cannot, then let the Almighty judge him because he alone knows.' " Commenting on his mother's advice, Sir Sayyid stated: "Since then I have never entertained the idea of revenge even against my worst enemies. I do not want even God to punish my wrong-doers on the Day of Judgement."

Respect for the elderly, regardless of social position, was maintained. A domestic servant was a helper, not engaged in servitude, and was looked upon as a member of the family. An infringement of this rule was never tolerated. The 12-year-old Sayyid Ahmad once slapped an aged servant who had served the family for many years. Mortified by the act of her brash son, the mother ordered: "Turn him out of the house, he may go where he may. He is no longer fit to live in my house." A maid turned him out, and left him out in the street. The boy went to his aunt's house in the neighborhood, who hid the "delinquent" lad in the attic. After a "solitary confinement" of three days, the aunt took her nephew to his mother and begged for her forgiveness. "He better ask the wronged servant for forgiveness," answered Sayyid Ahmad's mother. Folding his hands in humility and seeking forgiveness, Sayyid Ahmad beseeched the old servant, who forgave. He was thus readmitted into the house. "Undoubtedly a good mother is by far superior to thousands of teachers," was the fond reflection of Sir Sayyid.

By her conduct 'Azīz al-Nisā also demonstrated *noblesse oblige*. She maintained several helpless and indigent old ladies in especially built quarters adjoining her house. One of them, called by her abbreviated name, Zayban, once became sick at a time when 'Azīz al-Nisā was also stricken. Medication was equally divided between them, and when Sir Sayyid, who was then a subjudge in Delhi, purchased an expensive tonic for his mother, 'Azīz al-Nisā gave it to poor Zayban. Also, although Islamic law has enjoined *Zaka* (legal charity) at the rate of 2½ percent on one's possessions, 'Azīz al-Nisā regularly set aside 5 percent of the family income for charitable purposes and also advised her sisters and nieces to act accordingly. With this money she helped poor families marry their daughters, and gave allowances to helpless women. She encouraged second marriages for the young widows, and never considered it beneath her dignity to socialize with poor relatives or those who had married women of questionable reputation. "Be compassionate!" That was her motto.

In endeavoring to follow the normative conduct of the Prophet, 'Azīz al-Nisā developed a rational system of Islamic convictions. At age 38, her eldest son, Sayyid Muhammad Khan, died. A portrait in courage, she unrolled her prayer carpet and exclaimed: *"Khuda key marzīy,"* God's will was done. With tears running down her cheeks, she kneeled down to pray for God's compassion and mercy. In order to share her mourning one of her relatives decided to postpone the wedding of his daughter. Three days after the burial of her son, 'Azīz al-Nisā visited the sympathetic relatives and told them: "Go ahead with the marriage plans; the postponement is uncalled for, because [Islam] allows mourning for no more than three days. Who would criticize you when I urge you to celebrate the wedding on the appointed date?" Commenting on the impact of his mother's religious practices and beliefs, Sir Sayyid wrote decades after her death: "While today my religious convictions are based upon scholarly investigations, I do not find any of her convictions or practices smacking of *shirk* (associating anything with God) or *bid'ā* (impious innovations)." 'Azīz al-Nisā's religious "rationalism," simplicity, and the desire to eschew superstitions were very largely due to her family's exposure to Shah 'Abdul Azīz and his followers' philosophy,[10] which was also internalized by Sir Sayyid.

Sayyid Ahmad's formal education was strictly traditional, and was never completed. At age 5 he started learning the recitation of the Qur'ān, which was followed by lessons in elementary Persian texts, including the *Karīmā, Khāliq Barīy, Āmad Nameh, Gulistān* and *Bostān* of Sa'di. Subsequently, he studied some books in Arabic syntax, grammar, and logic, and a few elementary texts of mathematics, algebra, and geometry under the guidance of his uncle, Khawjah Zayn al-'Abidīyn Khan. Pursuing his desire for medical education, Sayyid Ahmad studied medicine in Hakīym Ghulam Haiyder Khan's clinic, and then practiced medicine under his supervision for some months.[11] When he was 18 years old, he gave up all formal education. The Delhi College no doubt was there; but it did not enter into his or his family's thinking as a suitable institution for his advanced education.

As a young man, Sayyid Ahmad was by no means a bright or disciplined student, and for many years he retained an uncomfortable feeling of being semieducated. Consequently, in 1846, when he was 29 years old, and occupied the position of Munsif (small-cause judge) in Delhi, he attempted to complete his education, but it did not advance very far. The Delhi College, though at the peak of its reputation, once again remained out of his consideration. However, for the first time he studied under the guidance of accomplished scholars in Delhi. He studied a few portions of *Maqāmāt-i Harīry,*[12] and a few odes from the so-called *Seven Mu'llaqāt*[13] from Mawlavi Faiz al-Hasan; for *fiqah* (jurisprudence) he studied *Sharh-i Waqayah*[14] and *Hidayah*[15] and for *usūl al-fiqah* (principles of jurisprudence) a few books including *Shashīy* [16] and *Nūr al-Anwar* [17] from Mawlavi Nawazish 'Ali. Mawlana Makhsūs Allah, grandson of Shah Waliy Allah, introduced him to the literature on the Prophetic traditions—some portions of *Mishkat al-Masabih,* [18] and *Sahīhy Muslim,* [19] and finally the book of Allah, *The Qur'ān.*

This strictly traditional education was neither comprehensive nor intensive, and after 1857 exposed him to the ridicule of his conservative critics, who considered him unqualified for modernistic interpretations of Islam. It is, however, doubtful that he would have ventured at all beyond the trodden path of tradition if in his earlier years Sir Sayyid had studied in an established traditional academy such as Madressah-i Farangiy Mahal in Lucknow, where *Dars-i Nizamiyya* held sway. His weakness was his real strength; unfettered by the discipline of rigorous traditional education, his mind by personal study and independent investigation reached out to new horizons of intellectual creativity and laid the groundwork for modern Islam.

Physically big and strong, Sayyid Ahmad as a young man also indulged himself in all the sensual pleasures and vices which occupied the spoiled youths of the *sharīf* culture in Delhi. Even his marriage at age eighteen failed to instill in him a sense of moderation and responsibility. Song and dance girls lured him to their private chambers; sometimes carefree friends engaged professional singers for private performances and entertainment, and Sayyid Ahmad joined the others in satisfying his aesthetic as well as his carnal appetites. "In the days of irresponsibility (*ghaflat*)," says Altaf Husain Hali, "with the exception of a few individuals, hardly anyone knew of his deeds. The members of the *sharīf* culture did whatever they did surreptiously; their actions were never exposed to the public gaze." [20]

Emergence of a New Man: 1838–1857

What turned this "carefree Mughal prince" into a responsible man, and a sensitive Muslim nationalist? The change was definite and came about in slow evolutionary stages, but was climaxed by the trauma of 1857.

The death of his elder brother, Sayyid Muhammad Khan, was a deep emotional shock. Their fraternal love and devotion was well-known in Delhi. In mourning and sorrow, Sir Sayyid gave up wearing fancy and fashionable clothing, started keeping a beard, and eschewed the company of his boon companions. In 1838 the death of his father reduced the economic ease of the family to austerity. Bahadur Shah's prime minister, Raja Sohan Lal, withdrew all the imperial grants including the land, and left the family with a meager pension for Sir Sayyid's mother. Semieducated, Sir Sayyid was ill-equipped for a position; mindful of his inadequacies, he asked his uncle, Khalil Allah Khan, who was then a Sadr Amin in Delhi, to teach him the routine of judicial proceedings. A few months later, he appointed him Sarishtadar (recorder) of the criminal department of his Court. In 1839 he was transferred to Agra as Naib Munshiy (deputy reader) in the office of the divisional Commisioner, Sir Robert Hamilton.

In Agra, Sir Sayyid made his literary debut, indicating that he was endeavoring to overcome his "timidity"[21] and lack of self-confidence borne of inadequate education. Permanent settlement was being introduced in some districts of the Agra Division. To expedite the settlement, and to streamline the administrative procedures, Sir Sayyid drafted a *Dastūr al-'Aml,* a transcript and analysis of the settlement regulations. *Jam-i Jam,* a Persian history of the Mughal dynasty, including the reign of Bahadur Shah, appeared in 1840, followed a year later by *Intikhāb al-Akhawayn,* a civil law digest, which he had prepared to achieve promotion to the position of Munsif (small cause judge). Sir Robert recommended him, but the Government's new policy decreed that the position be filled through a competitive examination. In December 1841, when he succeeded in the competitive examination, he was appointed Munsif at Mainpuri, but a year later was transferred to Fathpur Sikri, once a splendid capital of the Mughal Emperor, Akbar. He spent the next four years there in a house which was at one time the imperial apartment. In 1842

Bahadur Shah was persuaded by his prime minister, Hakīm Ahsan Allah Khan (who was also a collaborator with the British), to grant Sayyid Ahmad his ancestral titles. The titles, which once adorned the lords of the powerful Mughal Empire—*Jawad al-Daulah, Araf Jang*—were now bestowed upon a Munsif, whose monthly salary of barely 100 rupees was paid by the British East India Company. Several years earlier Sayyid Muttaqīy, Sir Sayyid's father, had demonstrated a greater sense of realism in rejecting these titles with an ironic remark—*where was the State, and the army* that the recipient of the titles was to fend.

Now Sayyid Ahmad turned to religion and the traditional Greco-Arab science, once popular among the Muslims. In 1843 was published *Jala'al-Qulūb bi-dhikr al-Mahbūb,* a biographical sketch of the Prophet Muhammad, and in 1844, *Tuhfah-i Hasan,* an Urdu translation of Shah 'Abdul Azīz's *Tuhfah Ithna Ashariyyā,* basically a sunni polemic against the Shi'a. *Tashīl fi Jarr al-Thaqīl,* an Urdu translation of a Persian treatise on mechanics, appeared the same year. Was there an intellectual relationship between these religious works and the long obsolete scientific study? None whatsoever; it merely reflected Sayyid Ahmad's fantastic creative energy groping to find an acceptable channel. From 1846 to 1854 he remained in Delhi as Munsif, while he spent several months in Rohtak (Punjab) in 1850 and again in 1853 as acting Sadr Amin.

Like an obedient and faithful son, Sir Sayyid each month gave 100 rupees of his salary to his mother, who had to manage a large household containing not only Sir Sayyid's family, but also his brother's widow and their children. To augment his income, Sir Sayyid turned to journalism. *Sayyid al-Akhbār,* an irregular periodical originally started by his deceased brother, was now taken over by Sir Sayyid. It was published for a while, and then became defunct; today none of its issues can be found. Subsequently, Sir Sayyid wrote six more books, including an Urdu translation of his grandfather's book on geometry, *Fawa'id al-Afkar fi A'mal al-Farjā* (1846) and trivia on Sufism, *Kalmāt al-Haq* (1850) and *Namīqah* (1852). *Qawl-i Matīyn Der Abtal-i Harkat-i*

Zamīyn (1848) was a traditional attempt to "disprove" the modern scientific view that the earth revolved around the sun. In 1850 was published *Risalah Rah-i Sunnat wa Radd-i Bid'at,* his passionate defense of Sayyid Ahmad Shahīd and his followers' religious views, which were then derogatorily called "the Wahhabi doctrines." *Silsilāt al-Mulūk,* a chronology of the Delhi kings from the ancient Aryan rulers to the contemporanious Queen Victoria, appeared in 1852, and was followed the next year by *Tarjamah-i Kimya-i Sa'dat,* an incomplete Urdu translation of al-Ghazzali's Persian work on ethics.

Once again a question may be asked about Sir Sayyid's works produced in this period of 1846–1854: did he apply any particular method or technique in composing these studies? Pecuniary advantage was the motive force for this "scholarly" activity, but like authors before and after him Sir Sayyid realized much to his disappointment that scholarly publications hardly ever bring financial rewards to the author. *Athār al-Sanadid,* an archeological survey of Delhi, which was first published in 1847, brought him recognition from the West, but no money. In fact, the publisher cheated him out of his share of the profits. However, the study stands out as a pioneering work demonstrating Sir Sayyid's vast knowledge of historical sources and his ability to present archeological evidence as a supplement to the understanding of history. The first edition also contained chapters on the birth of Urdu in India, and invaluable information regarding the traditional Muslim elites in Delhi, including such revolutionary leaders as Sayyid Ahmad Shahīd and Isma'īl Shahīd, whom Sir Sayyid had known as a young man.

A copy of the first edition of *Athār al-Sanadid* was presented by A. A. Roberts, a collector of Delhi, to The Royal Asiatic Society of Britain. The Society asked Roberts to translate it into English. For the English translation, Edward Thomas, who achieved recognition for numismatic studies, advised Sir Sayyid to revise the first edition of *Athār al-Sanadid.* The second edition was published in 1854, containing in English a preface and a brief account of the minaret which adorns the Qutab in Delhi. These portions were probably translated by Roberts in tedious victorian English; however, a celebrated French scholar of Urdu literature, Garcin de Tassy, who never visited India, rendered the second edition in French and published it in 1861. Tardily and grudgingly The Royal Asiatic Society of Britain made Sayyid Ahmad an honorary fellow in 1864. Sir Sayyid, no longer a "timid" man, also hoped that *Athār al-Sanadid* would "maintain his name for ages to come."[22] Being the first archeological survey of Delhi, the study deserved recognition, but whether it would assure an abiding place in archeology to the author remained a moot point. In 1855 a publisher of Delhi, Haji Qutb al-Din, published the first and the third volumes of Abul Faḍl's *Āin-i Akbari*, which Sir Sayyid had edited with great diligence. The second volume was sent to the publisher in 1857, but was destroyed in the press when Delhi was recaptured the following year by the British. Illustrations and pictures which were included by H. Blockmann in the English edition of Āin-i Akbari in 1873 had originally appeared in Sir Sayyid's edition.

In 1855 Sir Sayyid was transferred to Bijnore, where he witnessed and participated in the upheavals of 1857. If the wars of 1857 against the British had not broken out Sir Sayyid probably would have ended his life as a minor judicial official with a dozen mediocre books to his name. The trauma of 1857 provided the essential background to his greatness both in terms of his scholarship and his role of purveyor of modernity for the Muslims of India. Self-centered and self-seeking before 1857, Sir Sayyid's sensitive mind responded profoundly to this national as well as personal tragedy, which instilled in him a gnawing sense of remorse for his personal involvement on the side of the British against his own people. Subsequently, the psychological presssure for atonement which created in him an irrepressible urge to be helpful to his people made Sir Sayyid a new man. In a sense Sir Sayyid's real life started after 1857.

Sir Sayyid has shed considerable light on the development of his new orientation as a reaction to the events of 1857. "People have not yet forgotten the wretched days of 1857," said Sir Sayyid publicly several decades later,

I was in Bijnore in those days. A great misfortune befell the English officials and Christian men, women and children. Motivated exclusively by humanitarianism I helped them in their affliction. And what devastation did our own nation suffer! Many well-known families perished; the narration of these events cuts my heart into pieces. After the mutiny I cared neither for my home nor other possessions which had been destroyed. I grieved only at the destruction of our nation, and the suffering of the British which had been caused by the Indians. When our friend, the late Mr. Shakespeare, who shared our troubles, offered me as a reward for my loyalty to the British cause the Jahanabad estate of the Sayyids [23] which was then valued at Rs. 100,000 I felt grieved. I said to myself that there was no one more wretched than myself. Our nation suffered like this, and I, at their expense, should become a ta'luq-dār (estate-holder). I declined this offer and said [to Shakespeare] that I no longer desired to live in India.

At that time I did not think that our nation would survive or attain prestige. I could not bear to see the condition of our nation. For several days I remained in deep depression. Believe me, this grief aged me prematurely and my hair turned gray. When I came to Moradabad [in 1858]—which was in fact a big house of mourning for the death and destruction of our nation's well-to-do families—my grief was deepened. Then and there it occurred to me that my personal flight to a place of safety was contrary to all feelings of compassion and manhood. No, I must share the troubles of my nation; and whatever the afflictions there might be I must help to alleviate them. This is a national obligation. Then I decided not to leave the country, and dedicated myself to the national cause. [24]

Sir Sayyid emerged from the ordeal of 1857 not only as a loyal employee of the British Government, but traumatized into a staunch Muslim nationalist. Also, his feeling for national tragedy was deepened by the suffering of his family and close relatives, who lived in Delhi. The British rule had been ejected from Delhi on May 11, 1857; but by September 20 the British forces had recaptured the city. In September Sir Sayyid came to Delhi to see his mother. The old lady, along with her younger sister, had taken refuge in a shanty after the house was plundered by the British troops. He knocked at the door, and she cried out, "Why have you come here? All are being killed. You will be killed also!"[25] Thirsty and hungry for days, she asked her son to fetch her a drink. After hours of search, Sir Sayyid finally procured water from the Red Fort. On the way back he found old and emaciated Zayban, a ward of his mother, with a bowl in her hand begging for water. Sir Sayyid poured water into her bowl, some of it she spilled and some she drank, but persistently she pointed with her finger towards the shanty indicating that his mother needed the water most. After serving his mother and aunt, Sir Sayyid returned to the street and found that Zayban had died. He managed to take his mother to Meerut, where she died a few months later.

In the rage of reprisal and blind vengeance the victorious British soldiers indiscriminately slaughtered the loyal and the rebel. Sir Sayyid's uncle Wahīd al-Din Khan and his son Hāshim 'Ali Khan were "slain unarmed by the infuriated Sikhs three days after the assault" on Delhi. Sir Sayyid's relatives, along with the city's population, were driven out and took refuge at Nizām al-Din Awliya's tomb. Hindus were allowed to return to Delhi as early as January 1858, but the Muslims were kept out until 1859.[26] During this punitive period no more than 1,000 loyal Muslims were allowed to live in the city. Then some Muslims, who could pay an arbitrary fine and obtain a permit, were allowed to dwell in Delhi.[27] How was British justice dispensed? To try the guilty a Special Commission was established which "tried 3,306 persons of whom 2,025 were convicted. Of these, 392 were hung and 57 sentenced to life imprisonment. To this number must be added, first, all those who fell in the six days' fighting after the assault, and second, all those who suffered death without any sort of trial from maddened or reckless officers."[28]

Bahadur Shah was exiled .to Burma, and two of his sons were executed in his presence. This punishment was inflicted for their "rebellion" against the British and the execution of 50 British civilians, mostly women and children, who had taken refuge in the Red Fort. Asad Allah Khan Ghālib, a loyalist poet, described the fate of the king's family: "The male members of the royal household whom the sword spared are now each getting

Rs. 5 per month as a pension. Of the women, the older ones have become madams and the young ones are prostitutes."[29] Ghalib, who had composed a congratulatory ode to Queen Victoria on the reconquest of India, and described 1857 as *Rastakhayz-i Bayjah*[30] (unjustified insurrections), was finally moved to describe the Delhi Muslim's misery, and their oppression by the British:

> Surely today every English tommy is Almighty God,
> Now every man going from his house to the *bazaar* is panic-stricken.
> The marketplace has become a slaughter-house, and the house looks like a prison,
> The very particles of dust in Delhi thirst for the blood of Muslims.[31]

Sir Sayyid could not fail to be moved to the depth of his soul by the tragedy of Delhi, the destruction of the upper class to which he belonged, and the violent deaths of his own relatives. British anger at the death of innocent Europeans was justified and even their revenge against the guilty Indians was understandable, but was there any justification for the wholesale demolition of Muslim neighborhoods, including some monuments, the desecration of the mosques, and the execution of innocent citizens? "I cannot describe to you what a critical time it was," said Sir Sayyid of his response to these tragic events; "in that exuberant feeling of national love, which I myself can describe as madness, I could scarcely care what might happen to me. However, that was my very first lesson in [the development of] national love. My friends who shared my grief wanted me to restrain my emotions, and my heart would say to them [in the verse of a poet]":[32]

> *Harif Kawish mizhagan-i Khun rayzam n-eh nasih*
> *Badast awer rag-i janiy wa nashtir ra tamasha kun*

> O dear friend! You would never be able to bear
> the sight of blood in my tears [i.e., afflictions]

If you cut my veins you will see a
never-ending flow of blood [i.e., an endless grief]

Sir Sayyid's remorse was of a dilaectical nature, simultaneously reflecting love for his nation and devotion to the British, whose policy during 1857–58 and immediately after the reconquest of Delhi was avowedly repressive of the Muslims. This situation created in him acute emotional tensions throughout the next decade; however, these personal tensions could be resolved only if the Muslims and the British established an acceptable *modus vivendi*. In order to bring this about he endeavored to be a bridge of understanding between the sovereign and the subject. Initially, his agonized soul sought catharsis in acts of personal atonement supplemented by public prayers for *pax Britannia* in India.

In 1858, when Queen Victoria issued a proclamation of amnesty and religious noninterference, Sir Sayyid organized a public meeting of Moradabad Muslims to offer thanksgiving. Fifteen thousand Muslims congregated at the mosque, near Bulaqi Shah's shrine, on July 28, 1859, and joined in the prayer which Sir Sayyid had composed. The prefatory remark was indicative of the emotional release derived from the prayer. "As it is my heartfelt desire and prayer to God that our Government and the people of India be so connected together as to be of one accord in the administration of this country. Therefore, whenever I find such unanimity between them on any subject I become exceedingly glad of it, and wish to have it recorded for future remembrance." Consequently, the text of the speech along with the proceedings of the meeting were published separately and widely distributed. Most significantly, Sir Sayyid's prayer extolled the British as "just rulers" and "impartial governors," and the revolt of 1857 as the divine wrath:

O God! Our sins have multiplied exceedingly; our cursed deeds were countless in thy sight. We believe that thou wilt one day doubtless reward each man according to the deeds he has committed, for thou hast so promised in the books of thy true Prophets. On that day none can expect deliverance but through thy mercy and grace; for all men are sinners in thy sight. But within the last two years [1857–1858] thou hast looked down with wrathful indignation on thy helpless servants; this was undoubtedly the consequence of our cursed deeds. Lord! We repent our Sins. We beg thy forgiveness for our sins. Pardon our Sins O Lord! We beseech thee; Amen.

O God! We humbly acknowledge thy great kindness in having placed us under just rulers. For a hundred years thou hast continued to us, thy people of India, the blessed rule of just and impartial rulers. Thou hast shown us the evil tendency of our deeds by depriving us temporarily of our rulers, and hast now reestablished our Government, and given us back our just and impartial governors. We approach thee with hearty thanks for thy merciful kindness.[33]

The prayers were followed by acts of expiation. In 1860 famine devastated the northwestern districts of the former United Provinces (Uttar Pradish). On his request the British Government appointed Sir Sayyid the administrator of relief measures for about 14,000 famine-stricken people. Also, an infirmary was established to look after the sick. Disregarding all rules of hygiene and preventive care, Sir Sayyid daily visited the cholera patients, and insisted on changing the clothes of those who were suffering from diarrhea. Even when the patients' clothes were saturated with excrement he would gently hold them in his lap and help them wash their hands and faces or just make them comfortable, or arrange for them to have close haircuts.[34]

In early 1861 Sir Sayyid's wife died, leaving him with two infant sons, Sayyid Hamid (b. 1849) and Sayyid Mahmud (b. 1850), and a daughter. He denied himself a second marriage and resolved to sublimate his sex drive into the work of national reconstruction.[35]

The fact that feelings of remorse inspired him to achieve the highest ideals of modern liberal nationalism does not detract from the significance of Sir Sayyid's contributions to the Muslims' collective life. Remorse does not always inspire; it could just as well have led him to a sterile life of negativism and physical isolation. He had not been the only Muslim on the British side; others more educated and hierarchically more elevated had rendered equally important services to the British during

1857–58. But only Sir Sayyid felt this deep personal commitment to Muslim nationalism, which assured him an abiding place in Indic Muslim history.

The British no doubt valued his services, and rewarded him with a promotion to the rank of Principal Sadr Amin; in addition he received a *khilat* (robe of honor) of five pieces with three gems and a cash prize of one thousand rupees to compensate for the loss of his property in Delhi, which was estimated at Rs. 30,384. Shakespeare, Collector of Bijnore, in his confidential report of June 5, 1858, to R. Alexander, Commissioner of Rohilkhand Division, also recommended that Sayyid Ahmad "should receive a pension in perpetuity, or for his own life and that of his eldest son, of Rs. 200 per mensem. I make this proposal because I know that it is the wish of Syud Ahmud Khan to travel when he has passed a few years more in the service, and that he does not desire to have villages given, as their possession would fetter his movements."[36] Finally, the British Government granted him a pension of Rs. 200 monthly "for his own and his eldest son's lives."[37] Altaf Husain Hali has stated that Sir Sayyid wanted a pension in order to eventually settle in Egypt.[38] However, in April 1858 he was transferred to Moradabad, where he served until May 12, 1863. From there he was sent to Ghazipur; and in the following year he was assigned to Aligarh. Finally raised to the position of Judge, Small Cause Court, Sir Sayyid was once again transferred to Benares, where he remained until April 1869.

Political Socialization of Sir Sayyid: 1858–1870

This period of twelve years was a mental bridge in Sir Sayyid's political development in which traditional values slowly gave way to new orientations. The change to modernity was completed by his exposure in 1869–70 to the input structures of the British political culture, including specialized pressure groups, the media of communication, and political parties. In 1858, however, he started to demonstrate his political competence in criticizing the existing subject political culture, which in itself had entered a new phase of transition after the dissolution of the British East India Company. In Moradabad he not only completed *Tarīkh Sarkashīy-i Dhilla Bijnore* (A History of Insurrection in Bijnor District), but also developed his critique, *Asbāb-i Baghawat-i Hind* (The Causes for the Revolt of India), of the pre-1857 subject political culture. (Its detailed analysis is presented in a separate chapter.)

Here, it would suffice to say that Sir Sayyid held British imposed subject political culture primarily responsible for causing widesperad alienation of the subjects from the British Government, which had precipitated the catastrophic wars of 1857. Also, in its place he recommended the adoption of a mixed subject-participant culture for post-1858 India. Even this mild recommendation was resented by Cecil Bedan, the Foreign Secretary of the Government of India, who considered Sir Sayyid's critique inflammatory. Prudently enough, Sir Sayyid had sent in 1859 almost 500 copies of the *Asbāb* to the British Government in London, and only one to Lord Canning in Calcutta, and had not circulated even one to the public. In 1873, its English translation by Col. Graham and Sir Auckland Colvin was first published in Benares.

While Sir Sayyid was developing his ideas for the creation of an input infrastructure geared particularly to the needs of the Muslims in India, he simultaneously sought to assure the British Government that, contrary to the British misconception, a large number of Muslims had remained loyal to the British Government during 1857–58, and that the restoration of peace would increase their loyalty. In 1860–61 he developed the thesis in his *Risalah Khair Khawahān Musalmanān: An Account of the Loyal Mahomdans of India* that "in India there was one class of people above another, who from the principles of their religion, from habits and associations, and from kindred disposition, were bound with Christians, in their dread hour of trial and danger, in the bonds of amity and friendship, those people were the Mohamedans, and they alone!"[39] To explore areas of harmony and foster sympathetic understanding of Christianity among the Muslims, Sir Sayyid wrote *Tabīyn al-Kalām Fī Tafsīr al-Tawrāt wa al-Injīyl Ala*

Millat al-Islam: The Mahomedan Commentary on the Holy Bible, and published it in three parts in 1862 at his personal press in Ghazipur. Sir Sayyid, incidentally, was the only Muslim scholar to venture a commentary on the Old and New Testaments. To convince Muslims at the same time that *pax Britannica* did not make India *Dar al-Harb* (land of war) he published, as an appendix to *Tabīyn,* Jamal Ibn al-Abd Allah Umar al-Hanfi's (the Mufti of Mecca's) *fatwa* (decision) that "as long as even some of the peculiar observances of Islam prevail in [India], it is *Dar al-Islam* (land of Islam)."[40]

His relentless protestations of political loyalty to the authoritarian political system of British India enabled Sir Sayyid to develop an activist set of participant orientations and policies for the Muslims, and he persuaded the bureaucracy to be sympathetic to these orientations. This change found its initial expressions in the establishment of The Scientific Society, The British Indian Association, and a couple of elementary schools, where Sir Sayyid experimented with his educational ideas and evolved a comprehensive view of modernism. While the output structure of British Government, particularly the bureaucracy, was not yet prepared to accept the open and accelerated development of an input structure in India, the Liberal and enlightened members of the bureaucracy were inclined to lend their assistance in the creation of a participant infrastructure, which would not demand rapid change in the subject political culture of the British *raj.* This liberal element of bureaucracy was also convinced that India needed science first, and politics afterwards or perhaps never. In the post-1857 period some of them, including notably Col. Graham and Sir Auckland Colvin, supported Sir Sayyid and other Muslim causes, while some, particularly A. O. Hume and Sir Wedderburn and others, supported the All-India National Congress and the multifaceted Hindu renaissance.

The Scientific Society

These liberal bureaucrats had a deep faith in their modern European civilization, which was based upon science and technology.

They rightly saw science as a secret of their power and believed that it could deliver material benefits to the Indians. On January 9, 1864, at the first meeting of the Scientific Society, which was convened in Ghazipur at Sir Sayyid's initiative, Col. Graham, who later wrote Sir Sayyid's biography, alluded to its precursor in India:

Now within the last twenty years there have been several attempts to keep going a Society similar to the one the first meeting of which we are now holding, but which from the illness of the promoter or from want of funds or from the sudden outbreak of the Great Mutiny in 1857 have gradually or suddenly come to an end. These, however, were all, if I recollect aright, set on foot by philanthropical and earnest Englishmen and for this reason perhaps have not received from the nation in general that support which they deserved.[41]

Obviously, the desire to revive the Scientific Society persuaded the British to enlist the help of those Indians who demonstrated to a degree the development of participant orientations. For a police superintendent, Col. Graham was remarkably enlightened in appreciating the fact that India could profit from technology, even without going through the painful process of scientific discoveries with which Europe struggled during the previous two centuries. Addressing his audience on this subject, Graham added:

Look how England's wealth has increased with her education within the last century. She had great difficulties which we know only too well obstruct the spread of knowledge in this country. In those days she had no railways, no steam printing presses, etc., little but her own innate genius and unconquerable energy. . . . All the many aids to enlightenment which it took England many many years to invent, experimentalize upon, and finally to bring into general use are all at hand now. Steam, with its many models of application, is at the people's command, calling loudly for employment as a railway, a steam pump, or a steam press, that universal dissemination of knowledge. A desire to benefit by all these can only be thoroughly kindled in the minds of the natives of this country by bringing them and many other things prominently to view, which is the object of this Society.[42]

Consequently, the Scientific Society adopted the following objectives: (1) to translate into such languages as may be in common use among the people those works on arts and sciences which, being in English or other European languages, are not intelligible to the natives; (2) To search for and publish rare and valuable oriental works ("No religious work will come under the notice of the Society)." In 1867 two more objectives were added: (3) "to publish, when the Society thinks it desirable, any [periodical] which may be calculated to improve the native mind; (4) to have delivered in their meetings lectures on scientific or other useful subjects, illustrated when possible by scientific instruments." [43]

What kinds of books should be selected for translation? The issue revealed Sir Sayyid's preoccupation with the mystery of the rise and fall of nations. Having witnessed the demise of Muslim power in India, he, in contrast to Col. Graham, was naturally interested in the philosophy of history. "My dear compatriots," stated Sir Sayyid in his concluding remarks on January 9, 1863, "do not understand the past and have no light to see their future. What was yesterday, what is today they do not know; and they know not how tomorrow will dawn." He asserted, with not too much justification, that Asian scholars never wrote any history illuminating the birth and development of civilizations. They merely chronicled the kings' ascension to power and their deaths; then how could national morals be improved and characters developed? In order to achieve these goals one needed to fully appreciate in detail national character, its virtues and vices. "Let me make myself clear by an example," Sir Sayyid stated,

Now Sir Charles Treveleyan has proposed a topic for a competitive essay which would highlight the extent to which Arabs benefitted from Greek sciences during the times of the Abbaside Caliphs of Baghdad, and the Umayyad Caliphs of Cardova. Then he wants the essayists to demonstrate how Europeans benefitted from Arab contributions after the former awoke from the slumber of ignorance. Finally, a comparison be made between these two benign processes with a conclusion pointing to the possibilities of great benefits accruing to the Muslims in India as a consequence of their contact with Europeans at the present time.[44]

In October 1863, Sir Sayyid had delivered a lecture on the same theme before the Muhammadan Literary Society of Calcutta, which had been established by Mawlavi Abd al-Latif Khan to initiate modernism among the Bengali Muslims. Extracts from this speech were reiterated at the initiation of the Scientific Society. Highlighting the benefits to be derived from western modernism, Sir Sayyid had stated:

Insensibly we become assimilated to those with whom we associate. The higher intellect effects the weaker. Thus the study of an elevated literature will silently and little by little take effect on the man's nature, and the various elements of character will grow in correspondence with the influences that act on them. The student will learn to appreciate the temper with which great minds approach the consideration of great questions, he will discover that truth is many-sided, that it is not identical or merely co-extensive with individual opinion, and that the world is a good deal wider than his own sect, or society or class.[45]

A couple of decades later Sir Sayyid further refined this theme into a fully developed theory of diffusion.

The Scientific Society created the Directing Council and the Executive Council and B. Sapte, Collector of Aligarh, was elected President of both organs when his name was proposed by Col. Graham. Sir Sayyid and Col. Graham were elected secretaries of the Executive Council. Breakdown of membership in the Councils and the paid subscribers of the Scientific Society is given in Table 2.1.[46] The Executive Council was "the Government of the Society," whose members were the permanent residents of Aligarh since the Society moved there permanently

TABLE 2.1.

	Total	Europeans	Muslims	Hindus
Membership (1864) of the Councils				
Directing Council	16	11	4	1
Executive Council	9	3	3	3
Paid Members of the Society				
1864	109	14	—	—
1875	97	10	39	48

along with Sir Sayyid in 1867. As an advisory body the Directing Council had its members spread out in different parts of India. The Duke of Argyll (the Secretary of State for India) became the Society's Patron and the Lt. Governor of the N.W. Province Vice-Patron. Since November 1869 a well-known honorary member of the Society was the French scholar of Urdu literature, Garcin de Tassy. Sir Sayyid was not only the Secretary but was also a member of both councils; consequently, he very effectively manipulated the activities of the Society. Also, he was efficiently assisted by a capable and devoted friend, Raja Jaikishan Das.

What did the Scientific Society accomplish? Its planning and the approved projects reflected very largely Sir Sayyid's orientations toward science and their relevance to contemporary India. The Society translated forty European books dealing with history, political science, geography, meteorology, electricity, algebra, geometry, calculus, hydrology, and agriculture. For the Indian agriculture, modern agronomy was most significant. Consequently the Society undertook the first agricultural experimental project. In September 1864 Sir Sayyid applied for a Government grant for an experimental farm consisting of "The Government Garden," and adjoining "a piece of ground situated to the north of the Civil Courts" of Aligarh, where eventually the Society's building was constructed in 1866. The Government Garden was obtained, Sir Sayyid had assured the Government, in order "to improve the operations of husbandry and to introduce the European agricultural implements and machinery into India . . . to set up and arrange those implements so as publicly to show their working to the people." Also, Sir Sayyid had agreed that if the Society's agricultural experiments were given up the Society would relinquish possession of the Garden.[47]

In a memorandum of May 24, 1877, to the President of the Society, Sir Sayyid summarized the agricultural experiments; a few are noteworthy: (1) the Society for several years cultivated wheat and barley according to the methods prescribed in Scot Burn's work on modern farming and showed the results to Talukdars (estate holders) of Aligarh; (2) new instruments were used to cultivate corn by Burn's methods; (3) several vegetables were grown from newly developed European seeds and their seeds were distributed to farmers; (4) the Society cultivated American cotton seeds, and demonstrated their superior product.[48]

In 1865 Sir Sayyid decided to write a comprehensive work in Urdu on the scientific methods of cultivation suitable for India. Initially he suggested that the Society should examine "the various methods of cultivation now in vogue in these the North Western Provinces—to enumerate in detail the various crops of each district, their rotation, and the effect of each on the soil and the method of their cultivation. When this knowledge shall have been obtained it will be practicable to determine on scientific principles whether the various systems as pursued in each district were practically the best adopted to their several soils." Sir Sayyid also submitted to the Directing Council on July 27, 1866, for their approval 32 problems related to the methods of cultivation.[49] A great deal of research was conducted and the findings were published in several issues of the *Akhbar Institute Gazette,* which the Society had established in March 1866. But Sir Sayyid's book failed to see the light of day owing probably to his 16-month absence in Europe starting in 1869.

While the Society's publication program was successful, the agricultural experiments declined, due partly to the unsympathetic attitude of some bureaucrats and partly to the shortage of funds. The Aligarh Collector first of all reclaimed part of the Garden "for the Oudh and Rohil Khand Railway," and then allowed the construction of the Government dhillah school on another portion. When the Society failed to conduct agricultural experiments for two years, J. C. Colvin, the Collector of Aligarh, recommended to the Government in 1876 that the Garden be repossessed by the Government. However, B. W. Colvin, officiating secretary of the N. W. Province Government, decided "to allow [the Society] another year's grace before passing final orders."[50] Outraged by the district officials' attitude, Sir Sayyid commented:

To take this land out of the Society's possession would amount to a declaration that the Society should for the future entirely remove from its mind all thoughts of making agricultural experiments which may be calculated to benefit the country; and instead of any assistance being derived from the district authorities towards such useful objects, an obstacle will be placed in the way of their accomplishments. Whatever neglect the Society may have committed in making these experiments, its remedy did not lie in those measures which Mr. Colvin [the Collector of Aligarh] had adopted and which have caused a great disheartening to the Society.[51]

Dismayed by economic difficulties and the bureaucratic attitude, the Society finally transferred the Garden to the Government in November 1877.

Sir Sayyid's personal devotion to the Society, however, did not waver or diminish. His personal printing press which he had purchased in order to publish *Tabīyn al-Kalām* was made a gift to the Society. In 1866 Nawab Sikander Begum, the Ruler of Bhopal, sent a ring valued at Rs. 1000 to Sir Sayyid as a token of her appreciation for Sir Sayyid's contributions. On July 2, in a public ceremony, Sir Sayyid transferred this gift to the Society. To augment the Society's financial capability, he regularly transferred to the Society all fees which he earned for his legal lectures to advocates and vakils practicing civil law at the local courts. Also, Sir Sayyid succeeded in attracting permanent annual donations of Rs. 100 from Raja of Jodhpur; of Rs. 50 from Maharaja of Kopurthala, Maharaja Jaipur, and Nawab of Rampur. Nawab Kalbi Ali Khan made a gift of a gilded chair valued at Rs. 1200. Maharajas of Alwer and Indor and Nawab of Tonk made unspecified but generous contributions to the Society. Consequently, the Society's annual income, during the peak of its popularity, amounted to Rs. 10,850 (while at its initiation in 1864 its total assets were Rs. 2,716); and the Society had succeeded in constructing its building for Rs. 30,000 in March 1866.[52]

In dealing with the output side of the British Government, Sir Sayyid developed political orientations which had far-reaching consequences for the Muslims of India. Initially, to deal with the subject political culture he established the allegiant British Indian Association.

The British Indian Association

The inspiration for the name and the role of the association probably came from Calcutta, where the British Indian Association had been established on October 29, 1851. Of its 49 founding members, 47 were Hindu men, with one Hindu lady, Shrimiti Rasmure Dassi, and one Muslim, Shah Kabir Al-Din. Sir Sayyid's Aligarh British Indian Association started off with only 9 Hindu and Muslim founding members, each one a man of substance. The initiation took place on May 10, 1866, at the Scientific Society's office at Aligarh with a sizable number of local landlords and a few European officers in attendance. They listened to Sir Sayyid define the role of their elite association:

In order to get our rights from the Government the Indians must establish contacts with the [British] Parliament. During the East India Company's rule, India's great difficulty was this: all of its affairs had access to the Company's Court of Directors only and were scarcely settled by the Parliament. Now the Indian administration has been taken over by the Queen and Indian affairs will have connection with the Parliament. In order to adequately inform the members of the Parliament of our affairs and reasonable aspirations we should create channels of communication. Like those Englishmen who reside in India and have decided to create an association in England, similarly we should establish an association for all the Districts of the North-West in order to communicate our aspirations and objectives to the Government and the Parliament.[53]

In dealing with the British Indian Government Sir Sayyid soon recognized the limitations of the subject political culture: it would allow limited *association* of the Indians in the administration, but no effective *participation* in the decision-making processes of the Government. (The theoretical considerations relat-

ing to the roles of the subject and the citizen in the Government
are discussed in a separate chapter.) The Association asked the
Government to create local committees, starting first in Aligarh
District and then in other districts, for "the general control and
supervision of the [educational] system and for regulating the expenditure." The Government, in a resolution of July 14, 1866, denied that the Association had a right to play this role, but recognized "the desirability of enlisting the sympathies and obtaining
the cooperation of the resident gentry in the cause of education."[54]

In order to be sure that the Aligarh Educational Committee
would play the subservient role, the Government appointed several high district officials, including the Deputy Commissioner,
the Judge, Joint Magistrate, Assistant Magistrate, and even the
Civil Surgeon, in addition to the resident members of the Scientific Society. Subsequently, similar educational committees were
created in other districts. By 1872 Sir Sayyid realized that cir-
cumscribed participation had failed to create civic competence
among the nonofficial members of the educational committees,
and he complained of bureaucratic domination and private members' subservience. Responding to this protest the Government
modified rules of procedure in 1877, but the Indians' limited association could not be converted to effective participation in the
administration. In 1882 Sir Sayyid repeated his criticism of the
educational committees before the Education Commission, but
the Government's policy did not change.

On July 2, 1866, Sir Sayyid, as the Honorary Secretary of
the Association, protested to the Government of India the increase in the rates of book postage under the Post Office Act of
1866. Sir Sayyid called the increase of rates "a direct taxation on
knowledge." But in a letter of August 17, 1866, the Government
made short shrift of this argument in a terse sentence: "the
Governor-General in Council regrets his inability to comply with
the wishes of the Association in respect of the reduction of the
Book Post rate which is not regarded by His Excellency in
Council as excessive."[55] And the matter quietly ended.

The British Indian Association, however, entered into a dialogue with the Government on the most crucial issue of the Government's educational policy. On August 1, 1867, the Association sent a memorandum to the Government suggesting: (1) that a system of university education be established in which the arts, sciences, and other branches of European literature may be taught through the vernacular language of Northern India, that is, Urdu; (2) that examinations in the vernacular be held in those subjects in which the students were examined in English at the Calcutta University; (3) that, as with students in English classes, degrees should be conferred on those students who pass the same subjects in the vernacular; (4) and "that a vernacular university be created for the N. W. Provinces." [56]

In a letter of September 5, 1867, the Government of India discouraged the plan of mass higher education for lack of funds and the unavailability of scientific literature in the Indian vernacular. In a section of the local press the demand was made that should a "Vernacular University" be established in Northern India, Hindi rather than Urdu should be employed as the medium of instruction for the Hindus. Discouraged by the Government's negative reaction, practical difficulties of translating European works, and the demands of the champions of Hindi, Sir Sayyid abandoned his commitment to the Vernacular University. This change in policy subsequently made Sir Sayyid a zealot of education through the medium of English.

Another abortive plan of the Association was related to the encouragement of the Indians' travel to Europe and particularly Britain. The Association announced in 1868 assistance to persons "visiting Europe for educational and scientific purposes." Contributions were solicited, but the project did not catch popular imagination. Still most people in northern India considered social contacts with Englishmen polluting of their morals and religious integrity. The adventure of travels to Europe across the high seas however inspired Sir Sayyid's zest for life, new ideas and wider contacts with the centers of modernity.

Exposure to the West

Accompanied by his two sons, Sayyid Hamid and Sayyid Mahmud, a younger friend, Mirza Khuda Dad Beg, and a servant known only by his twisted name, Chajju, Sir Sayyid arrived in London on May 4, 1869, after spending five days in Marseilles and Paris.[57] Financially, however, Sir Sayyid was in a squeeze. For his European travels he had not only mortgaged his ancestral house in Delhi, but had also borrowed 10,000 rupees from a money lender at 14 percent interest rate for the first 5,000 rupees, and at 8 percent for the second 5,000 rupees.[58] "In order to come to England," wrote Sir Sayyid on July 28, 1869, to the Secretary of State (George Douglas Campbell, the Eighth Duke of Argyll, 1823–1900), "I have been obliged to sell and mortgage my property." He then requested "to be allowed full pay while on furlough." On August 5, Secretary of State in Council "agreed to grant him Rs. 250 per annum for two years in addition to his furlough pay."[59]

This "generous" grant that the Government had originally denied him in India, was somewhat larger than the Rs. 200 annual stipend of Sayyid Mahmud, who had been selected from the Northwest Province for one of the nine scholarships which the Government of India had awarded by its decision of June 30, 1868. The initiative for Sayyid Mahmud's selection was taken by Sir William Muir, against whose anti-Islamic presentation, *The Life of Mohammad,* Sir Sayyid was to publish an answer in London. Writing confidentially to Sir John Lawrence on January 6, 1869, Sir William had stated in the postscript of his letter: "Syed Ahmad is about to take his son (whom I am going to recommend for the N.W.P. scholarship) to England, an additional reason perhaps for encouraging his merits."

Despite Sir William's generally known anti-Islamic bias (and Sir Sayyid's open resentment of it), he privately maintained a generous and appreciative attitude toward Sir Sayyid. Probably Sir Sayyid was unaware in the summer of 1869 that Sir William had also initially sponsored Sir Sayyid for the award of the third class Order of the Star of India.[60] Consequently, Sir John

Lawrence, Governor-General of India, wrote to the Duke of Argyll on July 9, 1867: "Syed Ahmad . . . is a man of singularly liberal and enlightened views. He has at all times, and at no time more strongly than in the crisis of the mutiny in 1857, used his influence in uniting, by example and by word to stimulate those of his creed to loyalty, tolerance and enlightened action."[61] On August 6, 1869, Sir Sayyid received the Star at the India office from the Secretary of State, the Duke of Argyll.

While Sir Sayyid's official reception was elevated, he barely managed to maintain a standard of living in London corresponding to his status. He rented in May 1869 six rooms in a depressing row house at 4 Guilford Street,[62] Russell Square, which is located exactly seven blocks from the University of London. Not being able to afford the rent, Sir Sayyid moved after December to another low-rent row house at 21 Mecklenburg Square and occupied only a few rooms on the first floor. In this depressing house Sir Sayyid spent the remaining eight months, while Sayyid Mahmud enrolled at Lincoln's Inn of Law. Although he lived in the middle-class neighborhoods his association was mostly with the members of the British nobility and upper bourgeoisie. Lord Lawrence, the former Governor-General of India, visited him "once every month during his stay" and frequently invited him for dinners. Another old India hand, Sir John William Kay, who was then Secretary to the Duke of Argyll, was Sir Sayyid's frequent companion and their conversations often explored the dark contours of 1857. Sir Sayyid also cultivated Lord Stanley of Alderly, who because of his long stay in Turkey as Britain's ambassador had acquired a respectable knowledge of Islamic laws and history. His old friend, Col. Graham, who was on vacation in Britain, often visited him and once even lured him to the horse races at Derby.

In Britain, Sir Sayyid internalized some positive aspects of British culture, including the value system of modern scientific education, and the capitalistic form of economy underlined by social and political *laissez faire*. Positive aspects were highlighted by his extravagant admiration of Britain's dynamic culture, which was politically dominated and led by the nobility and upper bourgeoisie, and was materially based on science and technology. Although Karl Marx's *Communist Manifesto* was published in 1848 and *Das Kapital* had appeared (1867) shortly before Sir Sayyid's arrival in Britain, his thinking remained strikingly uncolored by Socialist ideology. In fact the economic conditions of Europe which were being deplored by the Socialists were lauded by him in his letters and his travelogue:

It is nearly six months since I arrived in London, and [I] have been unable to see many things I should have liked . . . [I] have been in the society of lords and dukes at dinners and evening parties. Artisans and the common working-man I have seen in numbers. I have visited famous and spacious mansions, museums, engineering works, ship building establishments, gun-foundries, ocean-telegraph companies which connect continents, vessels of war (in one of which I walked for miles, the Great Eastern Steamship), [and I] have been present at clubs and private houses.[63]

Staggered by the technological superiority of the British, Sir Sayyid felt humbled. Writing in his letter of October 15, 1869, Sir Sayyid described his impressions:

Without flattering the English I can truly say that the natives of India, high and low, merchants and petty shopkeepers, educated and illiterate, when contrasted with the English in education, manners, and uprightness, are as like them as a dirty animal is to an able and handsome man.[64]

Had Sir Sayyid examined the living conditions of Britain's working classes, he might have bracketed them and his compatriots with the "animals." This statement, which greatly offended his friends in India, truly reflected the humbleness of a member of an agrarian culture when confronted by the vitality of an industrial modern culture. Vicariously, however, Sir Sayyid identified himself with the "animals" of India. In order to achieve material progress Sir Sayyid accepted Western education for India. "This is entirely due," Sir Sayyid summed up his impressions in the same letter, "to the education of the men and women, and to

their being united in aspiring after beauty and excellence. If Hin-
dustanis [Indians] can only attain to civilization, it [India] will
probably, owing to its many excellent natural powers, become
if not the superior, at least the equal of England." [65]

Also, *laissez-faire* capitalism appeared to Sir Sayyid as the
most dynamic form of societal progress, since it enabled the
bourgeoisie to exercise full initiative. What did capitalism accomplish for Britain? A microstudy of its achievements was
made by Sir Sayyid during his visits to Bristol. In March 1870
some old stalwarts of the Indian Empire, including General Sir
Abraham Roberts, Sir Edward Strachey, and John Elliot Bitton,
invited him to Bristol and showed him the landmarks of the city.
A suspended bridge over the Avon at Clifton and the history of
its construction demonstrated to Sir Sayyid the enterpreneurial
skill, civic sense, and technical ability of the British bourgeoisie.

This bridge could not be constructed even by a king, yet the subjects'
determination, philanthropy, and technical know-how built it. The
honor of this nation is further enhanced in my eyes when I realize that
this construction was designed neither to be a king's castle, nor a lord's
manor, nor yet a mausoleum of someone's ancestor. This was built
only for the public's welfare. Can you imagine how unfortunate that
Indian feels who is determined to work for his country's progress, but
suffers in return his compatriots' harshness, and is also convinced of
their selfishness, self-centeredness, and prejudice. [66]

Sir Sayyid described in his travelogue how philanthropy, en-
meshed with the profit motive, gradually constructed the bridge.
In 1753 a wine merchant, Mr. Vick, endowed 10,000 rupees (Sir
Sayyid used rupees rather than pounds in his description) for the
construction of a bridge over the Avon, providing a link between
Bristol and Clifton. By 1831 the investment of this amount
yielded 80,000 rupees. Bristol and Clifton's citizens raised an additional 370,000 rupees to cover the cost of the construction.
With this fund, land and basic heavy equipment was purchased.
A foundation stone on one side was laid by Lady Alton on June
20, 1831, and on the other side by the Marquise of Northampton
on August 27, 1836. I. K. Brownell was appointed the project

engineer. In 1839 the construction, because of the shortage of funds, stopped. In 1860 the Civil Engineers' Institute of London purchased the assets of the bridge for 20,000 rupees and in the name of a joint stock company sold its shares of stock to the public. Consequently, 350,000 rupees were raised, a sufficient capital to underwrite the total construction of Clifton-Bristol bridge over the Avon. Finally, the bridge was open to traffic on December 8, 1864, and a small toll was fixed which eventually recovered the invested capital with some profit.

Savoring this romance of Capitalism, Sir Sayyid asked a rhetorical question: "Are these [Britons] the human beings or us—who are drowned in selfishness?" To this Sir Sayyid replied satirically:

How resourceful we are! At every step we demand that the Government should make arrangement for the education of our boys and our girls. We also expect that [the Government] should impart them necessary religious instruction. *Afsus, Sad Afsus, hazar afsus,* woe unto us a hundred times, nay a thousand times; we deserve to drown ourselves. We are not fit to appear in the company of any civilized people.[67]

Shorn of its rhetoric, the statement was indicative of Sir Sayyid's recognition of capitalism as a superior mode of production compared to the archaic feudal mode of India.

While Sir Sayyid remained enchanted with the dynamism of British culture, he also began to develop an awareness of his own cultural identity—a process of self-affirmation or self-realization called *Khudi* (ego) by the poet-philosopher Dr. Muhammad Iqbal (1877–1938) almost two generations later. In a letter of September 10, 1869, Sir Sayyid shed light on this aspect of his psychic development:

An intelligent and sensitive individual, after observing the folkways and mores of the Europeans, can adequately comprehend which customs and manners of the Indians, particularly that of the Muslims, are bad and need to be changed. [My] faith in the fundamental principles of Islam was strengthened more by exposure to the conditions of Europe and by gaining the knowledge of [European] scholars' views rather

than by going on a pilgrimage to Mecca—*nā'awz bi-Allah,* God forgive
me [for making this statement]." [68]

In another letter Sir Sayyid reported a similar mental change taking place in Sayyid Mahmud. "Tonight he said: 'after my arrival
in London I became a true and faithful Muslim by *tasdīyq-i qala-
bīy'* (that my heart verifies it)." [69]

Like them, Iqbal had a similar self-discovery, which he generalized in terms of the Muslim world:

> *Musalmañ ko Musalmañ ker diya tūfan-i mughrib nay*
> *Talatam ha'y darya say hay gawher key sayrabīy*

> West's typhoon turned a Muslim into [a true] Muslim
> The way waves of the ocean nourish a pearl in the oyster

These Indic Muslim leaders were not unique in the discovery of
their heritage in Europe; other Asian leaders including Ahmad
Sukarno, and Muhammad Hatta in the twentieth century, had
developed the profiles of their nationalism "in the libraries of
Europe." Sir Sayyid's sojourn in Britain enabled him to "discover" Islam as a political ideology whose value system, he came
to believe, was superior to the contemporary ideologies of the
West. The salient features of this value system Sir Sayyid summarized in a letter to a British friend: (a) egalitarian distribution
of national resources; (b) social radicalism; and (c) the republican
form of Government. [70] Islam, as an ideology, enabled him to
make a distinction between Muslims (whose historical role varied
from sublime to degenerate), and Islam as a doctrine of truth,
eternal in nature. Consequently, he committed himself to eman-
cipating the contemporary Indic Muslim society, defending Islam
against the attacks of the West and updating its doctrine in the
light of reason or nature.

The historical role of the Muslims, Sir Sayyid asserted, was
just and something to be proud of. "Englishmen have imputed
all kinds of bad qualities to the Muslim kings and the Muslim
states, and have written their histories with prejudice and lack of
justice. And our English-educated youth tend to look upon them

as 'historical truth,' " complained Sir Sayyid in London. This situation, he emphasized, must be rectified. Four issues particularly deserved to be placed in their true historical perspective: (1) The Muslims' conquest of Spain and their contributions to the world culture; (2) The Muslims' conduct in the eight major battles of the Crusades; and (3) a truthful presentation of the Prophet Muhammad's life and his mission before the Western audience. For the first and the second projects Sir Sayyid subsidized almost completely the works of sympathetic scholars, particularly that of John Devonport, who wrote a study defensive of the Prophet Muhammad.

Sir William Muir's biography of the Prophet Muhammad had outraged Sir Sayyid. "I am reading William Muir's book," wrote Sir Sayyid to Mahdi Ali Khan on August 20, 1869, "but it has 'burned' my heart; his injustice and bigotry has cut my heart to pieces. I am determined to write a full length study in refutation even if its preparation [in London] turns me into a pauper and a beggar."[71] While Sir Sayyid's attitude was defensive, Sir William Muir was motivated by the missionary zeal. "The work was first undertaken," revealed Sir William, "at the insistance of the Rev. C. G. Pfander, D.D., so well known as a Christian apologist in the controversy with the Mahometans, who urged that a biography of the Prophet of Islam should be compiled in the Hindustani language from the early sources acknowledged by [Muslims] to be authentic and authoritative."[72] Questioning the authenticity of Sir William's sources, Sir Sayyid finally published in London twelve essays—A Series of Essays on the Life of Mohammad (Trubner & Co., 1870). The production of the Essays cost him Rs. 3,948; the sale of its 20 copies along with the donations of his friends in India brought him Rs. 1,691. In order to pay the balance of Rs. 2,257 Sir Sayyid borrowed 3,000 rupees in London. In addition to using Latin, German, French, and English sources, for which he paid the translators handsomely, Sir Sayyid evolved his doctrine of nature, which constituted the theoretical understructure, the frame of reference of modern Islam.

For the emancipation of Indic Muslims a dual plan of social reforms and modern education was developed. In order to study the British educational institutions, he visited the universities of Cambridge and Oxford, as well as private preparatory schools including Eaton and Harrow. These educational "models" enabled him to develop the blueprint for the Muhammadan Anglo-Oriental College, which was ,established in 1877 at Aligarh. Subsequently, in 1920, the College became Aligarh Muslim University. However, Sir Sayyid abaodoned the Mughal India's concept of egalitarian mass education, and adopted instead Britain's pragmatic but aristocratic policy of advanced and elitist education.

Tooled with modern ideas and orientations, Sir Sayyid returned to India on October 2, 1870, and initiated his movement of modernism, now commonly called the Aligarh movement. He remained in the judicial service until 1876, and when in July his pension was granted he resigned his position, settling permanently in Aligarh. He spent the remaining years of his life struggling to modernize the collective life of the Indic Muslims till his death in 1898.

3

Perceptions of 1857
and the Theory
of Participatory Rule

SIR SAYYID'S VIEW of 1857 was not that of a historian—detached and dispassionate—but that of a participant and a partisan. Mindful of his assumed role as a historian, he endeavored to be objective in recording the events of 1857, but the framework of his objectivity did not extend to the nature of revolt against the British. In January, 1855, he was transferred from Delhi to Bijnor as Sadr Amin. Two and a half years later revolt broke out, drawing him into the vortex of tragic events. After the revolt was crushed in 1858, Sir Sayyid wrote in Moradabad the history of rebellion which took place in the district of Bijnor. He prefaced the narration with a prayer: "O God! enable me to complete this history truthfully, because partiality in historical composition is sheer dishonesty, and its effect lasts forever. The author of partisan history suffers damnation till the doomsday."[1] Viewed from the British perspective, Sir Sayyid treated the "rebels" as misguided law-breakers, and projected his con-

cept of historical objectivity as merely a factual narration of
events. To him the British authority was legal and legitimate,
and 1857 could not be evaluated as a justifiably violent attempt to
establish native rule. Despite the frequently used epithets and uncharitable remarks for the rebel leaders, he recorded their activities and policies accurately. They had, according to him, no case,
certainly no cause, and no legitimate grievance to challenge the
benign British *Raj*.

Upon mature reflection and observation of the events
beyond the Bijnor district, this simplistic view was greatly modified to eventually find an expression in a sophisticated theory of
politics, urging the British to transform India's subject political
culture into a mixed subject–participant culture. His personal involvement in the events of Bijnor left on his mind some indelible
impressions, which determined his attitude toward the issues of
Hindu-Muslim politics. Bijnor is therefore a watershed in the development of his Muslim nationalism, and an analysis of his normatively oriented actions must begin with Bijnor.

Revolt in Bijnor (what??!!)

Bijnor occupied the northwest corner of Rohilkhand or Bareilly
Division, and was a roughly triangular stretch of country with its
apex to the north. The western boundary was formed by the
river Ganges, beyond which were located the four districts of
Dehra Dun, Saharanpur, Muzaffarnagar, and Meerut. To the
north and northeast was the hill country of Garhwal, and on the
east the Phika river constituted the boundary, separating the district from Naini Tal and Moradabad. To the south was located
the Thakurdwara, Amroha, and Hasanpur tahsils (subdistricts) of
Moradabad. The total area of Bijnor in 1906 amounted to 1789.5
square miles.[2] According to the census of 1853 the total population of the district was 695,521 with 467,494 Hindus and 230,727
Muslims. The common language of the people was Urdu or the
so-called Hindustani dialect of western Hindi.

Among the Hindus, according to the census of 1900, there

were 66 castes, and half a century earlier there would have been no less. The property-owners were Rajputs, who owned about one-sixth of the district; Gujars (cattle-ranchers); Brahmans and Banias, who in addition to being money-lenders were engaged in agriculture. The Muslims primarily belonged to the Sunni sect; the Shi'ites among them were mostly Sayyids. The large estate-owners among the Muslims were Pathans, including Lodis, Ghoris, Bangash, and Muhammadzai; Shaikhs, whose ancestors had come from abroad; and also the Hindu converts who had been integrated with the descendants of the foreign-born Muslims; and the Sayyids. The vast majority of the population in Bijnor, however, consisted of the working classes, both among the Hindus (including Kahars, Barhais, Gadariyas, Kumhars, and Bhangis) and the Muslims (Julahas, Behnas, and Taylis).

Bijnor was considerably urbanized with its 1,975 villages; 1,900 of them containing a thousand inhabitants. The Bijnor District and the surrounding country was handed over to the British East Company in 1801 by Nawab of Awadh, and it remained under British control until 1857, when the rebels temporarily ejected their rule.

In this territorial laboratory of 1857, Sir Sayyid recorded the events from May 1857 to April 1858, when he was transferred to Moradabad with another promotion as Sadr al-Sadur.

Sir Sayyid's *History of Revolt in the District of Bijnor* deals with several issues: (1) Sir Sayyid's loyal support of the British cause; (2) Nawab Mahmud Khan, a hereditary chieftain and a descendant of legendary Nawab Najib-ud-Daulah, who became a focal point of revolt in the District, his defiance of the British authority, and his worsening relations with Hindu landlords, degenerating into Hindu-Muslim wars; (3) the eventual triumph of the British power, and recapture of the District.

Nawab Mahmud Khan, invariably described by Sir Sayyid as Na-Mahmud (the unblessed one), assumed *de facto* control of the district on May 20, 1857, and remained in authority for approximately four months. At first Sir Sayyid tried to persuade him to accept the administration in the name of the British, and to provide protection for the lives of the threatened British officials and their families. He succeeded in both objectives. On the night of June 6–7, 1857, Nawab Mahmud Khan accepted a letter of investiture, transferring power to him. This letter was drafted by Sir Sayyid on the order of Alexander Shakespeare, the Collector of Bijnor. It stated: "Depending upon the discretion of the Government, the administration of the District is transferred to you. You are required to administer the District efficiently, and to protect the property and other possessions of the Collector, and the Magistrate of the District."[3] The document was signed by Shakespeare.

The policy of Sir Sayyid, and his Hindu and Muslim colleagues, was to treat Mahmud Khan as a subordinate functionary of the British Government. Consequently, they initially extended limited cooperation to him but also worked out a plan of sabotage to thwart his ambitions. A committee for mutual consultation, consisting of Sayyid Ahmad, Pandit Radhakishan (Deputy Inspector of schools), and Sayyid Turab Ali (Tahsildar) was created. They agreed not to render individually any service to the Nawab unless the committee was consulted. Otherwise Ali as the Tahsildar would discharge only those of his normal functions for which he would receive the Nawab's urgent orders, and collect adequate revenue for the payment of the Government employees' salaries only. Enlisting the help of another Hindu Tahsildar, Bakhshi Ram, the committee instructed the tenant farmers not to pay their revenue directly to Nawab Mahmud Khan. Sir Sayyid, as a Small Cause Judge, continued to apply the English law to all *subjudice* cases; in fact when a case had to be referred to a superior English judge, orders to this effect were "dictated quite loudly in the court. People were thus made to realize the continued dominance and presence of the British rule."[4]

After the departure of the British officials from the District, Nawab Mahmud Khan's ambitions, which were known to the British and Sir Sayyid, became public. Despite his acceptance of the letter of investiture from Shakespeare, indicating his subordinate position to the British, Nawab Mahmud Khan established an independent state in the District of Bijnor. Both Hindus and Muslims supported him, and recognized his hereditary right to rule. This eventuality was fully anticipated by the British. To prevent this development, Shakespeare had unsuccessfully tried to convince the Hindu landlords to collectively assume responsibility for the administration of the District until the British returned victoriously. "In fact it was inconceivable," commented Sir Sayyid, "that people would accept anyone as their ruler other than Nawab Mahmud Khan."[5] Since in Bijnor the Hindus outnumbered Muslims two to one, Sir Sayyid's comment bore testimony to the Nawab's popularity among the Hindus. Partly due to his ineptness in leadership, and partly because of the Hindu landlords' loyalty to the British, Nawab Mahmud Khan forfeited this popularity among the Hindu masses. Ultimately Hindu-Muslim confrontation became unavoidable, resulting in Nawab Mahmud Khan's downfall. From behind the scenes, and with skill, the British officers pitted Hindus against the Muslims.

In order to stabilize his regime, Nawab Mahmud Khan needed to build an efficient administrative infrastructure which would fill the vacuum created by the expulsion of British rule. Recognizing Sir Sayyid's administrative talents, he tried to win him over by offering him an estate, which he assured would remain in perpetuity with his descendants. Not wavering in his loyalty to the British, Sir Sayyid instead tried to instill British loyalty in the Nawab. Sir Sayyid's attitude reflected his pragmatism as well as his deep skepticism regarding the fulfillment of the Nawab's ambitions. "I submitted," recorded Sir Sayyid,

Nawab Sahib! I can take an oath saying that I will be your well-wisher in all situations. If, however, you intend to grab power and land, and fight against the British then I cannot be your accomplice. By God Nawab Sahib, I say that British sovereignty cannot be eliminated from India. Even if the English were to leave India no one else would be able to establish his rule over India. If, according to your estimate, the British can be expelled, then you are the ruler and no one would challenge your Nawabship. On the contrary, if my views turn out to be right, then you would be looked upon by the Government as a well-wisher. Then you will bask in their favor and enjoy rapid promotions. If you want me to join you in the administration of the District, then obtain the authorization from the Collector. Also, agree with me that no business would be transacted unless we have the prior consent of the Collector.[6]

Nawab Mahmud Khan had hired both Hindu and Muslim employees, while he appointed his close relatives to the top administrative positions. However, the conflict between the Nawab and the Hindu landlords was precipitated by his demand that they surrender to him the British officials' belongings and the arrears of land revenue owed to the Government. Revenue was thus forcibly collected, while casualties were inflicted upon the Hindu landlords. In retaliation, the Hindu landlords entered into an alliance, and started to kill the Nawab's employees. By the end of July 1857 the clash of interests between the Hindu landlords and the Nawab Mahmud Khan degenerated into Hindu-Muslim conflict. Commenting on this development, Sir Sayyid recorded: "Before this fight, there was no bone of discord or religious conflict between the Hindus and Muslims of this District. Hindu landlords often employed Muslim servants; similarly, Nawab Mahmud Khan had hired several Hindu employees."[7]

With the clash of economic interests Nawab Mahmud Khan's officers raised the Muhammadi Jhanda (Muslim flag), and the Hindu landlords started to recruit an exclusively Hindu army to protect life, property, and *dharma* (religion). On August 5 the Hindu landlords attacked Nawab Mahmud Khan at Bijnor and defeated him. The Nawab fled, and the District fell under the control of the Hindu landlords. By the beat of drums, they had their collective rule proclaimed in the name of the British. Sir Sayyid recorded his reaction: "Two sovereigns cannot be content in one dominion, and here they trick us into believing that fifty sovereigns can rule in one district. This analogy should be paraphrased thus: ten paupers want to sleep under one quilt."[8] Prudently, the Hindu landlords clandestinely reestablished contacts with the fugitive British officials, and started administering the district with the help of Sir Sayyid, Muhammad Rahmat Khan, Deputy Collector, and other Indian officers of the British East India Company.

During these months of the turmoil, what did the Hindus think of Sir Sayyid's character? Crecraft Wilson's testimony on this question was eloquent:

Despite the bitter animosity between the Hindus and the Muslims of the District, and the eventual expulsion of the Muslim rule from the District in a show-down, when we wanted to transfer the District to Rahmat Khan and your care, all the big Hindu landlords complimented your gentility, good character, and loyalty to the Government. With great desire and joy they accepted you Muslims as their officers; in fact, they petitioned us to appoint you as officers over all the Hindus in the District.[9]

From the events of Bijnor, Sir Sayyid drew certain conclusions: (1) the British rule alone could maintain peace, law and order in the country, and the balance of power between the Hindus and the Muslims; (2) despite his personal popularity among, and friendship with, the Hindus, Sir Sayyid concluded that the Hindus and the Muslims were incapable of developing a political *modus vivendi*. Since they failed to forge a united alliance against the British during the crisis they were less likely to cooperate with each other in peaceful times; (3) the clash of economic and political interests between the Hindu and the Muslim elites often degenerated into religious conflicts; and (4) he concluded that particularly in India public opinion amounted to the propertied classes' views, and that they alone could influence the political processes. Lacking intellectual or moral capacity for self-rule, people in general cherished peace and desired not to be involved in political problems. Appreciating the neutral British Government, they were not opposed to the British *Raj*. Peoples' supportive role for the Hindu landlords, and Nawab Mahmud Khan was narrowly interpreted to mean merely unconscious and non-ideologically oriented partisan support. Stated Sir Sayyid,

The people of the district, who fought with the Nawab against the Hindu landlords certainly did not conceive of themselves as fighting against the British Government. Everyone looked upon it as a contest between the Nawab and the Hindu landlords as if the Government was out of the picture. While supporting the Hindu landlords, the Hindu populace also kept the British Government out of the focus of its attention.

Then, who was the real rebel? In February 1858 the issue was debated by the British military and civil officials. Sir Sayyid's view, that only those who would resist the returning British Army were rebels, became the British policy in Bijnor. Had the opposite view, holding everyone who had fought against the Hindu landlords as Nawab Mahmud Khan's partisans prevailed, hardly a Muslim would have survived in the District of Bijnor.[10] However, many Muslim landlords were ruined financially, especially Mir Sadiq Ali and Mir Rustam Ali of Chandpur, whose estate, valued at Rs. 100,000, was confiscated and offered to Sir Sayyid, who refused to accept it. A deep sense of remorse overwhelmed him, and Sir Sayyid recorded his feelings several decades later: "There was no one more wretched than myself. Our nation suffered like this, and I, at their expense, should become a landlord?" Perhaps incidents like this, highlighting the Muslims' sufferings, forced Sir Sayyid to take a more critical look at the causes of this revolt.

The Causes for India's Revolt

Contrary to the prevalent British view of the events of 1857 as a "grand mutiny," Sir Sayyid described it as a classic revolt in his well-known memorandum, *Asbāb-i Baghawat-i Hind* (The Causes for India's Revolt), which he sent to the British Government in 1858. Five acts of defiance, individually or collectively amounted to rebellion: (1) the subjects' fight or armed opposition to the Government; (2) disregard of the government's orders with a view to resisting its authority; (3) aiding and assisting the government's opponents; (4) engaging in infighting, indicating disregard of the government's prescribed rules; (5) and finally eliminating "from one's heart" loyalty for the government, and refraining from helping it in crisis. In 1857, Sir Sayyid stated, "there was not one of these forms of rebellion which did not find a place."[11] Unicausal explanations, holding either the Muslims or the Hindus responsible for the revolt, which were so commonly offered by the British in the post-1857 literature, were completely discarded by him. Instead he suggested that five main causes spawned the revolt: (1) the peoples' misappre..ension of the East India Company Government's intentions; (2) the enactment of laws, regulations, and procedures which were not in harmony with the Indians' mores, and their past political systems; (3) the government's lack of information about the peoples' condition, their folkways, and other "afflictions," which alienated the subjects from the government; (4) the inefficient management and disaffection of the Army; (5) the government's abandoning of those practices which were essential to the maintenance of good government in India.[12] Each of these causes was elaborated with examples.

First, Indians had erroneously believed that the Company's "Government intended to force the Christian religion and foreign customs upon Hindu and Muslim alike." This conviction, however, drew strength from the 1837 famine, when the missionaries, contrary to the Indians' expectations, raised the Hindu and Muslim orphans in the Christian faith. Moreover, Sir Sayyid maintained, British Army and civilian officers often attempted to proselytize subordinate Indians. Attacking Hinduism and Islam often in offensive language, the missionaries frequently preached in the bazaars and public fairs. In the missionary schools the teaching of theology became mandatory; students were quizzed on "who is your Redeemer." The truly Christian answers were applauded, and the writers were given prizes. People also suspected that the government's village schools were nurseries of the Christian faith, but they feared most the Christianization of the girls, especially Muslims who were urged to discard the veil.

Alluding to the government colleges' earlier traditional curricula, including Sanskrit, Arabic, and Persian, Sir Sayyid maintained that even the celebrated scholar of Delhi, Shah Abdul Azīz (d. 1823) had blessed them, because then English was

taught only as one of the languages. Slowly *Fiqh* (Islamic jurisprudence), and *hadīth* (the Prophet's Traditions) studies were
dropped in favor of sciences and other secular subjects, raising
the suspicions of Muslims who saw in these changes an attack on
Islam. Finally in a public letter, missionary Edmond asserted
Christianity's superiority over Islam and Hinduism by virtue of
the West's scientific, technical, and political superiority over the
East. His letter stated: "All India was now under one rule, that
the telegraph had so connected all parts of the country that they
were the one; that the railroad had brought them so near that all
towns were as one; the time had clearly come when there should
be but one faith, that we should all become Christians." [13] Although Bengal's Lt. Governor issued a proclamation assuring the
Company's neutrality in religion, it only put peoples' "suspicion
to sleep for a time." When reduced to abject poverty, Indians
believed that they would be given the final choice of Christianity
or hunger.

Second, the East India Company issued many laws and regulations which violated established Indian customs. In actuality,
however, these "strange" laws forced social reforms upon the Indians. Sir Sayyid charged that the Legislative Council in Calcutta
was "not free from the charge of having meddled with religious
matters." Undoubtedly the Religious Disabilities Act XXI of
1850 was prejudicial to both the Hindus and the Muslims. No
convert to Islam or Hinduism could inherit his parents' estate, although this disability did not apply to a Christian convert. Since
Hinduism did not accept conversion until the beginning of the
twentieth century, in practice this disability applied only to a
Muslim convert. However, the Hindu Widows' Remarriage Act
XV, passed in July 1856, was a truly humane act. Recognizing
the meager support for Act XV, which came mainly from
Bengal, [14] Sir Sayyid believed that in general the Act alienated the
Hindus. Married women achieved legal competence in criminal
actions as well as in civil proceedings, thus achieving freedom
from their guardians' control. For the restitution of conjugal
rights complicated procedures were adopted, causing years of
delay during which an abducted woman would give birth to two

or three children before she was reunited with her lawfully wed-
ded husband. Also, the civil courts' decrees often violated the
religious convictions of the litigants. These measures, Sir Sayyid
reasoned, shattered the Indians' traditional social fabric.

Economically, some elements of landed gentry were ruined,
when the Act VI of 1819 provided for the resumption of *la-kharāj*
(rent-free) lands. Sir Sayyid asserted that on "the flimsiest pre-
texts" many lands, which had been held rent-free for centuries,
were confiscated by the Company. Originally assigned by the
Mughal emperors, the rent-free lands were of various types: (1)
the *milk* land was granted in favor of scholars, pious and saintly
persons, or for the maintenance of a school, a mosque, a temple,
or a shrine. Also the rent was waived, indicating state's *ma'fiy*
(pardon) or *inam* (reward or benefaction). Many of these grants
were hereditary. In the case of another type (2) the *Jagīr* lands,
possession of estates was transferred temporary to some persons
for military or political services rendered to the State. Their rent
was never taxed. The *jagīr*-holders were *mansabdārs,* the Mughal
officers of State. The troublesome frontier tracts were also given
in *jagīr* to capable military chiefs, who utilized the rent for the
development of agriculture and for maintaining military or police
forces.

The Company, however, had charged that the three
categories of grants had been greatly abused by "impecunious
governors who had [during the period of Mughal decline] no
other way of meeting claims on their empty treasuries, by subordinate officials who had no right to make them. They were often
fraudulent, intended only to keep money out of the treasury."[15]
For instance, in Bombay, the Inam Commission found that
grants for political, religious, personal, or village service affected
Rs. 13,250,000 of the land revenue. The Commission reduced this
to Rs. 8,038,000.[16] In Bengal one fourth of all the land had been
transferred rent-free to the educational institutions. The Company spent £800,000 on resumption proceedings and permanently
gained an additional revenue of £300,000 a year. Almost all of
this land was held by Muslims and their scholastic institutions.[17]
Not challenging the legal status of these revenue-free lands, Sir

Sayyid maintained that the resumption proceedings alienated the people from the Government, and in all their proclamations the rebels listed two grievances against the British: "the interference in matters of religion, and the resumption of revenue-free lands."[18]

Sir Sayyid pointed out that the Sale Laws or Regulation VII of 1799 and Regulation V of 1812, long known as *quanūn haftum* (seventh) and *panjam* (fifth), also caused great mischief. To recover the arrears of revenue the Company authorized the sale of all or part of defaulting estates. Similarly bankers and moneylenders could obtain decrees from the civil courts, and have the bailiff auction lands to satisfy the decrees. To Sir Sayyid the British system of revenue settlements appeared burdensome and excessive when compared with the former settlements. Under the Muslim sovereigns the revenue was realized by sharing one-third of the actual crop with the cultivator. However, Emperor Akbar (1556–1605) "changed the payments in kind into payments," and divided the agricultural land into three categories: (1) the Polaj land was cultivated annually, and full revenue was charged on its produce; (2) the Parauti land allowed to lie fallow to regain its strength and the revenue on this land was levied in the years of its cultivation; (3) the Chachar land generally remained uncultivated from three to four years, and required capital investment for its fertilization. During the first year of its cultivation, "Akbar took two-fifths of the produce," but in the fifth year "he received his full share." The Banjar or barren land, lying fallow for more than five years, "was treated on still more lenient terms."[19] The cash value of the revenue was determined by reference to the current market price of the produce, which naturally absorbed inflationary as well as depressive trends in the economy. The British assessments, on the contrary, were permanently fixed without any regard to economic contingencies. Fallow land as well as fertile land paid revenue in the same proportion, thus reducing both the tenant and the landowners to greater financial straits. Many big landlords, the Ta'lukdār in the Awadh province, were also ruined when their "sovereignty in the villages" was dissolved and their lands were confiscated. They thus became the focal points of rebellion.

Most repugnant to the Indian custom was the introduction of stamped paper which, gradually rising in price, "reached its highest amount under Regulation X of 1829." As a source of revenue, the stamped papers were used for all financial transactions, title deeds, and for applications in the courts. Citing Mill's *Political Economy* and Lord Brougham's *Political Philosophy* in support of his argument, Sir Sayyid stated: "Besides the heavy expenses which this system entails, it tends greatly to hinder the actual administration of justice."[20] However, he focused his criticism on the civil courts of the Punjab, whose jurisdiction extended over Delhi and the adjoining areas. The laws enforced by the Punjab's civil courts were "very vague and sketchy," and no guidelines in the form of commentaries were available to the judges "for the purpose of explaining or elucidating the laws or adapting them to practice." Altogether Sir Sayyid blamed the civil courts "for having their share among causes of the rebellion," especially in regard to the transfer of civil rights and the issuing of decrees for debt to the money-lenders. To people the various gradations of appeal meant exorbitant expense rather than available channels for redressing grievances and obtaining justice.

Third, the British Government's ignorance of and indifference to Indian public opinion had no less of a share in fomenting the rebellion. Unlike former Muslim rulers of India, the British settled in India temporarily, and separately from the Indians. Consequently no communication between the governors and the governed developed. The reports of the subordinate district officials, which were the only source of information for the government, were highly superficial and unreliable, because their Indian informants, including "wealthy native gentlemen," had been reduced to the abject status of sycophants. Moreover, the British recruitment policies in the civil administration and the army denied opportunities for respectable careers to Muslims. According to Sir Sayyid, the Hindus, with the exception of the Kayasths, cared very little for the military service since most pursued the occupations reserved to their castes. Even the Brahman and the once warrior Kshatriya had become landlords, living off the land rather than by the book or the sword. Coming in the train of their conquering Emperors, the Muslims served as soldiers even when they "gradually settled down in India." The British Indian Army, composed mainly of South Indians from the region of Telingana, was looked down upon by the Muslim upper classes as an appropriate place of employment. Frustrated and unemployed, Muslims by the thousands joined the rebels "just as in a famine hungry men rush upon food." They got four or six pennies a day, while many received three pounds of grain daily instead of cash.

The British policies increased poverty in the country when some of the old practices of giving charitable pensions and stipends were abandoned. Referring to Emperor Shah Jahan's (1628–1658) coronation, Sir Sayyid stated that "no less than 400,000 bighas,[21] 120 villages, and tens of thousands of sterling were given away in presents." In addition to stopping this custom, the British forfeited the rent-free lands, thus denying a considerable source of income to the tenants and the landlords. The large-scale imports of the British manufactured goods ruined Indian artisans and craftsmen. Not able to compete with machines, these workers lost their traditional source of income, while the consumer paid artificially determined higher prices. A novel practice in India, the issuing of Government bonds on specified interest rates worked only to the advantage of the British Government, and the people never received any interest on their investments.

Sir Sayyid maintained that the consolidation of the British rule progressively pauperized those classes who had been prominent and prosperous under the Mughals. Just before 1857, the Indians had started to look upon every British triumph with sorrow. "When the British were victorious in Afghanistan, the people mourned. Why was this? Because they feared open interference in their religion. When, in addition to this, Gwaliar, the Punjab and Awadh were conquered, the people grieved much more." Moreover, in these states employment opportunities were available for the talented native men, while their markets absorbed the home-made products. With the overthrow of native rule, the Indian upper and middle classes sunk low, and the ar-

tisan was ruined economically. The fear of religious interference
by the British reinforced by the economic loss forged at least a
temporary alliance between the fallen middle and working classes
during the rebellion.

Fourth, Sir Sayyid greatly stressed the mismanagement in
the Indian Army, and the British disregard of and indifference to
the psychological changes wrought in Indian soldiers as a consequence of the successive British victories. Parenthetically, it may
be added that in 1857 the total military strength of British India
was 238,000, of whom 38,000 were British. In 1876 the army's
total strength was reduced to 190,087 but the British personnel
had increased to 66,509.[22] In view of the smaller number of British soldiers, Sir Sayyid maintained, the Indian soldiers "looked
upon the European portion of the army as a myth," and generally boasted that "they enabled the English to conquer Hindustan
[India] from Burma to Kabul." With self-confidence came the
arrogance of power, and the Indian soldiers often flouted army
discipline. In 1856, the British introduced greased cartridges for
the new Enfield rifle, which the soldiers had to bite in order to
insert them into the rifles. Rightly believing that cow's fat was
contained in the cartridges, the Hindu soldiers feared the loss of
their castes, and thus refused to bite them. Consequently a regi-
ment at Barrackpur was disbanded. The refusal to bite the cartridges was interpreted by other soldiers as a justifiable act, and
was followed by the Indian soldiers in general. Sir Sayyid summarized their feelings: "They felt that they had shed their blood
in its [the Company's] cause and conquered many countries for
it, that it wished to take away their caste, and had dismissed
those who had justly stood out for their right." In Meerut on
May 10, 1857, after watching the disobeying noncommissioned
Indian officers' "feet manacled," the soldiers rose and shot the
British officers and then went to Delhi. Recognizing the British
dependence on the Indian soldiers "the people also became riot-
ous. They no longer were in awe of the Government."[23]

As to why the rebellion did not break out in the Punjab, Sir
Sayyid offered several explanations. Freed from the Sikh misrule,
which became oppressive after Maharaja Ranjit Singh's death in

1839, the Punjabi Muslims suffered no injury from the British. While no longer wealthy, the Sikhs had retained their previous savings, and had not suffered the poverty which "Hindustan" had experienced. Moreover, the British officers immediately disarmed the native soldiers in the Punjab when the news of rebellion spread. All martially inclined Sikhs, Punjabi-Muslims, and Pathans had been taken into the British Army. Thus a respectable source of living was available to them, while it had been denied to soldiers in "Hindustan." In a nutshell the Punjab's circumstances were entirely different from those of "Hindustan."[24]

The Theory of Participatory Rule

The last point in Sir Sayyid's memorandum did not really explain the fifth cause of the 1857 rebellion, but elaborated a participatory view of Government, which, had the British applied it to India, would have prevented the outbreak of the rebellion. Drawing insights from Gabriel A. Almond and Sidney Verba, one might say that Sir Sayyid in reality wanted the British to gradually change India's subject culture into the mixed-participant culture. "In the mixed subject-participant culture a substantial part of the population," according to Almond and Verba, "has acquired specialized input orientations and an active set of self-orientations, while most of the remainder of the population continue to be oriented toward an authoritarian governmental structure and have a relatively passive set of self-orientations."[25] In a subject culture an individual is "a passive beneficiary or victim of routine governmental actions." A subject does not attempt to influence the legislative processes or the executive decisions of his government, but only seeks to be treated "fairly" within the framework of the governmental action. A citizen, on the other hand, participates in the formation of political decisions, and is a part of the democratic infrastructure.

In India, Sir Sayyid reasoned, the subject political culture had also operated to the disadvantage of the British Government in so far as it isolated it from the subjects, while as a foreign gov-

ernment it should have encouraged, to a limited extent the subjects' participation in the governmental decisions and actions.

[The British] Government could never know the inadvisability of the
laws and regulations which it passed. The people had no means of protesting against what they might feel to be a foolish measure, or of giving public expression to their own wishes. But the greatest mischief lay
in this, that the people misunderstood the views and the intentions of
the Government. They misunderstood every act, and whatever law was
passed was misconstrued by men who had no share in the framing of it,
and hence no means of judging its spirit. At last came the time when all
men looked upon the English Government as slow poison, a rope of
sand and a treacherous flame of fire.[26]

Not even a relatively free press, according to Sir Sayyid, could
be a substitute for the peoples' participation in the governmental
decisions, and the legislative processes.

    Sir Sayyid did not want the British to replace the Indians'
subject role by an exclusively citizen role, because it would have
amounted to making India free and sovereign, which was an un-
thinkable possibility for Victorian Britain. "To form a Parliament from the natives of India is of course out of the question,"
reasoned Sir Sayyid. "It is not only impossible, but useless." But
he saw no legitimate reason why the Indians "should be excluded
from participation in the Viceroy of India's Legislative Council."[27] Though momentous for its times, this suggestion was not
supported by any concrete method of the Indians' selection or
election[28] to the Legislative Council. Probably he thought in
terms of appointment of some prominent Indians to the Legislative Council. To him the goal of Indian participation in the legislative processes, rather than democratic means of participation,
was most significant. Sir Sayyid's "ideal" polity, and "model" of
democracy, Britain even after the Reform Act of 1832 was governed by "the educated ten thousand"; they alone formulated
public policy, chose parliamentary candidates, made laws, and
administered the State. After the further extension of the fran-
chise in 1867 and 1885, the British Government was still described as "Government of the people, for the people, by the *best*

of the people."[29] In view of this, it is doubtful indeed if Sir Sayyid could have understood in 1858 the implications of democratic elections inherent in his proposal. However, it must be emphasized that for Sayyid the Indian subjects' participation in the British *Raj's* legislative council as well as in the high administration was a key to political stability and to creating a relatively "popular" Government in India.

Consequently, Sir Sayyid considered the exclusion of the Indians from the high administrative services as another contributory factor for the rebellion. Despite his recognition of the competitive examination as the best means of creating an efficient bureaucracy, Sir Sayyid alluded to the British patronage system in a rhetorical question: "Are the best English statesman invariably those who have passed high examination? Are high diplomatic posts not often given to them on account of their birth and practical common sense, and sometimes even without the latter qualifications?"[30] Implicit here is a suggestion that by denying similarly high administrative positions to the members of the fallen Indian aristocracy the British policy forced them to throw off the alien yoke at the first available opportunity. The Muslim aristocracy, asserted Sir Sayyid, particularly resented their exclusion from the British administration since "a few short years ago they filled the most honorable posts under their government, and the desire and hope for such is still in them."[31]

Exclusion of the Indians from the Viceroy's Legislative Council and the high administration thus alienated the Hindu and Muslim elites from the British rule. Relegated to low and subservient positions, the Indians became objects of contempt for even the Company's meanest Europen employees. As members of the subject culture, the Indians were expected to be passively obedient to the British law, even if it was repugnant to them. To Sir Sayyid the rebellion of 1857 was spawned by the subject culture, which the British had superimposed on Indian society. In order to transform it into a mixed subject-participant political culture, Sir Sayyid exhorted the British not in the name of democracy, but in terms of Christianity's ethos, and the historical insights derived from the eight centuries of Muslim rule in India.

Like individual friendships the people and their government

should be knit together. To Sir Sayyid such a bond of friendship between the British and the Indians was entirely feasible and necessary for the government's stability. Racial and religious differences would have posed no insurmountable difficulties, if only the British had followed Jesus Christ's admonition: "Therefore all things whatsoever ye would that men should do to you, do ye even so to them, for this is the Law of the Prophets" (Mathew VII, 12). Also St. Paul explained this golden rule: "And the Lord makes you to increase and abound in love one toward another and toward all men, even as we do toward you" (Thessalonians III, 12). In view of this the Christian government was under the obligation to cultivate the peoples' friendship, but it never really seriously tried. The way a father loves his child before the child loves him, the British should have endeavored to win the peoples' affection; conversely it was not for the Indians to have wooed the British government. Frankly stated, the British "Government has hitherto kept itself as isolated from the people of India as if it was the fire, and they the dry grass."

The Muslim rulers of India, reasoned Sir Sayyid, were once, like the British, alien to India. Differing in faith and culture, the Muslims and the Hindus eventually succeeded in establishing friendship. Initially, and especially during the Turkish and Pathan dynasties' rule, the contacts between the Hindus and the Muslims were minimal.

A feeling of cordiality was first established in the reign of the Mughal Emperor Akbar [1556–1605], and continued till the reign of Shah Jahan [1628–1658]. . . . This feeling unfortunately ceased during the reign of Aurangzeb 'Alamgīr [1658–1707] owing to the rebellion of the Hindus, including that of Shivaji, the Maratha [1627–1680]. Roused to anger against all Hindus, 'Alamgīr ordered his provincial governors to treat them harshly, and to exempt none from paying *jizya*.[32] The injury done to the subjects, and their alienation [from the Mughal government] are only too obvious, and well known. Now the English Government has been in existence for more than a century, and to the present hour has not secured the peoples' affections.[33]

How could the British have won the affection and the loyalty of the Indians? Again falling back upon his historical knowledge of the Muslim rule in India, Sir Sayyid recommended two past practices. The Indians, especially the upper classes, since time immemorial, have enjoyed attending their sovereigns' courts. Thus brought face to face, they felt the sovereign's power, and relished the happy thought of enjoying the security guaranteed by his power. Continued by the Governor-Generals Lord Auckland (1836–1842) and Lord Ellenborough (1842–1844), this practice, regretted Sir Sayyid, gradually fell into disuse. Personal contacts between the ruler and the ruled disappeared, and mistrust and suspicions came in. In addition to holding the open courts, Sir Sayyid maintained, the Muslim kings spent public funds in rewarding the subjects' services to the State. "The nobles, and the people at large had honors and gifts, such as titles, money, land, and other valuables bestowed upon them with no sparing hand." Also funds were expended in rewarding "faithful servants, victorious generals, scholars, holy men, poets, recluse mystics, and indigent people."

Probably this policy also induced certain negative qualities of lethargy and indolence among these classes; and it is possible that the denial of access to state charity would have encouraged self-reliance, and private initiative resulting in their economic self-sufficiency. Nevertheless the sovereigns' liberality had won the subjects political loyalty. However, the Company's government discontinued this useful practice. Justifying this liberal policy, according to Sir Sayyid, was the prevailing view that God made the mortal kings

as a type of what He himself is in order that people on seeing their king should realize that there is the Greatest Sovereign, who created the worldly kings. Consequently, the wise ones have laid down the rule that the Almighty's good qualities including compassion, kindness and charity should also be reflected in earthly kings. That is why respectable thinkers have described the kings as *dhil-Allah,* the shadow of God. The kings should treat their subjects with that bountiful liberality with which the Almighty has treated the whole world, because man is slave to kindness.[34]

Sir Sayyid's term "kindness" should be interpreted to mean the British Government's willingness to allow the Indian subjects a role in the governance of their own country.

The extent to which Sir Sayyid's memorandum influenced the formulation of British policy after 1857 is not precisely known, although it can be stated most confidently that his views were seriously considered by the India Office in London. The Duke of Argyll, the first Secretary of State for India, showed to Sir Sayyid in 1869 in London the heavily marked and annotated original copy of the *Asbab,* tacitly acknowledging his influence on the India Office's thinking. More reflective of Sir Sayyid's recommendation was the Indian Councils Act of 1861, which made it possible for the three Indians—The Maharaja of Patiala, the Raja of Benares, and Sir Dinkar Rao—to join the newly created 18-man Legislative Council. In 1878 Lord Lytton appointed Sir Sayyid a member of the Legislative Council, and in 1880 his tenure was extended for two more years by Lord Ripon. Allen Octavian Hume's endeavors for the creation of the All-India National Congress, according to some sources,[35] received inspiration from Sir Sayyid's *Asbāb.* Both developments, and Sir Sayyid's attitude toward them, had far-reaching repurcussions for political developments in the first half of the twentieth century.

4

Muslim Reaction
to Modern Education

THE BRITISH GOVERNMENT of India, as well as Sir Sayyid, shared an impression that the tragedy of 1857, shattering the illusion of Muslim rule in India, had made the Muslim population withdraw into a purposive cultural isolation. To what extent did this withdrawal imply repudiation of the British educational system? Both wanted to make an objective assessment of the situation before a remedial policy could be adopted. Spurred by his own convictions and strengthened by his European observations, Sir Sayyid took the initiative in 1870. No conclusive evidence can be offered to suggest whether or not the British Government gave any initial encouragement. An appropriate contact between Sir Sayyid and the Government, Kempson, the Director of Public Instruction in the Northwest Provinces, was not known as a Muslim sympathizer nor even a moderate supporter of Sir Sayyid's modernism. In fact both looked at each other with suspicion and veiled antagonism.

Probably the initiative was independently taken, while it coincided with Lord Mayo's policy (formulated in 1871) of distributing among neglected Muslims an equitable share of opportunities in education and government. Containment of the influence of the modernized and articulate Hindu middle classes, who monopolized government jobs and modern professions, probably inspired Mayo's sense of distributive justice. Looked at from the Muslims' viewpoint, this fortunate coincidence significantly though partially explained the success of Sir Sayyid's endeavors. The Punjabi Muslims' collaboration with Sir Sayyid, offered popular acceptance to his ideas and made the final difference between the success and failure of his movement.

Sir Sayyid's Evaluation of Muslim Response to Modern Education

Sir Sayyid organized on December 26, 1870, the Committee for the Better Diffusion and Advancement of Learning among Muhammadans of India. The Committee was required to: (1) determine the Muslims' reasons for ignoring the study of Western sciences; (2) ascertain objectively the reasons why the Muslims did not take advantage of the educational opportunities offered by the British Government; and (3) recommend remedial action for eliminating the Muslims' objections and the Government-made obstacles in the educational system.[1] Also, the Committee offered cash prizes of Rs.500, Rs.300, and Rs.150 each for the three best essays answering these questions. For these awards Rs.1,102 had been collected in December 1870.[2]

Altogether 32 essays were submitted for judgement by a 19-man Select Committee,[3] with Sir Sayyid as its secretary. In July 1871 the Select Committee scrutinized the essays, indicating the endorsement of various findings by its own majority and minority. Ultimately Sir Sayyid's view prevailed, which sometimes contradicted even the essayists' empirically verifiable observations. The Select Committee's report was divided into three unequal parts, each one containing several headings and subsections. Exploring various contours of general Muslim reaction to modern education, Part II summarized the data. Part III contained Sir Sayyid's recommendations to found Muhammadan Anglo-Oriental College (MAO) at Aligarh.

Was the proportion of Muslim students less than that of the Hindus in Government schools and colleges? The findings were divided; the majority of the essayists indicated a definite imbalance, while a minority contradicted this view. The minority demonstrated that the percentage of Muslim students attending government institutions was in harmony with the percentage of the Muslim population in India. The Select Committee refused to accept the minority's statistical evidence and its related interpretations, and called it "erroneous." Instead, the tribes of India, including "the *Bhangis, Chamars, Bheels, Phansias, Kanjars,* and *Babarias* [who were] beyond the pale of civilization," asserted the Select Committee, could not be validly included among the Hindus, because "no Muhammadan tribes corresponding to them are included in the Muhammadan population." "If these tribes of the Hindus be excluded," suggested the Select Committee, "and if the proportion between the Hindus and Muhammadans of equal ranks be ascertained, a correct conclusion might perhaps be arrived at."

To Sir Sayyid even this mode of comparison was not quite valid. In the past Muslims nearly monopolized education and the professions. Their past status rather than the present proportion of population consituted the fair norm of comparison. "Amongst the Muhammadans who came to reside in this country," stated the Select Committee, "the number of families whose profession was learning was large, and thus the proportion of learned Muhammadans was larger than that of the Hindus of the same class." Judged against this background, Sir Sayyid determined "that the number of the Muhammadan children in Government Colleges and schools is not so large as it ought to be."[4]

Why did the Muslims object to sending their children to Government schoools and colleges? The essayists assigned various reasons including: (1) the want of religious education; (2) disbelief in religion, particularly Islam; (3) corruption of morals, absence of traditional politeness and courtesy among modern students; (4) depressed economic status of the Muslims; and (5) almost all the essayists attacked various aspects of the modern educational system, discouraging Muslims from modern education.

A consensus developed among the essayists and the Select Committee in accepting the secular nature of modern schools as the Muslims' primary cause of their antipathy toward them. The absence of religious instruction in the elementary Tehsily and Halkabandi schools particuarly kept Muslim students away, because traditionally all Muslim children initiated their learning process with the Qur'ān, and the specified rituals for prayers. What could be done to change this situation? Responses were sharply polarized along traditional and modern positions. Sir Sayyid's supporters, constituting a majority in the Select Committee, maintained "that it would not be advisable for the Government to introduce any religious instruction in its public institutions." Some feared that religious instruction, if introduced, would only be distorted and produce "false notions" about Islam. Since the Tehsily and Halkabandy schools were supported by a Government-imposed educational cess on the agricultural revenue, a minority deemed it proper to ask the Government for the introduction of religious instruction in these elementary schools.

Finally, Sir Sayyid challenged an established view that Muslims' elementary education commenced with religion. Traditionally, Muslim children were educated in Persian literature only, while even the study of Arabic included grammar, logic, and philosophy. At the middle levels of education Muslims acquired knowledge of Islam along with ancient Greek philosophy. However, the Select Committee unanimously rejected Sir Sayyid's view.

Almost all the essayists and the Select Committee agreed that English education undermined Muslim students' faith in Islam. Quite emphatically Sir Sayyid stated that "he had never yet met a man who knew English and who had still full respect for all the religious beliefs and venerations." To buttress his contention, he cited W. W. Hunter: "The luxuriant religions of Asia shrivel into dry sticks when brought into contact with the icy realities of Western sciences."[5] The Select Committee regarded the study of religion as a preventive to disbelief in Islam; they differed, however, regarding the mode of instruction. All members concurred on the necessity of making private arrangement for the study of Islam, but Sir Sayyid was doubtful if the private schools using the existing religious texts could provide the antidote to religious skepticism. New *'ilm alkalām* (dialectical theology) catering to rationality was needed. Motivated by this conviction Sir Sayyid later wrote several books on various aspects of Islam, but not a single member of the Select Committee in 1870–71 accepted his suggestions or even grasped the significance of his argument.

Modern education was also held responsible by some essayists for "corrupting" the morals and manner of the students. Specifically they charged that "humility, good breeding, and respect for elders and superiors [were] replaced by pride, haughtiness, and impudence." This transformation, however, was blamed on teachers who scarcely found time to cultivate good manners in students. The remedy was to be sought in the appointment of well-mannered instructors. The Select Committee was evenly divided in accepting the essayists' observations. Sir Sayyid and his supporters rejected them as mere assertions, and maintained that among modern students "love of truth and freedom, sincerity and simplicity of manners were very often to be found, that sycophancy and flattery, the meanest of human qualities is [absent]. . . . They are not generally slow in showing respect where such is necessary, but they refrain from servility and undue reverance." Obviously, the traditionalists' "humility" and "respect for elders and superiors" meant "sycophancy" and "flattery" to the modernists. Perhaps Sir Sayyid failed to gauge the impact of modernity's silent revolution on the personality of the new generations, as it was making them culturally marginal in their traditional environment. That the cultural split would not only be permanent but would continue to polarize Muslim society, remained beyond Sir Sayyid's sympathetic appreciation. Nevertheless, he cherished a hope that perhaps in the distant future the societal discord would vanish when the Muslim society was altogether modernized.

General economic backwardness was also considered, at least by a significant minority of the essayists, as a cause of Muslim aloofness from modern schools. With one member dissenting, the Select Committee categorically rejected this view. Instead of marshalling economic data in refutation, the Select Committee transformed the economic question into a cultural issue by posing a rhetorical question: "If Muslims could lavish large sums in the celebration of absurd and unreasonable ceremonies connected with their children," then why could they not "lay aside only one half of such sums for the education of their children"? Certainly this comment was more appropriate to the middle and upper classes than to the depressed working classes. In fact some of the essayists suggested "that the children of the lower classes should receive no education at all as was the case during the Muhammadan rule." This in their judgement would be reassuring to the "noble classes," who resented having their children share schooling with "boys of low parentage." Eight members of the Select Committee admitted to the existence of this bias, but disapproved of it as "most improper, unfair, and opposed to their religious precepts."

Sir Sayyid stated unequivocally that

nobility and meanness should not be held to consist in riches and poverty. A man of low manners, if he only be rich, is treated by the world at large with the same consideration shown to a member of an ancient family . . . [in order to economize] the rich and the noble however are not ashamed to travel by the railway in the same class of carriages which are crowded with the common people. All the creatures of God have equal rights. No man is entitled to allow one particular race of men to obtain the good things of this world, and to bar the rest from participating in them, and it is the duty of the Government to observe this divine law in all its integrity.

Despite this commitment to the concept of human equality, Sir Sayyid's subsequent statements and actions betrayed a degree of aristocratic disdain as well as sympathy for "the low man." That the society's structure rather than his own choice had placed the "low man" lower on the socioeconomic scale remained inex-

plicable to Sir Sayyid. Consequently both democratic and aristocratic values collided in his consciousness, placing him at times in
support of undemocratic policies while adhering in theory to democracy. Islamic egalitarianism and aristocratic exclusivity had
left indelible impressions on his mind. In dissociating himself
from the bias of the Muslim upper classes, he also suggested
rather ruefully that if they wanted to avoid the indignity of their
children having poor classmates then they could establish a special college of their own. "Let the tuition fee in that college be so
high that the boys whom they call mean may not be able to
enter." Simultaneously, however, Sir Sayyid warned them that
"the Government was bound to keep the colleges and schools,
established by it, open to all classes; were the Government to
make any distinction in admitting boys to its institutions, it
would be responsible before God, and would also be guilty, if
judged by the general laws of the Government."[6]

All the essayists attacked the modern educational system,
holding various aspects of it responsible for generating Muslim
antipathy. For conceptual analysis the criticism can be divided
into two categories: (a) curricular, and (b) the place of scientific
education. Fifteen objections, ranging from trivial to highly significant, were made in the first category. The critics objected to
the assigning of several texts "on certain subjects" with insuf-
ficient time for their explanation; the meagerness of the ratio of
faculty to students; the waste of half of the academic time in ex-
tracurricular activities; too much emphasis on arithmetic, history, and geography in elementary schools; lack of individual attention; and emphasis on general instruction regardless of
students' "natural inclinations and tendencies." Instruction in Arabic and Persian did not even develop knowledge of etymology
and syntax and failed to include suitable texts at the college level.
Books, particularly historical, were included which were not
only offensive in style to the Muslims but were also "inimical to
the religion of Islam," and Urdu was insufficiently taught.
Lastly, the critics deplored the teaching of the English language,
consuming several academic years without producing noticeable
mastery of the language. Also, they inveighed heavily against the

method of examination, which produced an incredibly large number of failures for minor scholastic deficiency.

Commenting on all these objections, the Select Committee spotlighted some points, especially concerning the teaching of history. Kempson's English translations of histories contained in *Tarīkh-i Āina-i Numā,* originally written by Baboo Siva Pershad, were taught in colleges as well as in schools. The Select Committee stated that it was "cordially hated by all" Muslims. On this subject a lengthy correspondence ensued between Sir Sayyid and the Government of India, which discussed not only the contents of these histories but also the place of historical study in modern education.

The Select Committee maintained unanimously that, judged against the calibre of the educated generation, modern education proved to be a failure in India. Very succinctly one member summed up the Committee's reaction: "For more than forty or fifty years the Government has been exerting itself by every possible means to instruct and educate the people of this country, but I have never heard of any person who became a great philosopher or a renowned and distinguished author. Why is the effect of education in India not similar to that in England?" The Committee cited Kempson to partially substantiate this claim: "A boy who begins English at the age of twelve cannot expect to matriculate with credit until he is twenty years of age and then he must be well taught, obliged to be regular at school and generally work very hard." Even then this high school graduate, Kempson had noted, was "of little use to native society in its present condition."[7] Muslims, the Committee believed, "who are accustomed to a very high standard of learning cannot be satisifed with it." Without making specific recommendations, the Committee advised the Government of India to change not the curricula but the mode of instruction in modern schools.

The management of public education, the Select Committee asserted, should not be exclusively controlled by the Government; instead "the Government should transfer all authority to the general public in India. Also it was maintained that the Educational Committees consisting of Indians and the British were "about as useful as the same number of wax figures in Madame Tussaud's exhibition" in London. General Muslim aversion toward Government schools would be further mitigated if Hindi and its Devanagri script were scrupulously kept out of those schools "where the majority of the population are Muhammadans," because they "would never like Hindi or Nagri." To emphasize this point, Sir Sayyid made a curiously emotional pitch:

For the good of Muhammadans it would not be advisable to make everything suitable to their circumstances. It would apparently be more beneficial that everything should turn against them, that all the village and Tahsily schools should be made Nagri [Hindi] schools, and that the language of the Courts should also be Nagri . . . [Muhammadans] would have no means left to satisfy their wants, and that they would then be no longer fit for any employment or to earn their bread by any means whatever.

Reduced to this condition, Sir Sayyid reasoned in a similar emotional vein, Muslims "would wake from their slumber and make endeavors for their own welfare," or they would be no more.

Finally, the Select Committee explored Muslims' reaction regarding scientific education. The conflict between *scientia* (human knowledge) and *sapientia* (Divine wisdom) was by no means new to the Islamic civilization, and the Select Committee was aware of the intellectual milieu which had nourished it. It was particularly intense during the tenth and eleventh centuries when some Muslim scientists endeavored to establish rationalism independent of the revelation.[8] To preserve the hierarchy between intellect and reason the devotees of *sapientia* reacted rather excessively, downgrading the complimentary role of *scientia*, which eventually turned the Muslim world "to a science of the soul" and blotted out the science of nature. Alluding to this development in the intellectual world of Islam, the essayists as well as the Select Committee noted "that in the works of canon law, *'ulūm 'aqliā* (intellectual rational sciences) as well as *'Ilm al-kalām* (scholastic theology) have been declared unlawful." An authoritative study of canon law among the Hanafite Muslims *Al-Durr al-Mukhtār Fī Shrah al-Tanwīyr al-Absār* was cited, containing an interdiction of scientific study: "The sciences, the study of which is forbidden by the laws of Islam, are philosophy, astrology, ramal (a branch of astrology), natural philosophy, magic and the sciences of supernatural exhibitions and prediction; logic, being a branch of philosophy, is also forbidden." [9]

Parenthetically, it may be added that *al-Tanwīyr al-Absār* was written in 1586 by Shams al-Din Muhammad Abdullah al-Ghuzzīy, who died in 1595. Considered a definitive work on canon law, it excited the imagination of many commentators, most well-known and influential among them being Qadi Muhammad bin Ali (commonly known 'Alā al-Din al-Haskafīy), who wrote *al-Durr al-Mukhtār* in 1660. Born in Damascus, and educated under the care of Fakher al-Din Zakarīya al-Muqaddasīy, Qadi Muhammad Bin Ali eventually achieved the position of the Grand Mufti of Damascus for five years, and died in 1677 at age 63. While not wholesomely complimentary, *Khulasat al-Athar's* description of the Grand Mufti's intellectual propensity, that "his knowledge overwhelmed his rationality," [10] certainly accurately reflected his negative orientation toward empirical phenomena.

In order to determine precisely the Indic Muslims' objections to the study of contemporary Western sciences, the Committee established these broad categories. First, recently developed sciences which did not exist among the ancient Greeks and the Muslims. Geology was most conspicuous in this class. Secondly, those sciences which existed in the Greek and Islamic civilizations, but whose underlying principles since then have "proved to be wrong and now principles have been established in their stead." Thus, the old and modern sciences have nothing in common except the name. In this category astronomy and chemistry were placed. Thirdly, some sciences matured by the Greeks and the Muslims which have developed more recently in the West with no divergence in the fundamental principles, but which have "been so much improved that they now seem almost to be new." Mechanics, which the Muslims called *Jar-i saqīl* and mathematics—arithmetic or Euclid—were mentioned in this category. [11]

Seven objections against their study were noted by the essayists. (1) Muslims generally considered the principles of modern sciences opposed to Islamic convictions. (2) Obligations of *zahud* (devotional worship), *'ibadāt* (prayers), and the Muslims' propensity for *taqlīd almadhhabīy* (unquestioned following of the precepts of faith, established by the four schools of sunnite Islam) [12] deterred them from the knowledge of sciences. (3) Generally conservative, the Muslims eschewed "anything new." (4) Muslims believed that modern sciences could be of no value in "business, trade, or professions of any class of people." (5) Taught exclusively in English, the study and command of modern sciences was well-nigh impossible without spending several exhaustive years in learning the English language. Moreover, the scientific literature was not available "in any of those languages which are commonly read by Muhammadans." (6) The Muslims were "utterly ignorant of the value and worth of the modern sciences." (7) Believing that the rational sciences "were brought to perfection" by them in the past, they ignored all modern sciences. [13]

Deploring *al-Durr al-Mukhtār's* impact in discouraging Muslims from the empirical study of natural phenomena, the Select Committee almost unanimously concurred in the view that Muslim society no longer regarded the scholars of rational sciences as men of learning. The Committee observed that Shaikh 'Abd al-Haq, the great *Muhadith* (traditionist), the family of Shah 'Abdul Azīz (d. 1823), and other well-known savants of the Khanqah of Delhi, never taught or read rational sciences. "And there was no doubt that this was one of the great causes of the decline of the intellectual sciences" among the Indic Muslims.

Of the seven objections, however, the Select Committee entertained the first one rather seriously, even though its observations were not unanimous. The majority denied its validity, "because no one knew how far the principles of the modern sciences were consistent, and how far inconsistent, with the beliefs of Islam." A five-man minority remarked that the assigned reason was quite true. "Many principles," they said, "such as those relating to the revolution of the Earth, and the heavens being an ether, as well as the facts relating to thunder, electricity, comets, and shooting-stars, were so well-known that even the pupils of the village schools understood them. The Muhammadans, contrary to the truth, regard them as matters connected with faith, and the Committee therefore believe that this false notion is a great obstacle to the introduction of the Modern Sciences." [14] The fifth, sixth and seventh observations for the Muslims' aversion toward the sciences were considered unanimously valid by the Select Committee.

Although the Committee's report was primarily designed to be analytical, some attempts were made to delineate the roles of sciences and the *fiqah* (canon law) in the contemporary Indic Muslim culture. Science dealt with material phenomena, which was subject to empirical verification, and th *fiqah* generally defined devotional rites and convictions, which was beyond the scope of the scientific method. An inference was drawn by Mawlavi Farīd-ud-Din, President of the Select Committee, that "it was not incumbent on Muhammadans to obey and act up to any precept of canon law which obstructed intellectual improvement in matters relating to this world, and that they should not act upon it though it may have been enjoined upon by the Hanafi Imams." [15] To illustrate this conceptual dichotomy, he stated that if agronomy developed techniques of more productive agriculture, Muslims ought to adopt them and should not allow a Hanafi jurist's view to have any relevance whatsoever in this matter. (In developing this distinction, Sir Sayyid and his associates had a slow but sure success. Once again *scientia* acquired coexistent legitimacy with *sapientia* in the Indic Muslim culture. In the second half of the twentieth century Muslims in India and Pakistan—traditionalists and modernists—have finally recognized a legitimate role for science.)

British Response to Sir Sayyid's Evaluation

Hardly any of the Select Committee's findings and evaluations were accepted by the British officials in the Government of the

Northwest Provinces. (The heartland of these areas were later organized into the United Province, which the Government of India rechristened as Utter Pradesh [UP] after 1947.) Demonstrating his interest in the Select Committee's report, the Governor General of India asked the Lieutenant-Governor of the Northwest Provinces for his comments. Consequently, Kempson, the Director of Public Instruction, was called upon to explain the reaction of the provincial government. He submitted two detailed reports on August 28, and September 3, 1872, to the Lieutenant-Governor, which were forwarded on April 12 and April 18, 1873 to the Governor General, with Colvin, Secretary to the Government of the Northwest Provinces, indicating his endorsement of the Lieutenant-Governor's views. The contents of these reports were confidential and were never made public; not even Sir Sayyid had an inkling of them. (They are being analyzed for the first time by this author.)

Marshalling statistical evidence, Kempson first challenged the Select Committee's assertion that the Muslims generally ignored modern education, and their number was proportionately smaller in the Government schools and colleges, as shown in Table 4.1.

TABLE 4.1. MUSLIM STUDENT POPULATION IN GOVERNMENT
INSTITUTIONS (1872)

	Student Population	
Institutions	Hindus	Muslims
Government Colleges	1,012	81
Government Zilla (High) Schools	2,438	448
Goverment Tahsily Schools	7,129	1,937
Government Halkabandiy Schools	85,356	16,603
Grant-in-aid Schools	8,771	2,688
Unaided Private Schools	36,368	17,354
Total	141,074	38,111

SOURCES: Department of Education, *Report on the Progress of Education in the North-Western Province During 1870–71.* Memorandum from M. Kempson to C. A. Elliott, Secretary to the Government of the NW Provinces, no. 1728, dated Naynoo Tal, 28 August 1872. Government of India, Home Department, *Proceedings: Education,* September 1873, no. 48, p. 689, I.O.L.

Quite justifiably, Kempson deduced from the data the following generalizations. (1) According to the 1870 Census, the proportion of Muslims to Hindus in the Northwest Provinces was 14 percent, while at Government aided and indigenous schools Muslim students were 21 percent of the total and were between 15 and 16 percent at Government schools, and 23 percent at aided schools. (2) At unaided schools the Muslim students constituted 32 percent of the total. A majority of the aided schools, however, were run by European missionaries and the Muslim student population in these schools were relatively larger than that of the Hindus. Perhaps the "comparative cheapness of the education given in this class of schools was an attraction to Muhammadans." (3) A "just proportion of Muhammadan students *does* attend the Government schools and the 'small minority' of the essayists were nearer the truth than the Select Committee thought." [16]

Invalidating Sir Sayyid's comparative norm that "the proportion between the Hindus and Muhammadans of equal ranks ought to be calculated," Kempson conceded that the actual number of Muslim students in the Government institutions might be small, but, he asserted, that was also the case with the Hindus. With some bitterness he added that "all special pleading on behalf of the Muhammadans alone is out of place." Referring to Sir Sayyid's suggestion that the British Government should extend financial assistance to the Muslims in establishing schools catering to their educational needs, Kempson stated unequivocally: "We do not want special schools and a special system of instruction for a single section of the community." Finally, Kempson stated that Muslim personnel in the administration was adequately represented, while "the majority of the more valuable appointments are held by Muhammadans." Citing the Official Civil List of July 1, 1872, he said: "I find that 50 percent of all appointments in the Civil List are held by natives, in the proportion of 30 percent by Hindus and 20 percent by Muhammadans." Was this, comparatively speaking, fair to the Hindus? Here, Kempson, instead of applying the norm of population ratio, accepted the comparative norm of the past Hindu status under the Mughal rule. "As a comparative statement," Kempson added, "that in the Emperor Akbar's time [1556–1605] about 15 percent of office-holders were Hindu; in Shah Jehan's reign [1628–1658] they were 16 percent, but under 'Alamgīr [1658–1707] the proportion fell considerably." [17] This statement was not documented at all.

Regarding the public management of education and Sir Sayyid's reference to the Indian members of the educational committees as "wax figures in Madam Tussaud's museum," Kempson was outraged and described Sir Sayyid's comment "as unfair and unsavory slander." Kempson did not believe that the Indian public was the appropriate authority for the management of education and he saw the educational committees as a forum of "native counsel" only. If Muslims wanted special committees of their own to supervise Muslims' education, how could the Hindus be denied this opportunity by the Government?

Why didn't modern education produce any great scholar or philosopher in India? Here Kempson's explanation was rather extraordinary: "Circumstance rather than a special course of study makes great men. Philosophers and other renowned men in European countries will generally be found to have been at a university or public school, but this is not the reason why they were great men." [18] Implicit in this statement was an assertion that modern universities merely taught skills, and intellectual excellence developed beyond the academic precincts only accidentally or rarely. One wonders if Kempson was quite aware of the implications of his thoughtless statement. Defensive and at times sarcastic, Kempson's rebuttal of the Select Committee's report was point by point.

Kempson's explanations, evaluations, and recommendations were endorsed by Colvin for the ultimate approval of the Government of India. In behalf of Sir William Muir, the Lieutenant-Governor, Colvin wrote a detailed letter on April 18, 1873, to A. C. Lyall, Secretary to the Government of India, not only defending Kempson, but adding the Government's evaluation of Muslims' orientation toward modern education:

There is nothing in the system itself which is repulsive to Muhammadans where they have a desire for learning; but there is unfortunately very little desire, and for the higher and more scientific and European teaching a large class of the Muhammadans entertains a positive dislike. Religious feeling and the natural desire of training of their children in the tenets of Islam and the literature of the East have no doubt something to do with the paucity of Muhammadans in our upper schools and colleges; but there is also wide-spread over the country an unreasoning, if not fanatical aversion from anything that is foreign and non-Muhammadan, and the study of English and of European philosophy and science is regarded with repugnance.[19]

Educational data clearly show that Kempson's evaluation, rather than Sir Sayyid's or Colvin's, was closest to the truth.

British Assessment of Muslim Reaction

While Bengal was the first province to fall under the rule of the British East India Company in 1757, the plight of the Bengali Muslims was also the first catalyst to rouse the British conscience. In May 1871 Lord Mayo, the Viceroy of India, commissioned Sir W. W. Hunter to write a book about the Bengali Muslims, asking him also to answer this question: "Are Indian Muslims bound by their religion to rebel against the Queen?" With the help of Professor Henry Blockman, Principal of Madressa Aliya, Calcutta, Hunter not only affirmatively answered the question (which was rebutted by Sir Sayyid) but also presented an objective portrayal of the disastrous consequences of the Government's anti-Muslim policies. Written in thirteen days, Hunter's *Indian Musalmans,* published in London in 1871, won Lord Mayo's approval. In a letter of September 8, 1871, to the author, Sir J. Fitz-James Stephen, a law member of the Viceroy Council, reflected the impact of the book on the British national conscience: "It shows the truth of an opinion I have often expressed that John Bull is a well-meaning giant, but very nearly blind."[20]

What did Hunter reveal about the Bengali Muslims? First, the Permanent Settlement of 1793 pauperized the middle and upper classes of Muslims; secondly, the British had systematically ejected the Bengali Muslims from Government positions, and thirdly, the Muslims had been almost completely excluded from the professions. Each of these assertions Hunter backed up with irrefutable statistics from the Government's own records.

During the Mughal Empire the Muslims generally occupied the higher fiscal administrative positions, while the Hindu bailiffs dealt directly with the cultivators. The Hindus thus staffed the subordinate revenue service under the Mughals and they took a percentage of the collected revenue before passing the collections to the Muslim superior officers. The latter were responsible to the Mughal Emperor, thus forming an essential link in the fiscal system. The British East India Company transformed the revenue administration with a series of changes introduced by Lord Cornwallis and Lord Shore, ending in the Permanent Settlement Act of 1793. Consequently, the British took over the functions of those Muslim officers who had formerly been the link between the actual collector and the Government. They were replaced by the British collectors with a fiscal police in each district; however, Hindu officers as subordinate collectors were retained to deal directly with the cultivators. Commenting on the consequences of the Permanent Settlement for the Muslims, Hunter stated: "It elevated the Hindu collectors, who up to that time had held but unimportant posts, to the position of landholders, gave them a proprietary right in the soil, and allowed them to accumulate wealth which would have gone to the Muslims under their own rule." [21]

Another major source of the Muslims' livelihood had been their positions in the judicial, political, or civil administration. They continued to hold them for some time after the province passed under the Company's rule. Muslim *faujdars* and *kotwals* officered the police; *qadis* (doctors of law) sat in the civil and domestic courts. Even when the Company attempted to administer justice by appointing trained British officers, the *qadis* sat with them as their authoritative advisors on points of Islamic law. However, during the second half century (1807–1857) of the Company's rule the situation changed, because Persian, the official language, gave way to English and Bengali in the judicial administration. All positions were then filled by the promising Hindu youth graduating from English Government schools.

Until 1839 Muslim lawyers (pleaders) were almost as numerous as the Hindus and English put together, the proportion being 6 of the former to 7 of both of the latter. But, since 1851, the scene started to change. Different fitness tests were introduced; of 240 pleaders of the Calcutta High Court admitted from 1852 to 1869, 239 were Hindus and only one was Muslim. Among the attorneys, proctors, and solicitors of the High Court in 1869, there were 27 Hindus and not one Muslim; among the barristers-at-law were three Hindus and not one Muslim. Again, in 1869, the statistics regarding the medical profession indicated: (a) among the graduates of medicine in the Calcutta University there were 4 doctors, 3 Hindu, 1 English, and no Mulsim; (b) among 11 bachelors of medicine, 10 were Hindus and 1 English; (c) the 104 licentiates of medicine consisted of 5 English, 98 Hindus, and 1 Muslim. The story, Hunter maintains, was the same in every profession[22] (for further statistics see the appendix). In consequence of the Company's rule in Bengal the Muslim upper and middle classes either disappeared or were submerged beneath the new Hindu upper classes which developed as the result of British policy.

Finally, the British Government decided to attack the Muslims' educational backwardness, and on August 7, 1871, "issued a resolution upon the condition of the Muhammadan population," regretting that "so large and important a class should stand aloof from cooperation with our educational system." The Government of India proposed the following means to gain acceptance and promotion of Western education among the Muslims:

(i) The promotion of secondary and higher education conveyed in the Vernaculars, coupled with a more systematic encouragement and recognition of Arabic and Persian literature. (ii) The appointment of qualified Muhammadan English teachers in English schools in Muhammadan districts. (iii) Any general measure which might be adopted without infringing the fundamental principles of the Government educational system.[23]

Muslim Education in Bengal and Behar

Responding to this resolution the provincial governments refused to recommend the adoption of special measures to popularize English education among Muslims, while their reports presented the first objective survey of Muslim educational progress, not only at the university and secondary schools levels, but also at the primary school level. Again, to begin with, in Bengal, the state of Muslim education was obviously disheartening, even though the provincial educational authorities were unable to present complete statistics. See Tables 4.2–4.5.

TABLE 4.2. UNIVERSITY EDUCATION: 1870–1871 (BENGAL)

	Hindu Candidates		Muslim Candidates	
Examinations	Successful	Failed	Successful	Failed
Entrance Examination, 1871	504	859	27	44
Fine Arts Examinations, 1871	166	268	1	18
B.A. Degree, 1870	56	95	0	2
Total	726	1,222	28	64

TABLE 4.3. COLLEGE EDUCATION ENROLLMENT

College	Hindu Students	Muslim Students
Dacca	108	2
Hughly (founded by a Muslim, Muhammad Mohsin)	130	21

TABLE 4.4. ZILLA (HIGH SCHOOL) ENROLLMENT: 1871

Zilla School	Hindu Students	Muslim Students
Chittagong	123	44
Noakhally	109	14
Mymensing	342	19
Burrisaul	347	27
Commillah	145	21

TABLE 4.5. RURAL SCHOOL ENROLLMENT 1871

Chittagong district	1,272	348
Sylhet district	1,344	208

In the absence of complete educational statistics, C. Bernard, officiating secretary to the Government of Bengal, estimated that in 1870–71 the percentage of Muslim students, particularly in the North Central Circle (most of the districts which are located in Bangladesh) of Bengal, in the total student population was as shown in Table 4.6.[24]

TABLE 4.6.

Levels of Institution	Percentage
University and College Examinations	5
Zillah or High Schools	6
Normal (teachers training) Schools	13
Aided Higher Class English Schools	2½
Aided Middle Class English Schools	7½
Aided Middle Class Vernacular Schools	20
Aided Lower Class Vernacular Schools	30
Day Patshalas	27
(Rajshahye Patshala)	40
Night Patshalas	35
(Jessore Patshala)	50

Hindu-Muslim educational disparity becomes most glaring when it is kept in mind that in the central and eastern districts of Bengal the census figures collected in January 1871 showed the Muslim population to range between 51 percent in Sylhet to 78 percent in Rajshahye and 81 percent in Bogra.

To help eliminate Muslim educational backwardness the Government of Bengal decided on July 29, 1873, to make modern education more palatable to Bengali Muslims. Consequently, the Bengal Government allocated Rs.93,000 (a grant-in-aid of Rs.38,000 to Calcutta Madrassah, plus Rs.55,000 from Muhammad Mohsin Educational Endowment of Hughaly) to found three new traditional schools at Dacca, Chittagong, and Rajshahye. Each of these schools, however, was to be headed by a European principal, who was to ensure "facility to Madrassah students who may elect to take English course of study and to read physical sciences." Also, the students were to be "taught Persian and Arabic and a reasonable amount of Muhammadan law and literature."

Despite the best intentions of the Government the experiment proved to be counterproductive; only a handful of students, even ten years after the founding of the madrassahs, ventured to appear in the English examination of high schools. In 1880, criticizing the performance of these schools, Sayeed Ameer Hossein, Secretary of the National Muhammadan Association of Calcutta, pronounced: "There is hardly any room for questioning that the Hoogly, Chittagong, and Rajshahye Madrassahs have proved failure."[25] He recommended abolishing these madrassahs, and instead suggested: "If the Anglo-Muhammadan College at Aligarh with its limited income of Rs. 22,000 a year can afford to maintain higher classes teaching up to the F. A. Standard, with a European principal, Bengal with its Rs. 93,000 devoted exclusively to Muhammadan education can rightfully claim to have a Muhammadan English College at the seat of Government."[26] However, the suggestion was never implemented.

Attached to Bengal for administration, the province of Behar contained a small Muslim minority. They were considered so insignificant numerically that the Bengal Government report did not bother to give their educational statistics. It was stated that "they have a full share of Government service. English education has not taken root there, and the Hindus of Behar have no advantage over them. . . . The competition they have to fear is rather that of the educated Bengalees, who come in and get many good things."[27] In 1872, ten Muslim students were enrolled at the Government College Patna, as against seventy Hindu students. And this was considered to be a satisfactory state for Muslim higher education in Behar.

Madras

Madras, another Muslim minority province in southern India, reflected Muslims' virtual exclusion from higher education. R. S. Ellis, Chief Secretary of the Madras Government, pointed out that in 1872 only one Muslim obtained the Bachelor of Arts degree and that during the last fourteen years Madrassah-i Azam and the Harris school, both institutions established for the exclusive education of the Muslims, did not send any students for modern education to Presidency College in Madras. Reflecting the Government's policy, Ellis admitted that the Government schools and "the scheme of instruction is framed with exclusive reference to Hindus. Except in the case of the Madrassah-i Azam and the Preparatory School at Mylapoor, the Muhammadan section of the population is practically ignored." [28]

What could the University of Madras do to encourage Muslims to pursue higher studies? On September 7, 1872, the Syndicate of the University adopted a resolution, providing the answer:

(1) The regulations of the University should not be modified with the views of encouraging a particular section of the population. . . ; (2) While the Syndicate deplored the undoubted fact of the Muhammadans being behind the Hindus as regards educational progress, they do not see that any steps can be taken by the University to modify this state of things. . . ; (3) Possibly some gold medals or other prizes for proved excellency in Arabic and Persian, where these languages enter the University, might be founded by the Government, if not by Mussulman gentlemen. . .[29]

Bombay and Sindh

In the Bombay Province the situation was considerably better. For the administrative purposes the British had not yet separated Gujrat, Maharashtra, Canarsee country and Sindh from Bombay. Commenting upon the political orientation of the Bombay Muslims, C. Gonne, Secretary to the Government of Bombay, stated in his communication of March 18, 1872, to the Government of India: "It would be an error to suppose that Bombay contains any large class of eminent or learned Muhammadans, cherishing a decaying literature and withdrawing itself from sympathy with an alien government." To Sindh this remark was not applied;

because it "is more analogous to the Punjab. [In Sindh] the Vernacular is Sindhi, but a knowledge of Persian is the distinguishing mark of a gentleman among the middle and upper classes. . . . It is still the medium of correspondence between educated persons; and its literature is cherished by Muhammadans who are adverse to the study of English."[30] These pro- and anti-English biases were fully reflected in the Bombay Province's student population (see Table 4.7).

TABLE 4.7. HINDU-MUSLIM STUDENT POPULATION: 1872 (THE BOMBAY PROVINCE)

| | Government Schools | | Private Aided or Inspected Schools | |
Areas	Muslims	Total Students	Muslims	Total Students
Gujrat	5,260	51,654	621	6,512
(Deccan and Concan)	2,107	45,679	300	8,886
Maharashtra				
(Khandeish and Nagur)	2,208	26,975	19	401
Canarese Country	1,857	27,504	—	—
Sindh	3,197	9,471	28	644

SOURCE: Government of India, Home Department, *Proceedings: Education*, 1873, p. 478, I.O.L.

In 1872, of the total population of the Bombay Province about 1 in 12 were Muslims; in Sindh the Muslims numbered 1,354,781 out of 1,768,627. The table shows that the Muslim students, being 1 in 10 in Gujrat, nearly 1 in 10 in Khandeish and Ahmadnagur, and 1 in 13 in the Canarese country, enrolled in Government schools in proportion roughly to Muslim population. In Sindh, Muslim students were 1 in 3 only, indicating their educational aloofness since the Muslim population constituted nearly three-fourths of the total.[31] Muslim student population in the Government colleges and English schools presented a rather discouraging picture, though the situation in Bombay was slightly better (see Table 4.8).

Here the Muslim educational lag was most conspicuous. While they enrolled in larger numbers in the lower schools, they hardly rose to the levels of high school and college. Surprisingly,

TABLE 4.8. MUSLIMS IN COLLEGE AND HIGH SCHOOLS, 1872 (BOMBAY PROVINCE)

Schools	Gujrat		Khandeish and Nagur		Deccan and Bombay		Canarese Country		Sindh	
	Muslims	Total	Muslims	Total	Muslims	Total	Muslims	Total	Muslims	Total
Colleges	1	35	—	—	13	592	—	—	—	—
High Schools	11	338	9	314	22	1,238	3	189	14	176
Higher Middle Schools			10	295	61	2,282	7	429	35	345
Elementary Schools	316	4,322	441	2,754	127	2,582	166	2,565	263	951

SOURCE: pp. 478–79, I.O.L.

however, in 1872 the University of Bombay listed one Muslim who earned a Master of Arts degree and two who earned the Bachelor of Arts. To "poverty and depressed social status," rather than antiwest bias, was attributed the Muslims' aloofness from the Government-established modern educational institutions.

The Territory of Awadh

With Lucknow as its capital, the territory of Awadh was annexed by the British in January 1856. Here Muslim Arabic-Persian culture had diffused profoundly, eventually evolving under the influence of the Hindus into the Urdu-culture, in which both Hindus and Muslims spoke Urdu and wrote it in Arabo-Persian script. Before 1857 a thin veneer of Western culture was also visible at least in the mode of living of the upper classes and the ruling Muslim dynasty. Some *nawabs* of Awadh had constructed English-style houses, and on ceremonial occasions wore western dresses. Muslims, as well as Hindus, did not spurn the modern schools, which were established after 1864 when the Government's Department of Education was formed.

Already in 1871 Muslims, in proportionately larger numbers than Hindus, were enrolled in English schools: "there were on the 31st March last 42,105 children at Government and other schools. Of these, 10,563 were Muhammadans, and 31,251 were Hindus. The total estimated number of Hindu children of a school-going age in [Awadh] is about 1,667,000 and of such Muhammadan children of a similar age there are about 200,000. (This calculation includes both boys and girls.) The male pupils then at Government and Aided schools is 36,092 of whom 27,770 are Hindu boys, and 8,119 are Muhammadan boys. The number of Hindu boys able to go to school may be estimated at 833,500 and the number of Muhammadan boys at 100,000. The percentage, therefore, of Muhammadan boys under instruction is 8.1, and that of Hindu boys only 3.3."[32]

TABLE 4.9.

English	2,699	Arabic	141
Urdu	17,009	Hindi	4,834
Persian	4,924	Sanskrit	123

    In addition to the teaching of English, in all government schools an Urdu-Persian curriculum rather than a Hindi-Sanskrit one was used. Why was this policy adopted? Browning, Director of Public Instruction, answered: "So long as Urdu is used in all official business, and whilst the vast number of Hindus are apathetic regarding all instruction except that which will bring them immediate pecuniary returns, and care for neither reading nor writing, Urdu and Persian will in [Awadh] be more studied than Hindi and Sanskrit."[33] For government schools only the proportion of language students in 1891 was as shown in Table 4.9.

    Canning College, the only advanced institute of modern education in Awadh, had 144 students enrolled, mostly in the oriental department of the College, while the Muslim youths of college-going age in Awadh was estimated at 9,000. In 1870 the city had a Muslim population of 111,397. Here the lag in higher education was obvious.

    To the educational authorities in Awadh the cause of the educational backwardness of India in general and that of the Muslims in particular was not the anti-British feeling or any other cultural or religious prejudice, but the mass poverty. In fact, Awadh's Director of Public Instruction, Browning, eloquently stated that the British Government was

already suffering from the want of a career for the educated. It has always seemed to me that the causes of there being no career open to many of our educated youths, are not that agriculture or trades are not taught in our schools, but are simply the unequal distribution of wealth, the poverty of the masses, the absence of a numerous and wealthy middle class, and the selfishness of the few who have money, and who do not care to spend it in an enlightened manner. Now our school[34] boys appeal to the Government for employment when they should appeal to the nation.

Central Provinces, Mysore, Coorg, and Berar

In much the same manner the British administrators in the Central Provinces reported that Muslims "as a class are alive to the advantages of education." Being only 2.5 percent of the population of the Central Provinces they send 3,249 students to Government schools, and 1,519 to private schools. The total student population of the Government schools was 46,993 and that of the private schools 36,543. Also, without supporting figures it was asserted that in high schools especially Muslim students' attendance was good.[35]

However, a rather sad picture of the Muslims, both educationally and economically, was presented in the province of Mysore. While other communities steadily improved their fortunes the Muslims reflected "a constant tendency to deteriorate."[36] Except for a miniscule middle class, most Muslims in Mysore were engaged in the rearing of silkworms. In the 1870s, attacked by a persistent bacteria, the worms perished and even the introduction of fresh stock did not substantially improve the worm-culture. With an estimated population of 189,272 in Mysore, Muslims were 4.7 percent of the total population, and most lived in abject

TABLE 4.10. MUSLIM PERCENTAGE OF THE TOTAL POPULATION, 1870

Bangalore	7.9	Hassan	2.4
Kolar	5.2	Shimoga	5.1
Toomkoor	3.7	Kadoor	3.6
Mysore	4.9	Chituldroog	3.1

poverty. In some districts of Mysore (as indicated in Table 4.10), the Muslim population was sizable.

While access to English and Canarese schools was available to the Muslims, they nevertheless established Urdu schools, where the course of studies included Persian and Urdu literatures and grammar, arithmetic, history, and geography. Most text books were not procurable in Mysore and were brought in from the Punjab. Browning, Chief Commissioner of Mysore, indicated "Urdu of the North-West was better adapted for educational purposes than the Dakhni of this part of India." See Table 4.11.

These figures show that at least a minority of Muslim children attended the Canarese schools. However, the Muslims' expenditure of Rs. 9,600 on private Urdu schools was matched by

TABLE 4.11. MUSLIM STUDENT POPULATION, 1870 (MYSORE)

	Urdu Schools		English & Canarese Schools	
Types	Number of Schools	Number of Students	Types	Number of Students
Government (Normal)	1	12	Government (English)	40
Government (General)	5	240	Government (Canarese)	178
Private Boys	51	1,575	Private (English)	27
Private Girls	3	161	Private (Canarese)	11
Total	60	1,988		256

SOURCE: Government of India, Home Department, *Proceedings: Education, 1873*, p. 552, I.O.L.

the Government's grant-in-aid of Rs. 7,700. In Colleges Muslim students were conspicuous by their absence.

A miniscule minority in the territories of Coorg and East and West Berar, the Muslims were in the 1870s "depressed in social and intellectual conditions." In 1872, they numbered 6,000 in Coorg, having migrated from Malabar and Canara. Only 28 Muslim boys attended the Central School at Mercara,[37] while in Berar (where a Hindu majority spoke Marathi) only a handful of adventurous parents sent their children to local schools. Responsible for the administration of Berar (technically a part of Nizam's dominions), Major W. Tweedie, First Assistant Resident, Hyderabad, assured the Government of India on April 16, 1872, of merely "a fair share of attention"[38] to Muslims' educational needs without offering a concrete suggestion.

The Punjab

Comparatively, the Muslims in the Punjab were more advanced in terms of English education than those in other provinces. This despite the fact that the Punjab came under British rule rather late in 1849, when the Sikh power was overthrown by the British conquest. Only 24 years later the Muslims had fully accepted modern education and cooperated with the British in making a switch to Urdu (as the medium of instruction and general education) from Persian. In the number of college graduates (5 percent during the academic year 1870–71 the Muslims were overwhelmingly behind the Hindus, although determined attempts were made during the 1890s by the middle classes to close this gap. However, the general picture of the Muslims' educational achievement was by no means dismal. Educational statistics support this view (see Table 4.12).

A noteworthy feature was the steady increase since 1861 of the percentage of Muslims in Zillah and aided schools, where English education was imparted (see Table 4.13).

In the teaching profession, however, the Muslim faculty in

TABLE 4.12. MUSLIM STUDENT POPULATION IN THE PUNJAB
(1870–1871)

Institutions	Muslims	Others	Total	Percent of Muslims
(I) *Studying English*				
Government Colleges	6	96	102	5.8
Government Schools, Higher Class	34	129	163	20.8
Aided Schools, Higher Class	639	1,677	2,318	27.5
Government Schools, Middle Class	334	1,001	1,335	24.8
Aided Schools, Middle Class	698	1,656	2,354	29.7
(II) *Vernacular & Oriental*				
Government Normal Schools	121	86	207	58.4
Aided Normal Schools	102	47	149	68
Oriental School, Lahore	12	18	30	40
Town Schools	2,410	5,466	7,876	30.6
Aided Schools of Middle Class	215	411	626	34.3
Government Schools, Lower Class and Village Schools	16,445	26,801	43,246	38
Aided Schools, Lower Class	2,910	7,074	9,984	29.1
(III) *Medical Schools*				
English Department	10	35	45	22.2
Vernacular Department	51	42	93	54.8
Total	23,987	44,539	68,526	35

TABLE 4.13. PERCENTAGE OF MUSLIM STUDENTS

Institutions	1861–62	1865–66	1870–71
Zilla Schools	21	23	24
Aided Schools	21	28	29
Town Schools	27	27	30

practically all institutions maintained its numerical preponderance over the Hindus (see Table 4.14).

Punjabi Muslims' Attitude Toward Modern Education and Sir Sayyid

Regarding the Muslim Punjab's educational attitudes and its general success, two salient questions may be asked: why did the

TABLE 4.14. MUSLIM TEACHERS IN THE PUNJAB, 1871

Institutions	Number of Schools	Hindu Teachers	Muslim Teachers
Primary Schools	1,057	427	771
Middle Vernacular Schools	79	78	126
Middle Anglo-Vernacular Schools	24	56	46
Normal Schools	3	4	11
Upper Schools	5	5	4
Colleges	2	6	2
Total	1,170	576	960

SOURCES: Government of India, Home Department, *Proceedings: Education*, 1873, pp. 526–27.

Punjab discard Persian as the medium of instruction and adopt Urdu instead of Punjabi, the language of the province? Also, why did the Punjab so easily adopt modern English education, while the Muslims in other provinces struggled to overcome their aversion to modern education? The answers to these questions offer the explanation for the success of Sir Sayyid's movement in the Punjab, and the Punjab's steady drive to modernity.

In answering these questions the Punjab's cultural and demographic background must be taken into consideration. Central Asia's gateway to India, the Punjab became from the second millenium B.C. to the second century B.C. the home of the Aryans, who founded the Hindu religion and culture in India; and the Persian and Greek conquerors. They were followed by the Parthians, who migrated from their homelands near the Caspian Sea, and settled in the Punjab. On their heels came the Scythian conquerors, who established another kingdom in the Punjab with Taxila as its capital. Behind them came the Kushans, of mixed Turko-Mongolian stock, who extended their dominions in Afghanistan and the Punjab. Like a tornado, around 460 A.D. the white Huns struck the Punjab, and they were followed in quick succession by less known Central Asian tribes. In the course of time, all of them were assimilated into the religio-social order of Hinduism.

With the advent of Islam a new series of invasions started,

altering the demographic shape of the Northwest and the Punjab. In 711 the Arabs conquered Sindh and approximately half of the Punjab up to Multan. However, the full impact of Islam was not felt by the Punjab until it was conquered by Sultan Mahmud Ghaznavi during 1024–25. He made the Punjab a provincial capital of his Indian dominions for a century and a half. Other Central Asian Turks (who, like the ancestors of Sultan Mahmud had accepted Islam and Persian culture in its new Islamic form) subsequently burst upon the Punjab and established the Delhi Sultanate (1192–1526) with the better part of Indian territory within its sway. Finally came the Mughals in 1526, who were overthrown by the British in 1857. These demographic changes have enabled the Punjabis to adjust themselves to the trauma of new stocks of people, who must inevitably bring new ideas.

Consequently, the steady stream of migrants swelled the ranks of the Muslim society in the Punjab. Commenting upon the spread of Islam in India, T. W. Arnold stated: "But the number of families of foreign origin that actually settled in India is nowhere great except in the Punjab and its neighborhood."[39] Although coersion played some role, the second major source of accretion to the Muslim society was persuasion, when Muslim Sufis (mystics) converted a large number of Hindus to Islam. Thus, for the first time in the Punjab, as elsewhere in India, the population was divided into two district cultural entities. There was considerable cultural give and take, but it stopped short of Hindu-Muslim synthesis, preventing the final assimilation of Muslims into the Hindu society.

The Sikhs, the third element in the Punjab's population, developed during the period of the Mughal rule. Desiring to unite the Hindus and the Muslims in quietist devotion to the pursuit of "Ultimate Truth," Guru Nanak (1469–1539), the founder of Sikhism, preached monotheism, universal brotherhood, and the equality of man, denouncing the caste system.[40] He was followed by nine more gurus, while the tenth one, Guru Gobind Singh, transformed the Sikh religious community into a distinct nation, differing from both Hindus and Muslims. During the decay of the Mughal administration in the Punjab, the Sikhs found the political opportunity, under Ranjit Singh (d. 1839), to establish a Sikh state in the Punjab. Although Ranjit Singh employed both Hindus and Muslims in subordinate roles, his rule was, in Percival Spear's apt description, "a minority dictatorship."[41] Considering the Sikh state a *dar al-Harb,* a land of war, Muslims led by Sayyid Ahmad Shahīd (d. 1838) and Mawlana Isma'īl Shahīd (d. 1838) initiated an armed struggle against Ranjit Singh, which ended in failure and the death of both leaders in the battlefield.[42] Finally, when the Sikh state was overthrown by the British in 1849, the Muslims in the Punjab received them with open arms as "liberators."

In 1871, the Punjab's total population was 17,574,784; Muslims numbered 9,331,360 (53 percent), and so retained a slight edge over Hindus (7,236,607), Sikhs, and other minorities (1,006,810). However, in the western half of the Punjab, Muslim numerical strength varied from 80 to 90 percent, while Hindus dominated the eastern half of the province.

Culturally, however, the Muslims set the tone in the Punjab. Until 1849, as with other provinces in India, Persian was the medium of instruction in the traditional Muslim schools, and remained the official language even at Ranjit Singh's court. The traditional Arabic-Persian curricula provided not only education in religion, but also in other rational sciences including philosophy, grammar, mathematics, geometry, and above all architecture. Men of outstanding creative ability in various disciplines produced by the traditional education are still a legend in the history of the Punjab and Muslim India, including a brilliant strategist, Nawab Sa'd Allah Khan[43] (d. 1656) of Chiniot, who was for 27 years Emperor Shah Jahan's prime minister and military strategist; Allamah 'Abd al-Hakīm (d. 1656) of Sialkot, who was noted for his excellence in rational sciences and was weighed twice in silver by Emperor Shah Jehan; the architect Ustad Ahmad Ma'mār (1059 A.H./1649) of Lahore, who designed and supervised the construction of the Taj Mahal and the Red Fort of Delhi;[44] and Shaikh Nizām, the distinguished lawyer of Lahore,[45] who headed the Commission of Jurists appointed by Emperor Aurangzeb Alamgir to compile the digest of Islamic laws, *Fatawa-i Alamgiri*.

However, these brilliant achievements were made at the expense of Punjabi, the spoken language of the people. Consequently, Punjabi remained devoid of any scientific or philosophic literature. Muslims hardly made any contribution to Punjabi's development as a vehicle of cultural and scholarly expression, although they retained it as a language of daily intercourse. However, during the periods of the Delhi Sultanate and the Mughal Empire some Sufi poets[46] wrote mystic poetry in "Punjabi" using rural idioms and the Arabic-Persian script, notable among them being Shaikh Farīd al-Din Mas'ūd Ganj-i Shakar (1175–1265). Grammatically and syntactically, Muslims' Punjabi is almost identical with Urdu, sharing a common grammar and 70 percent of the vocabulary. Truly, Punjabi was adopted by the Sikhs as their national language. Taking the 35 letters of the acrostic composed by Guru Nanak, his successor Guru Angad (1539–1552) adopted the letters from Devanagri and other north India scripts, and developed Gurmukhi (from the Guru's mouth)—a new script of Punjabi. In this script and language was composed the religious and secular literature of the Sikhs. Reflecting the Punjab's folk culture, Guru Nanak indeed was the first real mystic poet of Punjabi. Stylistically, he selectively adopted to his syncretistic poetic expressions the popular forms of *Vars* (ballads), *Brahmahs, Pauries,* and *Painti Akhari,* all having literary origins in Sanskrit, Prakrit, and Apbhramsa literatures. In addition to romances, Sikh poets composed some well-known ballads. With the exception of Guru Nanak's *Janam Sakhis* (Biographies), Punjabi lieterature, however, remained without prose of any significance until recent years.

Hindus in the Punjab, on the other hand, partially participated in the secular aspects of the Muslim educational system. This was necessitated in 1582 by Emperor Akbar's *diwan,* Raja Todar Mal's policy of changing the revenue records from Hindi to Persian. Motivated by the desire to obtain administrative positions in the Mughal administration, Hindus acquired a secular

Arabic-Persian education. During the nineteenth century, the British introduced some basic changes in the educational structure of the Punjab. Having dropped Persian as the British India's official language in 1835, the British eliminated it also as the medium of instruction in the Punjab's Government Schools.

British Educational Policy in the Punjab

In 1859–59 the British Government adopted Urdu, instead of Hindi, as the language of education in primary and secondary schools of the Punjab. To the British, the change from Persian to Urdu was logical, since the cultural affinity between the two was close, and Urdu was generally more in harmony with the Muslim coloring of the Northwestern Indic culture. In 1866–67, the Punjab administration explained this language policy, which was published in Britain's *Parliamentary Papers* of 1870:

There is one uniform scheme of studies for all town and village schools in which Urdu is taught. The scheme provides for eight classes, though comparatively few schools possess them. A town school must contain 50 boys, of whom 20 must be above the sixth, and some above the fourth class. All that do not come up to this standard are village schools. The study of Nagri [Devanagri script of Hindi] is carried on, as a rule, much more extensively in districts [Delhi, Guragon, and Karnal] that formerly belonged to the Northwest Provinces. The Nagri classes correspond with the town classes of Urdu schools, and the boys are, when possible, encouraged after finishing the Nagri course [Hindi] to continue their studies in Urdu and Persian. Many commence Urdu before they reach the first Nagri class. There are altogether in town and village schools 9,457 students who learn Nagri.[47]

What was the impact of British educational policy on the Punjab? The explanatory data for the 1850s and 1860s were also provided by the *Parliamentary Papers*. First, Captain Holroyd, Punjab's officiating Director of Public Instruction, stated: "Amongst the rural population of the Punjab, a knowledge of the Urdu language and of arithmetic has been widely diffused, and in many of our schools Persian is taught very much better than it could be learnt in the old *Maktabs.*"[48] Also the Punjab Government made special attempts to encourage the development of Urdu literature in general and the secondary schools texts in particular. In fiscal 1868–69, Rs. 10,000 were allocated for this purpose and a small amount was set aside for the purchase of the Aligarh [Sir Sayyid's] Scientific Society's journal. Guidelines were established for rewards to the authors of new Urdu books and the translators of English books into Urdu. Initially, emphasis was laid on producing Urdu textbooks for Vernacular schools, high schools, and the first two years of college education.

To create a pool of academic and literary talent in Lahore, Captain Holroyd made a recommendation in January *1862* to the Punjab Government to amalgamate the Delhi College with the Government College, Lahore.[49] This suggestion was carried out in April 1877. In 1874 the Punjab Government made a less successful attempt to renovate Urdu poetry, establishing a modern monthly *musha'ara* (poetical symposium) that, instead of a given hemistich (*radif*), invited poets to write poems on natural themes. In addition to including the best selections from the masters of traditional Urdu lyrical poetry in the secondary and high school texts, the Government hoped thus to create "Urdu poetry, aiming at moral instruction, and presenting a natural picture of feelings and thoughts."

Secondly, the number of traditional Muslim schools declined rapidly, especially in urban areas, because a sizable number of them were absorbed into the Zilla (district) schools. The prospects of regular salary lured many traditional teachers to the service of the new education department. Thirdly, learning of the English language gained wide acceptance since English Departments were attached to at least 53 town schools. These schools were "more largely attended both by the richer classes and by the children of Government officials than where no English [was] taught." In some districts, where "the principal people of the place" held aloof from English schools, poorer classes took advantage of the educational opportunity. Consequently, the modern school system provided opportunities for vertical social mobility to the lower middle classes of the Punjab. Also, as the British authorities perceived, the teaching methods in modern schools produced "habits of neatness, order, and cleanliness" in the rural population. Fourthly, the Punjab's agricultural classes, and particularly the gentry including Hindus, Muslim, and Sikhs, not only accepted the Government's language policy but also extended financial aid to the Government to spread education in the rural areas. Despite the Urdu-Persian curricular offerings of the new schools, Hindu students retained a numerical majority in the village and town schools. The following statistics in Table 4.15 support this.

TABLE 4.15. RURAL STUDENT POPULATION (PUNJAB 1866–67)

Schools	Muslims	Hindus	Others	Total	Agriculturists	Non-agriculturists
Village Schools	21,264	26,823	5,670	53,757	40,434	13,323
Town Schools	2,332	5,702	564	8,598	4,458	4,140

By 1905 the British educational policy had firmly established the supremacy of Urdu over Punjabi and Hindi. Even Hindu owners published their newspapers in Urdu, and Urdu newspapers outnumbered Hindi, Punjabi, and English newspapers in the province, as can be seen in Table 4.16.

Financial assistance to the Government schools was extended in the form of educational cess, paid by the landowners in addition to the land tax. Although willingly paid, the cess was not voluntary, but was assessed at the rate of 1 percent with the regular Government revenue from the agricultural lands. Regarding the cess the Punjab's attitude markedly differed from other provinces, particularly the northwest Provinces and Awadh, where the cess was "viewed with great suspicion by the people, who regard them as exactions." [50] That people should not be called upon to help the British Government in discharging its educational or other functions, was at least the Chief Commissioner's

TABLE 4.16. LANGUAGE SURVEY OF NEWSPAPERS IN THE PUNJAB, 1880–1905

Language	Number of Newspapers	Percent of Total
Urdu	343	81.86
English	24	5.73
Punjabi	19	4.53
Hindi	17	4.06
Mixed (more than one language)	12	2.86
Persian	2	.48
Arabic	1	.24
Sindhi	1	.24
Total	419	100.00

SOURCE: N. Gerald Barrier and Paul Wallace, *The Punjab Press* (East Lansing: Michigan State University, 1970), p. 159.

assessment of the Awadh's public opinion in 1861. On the other hand, the Punjab's landowners were relatively more cognitively oriented toward the British administration. In July 1857, Arnold, Director of Public Instruction, stated that the cess was "being levied in far the greater portion of the Punjab"; however, in 1864, Hoshiarpur, the only noncontributing district, offered its consent for the cess and joined the other districts in raising the amounts shown in Table 4.17.

Originally expended for the support of village schools in proportion to the amount of cess raised in each district, the allocative policy was changed in 1860. The cess collected annually in

TABLE 4.17. PUNJAB'S EDUCATIONAL CESS FUND (1856–1869)

Years	Amount (in rupees)	Years	Amount (in rupees)
1856–57	138,034	1863–64	210,000
1857–58	151,544	1864–65	210,000
1858–59	192,002	1865–66	210,000
1859–60	175,226	1866–67	212,710
1861–62	204,943	1867–68	207,422
1862–63	208,908	1868–69	210,083

SOURCE: *Parliamentary Papers, 1870*, p. 23.

all districts was then formed into one general fund and new guidelines for allocations were laid down. The first allocation was made to defray the expenses of *tehsiley* (town) and girls' schools; then 10 percent of the balance was set aside for the educational *moharers'* (clerks') salary; 4 percent for the incidental expenses of all Vernacular schools including the cost of prizes given by district officers; 6 percent for stipends of teachers studying at the teachers' training schools; 5 percent for the publication of the *Sarkari Akhbar* (the Government's newspaper, which was published in Urdu); and the balance was spent for the maintenance of village schools.[51]

In the middle of the 1860s, the Punjab Government decided to pay the salaries of the Chief Clerks and to bear the cost of the *Sarkari Akhbar*. It allocated Rs. 40,740 annually from the imperial revenue "for the maintenance of one 'model school' in each tehsil [sub-district] of the Punjab." This policy shifted the educational emphasis from the villages to the towns. While the funds were provided by the farmers—among them the Muslims owned a majority of the agricultural acres—the benefits of high school education were transferred to the urban middle classes. Despite the easy access to Government high schools, in hardly any district was the Muslim student population reflected in a majority, although it was by no means overwhelmingly outnumbered by the Hindus and others. Comparatively depressed economic conditions of the urban Muslims were mainly responsible for this disparity. Commenting upon the Punjabi Muslims' positive orientation toward modern education, Lepel Griffin, Officiating Secretary to the Punjab, wrote on February 21, 1873, to H. L. Dampier, Officiating Secretary to the Government of India:

In the Punjab proper, excluding the frontier districts, the Muhammadan population avail themselves of the educational opportunities offered to them to as great a degree in proportion to their members as the Hindu population. The Muhammadans of the Punjab are not generally a bigoted race. They do not appear, from statements made by the leading men of their creed, to entertain any religious objectives to their children attending Government schools, or indeed the Mission schools, where to a certain extent, religious [Christian] instruction is imparted.[52]

Other British administrators, including C. R. Lindsay, C. W. W. Alexander, Col. R. Maclagan, and even three Hindu members of the Senate of Punjab University College—Nobina Chandra Rai, Raja Harbans, and Rai Mul Singh—substantially concurred with Griffin's evaluation. Strictly traditional in their own educational training, but positively oriented to the benefits of modern education, the Muslim members of the Senate—Khan Bahadur Rahim Khan, Nawab Nawazish Ali Khan, Nawab Abdul Majid Khan, Faqir Shams-ud-Din, Muhammad Shah, Kalb-i Abid, and Muhammad Jan—ascribed relative Muslim backwardness in English education to lack of economic means. More modern educational opportunities for the Muslims was their recommendation:

We do not wish English education to lessen in any way, as it is a key to the treasures of all sciences and arts of the age, and men of every nation and occupation anxiously want it; for without this, according to the established rule of the Government, no one can rise up or obtain any high office; consequently the Government schools and colleges should remain open as usual to the Muhammadans for English education.[53]

In view of the Punjabi Muslims' positive response to modern education, it is not surprising that they enthusiastically participated in the Anjuman-i Punjab's movement for the creation of a modern university in Lahore, and extended enthusiastic cooperation to Sir Sayyid's movement toward modernity.

Muslim Contribution to the Punjab University and Cooperation with Sir Sayyid

Established in August 1865, the Anjuman-i Punjab, under the leadership of its Hungarian-born president, G. W. Leitner, initiated the movement for the establishment of a modern university in Lahore. Actually the British Government had wanted to "establish a single university for the Northwest Provinces and the Punjab, having its seat at Delhi,"[54] but the three Punjabi communities (through the Anjuman-i Punjab) and the British officials (in their private capacity through the "European Committee of Support") opposed this proposal stating that both the Punjabi public and nobility were in profound sympathy with advanced modern education, and had, since 1866, raised funds for the university in Lahore, while the Delhi public had demonstrated no financial evidence of support for the university. Consequently, in May 1868, Thornton, Secretary to the Government of th Punjab, submitted a proposal to the Government of India for the establishment of the university in Lahore. In addition to the study of Arabic, Sanskrit, and Persian, the university was to "diffuse Western knowledge through the medium of the vernaculars," that is, Hindi and Urdu.[55] This proposal reflected the suggestions of the Anjuman-i Punjab and the European Committee of Support, which included Sir Donald McLeod, the Lieutenant Governor of the Punjab, and seven high ranking British administrators. Sir Sayyid, it should be recalled, had submitted a similar proposal on August 1, 1867, which the Government had rejected in September 1867. How could the Government accept the Anjuman-i Punjab's and European Committee of Support's identical plan a year later?

This situation roused the wrath of Sir Sayyid, who first argued with the Punjab Government to accept Urdu's superior claim to be the only medium of instruction. When the Anjumani Punjab stated that a Hindu scholar, Babu Noveen Chander, had already endeavored to establish the superiority of Hindi, the Punjab Government rejected Sir Sayyid's suggestion. Subsequently, Sir Sayyid attacked the concept of an "oriental" university for the Punjab, and accused the Government of endeavoring to deny Indians the light of modern education. This argument reflected Sir Sayyid's shortsightedness, as he failed to recognize that the Hindu renaissance emphasizing Hindu cultural revival was unable to accept Urdu as the national language of India. At best, it would have tolerated Urdu as a Muslim version of Hindi. However, the use of both in the Punjab would have enabled their development as scientific languages, with the balance tilted in the favor of Urdu, since it was the language of secondary instructions and primary schools. Taught mostly in Urdu, Hindu high school graduates had to opt for Urdu as the medium of instruction in the university. To an extent, Sir Sayyid's criticism thwarted the flowering of this useful initiative when the Government developed the Oriental College in Lahore separately from the university, where modern education was disseminated in English, and Urdu and Hindi were offered as optional languages.

To blunt Sir Sayyid's opposition, the Anjuman-i Punjab and the European Committee mobilized the Punjabis to strengthen the Government in establishing a university in Lahore, reflecting their educational philosophy. In these efforts the Punjabi Muslims played a conspicuous role. In order to adopt supportive resolutions for the university, two significant meetings were held in Lahore on March 12 and May 25, 1868, in which representation was as shown in Table 4.18.[56]

TABLE 4.18.

Date	British	Muslim	Hindu	Sikh	Total
March 12	11	7	4	5	27
May 25	9	19	19	9	56
Total	20	26	23	14	83

The Punjab's endeavors for the creation of a modern university achieved a great significance when in 1869 Dr. Leitner released a list of donors and subscribers who had, since 1866, contributed funds to the Anjuman-i Punjab for the construction of Lahore University buildings. Quantitatively the Muslim donations reflected the extent of the Punjabi Muslims' positive orientation toward modern education (see Table 4.19).

Muslim donations acquire greater significance when it is realized that, compared to a sizable number of large Hindu and Sikh donors, only two Muslim nobles donated more than Rs. 500 to the University Fund of the Anjuman-i Punjab. Proportionately small Muslim donors were larger than the Hindu and the Sikh, and their donations of Rs. 2,292 were certainly larger than the Rs. 2,250 paid by the large Muslim donors. The smallest Muslim donation was four rupees only, indicating grass-root participation in the adventure of modern higher education. Table

TABLE 4.19. DONATIONS FOR THE PUNJAB UNIVERSITY, LAHORE (INCLUSIVE OF DECEMBER 31, 1869)

Donors	No.	Promised			Paid Subscriptions					
		Donations	Annual Subscriptions	Total	Donations	1866	1867	1868	1869	Total
Muslims	45	2,901	1,210	4,111	2,586	—	791	947	218	4,542
British	12	3,767	3,240	7,007	1,517	3,000	3,000	2,000	—	9,517
Hindus	51	79,541	3,599	83,140	68,137	24	397	291	174	69,023
Sikhs	46	79,442	3,196	82,638	12,596	2,000	757	772	742	16,867
Districts	5	4,178	2,139	6,317	4,178	—	2,118	21	—	6,317
Municipal and other corporations	2	1,051	513	1,564	51	—	500	—	—	551
Total	161	170,880	13,897	184,777	89,524	5,024	7,563	4,031	1,134	106,817

SOURCES: Condensed from "Account of the Lahore University, May 27, 1869: Statement of Contributions," Papers Relating to Education in India, *Parliamentary Papers*, 1870, pp. 358–62; Government of India, Education: Home Department, *Proceedings*, April 1873, pp. 149–55.

4.20, showing large donations puts in relief the extent of small contributions by the Britons, Muslims, Hindus, and Sikhs.

However, the inadequacy of the donated funds was soon realized, and the Anjuman-i Punjab established a voluntary standing committee, consisting of men of substance, in each of the Punjab's thirteen districts. Among the committee members, Muslim volunteers outnumbered both Hindus and Sikhs (see Table 4.21).

Regardless of the size of Muslims' donations, one fact stands out: the Punjabi Muslims' positive response to modern education was clearly established several years before Sir Sayyid launched the movement for the establishment of the MAO College at Aligarh. The Punjabi Muslims' loyalist attitude toward the British made the loyalist Sir Sayyid most welcome in the Punjab. This basic similarity in political and educational orientations thus firmly laid down the foundations of partnership between the UP and Punjabi Muslims, which lasted through the 1940s. In accepting Sir Sayyid as their leader, especially during the 1870s when the UP Muslims had ostracized him, the Punjabi Muslims provided a following for Sir Sayyid's leadership, and by their support made the decisive difference between the success and failure of his modernizing role.

Some Generalizations

In the light of the preceding qualitative and quantitative data a few generalizations may be offered. First, with the exception of Bengal, the Muslim student population in modern high schools was generally in harmony with the Muslim numerical strength in the provinces of India. Particularly in the inexpensive missionary schools of some provinces the Muslims even exceeded others in actual numerical strength. (This practice was observable in the Northwest Provinces [UP], the area of Sir Sayyid's activity.) Obviously this situation reflected the Muslims' pragmatic approach rather than blind negativism. Secondly, the number of Muslims in college and university education were discouraging,

TABLE 4.20. MAJOR PRIVATE DONATIONS TO THE PUNJAB UNIVERSITY, DECEMBER 31, 1869 (RS. 500 AND ABOVE)

Donors	Promised		Paid Donations	Paid Annual Subscriptions					Total of Paid Donations and Subscriptions
	Donations	Annual Subscriptions		1866	1867	1868	1869	Total	
(A) *Muslims (2)*									
Nawab of Maliyr Kotla	500	400	500	—	400	400	—	800	1,300
Nawab Nawazish Ali Khan	500	150	500	—	150	150	150	450	950
	1,000	550	1,000	—	550	550	150	1,250	2,250
(B) *British (8)*									
Sir John Lawrence, Governor General of India, retired	—	2,000	—	2,000	2,000	2,000	—	6,000	6,000
Sir D. F. McLeod, Lieutenant Governor of the Punjab	—	1,000	—	1,000	1,000	—	—	2,000	2,000
F. H. Cooper	750	—	—	—	—	—	—	—	—
C. U. Aitchison	500	—	500	—	—	—	—	—	500
T. H. Thornton	500	—	—	—	—	—	—	—	—
Col. R. Maclagan	500	—	—	—	—	—	—	—	—
A. A. Roberts	500	—	—	—	—	—	—	—	—
Dr. G. W. Leitner	617	—	617	—	—	—	—	—	617
	3,367	3,000	1,117	3,000	3,000	2,000	—	8,000	9,117

(C) Hindus (5)								
Maharaja of Kashmir	62,500	2,000	62,500	—	—	—	—	62,500
Raja of Jindh	11,000	—	—	—	—	—	—	11,000
Raja of Mandi	2,000	1,000	2,000	—	—	—	—	2,000
Raja of Farid Kot	1,000	—	1,000	—	—	—	—	1,000
Raja of Bilaspore	500	—	500	—	—	—	—	500
	77,000	3,000	66,000	—	—	—	—	77,000
(D) Sikhs (6)								
Raja of Kapurthala	10,000	2,000	10,000	2,000	—	—	2,000	12,000
Maharaja of Patiala	50,000	—	—	—	—	—	—	50,000
Raja of Nabha	11,000	—	—	—	—	—	—	—
Sardar of Kalsia	3,000	—	—	—	—	—	—	—
Raja Sin Man Singh	2,000	—	—	—	500	—	—	—
Raja Harbans Singh	1,000	500	1,100	—	—	500	1,500	2,600
	77,000	2,500	11,100	2,000	500	500	3,500	64,600
(E) Districts (4)								
Ludhiana	—	1,700	—	—	1,700	—	1,700	1,700
Gurdaspur	3,128	439	3,128	—	418	21	439	3,567
Lahore	800	—	800	—	—	—	—	800
Amritsar Municipal Fund	1,000	500	—	—	500	—	500	500
	4,928	2,639	3,928	—	2,618	21	2,639	6,567

TABLE 4.21. DISTRICT STANDING COMMITTEES TO RAISE DONATIONS FOR THE PUNJAB UNIVERSITY (ESTABLISHED ON JANUARY 17, 1870)

Districts	Muslims	Hindus	Sikhs	Total
Gujranwala	2	0	2	4
Sialkot	1	1	0	2
Gurdaspur	1	0	1	2
Amritsar	2	2	0	4
Multan	1	0	1	2
Jallandhar	1	0	1	2
Hoshiarpur	0	1	0	1
Kangra	0	1	0	1
Peshawar	0	1	0	1
Kohat	1	0	0	1
Rawalpindi	1	0	1	2
Ludhiana	1	0	0	1
Anbala	1	1	0	2
Total	12	7	6	25

but it was the result of widespread poverty among the Muslims rather than of religious prejudice. The Muslims' repudiation of modern education was a myth that Sir Sayyid himself created and then assiduously disseminated for popular consumption. The Punjabi Muslims' participation in modern education, and their cooperation in establishing the Punjab University in Lahore, reflected their awareness of the benefits to be derived from advanced Western education. Like Sir Sayyid, the Punjabi Muslim elites had been exposed only to traditional education, yet like him recognized the value of science-oriented education. In Bengal and Bombay the Muslim pioneers of modern education (including Justice Amir Ali, Abd al-Latif, and Justice Bader-ud-Din Tayabji) were educated in English universities.

Why did Sir Sayyid cultivate the myth of Muslim aloofness from modern English education? Sir Sayyid had offered an explanation. In rejecting the conception of proportionate Muslim student population in English schools, he had offered the norm of their past greatness, pointing toward the possiblility of Muslim greatness in the future via modernity. He wanted to see, not merely a "just" and proportionate representation of Muslims in modern schools, but their largest possible actual number. Thinking in terms of a Muslim renaissance in India, Sir Sayyid could do no less, and the "myth" became the catalyst in mobilizing the Muslim national will for a competitive coexistence in the future.

Thirdly, Sir Sayyid was by no means the only Muslim leader preaching the value of modernity among Muslims, although he was the most influential one. Even in Bengal, Sir Sayyid's contemporaries, including particularly Justice Amir Ali (1849–1928) and Abd al-Latif Khan Bahadur, had initiated the movement to spread modern education among Bengali Muslims; and Justice Bader-ud-Din Tayyabji (1844–1906) was active in Bombay. The Punjab, although lacking in leaders of comparable stature, had positively responded to modernity several years before Sir Sayyid traveled to Europe in 1869–70. In addition to the historical factors, the similarity of educational and political aims and widespread use of Urdu in the Punjab under the British initiative created an enduring partnership between Sir Sayyid and the Punjab. Precisely for this reason Altaf Husain Hali ascribed Sir Sayyid's success to the cooperation of the Punjab and the help of the British Government.[57]

Also, it is intriguing to hypothesize that even in the absence of Sir Sayyid modern education among Muslims would have spread, and that Sir Sayyid's ultraliberal *ijtihād* and provocative literary style in fact stiffened resistance to the acceptance of rationalism among the conservative elements of Muslim society. Even his ardent followers, particularly Shiblī Nu'manī, reacted in defense of some extablished Islamic convictions and practices, fearing that Muslim society might suffer from serious psychological and cultural dislocations. Consequently, Sir Sayyid failed to win acceptance for his *ijtihad* in his own province, while the Punjab's steadfast adherance to his religious and political ideas gave relevance to his mission of modernity.

Fourthly, the British Government of India did not believe that the Muslims all over India had repudiated modern education, although the provincial governments had pinpointed some areas of prejudice and educational backwardness. Here Sir Sayyid's perspective and the British Government's detached assessment of Muslims' educational status collided rather sharply.

While in sympathy with Sir Sayyid's liberalism and plans of modern education, the British Government was not overly anxious for him to launch the MAO College at Aligarh. Rightly the British Government detected Muslim opposition in the (UP) Northwest Provinces toward Sir Sayyid's plans. Writing a confidential letter in April 1873 to A. C. Lyall, Secretary to the Government, A. Colvin, Officiating Secretary to the Government of the Northwest Provinces, succinctly summed up the Lieutenant-Governor's policy toward Sir Sayyid:

But the success or failure of his [Sir Sayyid's] scheme will depend on whether he can overcome prejudice and render the higher teaching of an Anglo-Vernacular course acceptable to his own people. These are not wanting indications in the native press of a strong and growing opposition, and His Honour looks with some anxiety to the result. Meanwhile the attitude of the Government towards the movement is what it should be; the state stands by, looks favorably on, and is prepared at the proper moment to afford its aid in furtherance of the secular classes [in the MAO College].[58]

Finally, the force of data persuades us to conclude that the Muslim reaction to English education was by no means uniform. Determined by their historical experience and regional "character" the Muslim reaction to modernity varied from blind and self-defeating hostility to reasonable cooperation with British educational policy. In the provinces of Bombay, the Awadh, and the Punjab, Muslims' orientation was positive, while in Bengal, Sindh, and the UP (Northwest Provinces) the hold of tradition was generally severe, and the initial reaction to modern education was negative.

5

Mobilization
of National Will
for Modern Education

THE CHAPTER ON the Muslim reaction to modern education
has demonstrated, among other things, Sir Sayyid's commitment
to change the relational context in India. The change was to be
triangular, achieving for the Muslims a greater allocation of educational and material resources, and copartnership with the
Hindus in the political framework of India. For the realization of
this goal, Sir Sayyid endeavored to mobilize the Muslims' collective will for modern education, a prerequisite to participation in
political power. Any system of social action can be ultimately
explained in the light of ideas which motivate it. Sir Sayyid's
social actions may be analyzed in terms of two basic Parsonian
ideas: (a) existential, and (b) normative. The category of existential ideas contains the basic views determining the leader's understanding of the world around him. These ideas can be nonempirical or empirically verifiable. However, "the most general
type of norm governing existential ideas is that of 'truth.' "

Originally borrowed from the West, Sir Sayyid's faith in the "truth" of progress, and his collectivity-orientation yielding the concepts of Muslim nationalism, fall in the category of nonempirical-existential ideas.

"An idea," according to Talcott Parsons, "is normative insofar as the maintenance or attainment of the state of affairs it describes may be regarded as an end of the actor."[1] Subjectively determining Muslim backwardness in modern education, Sir Sayyid made a commitment to help change it in the not too distant future. His endeavors in this regard included the founding of the MAO College at Aligarh and the Muhammadan Educational Conference to widely diffuse modern education among the Muslims. This conceptualization, however, yields the 2 x 2 schematic table shown in Table 5.1.

TABLE 5.1.

Parsonian Ideas	Sir Sayyid's Actions
I. Nonempirical-existential	I. Faith in the "truth" of progress, and collectivity-orientation
II. Normative	II. Establishment of: (a) the MAO College; (b) the Muhammadan Educational Conference; and (c) the elimination of the traditional educational system

Role of Existential Ideas in Sir Sayyid's Actions

Along with some other elements of Western culture, Sir Sayyid internalized the value of progress as the most desirable integrative value of the Muslim society. Although cognizant of this value, the Indic Muslim culture had not given it primacy in its system of belief. As a dynamic leader, Sir Sayyid succeeded in making the concept of progress the focal point of the ideology of Muslim nationalism, which eventually gained general adhesion. (This ideology is discussed in a separate chapter.) Sir Sayyid not only assumed an obligation to accept all the dimensional implications of the concept of progress, but also made it the basis of his total system of action. Thus his conception of progress became the understructure, the frame of reference for the value-orientation of his concrete social actions. The concept of progress was not merely an instrumental belief, a conceptual means to an end for Sir Sayyid, but it involved his faith in the "truth" that the Muslims' collective salvation depended upon it. The directional orientation of his theory of progress, however, pointed toward modernity.

Theory of National Progress

Sir Sayyid analyzed the history of other civilizations in order to uncover the factors which are associated with progress. His studies led him to believe that progress has many dimensions. The most important of these are individual striving, inspired by love of nation and unhampered by governmental intervention and exposure to other civilizations, and the diffusion of new elements of culture.

Since Sir Sayyid's visit to Europe came only a few years after the publication of Darwin's *Descent of Man,* he came into contact with the view that isolated forms of life are relatively backward and that intercourse between species makes for progress. He adopted this idea and applied it to cultural development, stating that the march of civilization is essentially the result of intercultural contact. This became the cornerstone of his theory of progress, and made it logically possible for him to convince the Muslims of the need to adopt such Western traits as would further their own national development. He believed that it was the function of private associations, as opposed to government, to make certain that borrowed material traits and political and social values were properly integrated in the culture.[2]

Sir Sayyid did not feel that scientific inventions, dynamic organizations, and institutions flowed automatically or spontaneously out of the human mind. Thus:

The blind prejudice of Muslims is preventing them from emulating [Western] education, sciences and technology; Muslim society erroneously admires the blindness of those who are stubborn and haughty and considers all nations except their own inferior. There is not a single nation in the world which acquired excellence, material progress, and spiritual happiness entirely by virtue of its own efforts. Nations always benefit from each other; only bigots deny themselves the fruits of their fellowman's labour. They are like wild animals, happy in [the narrow life of] their flock, and are deaf to the sweet melody of the nightingale and the chirping of little sparrows, and know not how the garden [i.e., world] was laid out and what makes the flowers bloom. Prejudice and progress will never mix.[3]

And again:

Civilization is an English word which is derived from the Latin *civis* (citizen) or *civitas* (city). The reason for this derivation was the desire of citizens in antiquity to enter into a social contract for corporate living and to protect their lives, property, and personal freedom. Civilization in common parlance, however, connotes the advanced, cultured, and humanized form of Europeans, who stand in glaring contrast to the wild and barbarized peoples of North America, aborigines of Australia, Tartars and inhabitants of East Africa.[4]

After defining civilization, Sir Sayyid discussed five of 'those natural, political, and religious factors' which play a decisive role in the march of civilization.

1. *Natural Factors*
    "The fertile areas, abounding in food and water, attract settlers, and should *per se,*" asserted Sayyid, "be conducive to the development of civilization; the contrary, however, is the situation in some places. Look at the islands of East Asia, endowed with productive lands and hot climate. The inhabitants are lazy, ignorant, and brutish; similar is the case of the aborigines of South America and Africa."[5] Why did civilization not develop among them? They found abundant material goods but adapted themselves to them "as if they were animals or plants vegetating their existence in natural and pastoral surroundings." On the other hand, Sir Sayyid observed, the fertile deltas of the Nile and

the Tigris and Euphrates gave birth to magnificent civilizations, and the plains of Syria, watered by the Tigris and Euphrates, nurtured the very impressive civilizations of Babylon and Assyria. The Ganges valley in India produced arts and sciences, giving everlasting fame to the Indian civilization. These examples led Sir Sayyid to believe that natural factors, though basically necessary for, are not sufficient causes of, the rise of civilization.[6]

2. Intercourse Between Nations

Nations when separated by natural barriers fail to establish contact with other nations; like the inhabitants of Africa they are forced to forego the benefits of travelling. They are denied the light of intelligence and they learn no new techniques. "They reach a level of development," asserted Sir Sayyid, "and then stagnate. Living examples are the inhabitants of Tibet, Bhutan, Atlas mountains, the aborigines of Africa and America. For improvement in culture, diffusion of material and spiritual values is needed." He pointed out that the spread of civilization around the Mediterranean, the Greek islands, and Constantinople was due to the intermingling of peoples. Similarly the expansion of civilization in Europe, Asia, and Africa could be attributed to the mutual intercourse of different nations. The high level of civilization in Europe, Sir Sayyid concluded, was caused by maritime navigation in European rivers, including particularly the Rhine and the Elbe. Europeans traded frequently not only in material goods but in ideas, technical know-how, inventions, and even more. This exchange kindled new wants and desires for further development.

Sir Sayyid believed that maritime nations are temperamentally more suited to the diffusion and spread of civilization than settled nations. Thus the Phoenicians, Carthaginians, and ancient Greeks performed a civilizing role in their times by providing stimuli for social change to relatively static cultures. "In modern times," he believed, "the British, the Dutch, the French, and the Americans are performing a similar humanizing role."

Pointing to the various stages of the development of Islamic civilization, Sir Sayyid highlighted the role of diffusion. "The first base of learning was established by Caliph Abu Bakr (29 March 632–18 March 633) who appointed Zayd Ibn Thabit to compile the Qur'ān." The second stage of development, according to him, was reached when Muslim scholars started to collect the *hadith* (traditions) of the Prophet during the second century of the Islamic area (eighth century A.D.). Researchers, however, disagree as to who rightly deserves the credit for compiling the first work of traditions,[7] although Muslim scholars, including Sufyan b. 'Uyayna and Malik b. Anas in Medina, 'Abd Allah b. Wahhab in Egypt, 'Abd al-Razzaq in Yemen, Sufyan al-Thawri and Muhammad b. Faḍl b. Ghazwan in Kufa, Hammad b. Salmā and Ruh b. 'Abbada in Basra, and Hashim Wasit and 'Abd Allah b, Mubarak in Khurasan, published their treatises during this period.[8] Needless to say, toward the end of the second Islamic century Muslim rule had spread to all parts of the Fertile Crescent as well as India and Spain, providing intellectual stimulation and an exchange of ideas.

"The third stage of Islamic intellectual efflorescence," declared Sir Sayyid, "took place when the Greek arts, philosophy, and sciences were introduced to Muslims."[9] This momentous intellectual awakening in the history of Islam really got under way during the reigns of the 'Abbasid Caliphs Harūn al-Rashid (786–809) and al-Ma'mūn (813–833). This awakening was due in large measure to foreign influences, partly Indo-Persian and Syrian, but mainly Hellenic, and was marked by translations into Arabic from Persian, Sanskrit, Syriac, and Greek. Many of the translators were no doubt Christians, Jews, and Iranians, and there were also a few Indians. The best of these translators, Hunayn b. Ishaq (809–73), the Nestorian Christian from al-Hira, was paid in gold the weight of the books he translated.[10]

At the time of the Muslim conquest of the Fertile Crescent in the seventh century the intellectual legacy of Greece was primarily located in Edessa (al-Ruhā'), the principal center of Christian Syrians; in Harran, the headquarters of the heathen Syrians; in Antioch, one of the ancient Greek colonies; and in Alexandria, the meeting place of occidental and oriental philosophy. These cities served as intellectual centers radiating Hellenistic stimuli within the Muslim cultural complex. The apogee of Greek influence was reached under al-Ma'mūn. The philosophic tendency of this Caliph led to the establishment in 830 of the famous *Bayt al-Hikmah* (house of wisdom) in Baghdad, which combined a library, academy, and translation bureau.[11]

In absorbing the main features of both Hellenic and Persian cultures, Islam, in the eyes of recognized historians, occupied a significant place in the cultural unit which linked southern Europe with the Middle East. This culture was fed by a single stream—a stream with sources in ancient Egypt, Babylonia, Phoenicia, and Judea, all flowing to Greece and now returning to the East in the form of Hellenism. Later the Arabs in Spain (ninth century) and Sicily (tenth century) rediverted this cultural stream into Europe, helping to create the European Renaissance.[12]

Making an oblique reference to the personal insults suffered at the hands of the orthodox *'ulamā'*, Sir Sayyid pointed out that although in the initial stages students of Greek philosophy and sciences were declared heretics, "gradually reactionary forces gave in and the masters of Greek sciences were elevated to an honorable status [in 'Abbasid society]." The next higher level of intellectual development, according to Sir Sayyid, was attained when Muslim scholars made a successful endeavor to integrate "philosophic rationality with matters of faith, because they realized that without their compatibility *imān* (belief) could not achieve perfection." Sir Sayyid credited Abu Hamid al-Ghazzali (1058–1111) with this successful attempt at harmonization; his celebrated work, *Ihya 'ulūm al-Din* (the revivification of the sciences of religion) has achieved immortality. "He was also maligned and his book suffered vilification," Sir Sayyid mentioned with deep pathos, "but at last he was honoured with the title of the *Hujjat al-Islam* and his work was acknowledged as the standard text of Islamic philosophy." After al-Ghazzali very few works of this calibre were produced. Sir Sayyid maintained that the only outstanding contribution in modern times was made by Shah Waliy Allah (1703–62) of Delhi, who wrote *Hujjat Allah al-Balighah,* which is a unique contribution to Islamic interpretative thought. Against this background of Islam's relations with the West Sir Sayyid made a forceful case for renewed contact between the Indian Muslims and the British.

3. *Ability of Races for Refinement and Progress*

Sir Sayyid believed that nations are not all equally capable of benefitting from natural and social factors of progress; some nations are intrinsically superior to others. He did not support his assertion with any scientific data; he merely based his judgement on empirical observation of the cultural conditions of contemporary nations. He believed that the world is settled only by three main races, white, mongoloid, and negro, and that they are superior to each other in that descending order. "Humanity owes its progress to the white race, which in times immemorial radiated from central Asia to Europe and India," he maintained. For the spread of civilization Hindu India, he believed, played a valuable role. "Civilization reached ancient Iran, Syria, Chaldea, Phoenecia, Greece, and Italy from the heart of central India." His definition of the white race includes peoples of Europe, Ethiopia, North Africa, and all varieties of Semites. The following quotation illustrates his views on the negro:

Modern historians have tried to demonstrate that negro is capable of progress and a civilized mode of living but they failed to explain why the black man has made no significant contribution to civilization. In the dark areas of Africa there are no traces of bygone civilizations. There are plenty of fruit trees and natural resources including several lakes, which could facilitate navigation; nevertheless the people of Africa have remained wild and have never tasted the fruit of knowledge.[13]

The modern advancement of the African negro he attributed to the efforts of Europeans. Comparing the mongoloid races with the negro and the white he concluded that their intrinsic capacity was greater than the former, though much less than that of the white, the Chinese being the most advanced segment of the mongoloid race. He thought that the Chinese justifiably boasted about their scientific inventions of gunpowder, paper, and printing devices, and spreading the material and spiritual traits of their culture to the whole of south Asia and even to the ancient civilizations of Peru and Mexico. Sir Sayyid attributed the decline of the Chinese to the rigidity of their culture and the script of their language. He saw their renaissance only through elaborate contact with the modern West.

4. The Impact of Religion

Sir Sayyid considered religion as an essential prerequisite to progress. The monotheistic system of belief appears to have been his ideal. It is for this reason that he was partial toward Islam, considering other monotheistic religions based upon divine revelation (that is, Judaism and Christianity) bridges of progress. Monotheism, however, in his eyes does not have to be institutionalized the way it is in Judaism and Islam—Jehovah and Allah being the Almighty. It means belief in a unique, timeless, and merciful transcendental Creator of all the universe. To him the effective acknowledgement of Providence is religion. Idolatry in this context, being an artistic attempt to recognize the Lord of the universe, appears to be a facet of monotheism.

To Sir Sayyid idol worship indicates the romance in man's quest for religion, "raising idols to manifestations of nature, inspiring poets to compose lofty poems and spurring artists to creative endeavour."[14] This urge, he believed, impelled man to adorn Egypt, Chaldea, Greece, and Italy; art was the indicator of the excellence of their refinement.

If an organized religion like Buddhism, although well equipped with an elaborate code of ethics, does not affirm a positive belief in the Creator, it merely leaves the human soul drifting in eternal darkness. For this reason Sir Sayyid believed that the devotees of Buddhism made no significant contribution to the march of civilization. It is faith in God, he believed, that lights up the dark corners of the human mind and paves the way for advancement.

"Christianity preaches simplicity and humility, but after its inception," Sir Sayyid believed, its devotees "aspired to worldly glory, ostentation, and prestige." So much so that even the simple mode of worship was made ornamental, involving exorbitant expense. This was a worldly accretion to the other-worldly religion, although Christianity's overall impact on the decayed Roman world was therapeutic. "Islam has been maligned," Sir Sayyid believed, "quite erroneously as an impediment to progress and refinement." [15] He conceded that the Prophet Muhammad did not encourage the cultivation of such arts as sculpture and figure-painting, because he feared that the Arabs would revert to traditional idolatrous worship. However, in the eyes of Sir Sayyid, his injunctions against gambling, alcoholism, and other vices compensated for the loss of the fine arts. With this minor exception he considered the principles of Islam to be conducive to the march of civilization.

5. *The Role of Government: Laissez-Faire*

Sir Sayyid visualized a limited role for government in the advancement of civilization. Most important is individual progress, the sum total of which constitutes national progress. Even a benevolent despot is an unhealthy political institution, "because the citizens' creative spirit is stifled; totalitarian governments are worse since they misappropriate the fruits of poets' imagination and the artifacts of craftsmen with no distinction."

In England Sir Sayyid absorbed classical economic and political *laissez-faire* doctrines which had been enunciated by Adam Smith in *The Wealth of Nations*. The way economic determinism provides a key to the philosophy of Karl Marx is similar to the manner in which Adam Smith's doctrine gives a clue to the political reorientation of Sir Sayyid. For him England, France, and the United States were civilized because their citizens neutralized their governments in economic and political affairs. Limited and neutralized government, bound by law, was the guarantee of personal liberty. "Modern European sovereigns dare not imprison their citizens' intellect and creative faculties," declared Sir Sayyid. [16] In view of this it is obvious that he, quite consciously, became an apostle of *laissez-faire* philosophy among the Muslims of India.

The economic philosophy of Adam Smith is based upon

three assumptions. First, he assumed that the prime psychological drive in man as an economic being is self-interest. Secondly, he assumed the existence of a natural order in the universe which makes all individual strivings for self-interest add up to the social good. Finally he deduced from these postulates that the best program is nonintervention of government in the interplay of economic forces. Two of the most crucial questions in Adam Smith's philosophy are concerned with determination of the supply of labor and capital. The rising demand for labor, expressed in a rising rate of wages, increases the exertions of the workers in the short run and the number of the laboring population in the long run.[17] This leads to Smith's theory of population: rising demand—rising price—rising supply.[18]

Adam Smith's principle of supply and demand added a new dimension to the outlook of Sir Sayyid, providing him with a key to unlock the mysteries of history. If nations progress because of the diffusion of material and spiritual traits freely borrowed and integrated within their cultural complex, individuals and groups make their significant contributions to their national progress impelled by the laws of supply and demand. With this orientation Sir Sayyid attempted an interpretation of Muslim cultural and religious history. He believed that the development of Islamic theology, philosophy, and literature was conditioned by the laws of supply and demand. Since in modern times there is hardly any demand for those traditional avenues of learning, he advised Muslims to abandon them and apply themselves to western sciences and technology. He denounced 'ulamā,' who exhorted Muslims to shun western education, advising them "to retreat to bygone ages to such an extent that [at least in their material aspect of life] they would live in the age of the Prophet Muhammad, and his Companions."[19]

"It is an absolute principle of history applicable to all nations and epochs, admitting no exceptions," declared Sir Sayyid, "that when a commodity has value, it has demand. This principles is as relevant for material goods as it is for nonmaterial things."[20]

Thus recognizing the universality of the laws of supply and demand, Sir Sayyid also accepts the nature of Smith's 'economic man" (as distinguished from the tradition-bound man) as one who strives for maximum satisfaction with minimum sacrifice. What is really presupposed in his economic system is a man motivated by the desire for a maximum quantiative return for his investment. For Smith's "economic man" quantitative considerations must prevail over traditional values or political passions.[21]

Following this image of the "economic man," Sir Sayyid stated emphatically that:

Whatever is done in this world is done for some ulterior motive. Sometimes an individual is motivated by the reward of his labours, sometimes the desire to excel in a profession [galvanizes him]. Another time he strives after piety, very much valued by people. He may even try to benefit mankind without any desire for personal return, desiring in all sincerity closer relations with [and blessings of] God. Whatever is valued and consequently in demand will be most sought after by people.

Applying this postulate Sir Sayyid interpreted the rise and decline of literature, jurisprudence, theology, and philosophy in the history of Islam.

For example, [let us take the case of poetry] in the *Jahiliyāh* (pre-Islamic) period. With the advent of Islam falsehood and idolatry were condemned; euologies of the divine attributes of the idols, a notorious habit of the *Jahiliyāh* poets, were also forbidden. And God said: (Qur'ān, XXVI, 221–26)

> Shall I inform you,
> (O people!) on whom it is
> That the evil ones descend?
> They descend on every
> Lying, wicked person,
> (Into whose ears) they pour
> Hearsay vanities, and most
> Of them are liars.
> And the Poets,
> It is those straying in Evil
> Who follow them:
> Seest Thou not that they

Wander distracted in every Valley
And that they say
What they practice not?

This caused the downfall of poetry according to Sir Sayyid: "What Imam Fakhar al-Din al-Razi said in his *Tafsīr al-Kabīr* is noteworthy—'After Islam all poets gave up lies and became truthful.' "

The case of *hadiths* (traditions of the Prophet Muhammad) is similar. Thus:

It is the most sacred of all Islamic lore, yet the Caliphs Abu and Bakr and 'Umar had forbidden people to narrate a *hadith*. The latter even whipped offenders and imprisoned Ibn Mas'ūd, Abu Dardā' and Abu Mas'ūd Ansarī for narrating traditions. In fact Abu Bakr put to flame all those traditions which he had collected. Evidently the collection of traditions started in earnest only after the death of the Caliph 'Umar (644). Naturally those Companions of the Prophet who could narrate the largest number of traditions became most venerable: the same was the case of the Companions of the Companions.

In order to gain public esteem people fell to the temptation of contriving false traditions. The narrators of traditions enjoyed their preeminence until scholars and specialists compiled all sound traditions with utmost care. In this gradual process the "six sound works" of tradition were put together. "Then the narrators lost their value and their demand. A new era was ushered in when the compilers and their works gained importance. Then their students and disciples were valued, but in modern times commentaries on the books of *hadith* are available, freeing the people from *hadith* teachers." Sir Sayyid believed that this proved the validity of the laws of supply and demand.

In a similar manner Sir Sayyid analyzed the rise and decline of *fiqh* (jurisprudence). The founding of four schools of jurisprudence started the decline of *ijtihad*. People began to follow the four *Imams* blindly and became lost in the labyrinth of *taqlīd* (imitation). The philosophy of Islam, which, Sir Sayyid contends, was largely borrowed from the "idolatrous Greek," rose in demand when it was valued, but lost its importance when the *'ulamā'* deposed *fiqh* and Greek dialectic from the commanding positions they had usurped. The *'ulamā'* developed *'ilm al-kalām* (theological dialectics) to replace the Greek influence; when *'ilm al-kalām* had fulfilled its function it lost its value and consequently there was no more demand for it.

He deplored the fact that numerous *madaras* (colleges) and *makatıyb* (schools) still offered courses which were hopelessly inadequate for the needs of the scientific age. "All of them are in a bad condition," Sir Sayyid pointed out,

because they are no longer in demand; they are declining rapidly and will no doubt destroy their progeny [by ill-equipping them for the modern technical age]. The small group of Muslims who are dedicated to acquiring modern scientific education through the English language are maligned. They nevertheless very patiently reason with them, saying that in the former times our forefathers acquired those things which were in demand, now we strive after those which are in demand—our outlook is not different from that of our forefathers.[22]

Structured rigorously within the framework of valid knowledge, Sir Sayyid's theory established justification for the selective orientation and reordering of cultural values among the Muslims. Progress and cultural change became the keynotes in his value orientation, reflected particularly in his normatively oriented actions for education.

Sir Sayyid's Normatively Oriented Actions

For precise conceptual analysis, Sir Sayyid's normatively oriented actions may be divided into two chronological sequences: (a) 1859–1870 and (b) 1870–1898. As conceptions of the desirability for the Muslim culture, his actions revealed two sets of values. In the first period his educational endeavors were motivated by traditional values, reflecting his belief in egalitarianism, *noblesse oblige,* and a conviction that even widespread traditional education led to progress. Before these values were modified or totally abandoned in favor of modern values, Sir Sayyid defended them most passionately, and expected that, at each stage of their application, the Muslim society should accept them as progressive. From their vantage point his traditional critics charged that he was incapable of being consistent and only vaguely committed to his values. Viewed in historical perspective these changes in his value-orientation (even his volte-faces) were unavoidable hazards of a modernizing leader who was trying to shake loose from his own traditional moorings, and had to gradually "feel" his way to modernity. If consistency is a virtue, then it may be stated to Sir Sayyid's credit that his normatively oriented actions were always in harmony with his normative ideas. Change, a symbol of progress in his frame of reference, amounted to inconsistency in his critics' eyes; who regarded the process of change as disintegrative of the Muslims' cultural solidarity. This basic dichotomy in their frames of reference eventually hardened attitudes, making cooperation between his followers and the traditional opponents an impossibility.

Early Educational Experiments: 1859–1870

Sir Sayyid's earliest educational experiment was the founding of the Muradabad Panchayatiy Madressa on November 5, 1859. The school report of January 1, 1860, showed a student population of 175; Muslims being 103 and Hindus 72. All four classes were taught in Urdu and for the sixth to seventh grades of classes I to IV Persian texts included Sa'di's *Gulistān, Bostān,* and *Amad Namah, Anwar Sahelīy,* and *Karīyma*—the traditional books which Sir Sayyid had studied with his mother and grandfather. What was progressive about this school in Sir Sayyid's eyes? It reflected Sir Sayyid's perception of modern education catering to mass literacy needs, and social equality.

　　As a president of the Local Committee, which had helped Sir Sayyid in starting this school, he emphasized these ideas in his speech delivered at the school's annual examination of 1860. Social equality implied that poor and rich students should study in public schools because it created in them a sense of healthy competition. Calling the attention of his wealthy supporters, Sir Sayyid said:

Do not for a moment think that it is in the least degree derogatory for the landlord's children to study at a public school. Think of the Hindu Patshalas (schools) of a former age, and read the history of the Muslims, and you will find that high dignitaries regarded their children's education in large public schools as a great honor. For all our contemporary eminent Pundits and Mawlavis, and even those who lived before us, and whom all you great men hold in high esteem, received their early education and acquired their profound learning at public schools and not at their own houses.[23]

To highlight the respectability of public education, Sir Sayyid maintained that:

I have placed my own son in this school [and I] see my son seated among his poorer companions and answering the questions of the examiners and meekly putting forth his hand to receive from yours the prize of a book for his accomplishments as a student. All these things I regard as adding to, and not detracting from dignity. It is therefore a matter of astonishment if any dignitary should look upon it seriously as *infra dignitatem* to send his son to a public school.[24]

Reflecting his ingrained class consciousness, Sir Sayyid advised the students "to look around and see the great and rich men of the city here assembled, who took all this trouble on your account and have interested themselves in a liberal and friendly spirit solely for your benefit in establishing this school."[25] Two years later the Government established a high school in Moradabad, and the Panchayatiy Madressa was absorbed into it.

In 1864 Sir Sayyid graduated to a still higher conception of national education when he established an English high school in Ghazipur, which was subsequently christened as Victoria High School. In cooperation with the Hindu and Muslim landlords of the district he prepared a budget of Rs.80,000 for the school building and the faculty. When Rs.17,300 were raised through large and small donations he laid the foundation stone of the school building. On this ceremonial occasion, Sir Sayyid explained the educational philosophy of this publically owned school: (1) the school was nonsectarian both for the student body and for the members of several administrative committees, except that the Hindus' sensitivity for the caste system was respected, and religious education was imparted separately to both Hindu and Muslim students; (2) the education of arts and sciences essential for the modern professions was undertaken; (3) the Hindus and Muslims through self-reliance and mutual cooperation would finance the educational programs and the Government's help or special favor would not be solicited. Also, special provisions were made for the instruction of English, Arabic, Sanskrit, Persian, and Urdu but not Hindi. (The district's Hindu population did not protest the exclusion of Hindi.) Raja Dev Narain Singh, an influential landlord of the district, was made the patron and visitor of the school by popular demand.

For the first time Sir Sayyid publicaly emphasized the importance of the English language, and offered several pragmatic reasons for its cultivation: (1) Indians could not hope to gain government jobs without the knowledge of English; (2) participation in modern trade and international commerce was not possible without it; (3) international politics and the relative development of other countries remained unknown; (4) and finally, the Indians could not be effective in the political processes of India even if the British Government offered them a generous share.[26]

Sir Sayyid also knew that modern scientific knowledge was available in English, but he did not yet espouse the cause of English as the medium of instruction. He believed that modern knowledge could be acquired only through the mother tongue and for this purpose he had already established in 1863 the Scientific Society, which had undertaken to translate Europe's scientific literature into Urdu. In 1867 Sir Sayyid developed a plan for a truly national and modern university and the British Indian Association entered into a dialogue with the Government on the crucial issue. On August 1, the Association sent a memorandum to the Government suggesting:

(i) that a system of university education be established in which the arts, sciences and other branches of European literature may be taught through the vernacular language of Northern India, that is, Urdu; (ii) all examinations in the vernacular be held for those subjects in which the students were examined in English at the Calcutta University; (iii) that like students in English classes, degrees should be conferred on those students who pass the same subjects in the vernacular; (iv) finally, the Association suggested "that a vernacular department be attached to the Calcutta University, or an independent vernacular university be created for the Northwest Provinces." [27]

Besides Sir Sayyid, the memorandum was signed by four Hindu and five Muslim members.

The British Government of the Northwest Provinces was unsympathetic to this plan. In fact, Kempson, the Director of Public Instruction, recorded a very uncharitable remark on the proposal:

when upper India is placed under a separate governor, and when native society shows itself willing to create educational or other philanthropical endowments, instead of wasting money on the pilgrimages and Punjas [a pejorative reference to Muslims' spending money on the pilgrimages to Mecca, and Hindus' spending their resources on devotional rites] and marriage festivals, I think a university, worthy of the name, involving residence, *esprit-de-corps,* and encouraging physical as well as mental training may be found.

In a letter of September 5, 1867, Bayley, Secretary to the Government of India, discouraged Sir Sayyid's plan of national education on more elevated academic grounds. He drew a broad distinction "between the vernacular language as a necessary and only medium of instruction of a popular kind, and the English language as an essential requisite for education of a high order." Emphasizing the unavailability of scientific literature and texts in Urdu, he maintained that the real object of university education was "to prepare and fit the mind for the pursuit of knowledge in the wide sphere of European science and literature," and that it could be accomplished only "through the medium of the English language." [28]

Also, a demand was raised in the local press that should a "vernacular university" be established in Northern India, Hindi rather than Urdu should be employed as the medium of instruction for the Hindus. Discouraged by the Government's negative reaction, the practical difficulties of translating a large number of scientific works, and the demands of the champions of Hindi, Sir Sayyid abandoned his commitment to the vernacular university. This change in policy subsequently made him a supporter of education through English. Intellectually, however, he remained convinced that modern education, through the medium of English, would not produce in India a rational approach to life and truly creative scholarship, and that people in general would remain ignorant.

On August 31, 1869, after spending three months in Britain, Sir Sayyid submitted to the Secretary of State for India a memorandum—*Strictures upon the Present Educational System in India* [29]—stating that this system "must forever remain a useless one unless some effective changes be introduced." Basing his arguments upon a normatively structured paradigm determining "progressive and retrogressive movement of education in any country," Sir Sayyid developed his critique.

Pyramidal in shape, Sir Sayyid's paradigm envisaged the aim of a truly progressive educational system productive of three educated strata. The pinnacle was occupied by the intellectual elite or the creative scholars—"men by whose labors the onward march of the arts and sciences is daily promoted and increased . . . [the best of them] are the benefactors of mankind." The teachers stood in the middle and transmitted to "their fellowmen the knowledge thus acquired by themselves." The third layer of the pyramid he divided into three subdivisions: first came the professionals in "a certain ascertained proportion to the whole population." Secondly, administrators "competent to manage the secular affairs" were to receive education, developing in them the capacity "to benefit from the ever-increasing body of scientific knowledge." Thirdly, the working classes were to be literate and their training was to increase the efficiency of "their manual labor." [30]

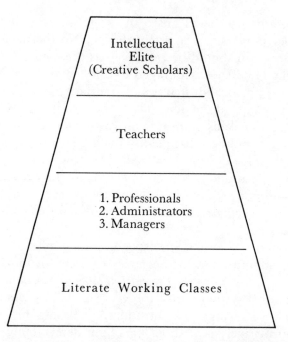

FIGURE 5.1 SIR SAYYID'S PARADIGM OF PROGRESSIVE EDUCATION

This educational paradigm, Sir Sayyid believed, allowed three generalizations: (1) if a society contained two educated classes only, the highest and the middle ones, then society as a whole "must be regarded as being in mental darkness," although it might be possible that in the future "the full rays of intellectual light" would benefit the society; (2) if a society produced only the lowest class or "should there be so few educated men of the highest and middle classes as to bear no appreciable proportion to the entire population," then such a country was in an inferior stage of development compared to the one mentioned above; (3) if a society lacked the highest and the middle classes of intellectuals, or should it be found wanting in "the first branch of the lowest class," or should have the second and third strata of the literati only, then that society must be viewed "in a state of total darkness or intellectual death." Very little hope for its development could be maintained.

What were the accomplishments of the traditional Hindu and Muslim systems of education in India? Sir Sayyid maintained that both had excelled the one established by the British in producing many creative scholars of the highest and middle strata. Their number, compared to the then existing population of India, "bore a just proportion"; however, those belonging to the lowest strata were so few that no valid comparison could be made. Sir Sayyid admitted that it was a great deficiency in the traditional educational system. Then Sir Sayyid asked the crucial question: what has the British modern educational system in India accomplished? His indictment of the system's failure was sweeping. After nearly a century in operation, the modern system has not produced one learned person who could be considered a member of the highest or the middle class. The modern system, Sir Sayyid maintained, produced only letter-writers, copyists, signal-men, and railroad ticket-collectors. Only a handful reached the stratum of education and their number bore no "sensible proportion to the whole population of the country." Among them a few were struggling to find their way to the first rung of the lowest class of education and "we may hit upon a small number whose abilities entitle them to . . . the middle class of education and it is upon these only that Bengal rests its claim to be regarded as dispenser of the light of European knowledge."[31]

Finally, Sir Sayyid emphasized that Britain made a commitment to modernize India, but the policies adopted for this purpose were inappropriate. First, Britain promised political equality for "natives and Europeans in every respect identical." Secondly, Britain "despoiled us of our mother tongue and our hereditary sciences, compelling us to learn the English language and the European sciences."[32] Since political equality and the participation in the political processes were contingent upon the acquisition of modern education through the medium of the English language, the British policy was inherently counterproductive. Sir Sayyid's memorandum was read by I. C. Melvell, the Undersecretary of State for India, who recorded a rather terse comment on the "Minute Paper": "It seems to call for no particular remarks." Sir

Sayyid's bold yet modest suggestion for a national and modern education in India was consigned to oblivion by the British Government. Subsequently, he made no more futile attempts to change the British educational system, but made the best of it by adapting it to the Muslims' needs.

Stratified Education for a Differentiated Social System: 1870–1898

Sir Sayyid had observed in Britain a highly stratified society maintaining a hierarchical educational system preparing various classes to play differentiated roles. The value of social equality adhered to by Sir Sayyid in founding the Muradabad Panchayatiy Madressah in 1859 found no expression in Victorian Britain's social and educational systems. In another aspect the British and Muslim social systems appeared to be similar: the aristocratic classes played the leadership roles in both. After his return from Europe in 1870 most of the traditional values were modified or subordinated to modern ones. Sir Sayyid recognized the structure of the Muslim social system as "a differentiated system," calling for the play of differentiated roles. In 1872 an incisive analysis of the social system and a plan of stratified education for the Muslims were published by him in the issues of *Tahdhib al-Akhlaq,* and in the *Report of the Members of Select Committee for the Better Diffusion and Advancement of Learning Among the Muhammadans of India.*

Dividing the Muslim social system between the bourgeoisie and the working classes, Sir Sayyid identified five collectivities of bourgeoisie. First, a collectivity "aspire[d] to high positions in the service of Government, to have a share in the management of the country, . . . and thus to do good to their fellowmen." The second collectivity preferred "to live by commerce or by some profession," or wanted to engage in trade and invest money in the development of modern industries. The third one wanted to manage personal property, including real estate and agricultural lands. The fourth collectivity was interested primarily in liberal arts and sciences. Finally, the last one wanted to devote itself to acquiring a mastery of religious scholarship. Among the working class, however, Sir Sayyid admitted, a degree of education was necessary. In addition to this, he asserted, all classes desired religious education for their children.[33]

Reflecting a dualism of ideal and real, Sir Sayyid and his colleagues in the Select Committee evolved a stratified educational system oriented to creating personnel equipped to play differentiated roles (see Figure 5.2). To Sir Sayyid, a dualism of ideal and real in the proposed educational system was essential for practical and ideological considerations. In eliminating the traditional and mass systems of education he would have earned the disapproval, even the condemnation of his traditionally oriented colleagues in addition to reflecting a disregard for the need disposition of the total social system. Consequently, the goal of mobilizing the Muslim national will would not be achieved. Practically, however, he realized the impossibility of implementing the entire plan

```
┌─────────────────────────────────────────┐
│        Modern System, creating           │
│  (1) Administrators   (2) Managers        │
│  (3) Professionals    (4) Teachers        │
└─────────────────────────────────────────┘
```

```
┌──────────────────────────────────────────────────────────────┐
│  Traditional & Modern System: Urdu & Arabic-Persian Colleges, creating │
│       (1) Medium grade Judicial officers  (2) Litterateurs      │
│       (3) 'Ulamā' (religious scholars)                          │
└──────────────────────────────────────────────────────────────┘
```

```
┌──────────────────────────────────────────────────────┐
│  Mass System (Private Muslim Schools) maintaining      │
│     (1) Secondary schools   (2) Primary schools        │
│     (3) Hafzīy Makatiyb (Training schools for the memorizers │
│         of the Qur'ān)                                  │
└──────────────────────────────────────────────────────┘
```

FIGURE 5.2 SIR SAYYID'S PARADIGM OF A STRATIFIED EDUCATIONAL SYSTEM

for lack of material resources. "There is a gap between the real [which is attainable], and ideal [which it is desirable to achieve] in our planning," counseled Sir Sayyid with his colleagues in the Select Committee, "but when you initiate the construction of an edifice, you complete the blueprint first, the ideal of your endeavors, and then raise the structure gradually, [the realizeable "real" of the endeavors]."[34]

Weighed on a scale of prestige and utility, the modern system of education became the focal point of Sir Sayyid and his colleagues' concrete action. A comparative glance at Sir Sayyid's paradigms of progressive and stratified educational systems reveals that he did not expect the latter to produce truly creative scholars, "the benefactors of mankind." To him the alien medium of instruction and the underdevelopment of the modern educational system in the Indian environment were the main obstacles. But the modern system was most suited to creating Government officials, business and industrial managers, professionals, and college teachers. In terms of political and economic power, they alone would be equipped to bring change in the relational context of Indian collectivities, eventuating a subjectively determined position for the Muslims.

According to well-established patterns, the modern educational system was designed to be liberal and scientific. Liberal education consisted of: (1) Islamic studies—law, jurisprudence, Apostolic Traditions, principles of Traditions, Commentary on the Qur'ān, the Prophet's biography and dogmas; (2) literature—grammar and syntax of Urdu, Persian, Arabic, English, and Latin, history, geography, ethics, psychology, logic, philosophy, political science, and public administration; (3) mathematics—arithmetic, geometry, statistics, and advanced mathemetics; (4) natural sciences—thermodynamics, hydrostatics, dynamics, pneumatics, optics, electricity, astronomy, heat, accoustics, and natural philosophy. Scientific education included engineering, veterinary science, anatomy, zoology, botany, geology, minerology, and chemistry.

Conceptually one last attempt was made to "nationalize" the modern system of education. As a coequal with the English College an Urdu College was proposed, where modern liberal and scientific education was to be imparted through the medium of Urdu. However, the students retained the option of studying English, Arabic, and Persian as one of the secondary languages. The outstanding students majoring in Arabic or Persian could seek admission in the Arabic-Persian College for advanced language studies.[35] Obviously one aspect of Sir Sayyid's plan was oriented to integrating the modern with the traditional systems of education, although he repeatedly denounced the traditional syllabi, the *Dars-i Nizamiya,* and committed himself not to introduce it in either one of the proposed colleges.

Sir Sayyid's proposed mass structure of education was also hierarchical, with high schools for every district and large town, and a *maktab* (Primary school) in every village; and *hafaziy makatiyb* in a few selected towns, where religiously oriented young boys would be taught to memorize the Qur'ān. Following the pattern of the Urdu College the secondary school students would be instructed in sciences, and learn English, Persian, or Arabic as a second language. The students in a *maktab* would learn Urdu, some Persian, elementary English, arithmetic, and the Qur'ān in six months according to a newly developed method. Besides these subjects the boys would learn to pray, and internalize the Islamic doctrines contained in *Rah-i Nijāt* and *Haqīqat al-Salwāt.*

Parenthetically, it may be added that by the 1890s Sir Sayyid had forsaken the concept of mass education through the primary schools, and the relevance of *hafaziy makatiyb* to a newly developing modern Muslim society. Speaking in 1893 he compared the graduates of Colleges and Universities to "the shining stars twinkling against the dark background in 'black' skies." They alone could help the Muslims achieve high standards of national progress. He urged the Muslims to pool their financial resources in order to establish modern high schools with European headmasters, preparing the students for advanced modern education.[36]

It may be explicitly stated that even during the 1870s in implementing the educational system primacy was given to the role of modern educated personnel. However, Sir Sayyid's conception of the role-system can be best analyzed in terms of (a) the allocation of resources, facilities, and rewards, and (b) the allocation of personnel to various roles.

(A) The Allocation of Resources, Facilities, and Rewards

The blueprint for the modern educational system had been developed by Sir Sayyid in London. Although the existence of the Mohammadan Anglo-Oriental College Fund Committee (with Sir Sayyid as its life secretary) was formally announced on December 26, 1870, it had been registered in early 1869. Along with Sir Sayyid, his coworker (and son) Sayyid Mahmud had conceived the three colleges to be located on a single campus, constituting the nucleus of a university patterned after "the system of Oxford and Cambridge, combining instruction with residence under a certain discipline." Actually the Fund Committee allocated all financial and material resources to the establishment of the modern (English) College only. Among other factors, this commitment elicited British support.

In October 1869 the Fund Committee circulated an open letter to the British public appealing to the British value-orientation indicating that the proposed college would not only create personnel for Government employment, but would be an English institution "for the enlightenment and refinement of the intellect." Also the Muslims would be reoriented to regard the British as friendly rulers rather than rivals in order "to make [their] future generations better citizens and better subjects." Lastly, £150,000 were estimated to be the adequate outlay for the College, "of which about a fifteenth part has already been raised", including Lord Northbrook's (Viceroy of India) donation of £1,000.[37]

Initially in India also, Muslim and non-Muslim donors responded with financial generosity. In addition to a cash donation of Rs. 20,000 Nawab Muhammad Kalb-i Ali Khan, the ruler of Rampur State, endowed to the MAO College agricultural land valued at Rs. 30,000, yielding annual income of Rs. 1,000.[38] Five large Hindu and Sikh donors gave Rs. 6,900 with the Sikh Maharaja of Patiala and the Raja of Vizianagram contributing Rs. 3,000 each.[39] Among the British officials Sir William Muir and Justice Spencky of the Allahabad High Court donated Rs. 1,000 each. By 1873 the Fund Committee had collected Rs. 100,000[40] and by October 1874 the donations totaled Rs. 200,000, with total assets valued at Rs. 325,000,[41] ensuring the establishment of a university on a modest scale. In February 1873 the Fund Committee petitioned the Government of India to charter a non-denominational but Muslim university at Aligarh.[42] On the suggestion of C. A. Elliot (Secretary to the Northwest Provinces Government), that the term University might "encourage the idea of independence or rivalry with Calcutta University," the Government of India forbade its use.[43] Consequently, the name of The Muhammadan Anglo-Oriental College at Aligarh was substituted.

Despite the shared value-orientation between Sir Sayyid and the British Government the British bureaucratic elite in the U.P. (Northwest Provinces) was not entirely sympathetic to Sir Sayyid's methods and his goals. This became evident when the Fund Committee petitioned the provincial Government to allocate the site of a former British military base at Aligarh, consisting of 75 acres, for the College campus. Two district Collectors of Aligarh, Montague and his successor Colvin, opposed the petition and created a negative consensus among the British officials of the Government. To determine the issue finally the Governor of the Province, Sir John Strachey, visited the site on January 6, 1875, and endowed the land to the Fund Committee, providing that the blueprint of the buildings would be approved by the Government, and the land and the buildings would revert to the Government if the Fund Committee's goals were not achieved.[44] When the Fund Committee accepted these stipulations in February 1875 the endowment of land was transferred to Sir Sayyid.

However, Sir Sayyid's modernizing crusade started to yield diminishing returns, both in terms of social solidarity and financial support, particularly from the Muslims of his own province.

On December 24, 1870, one month and 22 days after his return from Britain, Sir Sayyid started to publish the weekly *Tahdhīb al-Akhlaq,* and made it an instrument for the diffusion of his modern values, eliciting an intensely negative response from some segments of the religiously conservative Muslim middle classes. Not opposed to learning English and acquiring modern education *per se,* his opponents (including some who occupied "responsible" positions in the Government and were his potential supporters) disapproved of his innovative doctrines in Islam. (These doctrines are discussed in a separate chapter.) More like an impatient reformer than a leader aiming to create a national consensus for the value of modern education, Sir Sayyid squandered the support of this "conservative" collectivity. A delay of four or five years in the *Tahdhīb al-Akhlaq*'s publication would have accelerated the mobilization of the Muslims' will for the establishment of the MAO College. Much against his hope, the *Tahdhīb al-Akhlaq,* at least until 1875, proved to be counterproductive. Not respecting their sensitivity to the "new," Sir Sayyid categorized his opponents as *khabīyth al-nafs wa bad batan* (psychic perverts and ill-intentioned), *hassad* (jealous), *khud parast* (self-centered), *tat-pūnjiya akhbar nawīys* (yellow journalists), *be-tamīyz* (incapable of making a distinction between his personal views and national goals), and *na-dān* (the uninformed Muslims).[45]

In order to win over the last two "opponents," Sir Sayyid committed a serious tactical error. On February 10, 1873, the Fund Committee issued an interrogatory to the *'Ulamā',* soliciting their opinion about the validity of modern education for the Muslims:

what are your opinions regarding: (a) the proposed College, where Muslims would be educated in religious and secular sciences, and the teachers and scholars would be financially compensated. (The outline of the proposal is added for your reference). (b) In the light of the *shari'a* (canon law), would it be proper for the Muslims to give financial assistance toward the establishment of this College or to selectively donate funds for the instruction of certain disciplines. (c) Finally, of all the arts and sciences enumerated in the curricular offerings of the College, which disciplines merit Muslims' donations, and which don't.[46]

This step legitimized the *'Ulamā's* role in the allocation of resources to the proposed College. Stung by his frontal attacks on the traditional educational institutions and the value-orientation of the *'Ulamā'*, the traditionalists published their own interrogatories highlighting two points: "(1) were Muslims allowed to support a College whose founder divided institutions of Islamic learning; (2) especially when he sought to legitimize beliefs, contravening the Muslims' *ijmā'* (consensus), the prophetic traditions and well-established juristic interpretations."[47] The texts of the interrogatories and their answers, which were published by Imdād al-Ali (the Deputy Collector of Kanpur and like Sir Sayyid a recipient of the K.C.S.I.) in *Imdād al-Afāq bahajam ahlah-nifaq ba-Jawāb Parchah Tahdhīb al-Akhlaq,* would reveal that *'Ulamā'* did not forbid modern education via English. They merely criticized Sir Sayyid's "deviant" convictions, and despite his assurances that his books would not be included in the course offerings, the *'Ulamā"s* fears were not allayed and they continued to emphasize that a "deviant" Muslim educator would not create "true" Muslim students, and the latter could not possibly escape exposure to Sir Sayyid's "un-Islamic" ideas. (This situation was reminiscent of a similar development during the 1940s, when a segment of the *'Ulamā'* maintained that the modernized, or perhaps Westernized Muslim leaders would not be able to create a "true" Islamic State of Pakistan). In both cases the charge was well founded insofar as "true" in the *'Ulamā's* perspective was coequal with their interpretations of Islam.

Even the interrogatory which was taken to Mecca by Ali Bakhsh Khan, a sub-Judge of Gorakhpur, accused Sir Sayyid of: "denial in the existence of *Iblīs* (Evil Personified); the Prophet Muhammad's physical ascension to the heavens; the creation of Adam and Eve; and maintaining that Muslims' religious learning was of no avail."[48] Not knowing personally Sir Sayyid and his plans in detail and relying rather excessively on Ali Bakhsh Khan's representation, the Mecca jurists (including Shaikhs Abd al-Rahman, Ahmad bin Zaiyn, Muhammad bin Abdullah, and Husain bin Ibrahīym) representing the four schools of Islamic jurisprudence, stated rather mercilessly: "No assistance to his plans could be allowed. May Allah destroy [the institution] and its founder." [49] A similar decree was obtained from the Medina jurists.

Most of the bitterness against Sir Sayyid brewed in the Uttar Pradesh (U.P.) where his opponents established counter-journalism including *Nūr al-Afāq* and *Nūr al-Anwār* from Kanpur; *Loh-i Mahfūz* from Moradabad; *Tayravin Sadiy* from Agra; and *Imdād al-Afāq, Shihāb-i Thāqib,* and *Ta'īyd Islam* from other cities of the U.P. Merely a handful of the Aligarh landlords rendered financial assistance and offered their cooperation to Sir Sayyid.

While Sir Sayyid was depressed by his negative response, the Anjuman-i Punjab and Anjuman-i Islamia Punjab invited him on Muhammad Barkat Ali Khan's initiative to visit the province. In 1874, accompanied by Muhammad Sam'īy Allah Khan, and Muhammad Mushtaq Husain, Sir Sayyid visited the Punjab.[50] Sir Sayyid achieved a wide exposure in the Punjab and collected large but unspecified donations for the construction of the MAO College. During January 22–February 4, 1884, Sir Sayyid visited again five districts of the Punjab, and the Sikh princely state of Patiala, and collected Rs. 9,742 for the building program of the MAO College.[51] However, deploring the indifference of Bengali Muslims, and that of his own province, Sir Sayyid commented on the Muslims' low sense of solidarity obligation: "When I realize that the Muslims of the Punjab extended to me their profound sympathy and hearty cooperation, and have earned the title of *Zindah dillan-i Punjab* (the heartbeat of the Punjab) I acknowledge unhesitatingly their awareness [of solidarity obligation]." [52]

Acknowledging his partnership with the Punjabi Muslims, Sir Sayyid commented in a private letter: "Unlike the people of our province, the Muslims of the Punjab are alive. A feeling of national welfare, and a consciousness of solidarity obligation, have developed in them so profoundly that if their orientation is directed properly the qawm, (Muslim nationality) would benefit from it immensely." [53] However, the Punjab also had its anti–Sir Sayyid mavericks in *Akhbār Rafīq-i Hind* and *'Ashā't al-sunnat,* who denounced his religion liberalism, but his more influential supporters including the *Punjabi Akhbār, Koh-i Nūr, Akhbār-i*

'Am, Patiala Akhbār and Akhbār Anjuman-i Punjab widely diffused his modern Islam and mobilized the Punjabis in support of the MAO College.

To augment his funds for the College, Sir Sayyid also resorted to some unorthodox techniques, including variety shows, in which he preached messages of national awakening and also sang his own Persian lyrics. At an exhibition in Aligarh he sold books, and sometimes "begged" money as a national volunteer. Finally, in an act of defiance which appalled even his steadfast supporters, he obtained in 1878 the Government's permission to establish a lottery with 15,000 coupons priced at Rs. 2 each. Ten thousand rupees were distributed for seven different prizes, and Rs. 20,000 were saved for the College.[54]

While ingenuity in fund raising enabled him to accumulate sufficient capital for the construction of the MAO College, the intensity of opposition in the U.P. finally persuaded him and his colleagues to postpone the fulfillment of their ambitions until 1877; but in May 1875 a high school at Aligarh was started with eleven students. Samī'y Allah Khan supervised the school until July 1876, when Sir Sayyid came to Aligarh after voluntarily retiring from the judicial service. Finally, on January 8, 1877, Lord Lytton laid the foundation stone for the first building on the campus of the MAO College at Aligarh. Like the high school, the MAO College was an affiliate of Calcutta University, but in 1888 the College became affiliated with the University of Allahabad. In his letter of October 31, 1888, to the Registrar of the Allahabad University, Sir Sayyid submitted the following statement regarding the allocation of funds and faculty at the MAO College.[55]

The annual scholarship funds, Sir Sayyid stated, were not included in the above statement. Their inclusion, besides some miscellaneous funds, indicated the round figure of Rs. 50,000 in the annual budget. Among the faculty, English professors included the principal (head) of the College, who was educated at Cambridge; an Oxford graduate who taught English literature, and another Cambridge graduate who tutored in philosophy. An Indian, holding a Master of Arts degree from Calcutta Univer-

TABLE 5.2. STATEMENT OF ANNUAL INCOME (1888)

Source	Amount
1. Income from estate endowed by Nizam of Hyderabad	10,000
2. Income from the endowment of Nawab of Rampur	1,200
3. Government of India's promisory notes yielding interest	3,000
4. Maharaja of Patiala's cash gift	1,800
5. Income from Sir Salar Jang (Hyderabad) endowment	1,200
6. Raja of Mahmudabad (Amir Hasan Khan) endowment	600
7. Nawab Safder Ali Khan's (Rampur) cash gift	200
8. Raja of Vizianagram's cash gift	240
9. Rent from the MAO College real estate	800
10. Government of India's grant-in-aid	1,500
11. Local Municipal Aid	1,500
12. Tuition Fee	5,000
Grand Total	27,040

sity, taught mathematics; two Muslim professors offered Persian and Arabic, and a pandit taught Sanskrit.

From 1888 to academic 1895–96 the MAO College's budgets registered a steady increase in the annual income, enabling the trustees to allocate more funds to various categories during this period. However, a steady decline both in income and spending set in afterwards reaching a climax in the year of Sir Sayyid's death in 1898. See Tables 5.3 [56] and 5.4. [57]

What caused the decline in the financial resources of the College? In 1895, Sham Bihari Lal, a Hindu accounts clerk, who served Sir Sayyid from 1883 to July 1895, embezzled Rs. 115,000 from the College funds deposited in the Aligarh banks. Also, the College had to pay unusually high interest on Rs. 50,000 which had been borrowed for development purposes. [58] Lal committed suicide in prison and hardly a penny was recovered. Negative publicity about the mismanagement of funds dried up sources of contribution; consequently new buildings remained incomplete for some years, the construction of newly proposed ones was postponed, and the allocation of resources to all the categories of activity was severely curtailed.

Lastly a basic question about Sir Sayyid's decisional orientation may be asked. Was the MAO College designed to be an

TABLE 5.3. STATEMENT OF INCOME (1893–1898)

Sources of Income	1893–94			1894–95			1895–96			1896–97			1897–98			1898–99		
	Rs.	A.	P.	Rs.	A.	P.	Rs.	A.	P.	Rs.	A.	P.	Rs.	A.	P.	Rs.	A.	P.
1. Grants and Endowments	41,083	13	11	43,150	0	0	43,750	0	0	43,800	0	0	44,512	13	1	44,928	0	0
2. Interest on Investments	2,009	12	0	2,180	0	10	49	8	0	1,735	8	0	1,720	6	0	1,710	8	0
3. Tuition Fees	11,431	5	0	13,231	11	0	19,469	4	9	16,079	3	6	15,419	7	6	13,729	10	6
4. Dormitories and Bungalow Rents	7,213	7	3	8,695	8	6	10,239	12	0	7,863	3	9	7,068	9	9	5,986	7	3
5. Scholarships and Prizes	5,701	1	11	6,561	2	8	5,633	6	9	5,582	11	2	4,750	7	8	3,262	4	0
6. Medical Fees	2,177	13	9	2,934	6	3	2,162	13	7	1,564	6	11	1,104	15	0	976	11	0
7. Aligarh Institute	—			—			—			—			—			—		
8. Miscellaneous	5,332	13	5	4,229	1	3	2,210	15	7	2,442	13	1	2,170	10	4	1,594	13	4
Total	74,950	3	3	81,682	14	6	83,515	12	8	79,067	14	5	76,747	5	4	72,830	2	8

TABLE 5.4. ALLOCATION OF FUNDS (1893–1898)

Categories of Allocation	1893–94			1894–95			1895–96			1896–97			1897–98			1898–99		
	Rs.	A.	P.	Rs.	A.	P.	Rs.	A.	P.	Rs.	A.	P.	Rs.	A.	P.	Rs.	A.	P.
College and School	42,982	14	10	46,505	12	5	48,009	8	10	48,414	3	8	50,802	14	0	40,842	3	5
Law Class	5,047	15	9	3,997	2	0	3,712	13	0	3,360	0	0	2,772	4	0	1,860	0	0
Honorary Secretary's Office	2,181	4	3	1,791	13	6	2,037	4	5	2,691	11	4	2,371	15	10	2,239	2	1
Accounts Office and Dormitories																		
Establishment	1,481	10	3	1,807	3	2	1,753	0	0	2,163	0	0	2,090	15	9	2,125	5	0
Dispensary	2,040	5	3	2,202	—	2	1,975	4	7	2,257	14	0	1,915	10	8	1,919	0	9
Riding School	—			—			—			—			—			—		
Repairs and Sanitary Improvements	1,318	7	0	2,040	5	6	1,204	12	3	1,425	10	9	1,678	3	9	1,675	4	9
Aligarh Institute	523	13	0	350	0	0	728	2	6	600	0	0	550	0	0	2,020	3	3
Printing	138	2	0	704	6	0	401	1	6	829	9	6	604	5	6	1,167	11	6
Mosque	654	3	0	1,106	0	0	1,514	0	0	1,274	14	3	1,322	4	0	1,275	15	0
Scholarships and Stipends	6,743	14	0	7,196	8	3	6,182	13	9	5,443	9	0	3,949	4	0	4,119	15	0
Miscellaneous	9,248	15	11	8,747	2	11	8,802	11	6	12,140	8	6	10,519	2	10	3,696	10	0
Total	72,361	9	3	77,933	14	2	76,321	8	4	80,601	1	0	78,579	0	4	66,941	6	9

exclusive institution for the bourgeoisie? The answer can be found in the allocation of funds to underpriviledged students as against the funds raised in tuition from the scions of the affluent middle classes during 1893–1898. See Table 5.5.

During 1893–95 scholarship funds allocated to needy students were slightly more than 50 percent of the collected tuition amount; this figure declined sharply in the academic year 1895–96 because of the economic crisis generated by Lal's embezzlement. However, the annual average for the period of 1893–98 was 30 percent. Nearly one third of the student population at the MAO College was supported by public funds. Needy students belonged to the lower middle or "impoverished" upper classes, who passed under the rubric of *Sharif Khandani* (refined and cultured Muslims). However, the "low" or working classes hardly benefitted in any appreciable degree. Off in the distant future, they awaited the dawn of another social revolution, and the development of a new orientation in the Muslims' value-system.

Even after Sir Sayyid's death in 1898, the orientation of this policy remained steady. From 1898 to the academic year 1902–3, Muhsin al-Mulk (Sir Sayyid's successor as the Secretary of the Board of Trustees) collected Rs. 106,399.5.9 in tuition fees, averaging annually Rs. 21,279.13.11. For the same period Rs. 33,292.7.3 were collected for the scholarships, averaging annually Rs. 6,658.7.10. Against these amounts for the same period Rs. 35,236.0.0 were disbursed as stipends and scholarships, averaging Rs. 7,047.3.0 or roughly 30 percent of the total tuition fee paid by economically well-off students.[59]

In addition to being a center of modern education, and eventually a brain trust of Indic Muslim politics, the MAO College became an instrument of vertical social mobility for the sons of the lower and middle classes, who acquired modern professional skills to play differentiated roles.

(B) *The Allocation of Personnel to Various Roles*

How were the role-types to be distributed between various personnel? Sir Sayyid had a conception of the functions of various

TABLE 5.5. TUITION FEES PAID AND SCHOLARSHIP FUNDS COLLECTED (1893–1898)

	1893–94			1894–95			1895–96			1896–97			1897–98			Total			Annual Average		
	Rs.	A.	P.	Rs.	A.	P.	Rs.	A.	P.	Rs.	A.	P.	Rs.	A.	P.	Rs.	A.	P.	Rs.	A.	P.
Tuition Fees	11,431	5	0	13,232	11	0	19,469	4	9	16,079	3	6	15,419	7	6	76,331	15	9	15,266	6	5
Scholarship Funds	5,701	11		6,561	2	8	5,633	6	9	5,582	11	2	4,750	7	8	28,228	14	4	5,645	12	5
Scholarships Disbursed	6,743	14	0	7,196	8	3	6,182	13	9	5,443	9	0	3,949	4	0	29,516	1	0	5,903	3	5

roles needed in a modern society. In view of India's economic development, and his personal commitment to help change the relational context for the Muslims' position in India, Sir Sayyid considered technical education and skills irrelevant. He viewed their relevance only after the modernization of the Muslim mind had been achieved. In 1890, at the fifth annual session of the Muhammadan Educational Conference at Allahabad, Sir Sayyid proposed a resolution that technical education should not be promoted by the British Government at the expense of education in liberal arts and sciences.[60] Again, in February 1898 a few weeks before his death, he wrote an article indicating why technical ed-

TABLE 5.6. CIVIL LIST OF OCTOBER 1893

	North West Provinces & Awadh		Total of all Provinces			Percentage	
	Muslim	*Hindu*	*Muslim*	*Hindu*	*Total*	*Muslim*	*Hindu*
Railway	0	5	0	6	6	0	100
Telegraph	0	0	4	6	10	40	60
Paper	0	0	0	1	1	0	100
Marine	0	0	5 (in Burma)	1	6	83.3	16.7
Salt	0	0	1	5	6	16.7	83.3
Miscellaneous (technical)	0	0	0	12	12	0	100

ucation for the Muslims was premature.[61] This view was in harmony with the prevailing Muslim orientation in 19th-century India. Consequently, until the beginning of the 20th century the Muslims were conspicuously absent from specialized roles in practically all the technical departments of the provincial and central governments. See Table 5.6.

Sir Sayyid's educational system was designed primarily to create role-types for government administrators and managers, and modern professionals including lawyers and doctors. In allocating personnel to various grades of education, he revealed the allocative criterion shown in Figure 5.3.

Despite his diminishing emphasis on elementary education,

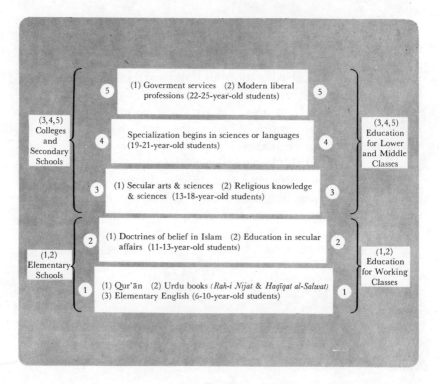

FIGURE 5.3 DIFFERENTIATED EDUCATION FOR THE PRODUCTION OF
ROLE-TYPES

Sir Sayyid maintained that with literate working classes "Hindustan would become a part of paradise."[62] At Aligarh, Sir
Sayyid's allocative decision had practical relevance only for the
third, fourth, and fifth tier of this paradigm. In admitting students to various departments no religious criterion was applied;
non-Muslims in general and Hindus in particular retained a significant representation in the student body from 1875 to 1898,
and this situation did not change under Sir Sayyid's successors
even to this day. From 1875 to 1878, before the MAO College
started, total student population in the high school was 481, and
72 among them were Hindus, averaging 18 annually compared
to the Muslim average of 120.2 (for the remaining years, see
Table 5.7).

TABLE 5.7. RELIGIOUS COMPOSITION OF THE MAO COLLEGE
STUDENTS (1877–1903)

| Degrees | Period | Number Passed | | | Hindu Percentage of Total |
		Hindu	Muslim	Total	
High School	1877–1878	4	6	10	40
	1879–1883	19	36	55	34.5
	1884–1888	27	43	70	38.5
	1889–1893	22	69	91	24.1
	1894–1898	9	86	95	9.4
	1899–1903	18	63	81	22.2
Total		99	303	402	24.6
Fine Arts (F.A.)	1880–1883	14	9	23	60.8
	1884–1888	20	17	37	54.0
	1889–1893	15	62	77	19.4
	1894–1898	18	85	103	17.4
	1899–1903	14	104	118	11.8
Total		81	277	358	22.6
B.A.	1882–1883	1	2	3	33.3
	1884–1888	9	7	16	56.2
	1889–1893	7	25	32	21.8
	1894–1898	12	77	89	13.4
	1899–1903	7	110	117	5.9
Total		36	221	257	10.1
M.A.	1888	0	1	1	0
	1889–1893	1	3	4	25
	1894–1898	0	7	7	0
	1899–1903	1	1	2	50
Total		2	12	14	14.2
D.Sc.	1901–1903	1	1	2	50
L.L.B.	1892–1893	4	1	5	80
	1894–1898	4	18	22	18.1
	1899–1903	2	3	5	40
Total		11	23	34	31.2
Grand Total		229	836	1,065	21.5

SOURCE: Mohsin al-Mulk, *Progress of the Muhammadan Anglo-Oriental College* (Aligarh: Board of Trustees Budget Meeting, August 4, 1903). I.O.L., Table no. 3.

The MAO College was to create a new value system among the Muslim students. First, a consciousness of Muslim nationality, national solidarity, and solidarity obligation must be instilled. Secondly, their dedication to Islamic religion should be

TABLE 5.8. NUMBER OF MUSLIM AND HINDU STUDENTS AT THE MAO COLLEGE: 1879–1900

Year	Muslims							Hindus			
	High Schools	Colleges	Law Students	Law Students in Art Classes	Boardees	Day Scholars	Total	Schools	Colleges	Law Students	Total
1879	112	15			27	100	127	26	7		33
1880	164	16			14	33	180	34	8		42
1881	232	27			172	87	259	43	15		58
1882	219	27			182	64	246	40	14		54
1883	210	38			163	85	248	41	18		59
1884	220	52			168	104	272	55	25		80
1885	221	39			160	100	260	53	20		73
1886	224	53			147	130	277	76	22		98
1887	208	41			118	131	249	68	22		90
1888	169	49			114	104	218	62	20		82
1889	194	65			151	108	259	40	23		63
1890	190	79			163	106	269	40	19		59
1891	208	102	6	47	195	121	316	46	26	19	91
1892	214	102	37	66	216	137	353	22	38	29	89
1893	241	121	48	69	230	180	410	20	41	0	61
1894	295	152	20	61	270	197	467	65	28	0	93
1895	360	205	14	85	329	250	579	72	37	0	109
1896	304	202	24	94	333	197	530	57	27	0	84
1897	213	159	21	51	256	137	393	34	25	0	59
1898	179	144	20	22	234	109	343	23	17	13	53
1899	255	174	27	36	325	131	456	38	17	10	65
1900	281	176	31	48	369	119	488	48	16	16	80
Total 1879–1900	4,913	2,038	248	579	4,336	2,730	7,199	1,003	485	87	1,575

SOURCE: Mohsin al-Mulk, *Progress of the MAO College*, Table no. 1.

strengthened so that they remained loyal to the *shihadah, La illa illa Allah Muhammad-ur Rasūl Allah* (there is no God whatsoever but Allah and Muhammad is his Prophet). Thirdly, values emphasizing honesty, truthfulness, and compassion for others must be internalized. Fourthly, Sir Sayyid maintained that Arabic and Persian literary and cultural traditions should be maintained in order to counterbalance the corrosive impact of modern English education. Lastly, primacy was given to the value of Muslims' solidarity obligation in the boarding houses, where the students were made to realize that only with mutual help and the development of ingroup orientation, nations were born. Cultural life in

TABLE 5.9. PROVINCIAL AND FOREIGN STUDENTS AT THE MAO COLLEGE: 1893–1903

Year	Agra	Awadh	Punjab	Bengal and Bihar	Madras	Bombay	Hyderabad Deccan	Central Provinces	Foreign Countries
1893	218	0	90	8	0	2	6	5	14
1903	220	81	95	44	15	12	15	14	35

SOURCE: Mohsin al-Mulk, *Progress of MAO College,* p. 2.

the dormitories was structured to keep their motivational orientation alive; physical development and intellectual growth were considered inseparable.[63] To Sir Sayyid a modern Muslim reflected in his personality a refined synthesis of philosophy, natural science, and the *shihadah,* the confession of Islamic faith.[64]

This synthesized and ideal role-type was not easy to produce, but the MAO College succeeded in creating personnel equipped to assume specialized professional roles (see Table 5.8).

The Punjabi Muslims sent the largest contingent of students to Aligarh. However, if the 1903 figures are compared with those of 1893, in addition to students from other Indian provinces, several from foreign lands (including Somalia, Uganda, Mauritius, Cape Colony, Iran and Arabia) are also visible (see Table 5.9).

In 1893, compared to the U.P. students, the Punjabi Muslim students were 42 percent, and 40 percent of all the provincial students. Perhaps due to the availability of relatively more widespread educational opportunities in the Punjab toward the beginning of the 20th century, their percentage at the MAO College declined. This is supported by the statistics for 1893–1897 when 77 Muslims graduated both from the Punjab University and the MAO College, while during 1898–1902, 123 Muslims graduated from the Punjab University against 113 Muslim graduates of the MAO College. Also, during these periods the number of Allahabad University's Muslim graduates exceeded the Muslim total of the MAO College graduates. A comparison of the MAO College graduates with other universities' graduates highlights the relative success of Sir Sayyid's modernizing endeavors (see Table 5.10).

The data suggest several intriguing possibilities, and challenge some established notions regarding Sir Sayyid's role as a modernizing leader. From 1882 to 1898 Muslim graduates of the MAO College totaled 122, while those of Allahabad University were 250. This period witnessed in the U.P. the most acrimonious opposition to Sir Sayyid's religious liberalism, climaxed by a split in 1889 with his most reliable associates, who were led by Sami'y Allah Khan. And then Lal's embezzlement of the College funds in 1895 almost bankrupted the MAO College. Despite these developments the U.P. Muslim students attended modern institutions, and during 1882–1892 their graduates (250) of Allahabad University exceeded the Muslim graduates (182) of the Punjab University. The disparity becomes even more significant when the population ratio is taken into consideration. In the U.P. Muslims were 13 percent of the total population, while in the Punjab they constituted a majority of 60 percent. The latter were also known to be in sympathy with Sir Sayyid and maintained a positive orientation for modern education. This situation clearly substantiates the British officials' assessment that the Muslims in India were responding positively toward modern education, while Sir Sayyid had challenged this evaluation. Moreover, the data support the view that the U.P. Muslims' opposition focused on Sir Sayyid's religious orientation and was not directed against English education, although in the popular imagination no distinction between the two has been maintained.

TABLE 5.10. MAO COLLEGE GRADUATES (B.A. & M.A.) COMPARED TO OTHER UNIVERSITIES' MUSLIM GRADUATES (1882–1902)

Year	Number of Muslim Graduates from Various Universities						MAO College	Percentage of Muslim Graduates	
	Calcutta	Madras	Bombay	Punjab	Allahabad	Total		All-India	Allahabad University
1882–87	80	12	7	11	0	110	10	9.9	0
1888–92	90	9	7	44	53	203	17	8.3	32.7
1893	23	2	3	15	25	68	11	16.1	44
1894	23	6	4	20	40	93	18	19.3	45
1895	22	3	4	6	45	80	20	25	44
1896	22	8	5	15	28	78	20	25.6	71.4
1897	17	7	2	21	27	74	8	13.5	37.3
Total 1893–97	107	26	18	77	165	393	77	19.5	46.6
1898	17	5	3	20	32	77	18	23.3	56.2
1899	30	4	10	28	43	115	22	19.1	51
1900	26	2	6	19	33	86	21	24.4	63.6
1901	24	0	5	23	37	89	22	24.7	59
1902	24	7	0	33	47	111	30	27.2	63
Total 1898–1902	121	18	24	123	192	478	113	23.7	58.8
Grand Total	398	65	56	255	410	1,184	217	18.4	52.9

SOURCE: Muhsin al-Mulk, *Progress of MAO College*, statement no. III (a).

From 1898 to 1902 Muslim graduates in Bengal totaled 121, against 121 of the previous period of 1893–1897. For the first 5-year period, Muslims in northern India (including the Punjab and the U.P.) produced 319 graduates, and for the second period 438. (This disparity remained stable until 1947, when an overwhelming number of educated Muslims from the U.P. migrated to West Pakistan. This substantially explained the underrepresentation of the Bengali Muslims in the administrative infrastructure of Pakistan.)

Finally, how far did the MAO College effect change in the relational context of the three major Indian collectivities—the British Government, Hindus, and Muslims? By 1900, the MAO College succeeded in placing a sizable number of its personnel in the administrations of the British as well as the princely states of India (see Table 5.11).

TABLE 5.11. ALIGARH GRADUATES IN GOVERNMENT SERVICE (1882–1900)

Department	Rank	Number
Imperial Service	I.C.S.	1
Civil Service	Gazetted Officer	1
General Administration	Deputy Collector & Extra Assistant Commissioner	11
Revenue	Naib Tahsildar	16
Medical	Civil Surgeon	1
Judicial	Judges	2
	Munsif (Sub-Judge)	7
	Sarishtadar (Reader) & Head Clerk	64
Police	Inspector & Sub-Inspector	29
Opium	Assistant Sub-Deputy Agent	2
Salt	Assistant Superintendent	5
Railway	(designation not known)	5
Education	Inspector	31
	Princely States of India	
General Administration	Officers (of unspecified rank)	49
Judicial	Lawyers	37
Revenue	Tahsildar	20
Army	Officers	7
Grand Total		288

SOURCE: Hali, *Hayat-i Javid,* p. 436

Obviously, this was a limited share in the administrative power of the country. Already in 1893 Muslim parents were beginning to bemoan the unemployment of their sons, who had acquired bachelor or master of arts degrees from Aligarh and other universities. The static Indian economy and the British bureaucracy could hardly absorb the college graduates, and Sir Sayyid was disturbed by their unemployed surplus. Dealing with this problem in 1894, Sir Sayyid suggested that the Muslim graduates should turn to trade and even venture to travel abroad for lucrative international commerce. Mixing sarcasm with practical wisdom, he advised the graduates to be frugal and engage in cooperative business, "instead of succumbing to petty jealousy, haughtiness, and mutually destructive rivalry."

Also, Sir Sayyid recognized that Indian universities were not developing in the students a spirit of free enterprise and self-reliance, nor were they creating men of high intellect.[65] In fact he had foreseen this possibility as early as 1870; in lamenting the consequences of the educational system in 1894 he was merely expressing his frustrations and despair. His well-meaning counselling could hardly change the "conservatism" of Muslim graduates' new orientation, which had led them to the garden path of the security of Government employment, and the glitter of a modest share in the bureaucratic control. The crusade for modern education created economic problems for the modern educated personnel, generating social pressures on the leaders and finally forcing the leadership role to initiate a political struggle for a fixed Muslim share of the Government jobs. (The politics of education were channeled by Sir Sayyid through the Muhammadan Educational Conference.)

All-India Muhammadan Educational Conference (1886–1937)

Established in 1886 with the title of *Muhammadan Educational Congress,* Sir Sayyid sought to transform the restless sweep of Muslims' energy (now accentuated by the rising expectations of the modern educated youth), into a concrete national organization. Also, this organization was to combine the functions of articulation and aggregation of the Muslims' educational, economic, and political interests, while enabling them to define their role in the imperial polity of British India. Finally, the Educational Congress aimed at politicization of the Muslim masses, since it involved a large number of them on a sustained and controlled basis. Thus, categorically Sir Sayyid renounced his apolitical role, recognizing the establishment of the All-India National Congress in 1885, heralding a competitive political environment in India. In 1890, Sir Sayyid persuaded the annual convention of the Educational Congress at Allahabad to adopt *Conference* for *Congress*[66] in order to reduce the competitive edge of the Muslims' organization. But the "new" conference did not change its firm "political" orientation, generating a struggle for power between the National Congress and the Educational Conference, and its ideological successor, the All-India Muslim League, which was established by the Conference's leaders in 1906 in Decca.

Some scholars have argued that "Sir Sayyid had been too overcautious in advising the Muslims to stay aloof from political activities."[67] This statement hardly applied to Sir Sayyid's leadership from 1885 to 1898. From 1886 to 1898 the Educational Congress was pitted against the National Congress. On December 28, 1887, while the National Congress met in Madras, Sir Sayyid utilized a public session of the Educational Congress at Lucknow, to oppose the Muslims' participation in the National Congress. Also, he rejected the principles of elections for the viceroy's legislative council, and the scheduling of the competitive examination in India for the Indian civil service. On March 16, 1888, he reiterated more vigorously his opposition to the National Congress in a public meeting at Meerut. The struggle for power had already begun.

Sir Sayyid was acutely aware that the National Congress' demands were an exercise of power. To protect Muslims' national interests (the way he perceived them), he attempted to organize them in a power equation, not in a communal Hindu-Muslim confrontation, but in the alignment of class interests. In order to neutralize the National Congress' rising power, Sir Sayyid organized in August 1888 the Patriotic Association. Hindus, as well as Muslim land-owning classes in Bengal, Bihar, Madras, Bombay, Awadh, the Northwest Provinces, and the Punjab, extended their support to the Association. The Patriotic Association started sending memoranda to the British Parliament, articulating property owners interests, which Sir Sayyid believed were in harmony with those of the Muslims, and to state that the National Congress lacked "national" representative capacity. However, the regional Islamic associations were most conspicuous in the Patriotic Association's system of action. Gradually, the Hindus' role virtually disappeared, and Sir Sayyid's leadership came to be identified with the "Muslim" Congress.

The change in name did not alter the Educational Congress' latent political functions of Muslims' interest articulation, and aggregation; but its manifest functions remained educational, including departments for: (1) elementary and secondary education; (2) female education; (3) development of the Urdu language; (4) business administration and technical education; (5) social reforms, and (6) general education, including adult literacy. At its first two sessions in 1886 ten resolutions were adopted which became the "ten commandments of modernity's Torah."[68] The Conference was to: (1) disseminate European sciences and literature among Muslims, and adopt plans for higher education; (2) encourage research on the past academic accomplishments of the Muslims, and publish them or arrange lectures on them in English or Urdu; (3) commission the biographies of renowned Muslim scholars and authors in English or Urdu; (4) locate and publish the rare works of Muslim authors; (5) subsidize research on controversial or episodic events in history, involving Islam; (6) commission monographs or lectures on matters of statecraft; (7) commission the collection and publication of Muslim emperors' proclamations, orders, and decrees; (8) arrange for religious instruction in English schools established by the Muslims; (9) investigate the educational level of traditional religious institutions, and adopt means of improving their performance; (10a) investigate the level of elementary education in *makatib,* and determine the causes of their decline in order to strengthen their syllabus for the common-man's education; and (10b) adopt much the same course of action for the *Hafizy Makatib,* where young students learned to memorize the Qur'ān.[69]

The Educational Conference existed from 1886 to 1937, completing half a century of very productive tenure. A brief review of its elaborate infrastructure for politicization as well as its "educational" policies, which had profound political implications, is in order. The Conference decreed to meet every December in Muslim majority and Muslim minority provinces. In some cities it met more than once: Aligarh 10, Lahore 4, Delhi 4, Lucknow 3, and Bombay, Calcutta, and Madras 2 each. In addition to Lahore the Conference met in the Punjabi cities of Amritsar in 1908, Rawalpindi in 1914, and Rohtak in 1931. In Sindh the Conference held its session in Karachi in 1907, and then in Khairpur in 1919. The 1909 annual session was scheduled to be held in Peshawar, but the Muslims of Burma pleaded the precariousness of their minority status to lure the Conference to Rangoon. The "Pakistan" provinces thus attracted 9 annual sessions out of a total of 45, since 5 scattered annual sessions in the period of 50 years were not convened for a variety of reasons. The minutes of the annual sessions indicated that hundreds of thousands of ordinary people attended each meeting, while the leaders presented their deliberations in speeches and resolutions. Leaders came from different provinces as "delegates" and "visitors." During Sir Sayyid's secretaryship (1886–1898) only 61 delegates and 150 visitors came to the first meeting of the Conference in 1886; the highest number was reached in 1890 at Allahabad with 1,014 delegates and 95 visitors.

In 1896–1897, just before his death, Sir Sayyid's popularity was at its lowest,[70] and the 1897 annual meeting was skipped. To these 45 annual sessions came altogether 35,934 leaders from various provinces; and in 1909 the distinction between the delegates and the visitors was abolished. Sometimes the Conference's annual meeting coincided with the All-India Muslim League, and other regional organizations of the Muslims. Like the U.P. Muslims, the Punjabi and Pathan leaders remained most conspicuous both as presidents and delegates. Most of the Conference's leaders were educated in the West, and had very successful careers in the practice of law and, the academic world. They used sophisticated techniques to articulate the Muslims' interests. Employing the "idiom" of the British parliamentary politics, they received the most sympathetic treatment from the British Indian Government.

The Conference also decreed that in every major city and town new committees should be created in order to maintain communication links with the general population. Where Muslim associations already existed they were to assume the committees' role. They were required to send delegates to the Conference's annual meetings, with data pertaining to the following items: (1) Muslim population in each district; (2) Muslim students in (a) government elementary and secondary schools, and colleges, and (b) Muslim students' proportion in missionary and other private institutions; (3) Muslim students in traditional religious institutions, where the Qur'ān, *hadith,* and other secular education was imparted; (4) female educational facilities maintained by various Muslim associations; and (5) well-known industries in each district owned by the Muslim communities. Uneven in quality and thoroughness, the delegates' reports contained an abundance of information on these points, and they were discussed often with verbal overkill. Also, these reports reflected the development of new institution-building skills among the Muslims. In the 1930s–40s these associations and local educational committees became the popular base for the political programs of the All-India Muslim League.

During the period 1886–1937, there were 582 resolutions adopted, articulating Muslims' educational, cultural, and religious grievances as well as demands. Some were trivial, while some had deeper implications for Muslims' progress and their share in the Indian bureaucracy. Only a few significant resolutions in the latter category are reviewed here. Collectively, they reflected an evolving Muslim policy for the national culture in regard to (1) education, and (2) the role of the Urdu language.

Clearly these issues demonstrated the cultural bias of north-western Muslims, who expected the Muslims from the east, especially Bengal, Bihar, and Bombay to accept their orientations. Bombay and Bihar Muslims followed the conference's leadership; Bengali Muslims remained lukewarm on the language issue, while they fully cooperated in political matters when the All-India Muslim League was launched in 1906 from Decca.

(1) *Educational Policy:* This policy was national in scope, and provincial in emphasis. The problems of the U.P., Punjab, Sindh, Northwest Frontier, and Bengal were sharply focussed. Increasingly, the Muslim female education was accepted. Along with modern education the need for Islamic education, and the *'ulamā's* cooperation with the modernists was recognized. Especially, after Sir Sayyid's death in 1898, the conference's leadership initiated the policy of involving the British government in implementing its policy. This approach sharpened Hindu-Muslim tensions, although it is difficult to determine the extent to which the British government accepted the Muslims' demands.

In 1898, to honor Sir Sayyid's memory the Punjab invited the Conference to meet in Lahore. Appropriately, a resolution was adopted to develop the MAO College into Aligarh Muslim University. To supplement the endowed property of an Aligarh Muslim, Haji Ahmad Saʿīd, valued at Rs.350,000 yielding monthly income of Rs.1,000, the Punjab Muslims contributed a substantial sum of money to found the University. In Lahore and other cities subcommittees were established to collect donations, but for the first time a condition was attached making Islamic theology a mandatory course for graduating Muslim students. In 1899 and 1904 resolutions were adopted to establish colleges of science and engineering at Aligarh. In 1902 a proposal was adopted to add a school of law to the proposed university. Finally, in December 1920, the British government issued the charter to recognize the MAO College as Aligarh Muslim University.

Modernization also rang alarm bells for Sir Sayyid, because Muslim students who went to Europe became "deculturized." In 1892 he moved the resolution to express national disapproval of some young students' tendency to marry European girls. A year earlier he had favored a resolution suggesting that Muslim students younger than age 20 (with the exception of the competitors for the ICS), should not be sent to Europe for education unless someone to act as parent surrogate accompanied them.[71] Also, Sir Sayyid endeavored to establish a rapprochment with the *'ulamā'* (traditional religious teachers and scholars). In 1893–94, the Conference urged Muslims to financially support Nadwat al-'ulamā' of Kanpur, and asked the British government to offer scholarships to Muslim students for the study of Arabic as a second language. To follow up on this strand of policy the Conference invited in 1910 the "progressive" *'ulamā'* to participate with the modernists in national seminars to "enlighten" Muslim cultural orientations. In 1915 an unusual suggestion was made asking the Government to establish in every division of the Indian provinces teachers' training schools for the *'ulamā'* and to provide them special incentives to enroll in these schools. The trained *'ulamā'* would then be employed in Islamic schools. A large class of *'ulamā'* equipped to teach only in elementary schools would thus find secure employment.

This conciliatory stance elicited positive response from the higher echelon of the *'ulamā'*. In March 1937 Maulana Husain Ahmad Madni, of Deoband's well-known Dar al-'ulūm, made some practical suggestions to establish symbiotic relationships between the *'ulamā'* and the modernists. In 72 years of its existence Dar al-'ulūm Deoband had educated approximately 13,000 scholars; additionally, Arabic-Islamic seminaries were producing annually several thousand *'ulamā'* with no visible means of employment. These "national leaders and spiritual guides," Madni admitted, added to a national malaise. The Conference, he complained, had neglected them, complaining instead that sound and progressive *'ulamā'* were not created. Without economic security, independent and self-respecting *'ulamā'* could not exist. To remedy this "deplorable situation," Madni presented a 12-point program: (1) Aligarh Muslim University should allow the graduates of Arabic schools to earn bachelor of arts' degrees after passing an English language and literature examination; (2) the Government should exempt or subsidize Arabic schools graduates' travels by the railroads like the university students; (3) to appear in the L.L.B. examinations the knowledge of Arabic, corresponding to the levels of high school, bachelor's or Master's degrees, should be recognized; (4) a substantial number of scholarships should be awarded to Arabic students for the study of English and vice versa; (5) the court language, instead of English, should be a national language; (6) for employment in the courts' registration departments Arabic degrees should be recognized by the Government; (7) Islamic-Arabic education should be mandatory for all senior appointments to the administrations of Muslims' religious endowments; (8) for the appointment of civil judges, who apply shari'ā laws of inheritance, Islamic-Arabic training should be a prerequisite; (9) the Government must create a system of Muslim courts; (10) in specialized schools of arts and technology, Arabic graduates should be admitted; (11) in departments of irrigation, agriculture, and trade Arabic graduates should be employed; (12) and finally, students majoring in Arabic in modern universities should be encouraged to spend some time in traditional Islamic-Arabic institutions of advanced studies.[72]

Madni's exceptionally practical and wise approach became a cry in the wilderness. Three years later, in 1940, the Muslim League adopted the "Pakistan resolution," completely transforming the Indian political environment. Traditional 'ulamā' of the Deoban school supported the National Congress, and the modernists through the Muslim League opted for Pakistan; thus, a unique opportunity to harmonize the traditional Islamic educational values with modernism was lost.

Another salient strand of the educational policy related to gaining a substantial participatory role in educational decision-making. In 1904 the Conference demanded the appointment of 15-man advisory committees in each province to assist the directors of public instruction, not in administration, but in determining educational policies, i.e., establishing the syllabi, tuition fees, promotions to higher grades, rules for final examinations, and grants-in-aid to privately maintained schools. Also, the Conference asked the Government to appoint special Muslim inspectors of schools in each province to ascertain Muslim educational progress. The provincial directors were called upon to periodically report on the performance of new Islamic colleges and schools and their financial conditions. Moreover, they should review their own efforts on the Muslims' behalf, which the Conference believed was mandated in 1882 by the government's Educational Commission.

In 1916 the Conference increased its demands for Muslim quotas in the government institutions: 40 percent representation in all "normal and training schools"; 50 percent and 30 percent admissions in all government colleges and schools, especially in Bengal. During 1927–31 a demand for the appointment of Muslim vice-chancellors at Agra, Allahabad, Lucknow, and Punjab universities was made, and the Government was asked to allocate funds annually for one Muslim student to pursue technical graduate studies in European or American universities. The extent to which the Muslims were politicized in the 1920s can be gathered from the Conference's suggestion in 1928 that military training in all schools should be compulsory. Not unexpectedly, the British Government turned it down as inappropriate.

Quite appropriate, however, was the Muslim modernist leadership's gradual emphasis on female education. An 1891 resolution, which Sir Sayyid had approved, suggested female education in religion so that "the future generations benefit from mothers' superior moral training." Eight years later the Conference recommended the establishment of secular educational institutions for girls to be supervised by provincial Islamic committees. In 1900 they specifically accepted the additional studies n mathematics, history, geography, ethics, and metaphysics. Sixteen years later the Conference urged the necessity of establishing girls high schools in every district of all provinces; only in 1927–28, the leadership recognized Muslim female education in the universities and colleges, but urged the government to exempt them from the compulsory attendance of lectures. Simultaneously, the principle of free and compulsory secondary education for all Muslim girls was accepted, and the government was urged to provide free luncheons and transportation to economically disadvantaged girls. Finally, in 1932, the Conference demanded the appointment of Muslim female faculty members at all government colleges and universities. Obviously, the Muslim modernist leadership changed its traditional orientation for female education rather slowly, and did not recognize the principle of equality in modern education until the 1930s.[73]

(2) *The Role of the Urdu Language:* The record of the Conference reflected an alliance between the U.P. and the Punjab leaders for the promotion of Urdu, not only as the medium of instruction in the schools, but as the language of the courts. In 1899 a resolution demanded specifically the adoption of Urdu (in Arabic-Persian script) to be the official language in the Northwest Provinces, and Awadh. Gradually, this demand brought within its scope the southern provinces of India, where the Muslims were a miniscule minority. In 1901, the Madras government was asked to allow Muslims to use Urdu in the competitive examinations for employment in the provincial bureaucracy. Also, Sindh gained the focus of the Conference's attention, and the Bombay government which administered Sindh was urged to teach Urdu to Muslim students whose mother tongue was not Urdu, and to prepare special textbooks in Urdu for them. By 1917 the Bombay government implemented this Muslim suggestion. However, the general campaign for Urdu elicited negative reactions from the Hindus, who started to demand the expulsion of Urdu in favor of Hindi from educational institutions. Consequently, Muslims established the Urdu Defense Association in 1900. Three years later, when the Conference met in Delhi from December 30, 1902 to January 3, 1903, it created a department for the progress and protection of Urdu as the Muslims' national language. Subsequently, this department came to be known as Anjuman Traqqi Urdu (Association for the Progress of Urdu).[74] In 1918 the Conference appointed a national committee, consisting of Dr. Zia-ud-Din Ahmad (U.P.), Qadi Kabīr-ud-Din, and Ibrahīm Haroon Jafar (Bombay) to prepare a comprehensive plan for the promotion of Urdu in Muslim minority provinces. Simultaneously, however, the universities of

Bombay, Calcutta, and Mysore were urged to allow non-Urdu-speaking Muslims to opt for Urdu as a second language, and to establish one government college and one high school, especially in the Bombay province, to teach Arabic.

In the Punjab, where Urdu had been established as the provincial language, Hindus demanded the adoption of the Punjabi language instead of Urdu. In a speech at the Punjab University's commencement exercises in 1909, Dr. P. C. Chatterji demanded that Punjabi, as the spoken language of the Punjab, should become the medium of instruction. At the annual meeting of the Conference at Amritsar in 1908, Punjabi Muslims, under Mian Muhammad Shafi's leadership, indicated that the adoption of Punjabi would be detrimental to the Punjab's interest since Punjabi was the least developed language.[75] They urged that Urdu should continue to be the language in the Punjab's schools.

During the 1930s the Urdu-Hindi controversy became a symbol for the struggle of power and national self-assertion involving the National Congress and the Muslim League. Actually, Urdu developed in India during the Muslim rule from the eighth to the twelfth centuries, when the Persian, Arabic, and Turkish speaking Muslims adopted Hindi in the Arabic script. Two stages in the development of Urdu are indicated: (a) Lahori-Urdu, beginning in 1027 and consisting of old Punjabi overlaid by Persian; (b) Lahori-Urdu, beginning in 1193 overlaid by old Khari (which was not very different then from old Punjabi) and further influenced by Persian; all of this evolving into Delhi-Urdu. Just as the New Persian language in Iran evolved out of the Pahlavi in the Arabic alphabet in the ninth century, and became an entirely different language, similarly Urdu, under the impact of Persian and Arabic, developed into a separate language from Hindi during the twelfth century.[76] Muslim scholars and political leaders definitively asserted the separate identity of Urdu in 1934, when Moulavi 'Abdūl Haq, Secretary of the Anjuman Traqqi-i Urdu, stated that "Urdu and Hindi are no longer the one and the same language." Bharatiya Sahitya Prishad, a national Hindu organization, reacted to the Muslims' claim, saying "Hindi alone deserves to be the national language of India."[77]

In 1937, attempts were made by the Congress and Muslim leaders to achieve a compromise solution of the Urdu/Hindi conflict. Representing the Congress, Rajindera Prashad signed a memorandum of undersanding with Moulavi 'Abdūl Haq, admitting that "India's national language should be Hindustani, written in Urdu [Arabic] and Devanagri [sanscrit] scripts. It should be the medium of instruction, and be the language of the government."[78] Ten years later, when freedom dawned, and Pakistan emerged, Urdu became the national language of the Muslim state, and India declared Hindi to be its language.

6

Theory of Muslim Nationalism

AMONG THE NONEMPIRICAL existential ideas of Sir Sayyid must be included his concepts of Muslim nationalism. One of the problems in understanding nationalism has been a lack of agreement on a clear-cut and all-embracing definition of nationalism. Here and elsewhere, this author has adopted Hans Kohn's concept as a working definition. Kohn says: "Nationalism is first and foremost a state of mind, an act of consciousness . . ."[1] The "corporate will" of the Muslims (to use Kohn's phrase) was a cumulative historical growth in the Indian environment, and found its clearest expression in Sir Sayyid's works. In this chapter an attempt is made to present (1) Sir Sayyid's conception of Muslim nationalism; (2) his attempts to strengthen Muslim political consciousness, and (3) his attitude towards the Hindus, and the All-India National Congress.

Sir Sayyid's Definition of Nationalism

Sir Sayyid discussed the concept of nationalism in the terminology of nineteenth-century Europe, and like Henry St. John Bolingbroke (1678–1751), enunciated the creed of aristocratic nationalism. This was a logical development since he was a scion of the Mughal nobility whom the vicissitudes of history had exposed to Western ideas. After a 16-month stay in Britain and other parts of Europe (1867–68) Sir Sayyid evolved a *melange* of the Western ethos with his Islamic heritage.[2]

Unlike most Western scholars who look upon nationalism as an acquired characteristic, Sir Sayyid believed that it was an instinct. In fact, national solidarity and the urge for mutual help distinguished man from animal. An individual lacking in national sentiments remained less than a man.[3] A mutual feeling of solidarity with those who share many common traits is the quintessence of Sir Sayyid's definition of nationalism.

Sir Sayyid made a clear distinction between a nation and a nationality although he used the Arabic word *qawm,* for both concepts. This has confused his critics and followers alike, and has been the source of endless polemics between the protagonists of Muslim separation and the champions of Indian national unity. According to Sir Sayyid *qawm* (in the sense of a nationality) can be located internationally or locally, and it can be created by ethnic ties or shared spiritual or religious values. Muslims all over the world were a nationality because of their adherence to the *Shihadeh-La ilaha illa-i-Lah Muhammadur Rasūlu-i-Lah* (no God whatsoever but Allah; Muhammad is the messenger of Allah). Sir Sayyid maintained that "to Islam it was irrelevant whether a believer was white or black, Turkish or Tadhjik, an Arab or a Chinese, a Punjabi or a Hindustani." The Qur'ān is explicit in enunciating the doctrine of the Muslim brotherhood: *"Innamā al-muminūn akhawatū fasalhahū bayn-a akhawiykum waa-taqū Allah l-a'lkum tarhamūn."*[4]

The Believers are but
A single Brotherhood:

So make peace and
Reconciliation between your
Two (contending) brothers;
And fear God, that ye
May receive mercy. (49:10)

In the light of the Qur'ānic dictum "Muslims all over the world were the progenies of a spiritual father."[5]

Sir Sayyid was aware that, despite that allegiance to a common creed, Muslims differed in their geographic locations and historical experiences. Consequently, he maintained that the Muslims' historical encounter with the Indian situation had moulded Indian Muslims into a distinct nationality. Muslim political power in India, from the advent of the Arabs in the eighth century to the heyday of Mughal power in the seventeenth and eighteenth centuries maintained Muslim preeminence in politics, economics, and education. In the nineteenth century, Sir Sayyid lamented, the Muslim nation was decaying rapidly and the greatest obstacle to its resurgence was its lack of social solidarity.

Love of Nation or Love of Land: In 1872 Sir Sayyid was invited by the Honourable Mawlavi Muhammad Abul Latif, the founder of the Muslim Literary Society, to deliver a lecture in Calcutta on patriotism. Speaking in Persian he defined instead his view of nationalism—the love for one's own nation. "Love," asserted Sir Sayyid, "is like a pyramid." On the top of the pyramid is the noblest form of love—love for the universe, implying a tender concern for even leaves of grass. "This kind of love is unattainable, unless God of the universe opens the portals of his blessings."

The second kind of love is for those who "share human qualities with us"—the love of mankind so beautifully described by the famous Persian poet Shaykh Sa'di Shirazi:

Banī Ādam a'dhayi' yak diygar-and
Kah der afrīynash z-yak jawhar-and
Chaw a'dhaway baderd awarad rawzgār
Diyger a'dhaw-ha rā namanad qarār

People are organically related to each other,
Since their creation is from the same soul.
When a limb is afflicted with pain,
All other limbs do not remain tranquil.

"Lofty though this sentiment is," Sir Sayyid maintained, "it is
less noble than the first kind of love, and far too elusive a quality
to be comprehended."

"At the bottom of the pyramid," said Sir Sayyid, "is placed
a sentiment which I call love of nation, which I understand and
am capable of." [6] It was the love of the Muslim nation, he stated,
that had motivated him to undertake an extensive program of educational, cultural, and political reform among the Muslims.

To this end he had decided, while still in London, to establish a monthly journal. He had the title block made in London, giving the Journal the hybrid name of *The Tahdhīb al-
Akhlāq; Muslim National Reformer.* The first issue of the Tahdhīb
was published on December 24, 1870. It discussed Tunisian–Arab
nationalism, which was deeply influenced by western thought.
One of the Tunisian newspapers, *al-Ra'īd al-Tunisī,* which was
read by Sir Sayyid quite regularly, carried the following motto
on its front page: *"Hubb al-watan min-l imān faman yas'a fi 'imrān
biladah innamā yas'a fi a'zaz dīnah."*

> Love of the native land is a part of Faith.
> Whosoever strives for the progress of his country, really endeavors
> to raise the honour of his religion.

Sir Sayyid commented that the motto was suitable for Tunisia,
where one nation occupied the native land, but that it had to be
modified for application to India, where the native land and the
nation were not synonymous. Accordingly, he adopted the
motto with suitable revision: *"Hubb al-qawm min-l imān faman
yas'a fi a'zaz qawmat innamā yas'a fi a'zaz dīnah."*

> Love of the nation is part of Faith.
> Whosoever strives for the progress of his nation [7] really endeavours
> to raise the honour of his religion.

"Man is not only a social animal," declared Sir Sayyid, "he is essentially a national animal. Animals when they flock together indicate a preference for their kind, but are incapable of mutual help and consideration. On the contrary, man is capable of cooperative endeavour, but if he does not partake in the solution of national problems and demonstrate national love, he is inferior to the dumb animals."[8]

Sir Sayyid described the charitable activities of pious Muslims inspired largely by the hope of salvation in the next life, instead of the desire to help the fellow man in this life, as blatant selfishness. "Virtuous deeds are only those," declared Sir Sayyid, "which meet the problems of the Muslim nation and are motivated by the love of nation." The grand mosques and monuments and religious *madares* and *makatīb* which were supported by charitable endowments from the Muslim nobility were to Sir Sayyid symbols of their greed, masked for a facade of piety, betraying only the builders' lack of concern for the collective well-being of the Muslims.[9] He exhorted Muslim intellectuals to lead the cultural revolution, stressing the Muslims' social solidarity and accepting such innovations as would place the nation again in step with the modern world.

Factors Weakening Muslim Nationalism

In his essays and speeches Sir Sayyid comprehensively dealt with the contributory factors which weakened Muslim nationalism (a few salient ones may be discussed here). He believed that contemporary Muslim society was oriented towards the past, while the Indian political environment had been completely changed by British rule. "Muslims came from abroad to settle in India. They contributed to the advancement of sciences, although many of them they had learned from the Greeks. Then Europe benefitted from the Muslims' endeavours. Today our young men, instead of endeavouring to make their own contributions, take pride in the achievements of their ancestors."[10] This attitude, he believed, led to patterns of escapism, instead of a constructive approach to real conditions.

No distinction, Sir Sayyid pointed out, could be validly maintained between Islam and the Muslims. Islam, as a culture-making force, was identical with its adherents, especially the Indic Muslims. "If culturally we are degraded, Islam is degraded. When our forefathers achieved distinction on the scale of civilization, Islam radiated with glory. Today we are backward and the underdogs; every one tramples us under foot." Referring to his book, *Athar al-Sanadid,* Sir Sayyid lamented that it contained descriptions of Muslims' monuments in India which "reflected the grandeur of our ancestors; today they deserved to be viewed only with anguish. We are the decadent descendants who failed to preserve them. [Delhi], the capital, where our forefathers ruled for centuries, today the Muslims can gaze on it with shattered hopes and sorrow"? Then comes the exhortation: "If you desire heavenly blessings then uplift yourself . . . you build mosques and care not if the worshippers remain; you build monasteries and care not for the security of the occupants. You relish the plans for building the house of God with bricks and stone, and care not for the living house of God, your fellow man." In a similar rhetorical style Sir Sayyid admonished: "no worship, no charity, no good deed is better than the love of your *qawm* (nationality."[11]

Unlike most contemporary Muslims Sir Sayyid firmly believed that national progress was a dynamic process. Otherwise nations, like the Indic Muslims, tended to stagnate. National progress was achieved in slow evolutionary stages. Indic Muslims, on the other hand, completely lost sight of this reality, that contribution to national progress must be made by all strata of society, although the upper stratum bore a special responsibility. To illustrate this thesis, Sir Sayyid referred to British history:

Among the British upper classes several individuals made notable achievements and commanded respect, but the lower strata also made significant contributions to [British national progress]. In the histories only the names of generals and military commanders are preserved, but the victories were won by the industrious and brave commoners. Their contribution to the advancement of civilization and culture is equal to that of notable men whose names are preserved by the historians.[12]

When contrasted with the traditions of advanced European countries, Sir Sayyid observed, Indic Muslim classes showed no empathy with each other.

Among the political institutions which decisively weakened Muslim nationalism in India was the Caliphate. Although Sir Sayyid wanted to protect the Muslims' integrity by emphasizing their distinction *vis-à-vis* the Hindus, he also wanted to cut the silver cord which tied them to the international fraternity of "all believers," personified in the caliphate.

Muslim Nationalism and the Caliphate: From the advent of the Arabs in Sindh (711) to that of the British, Muslim citizens and kings of India considered the Sunni Caliphs, i.e., the Umayyads (661–750), 'Abbasids (750–1258) and Ottoman Turks (1517–1924), as the *de jure* sovereigns of the Sunni Muslim world.[13] The depth of the Indic Muslims' attachment to the Caliphate can be illustrated by the following incident which took plate during the reign of Sultan Rukn-ud-Din Firuz Shah (1235–1236). Taj Rezah, a poet of considerable merit,[14] was waylaid and robbed in one of the parks of Old Delhi. He petitioned the Sultan for redress like a good poet, in elegant Persian verse. Echoing contemporary Muslim sentiment, he threatened to go over the head of the Sultan, and take his case to the Caliph at Baghdad if he failed to obtain justice and appropriate compensation at the Delhi Court.[15]

> I come here to seek redress for the injustice done to me
> I implore the Sultan to compensate me.
> If, however, I fail to obtain redress for the injustice done to me,
> Then I will leave this God-forsaken land.
> I will repair to Baghdad and petition the Leader of the Faithful,
>   the Caliph.
> And with the flood of my tears will inundate another Tigris.
> But I know such an occasion will not arise,
>   Because our Sultan is a just monarch;

He is Rukn-ud-Din (Firuz Shah), the axis of justice,
    From him these dominions derive stability and order.

The institution of the Caliphate emphasized the ties binding all Muslims regardless of ethnic and territorial diversity. Religious and political allegiance was pledged to the "Community of Believers," thereby weakening regional loyalties and retarding the incipient development of nationalities in the modern sense.[16] The effect of the Indian Muslims' attachment to the Caliphate was twofold. It precluded any significant Hindu–Muslim cooperation (a prerequisite for the development of a joint Hindu–Muslim nationality), and at the same time impeded the development of a true nationalism among the Muslims of India. Sir Sayyid endeavored to strengthen the social solidarity among the Muslims by emphasizing their differences with the Hindus, and at the same time to shift the focus of political allegiance from the Caliphate to the Muslim nation in India. This process ultimately led to the development of Pakistani nationalism, articulated by Dr. Muhammad Iqbal[17] and Chaudhari Rahmat Ali,[18] and widely propagated by the All-India Muslim League.

The classical theory of the Caliphate stressed that since there was one God and one law there must be only one ruler. Some jurists, including al-Baqillani, Ibn Rushd, and Ibn Khaldun, believed that two or more Caliphs might legitimately rule since the regions of Dar al-Islam had become very extensive and widely separated.[19] According to this view, each Caliph would enforce the law in his dominions according to the ultimate objective of Islam. Sir Sayyid's interpretation struck at the roots of the institution of the Caliphate; he asserted that the true Caliphate had ended thirty years after the death of the Prophet Muhammad, and that no Muslim sovereign after the Caliphate of Ali b. Abi Tālib (656–661) could legitimately be regarded as his successor (Khalifah, i.e. Caliph) "The Prophet of God performed three functions: Nabūwwah, receiving revelation for the Shari'a from God; propagating them among the people, and exercising political authority for the defense of the Muslim Community, and to defeat its enemies."[20]

Sir Sayyid reasoned that Muslim jurists, traditionists, and *'ulamā'* could perform the second function of the Prophet. It is for this reason that some commentators of the Qur'ān, while explaining the significance of the Qur'ānic injunction—"Obey God and His Prophet and those who are charged with authority among you"—have included the *'ulamā'* in the category of *ulil-amr*, people in position of authority. Muslim sovereigns enjoying independence in their dominions can perform the third function of the Prophet, provided they demonstrate the "overt and covert piety" of the Prophet, and also comply with the dictates of the *Shari'a*. However, even then their sovereignty would extend only over those Muslims who lived within their jurisdiction, and could enjoy their protection. The effective exercise of authority was the quintessence of sovereignty for Sir Sayyid. The citizens of the Umayyad Caliphate in Spain during the tenth century owed no allegiance to the Caliphs of Baghdad, and the citizens of the Fatimid Caliphate of Cairo (909–1171) of course openly spurned the Caliphal claims of Cardova and Baghdad.[21]

Sir Sayyid's theory of the Caliphate suited the political situation of the Indic Muslims. Discouraging their exuberant loyalty to Sultan 'Abdūl Majīd (1839–1861) of Turkey would dilute the influence of the Turkish Foreign Office among the Muslims of the subcontinent, and at the same time would enable them to concentrate their attention on their own national problems. "We cannot possibly be considered subjects of the Turkish Caliph," declared Sir Sayyid,

His sovereignty does not extend over us. We are residents of India and subjects of the British Government, which has guaranteed us religious freedom. Our life and property is protected and our personal affairs—marriage, divorce, inheritance, endowments and wills—are administered according to the *Shari'a*. In such matters even Christian judges are forced to apply the Islamic laws to Muslim litigants.[22]

His endeavours to sever the Muslim attachment to the Turkish Caliphate were greeted with suspicion and distrust. The pan-Islamic movement led by Jamal al-Din al-Afghani and the Turkish Sultan countered Sir Sayyid's efforts at every turn. For the

majority of the Muslims the final break with the Caliphate did
not take place until the 1920s when the Caliphate ceased to exist.

Abolition of the Caliphate by the Turkish Republic left the
Muslims of India without a generally accepted focus of orienta-
tion. Some joined a general *hijrah* (migration) in the direction of
Afghanistan, eventually drifting into the Soviet Union and
adopting Communism.[23] A sizable number joined the All-India
National Congress, putting their hopes in the development of a
strictly territorial nationalism.[24] The majority identified with the
All-India Muslim League, which was the spiritual progeny of the
Aligarh Movement. Sixteen years after the official termination of
the Ottoman Caliphate in 1924, the All-India Muslim League
passed the "Pakistan Resolution" in Lahore, demanding the partition of India.

Sir Sayyid's Image of Democracy

Sir Sayyid was an enthusiastic admirer of western civilization as
represented by Britain. His exuberant language often misleads
scholars into thinking that he was slavish in his adulation. A critical analysis of his works shows that his political thought includes a blend of the west with traditional Islam. During his stay
in London Sir Sayyid corresponded with a noted Briton, freely
expressing his views on constitutional matters.

"A popularly elected President," declared Sir Sayyid, "is
preferred by Islam. A degree of radicalism is preached by my
religion, and it does not tolerate personl rule, not even the limited monarchy is acceptable; hereditary monarchy is altogether
rejected. Sir Sayyid also expressed egalitarian views regarding the
ownership of the means of production, saying that

The founder of Islam did not favour the concentration of wealth in a
few hands. For this reason the Prophet enacted the law of inheritance
which emphasizes the equal distribution of the real estate among heirs.
Because no matter how large an estate, it would dwindle to smaller
fragments in one or two generations, thus effectively preventing the ac-
cumulation of wealth in a few families.[25]

It should not be understood that his egalitarian views were in any way influenced by Marxism. In fact the economic conditions of Europe, against which the socialists were protesting, were lauded by him in his travelogue.[26]

(a) *Supremacy of Law:* Sir Sayyid's belief in the necessity of an impartial and supreme law is the key to his image of democracy. He rejected the British monarchy but looked upon the British regard for the impartiality and supremacy of law as the acme of civilized administration. "Queen Empress Victoria of Great Britain, Ireland, and India," asserted Sir Sayyid, "is the sovereign of law; her will does not constitute law and she is helpless to do anything at her personal discretion. The Viceroy of India is responsible more to the Queen's ministers and the British Parliament and the people than to Queen Victoria herself." Sir Sayyid pointed out that the Viceroy of India was likewise bound by law in his position, and was subject to recall by the British Cabinet and Parliament. If he is guilty of malfeasance, the way Warren Hastings was, British people are "louder in raising their critical voice" than the indigenous people. Hastings was impeached in the British Parliament and his services were not appreciated until the clouds of doubt regarding his integrity were removed. He then compared the British regard for law with that of the Mughals. "The Mughal king was an autocrat," he said, "his will commanded the statutes of law and he was responsible to no one. There was no parliament in Mughal India, although the court was held daily where the ministers and nobles outdid each other in tailoring their opinions to suit the will of the sovereign."[27]

From the reign of Akbar (1556–1605) to that of Aurangzeb (1659–1707) the prerogatives of the *'ulamā'* were withdrawn, although in pre-Mughal times the Shari'a was respected. In theory and practice the Mughal king could disregard law and justice. Capital punishment could be executed at his will, and the offenders' wives and children could be sold into slavery. A hereditary nobility which might have protested against the excesses of the sovereign did not exist. "The British Government was also despotic," commented Sir Sayyid, "but the rule of law was its ideal, both for the people of Europe and Asia." He congratulated his countrymen for having acquired the privilege of being ruled by a responsible government of law.[28]

(b) *Separation of Religious and Secular Affairs:* Although Sir Sayyid never openly questioned the supremacy of the *Shari'a,* he nevertheless advocated separation between matters religious and political. "It is the duty of a government," he declared, "to protect the rights of the citizens pertaining to their private ownership, professions, and ways of earning a livelihood and freedom of religion and opinion, nor should it weaken any of them with state powers. It must shield the deserving weak against the undeserving powerful citizens. All citizens must enjoy the fruits of their talents." In a civilized state, he reasoned, "the Government itself, like her citizens, both high and low, should be equally subject to the laws, and the laws should protect with equal impartiality the rights of all citizens (regardless of their race, colour or creed)." He indicted the contemporary Muslim states, "because they do not distinguish between religion and religious injunctions. They believe that secular affairs cannot be settled unless religion sanctions them, and even secular problems cannot be solved in new ways.[29]

Sir Sayyid believed that "religion" intruded to a ludicrous extent in the administration of Muslim states. Can Muslim soldiers, from the religious standpoint, wear tight-fitting uniforms and use a certain type of bazooka; would the use of railroads be allowed by religion? He pointed out that such questions plague the Muslim mind. The enmeshing of religion and state, in his view, was mainly responsible for the political unrest and insurrection of non-Muslim nationalities in the contemporary Ottoman Empire. "Spiritual or religious matters," he asserted, "cannot have any connection with worldly affairs. A true religion only states cardinal principles comprising ethical values and only incidentally deals with the problems of the world. Islam, as a true religion, is based upon this dichotomy and the Prophet upheld this distinction in his well-known statement: *"Ma ata kūm min amer-i dīnakum fakhazū wa ma naha kum 'inah fa-antahū."* "In all religious matters accept divine injunctions and refrain from those actions which are forbidden."

He believed that the principle of separation of church and state was followed by the four orthodox Caliphs but was gradually abandoned by Muslims to their own detriment. He criticized the religious zealots who interpreted all aspects of life in the light of religion. This enveloping tendency led the *'ulamā'* to formulate four schools of *Fiqh,* which have become the infallible dogma of Islam in the eyes of the common man. To him this development was not an unmixed blessing because it gave rise to four serious problems within the body-politic of Islam: (1) Islam was accepted as relating to all secular problems; (2) the *'ulamā'*'s personal *ijtihād* and *qiyās* was elevated to the status of dogma; (3) in modern times criticism of the four schools of *Fiqh* is tantamount to opposition to Islam; and (4) the *'ulamā'* deny the need for new legislation to cope with contemporary conditions.[30]

Sir Sayyid believed that since the Caliphate degenerated into a hereditary monarchy, Muslim governments ceased to be subject to the sovereignty of Islamic law. He considered the extreme intrusion of religion into secular affairs as the overriding factor in the lack of national progress among the Muslims.

Sir Sayyid analyzed the history of other civilizations in order to uncover the factors which are associated with progress. His studies led him to believe that progress had many dimensions; the most important of these were individual striving, inspired by love of nation and unhampered by governmental intervention, and exposure to other civilizations and the diffusion of new elements of culture.

Aristocratic Nationalism

Sir Sayyid, despite the democratic consequences of his movement, was an aristocratic democrat, and his nationalism was essentially based upon an enlightened conception of *noblesse oblige.* He encouraged understanding and solidarity between the lower and upper strata of Muslim society, but by no means desired to eliminate class differentiation. An enlightened bourgeoisie, in his view, created the political and intellectual climate in society which enabled the lower classes to lead a relatively prosperous and contented life and to make their contribution to the national progress. This hierarchical view of society which was the hall-mark of eighteenth- and nineteenth-century capitalistic Europe, blended harmoniously with the aristocratic background of Sir Sayyid.

It is, therefore, not surprising that his movement aimed pri-marily at uplifting the Muslim bourgeoisie, and he by and large sought their help. Muslim aristocrats were his advisers and co-workers and the common man was the follower. While Sir Sayyid was never indifferent to the plight of the impoverished Muslim masses, he lamented most the degradation of the aristo-crats. These aristocrats were essentially the heirs of the decadent Mughal nobility; former *mansabdars* (men of rank), including the descendants of well-known *qadis* (judges), *muftis* (jurists), scholars, and poets. They constituted the core of traditional Mus-lim aristocracy. Referring to their economic and cultural back-wardness, Sir Sayyid maintained that "if their noble families dis-appeared from India and the *nouveau riche* replaced them, India would eventually suffer and be deprived of enduring prestige."[31] Their conditions, however, could not improve unless they rea-lized their precarious position.

I have met the grandson of Insha Allah Khan[32]—who insisted that he was Insha's grandson—but one could never believe, just looking at him, that he was the grandson of an illustrious man. Also, I have known princes of the royal blood, whose only insignia of royalty was that their sole occupation was the training of partridges for fight and pigeons to obey their whistles. This Muslim nationality (*qawm*) de-served to be destroyed—God forbid that such men should have ruled over us. (We could not have lived like human beings.) If this be the condition of our princes, then one can easily imagine the condition of the Muslim masses.[33]

This concern for Muslim aristocracy is reflected in Sir Sayyid's political and educational endeavors. In order to preserve the estates of the aristocracy Sir Sayyid published in the *Tahdhīb al-Akhlāq* the draft of a bill, *Islami wakf l-awalad* (Islamic family endowment), which he intended to introduce in the Viceroy's Legislative Council if sufficient support was obtained. The intent of the bill was to make family estates inalienable. The bill contained 33 clauses and Sir Sayyid visualized the following advantages likely to accrue to the Muslim aristocracy. (1) Muslim estates would not suffer fragmentation, and would remain in perpetuity with the descendants of the *wākif* (who made the family endowment). (2) The proposed bill would equally benefit sunni and *shi'a* families. (3) With family property preserved in perpetuity, the succeeding generation would learn to maintain a fitting standard of living on assured incomes.[34]

Sir Sayyid did not seem to realize that the family endowments would also have other results. Instead of providing incentives for progress, unearned income might smother industry and eventually breed lethargy and further degeneration among the scions of aristocracy. In addition to the idea of family endowments, Sir Sayyid published several schemes for improving the fortunes of rich families. "In India," Sir Sayyid maintained, "people with exalted status set examples of good conduct, because the common man looks up to them." The rich were under the dual obligation of undertaking social reforms and simultaneously increasing their wealth in order to augment their prestige among the people.

Consequently, he suggested five steps to accomplish these ends: (1) On agricultural estates, irrigation canals and roads were to be constructed. If small landlords were unable to defray their expenses, they should form cooperative associations and ensure that fallow land is brought under cultivation. (2) Landlords should obtain a charter from the Government to establish a private agricultural institution.[35] This was a common practice among English landlords, Sir Sayyid pointed out, and deserved to be emulated. (3) English landlords, on their own initiative, hired engineers, geologists, and other technicians to survey the mineral wealth hidden under their lands. They discovered this wealth and then exploited it to their advantage. Why could not the Muslim and even Hindu landlords do the same? (4) In Australia colonists used their imagination and skill in breeding wool-bearing sheep and imported the best quality sheep from abroad. Why could not rich men of India (for example, the Maharaja of Bardawan and the Raja of Patialia) follow their example? (5) Lastly, Sir Sayyid advised the aristocrats to invest their wealth in establishing modern industries. The possibilities of international trade could also be exploited by them for their enrichment.[36]

Concept of a Nation

Like Bolingbroke, Sir Sayyid regarded nationalism as the most natural and reasonable means not only of safeguarding Muslim national interests but also of achieving amiable relations with the Hindus. His attitude towards the Hindus, for the purpose of conceptual analysis, can be divided into two unequal periods: (a) from 1857 to 1884, and (b) from 1885 to 1898.

First Phase. In describing the peoples of India (including both the Hindus and the Muslims) as a nation he again used the word *qawm*, which in his terminology also connoted a nationality. Sir Sayyid maintained that

the word *qawm* is used for the citizens of a country. Various peoples of Afghanistan are considered a *qawm* (nation), and different peoples of Iran are known as Iranis. Europeans profess different religions and believe in different ideas, yet they are all members of a single nation. In a nutshell, since the olden times the word *qawm* (nation) is used for the inhabitants of a country, even though they have characteristics of their own.[37]

Sir Sayyid reiterated the same view in numerous speeches which he delivered before mixed audiences. In 1884, replying to a welcome address presented by the Indian Association of Lahore (whose President was Sardar Dayal Singh), Sir Sayyid said:

By the word *qawm*, I mean both Hindus and Muslims. That is the way in which I define the word nation(*qawm*). In my opinion, it matters not whatever be their religious belief, because we cannot see anything of it;

but what we see is that all of us, whether Hindus or Muslims, live on one soil, are governed by one and the same ruler, have the same sources of our benefits, and equally share the hardships of a famine. These are the various reasons why I designate both the nationalities that inhabit India by the term "Hindu"—that is, the nation (*qawm*) which lives in India.[38]

In emphasizing the factor of common territory, equally shared by the Hindus and the Muslims, Sir Sayyid posed rhetorical questions: "O! ye Hindus and Muslims! Do you live in any country other than India? Don't you get cremated on or buried under the same sod? If you do, then remember Hindu and Muslim are merely religious terms—the Hindus, the Muslims, and even the Christians constitute one nation by virtue of living in the same country."[39] The common territory, in the eyes of Sir Sayyid, thus imposed upon all inhabitants of India the obligation of mutual cooperation and unity in order to ensure the common good.

Reiterating the concept of an Indian *qawm* (nation) Sir Sayyid made the famous statement:

I have said it many times and I say it again that India is like a beautiful bride blessed by two attractive eyes—the Hindus and the Muslims. If they maintain enmity or hypocritical (*nifāq*) relations with each other, [the bride] will look one-eyed. So! Inhabitants of India, do as you will—make this bride crosseyed or one-eyed [or preserve both her eyes].[40]

The theme of Hindu-Muslim cooperation permeated his messages until 1885. This, however, does not mean that he was not subjected to any strains by the resurgence of Hindu nationalism, embodied especially in the form of the Arya Samaj, Bharata Warsha National Association, Tilak's Shivaji festivals, and the formation of various anti-cow-killing societies. None of these developments stirred him so deeply as the question of an official language for India. In 1867 the Hindus started to press for the use of Hindi in place of Urdu in the courts. Hindu *sabhas* (associations) sprang up in Benares and elsewhere in India with a central office in Allahabad to promote the adoption of Hindi as the official language of India. Sir Sayyid argued that Urdu, although it developed during the period of Muslim rule, was a product of Hindu-Muslim intercourse and was widely spoken in India by Hindus and Muslims.

Commenting on the demand of the Hindus for the adoption of Hindi, Sir Sayyid wrote from London on 29 April 1870 to his collaborator and friend, Mahdi Ali Khan:

I understand . . . Hindus are roused to destroy the Muslims' [cultural] symbol embodied in the Urdu language and the Persian script. I have heard that they have made representation through the Hindu members of the Scientific Society[41] that the Society's *Akhbār* [Journal] should be published in the Devanagari rather than in the Persian script, and that all translations of [foreign language] books should likewise be in Hindi. This proposal would destroy cooperation between the Hindus and the Muslims. Muslims would never accept Hindi and if Hindus persistently demanded the adoption of Hindi in preference to Urdu it would result in the total separation of the Muslims from the Hindus.[42]

This foreboding, so forcefully but privately stated, occurred 15 years before the creation of the All-India National Congress. Publicly Sir Sayyid maintained cordial personal relations with the Hindus and continued to encourage a Hindu-Muslim entente in educational and cultural matters. However, during his stay in London he came to believe that the separation of Muslims from Hindus might be beneficial for the Muslims. He expressed this view in no uncertain terms to Mahdi Ali Khan in his letter of 1870:

If, after separating from the Hindus, the Muslims were to establish their own businesses Muslims would benefit more than the Hindus. The Hindus would be the losers. Two factors in this regard I take into consideration—my personal propensity of wishing well for all the peoples of India, be they Hindu or Muslim. Secondly, I fear . . . that Muslims certainly do not rationally evaluate their loss (as well as their gain). They are jealous and vindictive and engage in vanity more than the Hindus; they are poorer too and for these reasons they are not capable of doing anything constructive for self-help.[43]

Implicit in this letter is an assertion that in the balance, cooperation with the Hindus was not altogether without benefit to the Muslims. This indeed was true; Hindus made sizable contributions to the construction fund of the Muhammadan Anglo-Oriental College at Aligarh, and extended a measure of cooperation to his educational policy.

Sir Sayyid's endeavours on behalf of the Muslim *literati* in securing government jobs were another source of friction between his movement and Hindu leadership, especially that of the Arya Samaj. In 1882 the National Muhammadan Association under Sir Sayyid's guidance had sent a memorandum to the British Viceroy, Lord Rippon, soliciting two special considerations for the Muslims in governmental appointments because they were grossly underrepresented in all echelons of the British administration.[44] (1) In appointing Muslims to Government positions, especially in the judiciary, the requirement of a university degree (such as Bachelor of Law from Calcutta University) should be waived. They should be given comparable tests instead of having a strict degree requirement.[45] (2) Since Muslim parents were generally impoverished and were often compelled by penury to withdraw their children from school, the Government should make special arrangements for their education.

The British Government was not receptive to these suggestions; consequently, in 1883 Sir Sayyid created the Muhammadan Civil Service Fund Association to train young Muslims of 19 in England with a view to their eventually entering the Indian Civil Service (I.C.S.), or obtaining medical, engineering, and law degrees from British universities. Sir Sayyid had hoped that at least 500 generous Muslims would agree to donate Rs. 2 monthly, raising the annual total to Rs. 12,000. Only 299 members joined the Association who donated Rs. 2 monthly for some time and thus Rs. 4,000 were raised. After some time, however, these contributions stopped altogether and the Association became defunct. This stillborn venture, nevertheless, created suspicions among, and demands from, the Arya Samaj leaders who indicated that if Sir Sayyid were truly a patriot he would not exclude Hindus from his beneficial plans.[46]

In addition to other political developments in the country the failure of the Civil Service Fund Association probably stimulated Sir Sayyid to found the Muhammadan Educational Congress in 1886. To a very large extent the Muhammadan Educational Congress operated as a rival of the All-India National Congress (which had come into existence in 1885) even though Sir Sayyid substituted the word *Conference* for *Congress* in 1890 to lessen the impression of rivalry between the two organizations.[47]

Second Phase. Sir Sayyid's policy towards the All-India National Congress has become a moot point. Indian nationalists (particularly the vocal section of Indian Muslims) attributed Sir Sayyid's opposition to Congress as "senility" and an indication of the influence over his thinking wielded by Mr. Theodore Beck, Principal of the Muhammadan Anglo-Oriental College.

Sayyid Tufayl Ahmad Manglorī, writing during the 1940s and relying exclusively upon the undocumented testimony of Mir Waliyat Husain (a one-time associate of Sir Sayyid) has stated that Beck wanted to accomplish three things: "He wanted to turn Sir Sayyid away from the Bengalis;[48] isolate him from the national political movement (i.e., the All-India National Congress) and eliminate Mawlavi Sami'y Allah Khan, who was an influential confidant of Sir Sayyid."[49] In order to achieve these aims, according to Manglorī, Beck succeeded in gaining full control of *The Institute Gazette* and thus "started writing editorials in *The Institute Gazette,* which were in opposition to the Bengalis and their movement (the Congress); however, these editorials were attributed to Sir Sayyid. This started an open fight with the Bengalis since they started to publish derogatory statements about Sir Sayyid."[50] Manglorī also stated that because of his opposition to the Congress, especially after the Lucknow (1887) Session of the Muhammadan Anglo-Oriental Education Conference, the British Government knighted Sir Sayyid.

Repeating almost verbatim the accusations of Manglorī, Dr. Abid Husain made in 1965 an intemperate attack on Sir Sayyid's policy regarding the Congress, saying: "The Mohammadan Defense Association[51] was the sickly child of Sir Sayyid's old age and expired in 1900 with the death of Beck, but the seed of communalism which had been sown was to sprout six years later in the form of the Muslim League."[52]

These accusations obviously belittle Sir Sayyid's independent judgement. Sir Sayyid was a cautious Muslim leader, but to accuse him of being a satellite thinker is an extreme example of partisan injustice. In order realistically to evaluate Sir Sayyid's role one must understand his fundamental convictions about British rule in India. Sir Sayyid believed that sovereignty was established by blood and tears, and that the conqueror enjoyed this capability as a gift of God. This gift was not reserved for a particular nation; indeed different nations shared in this divine blessing during different epochs in history. The sovereign guarantees peace and public tranquillity, and thus creates a favorable social milieu for national progress.

The British rule was viewed as being there to stay, and the Indians certainly did not have the capacity to crush it. In fact Sir Sayyid believed that "in order to make all-round progress the British rule in India was indispensable for a long time—if not forever."[53] In retrospect, this appears to be a very conservative, if not reactionary statement. However, when one examines the views held by most Indian leaders of the period, the statement assumes a different cast. On the eve of the Boer War (1899–1902) Mahatma Gandhi declared that "my loyalty to the British rule drove me to participation with the British in that war. I felt that, if I demanded rights as a British citizen, it was also my duty, as such, to participate in the defense of the British Empire. I held then that India could achieve her complete emancipation only within and through the British Empire."[54] While in India at the time of World War I, Mahatma Gandhi campaigned for the British Government to enlist young Indians in the British Army. Explaining his reasons for this he wrote a letter to the British Viceroy, climaxing his arguments with the declaration that "I love the English nation, and I wish to evoke in every Indian the loyalty of Englishmen."[55]

In the nineteenth century, especially after the British triumph in 1857, Sir Sayyid could see the British rule in India as an immutable factor of history. He believed that with the passage of time the severity of the British rule, and especially their racial exclusiveness, would mellow and perhaps disappear altogether. Did not the Muslim rule during the period of the Delhi Sultanate remain exclusive of the Hindus? The situation changed, Sir Sayyid reasoned, with the advent of the Mughals. He believed that no conqueror ever established a representative government in a colony. Colonial government organized representatively was a contradiction in terms.[56]

In his view a representative government could be organized only in a national state. Therefore a demand for a representative government in India in the immediate or distant future amounted to Sir Sayyid as a demand for the withdrawal of British rule. Political agitation (no matter how restrained or sedate) for a representative government, filled him with a fear of British retaliation especially against the Muslims, who were already branded as the chief culprits of the Indian mutiny. This fear, perhaps exaggerated, was one salient factor of his opposition to the Congress. The record shows that for three years after the founding (1885) of the Congress, Sir Sayyid maintained complete silence about its activities. It was only in December 1887, when the third annual session of the Congress was held at Madras with increased participation of southern Muslims, that Sir Sayyid denounced the Congress.

Despite Sir Sayyid's expressions of solidarity with the Hindus and his serious attempts to develop an enduring relationship with them, especially in educational and cultural matters, he did not believe they could coexist politically and share equally the sovereignty of India after the hypothetical British withdrawal. He believed that their withdrawal would create a vacuum of power, ensuring a struggle for hegemony between the two contenders—Hindus and Muslims. This would be retrogressive and disruptive of the political climate in India, which Sir Sayyid viewed as favorable to the educational and cultural progress of the Muslims. For this reason he believed "even if I were appointed the Viceroy of India, I would endeavor just as well to strengthen the rule of Queen-Empress in India."[57]

To keep the British sovereignty beyond public account-ability, he suggested that the annual budget, containing fun-damental policies regarding the defense forces and the sovereign's foreign relations, should not be subjected to public debate. In emphasizing this point, Sir Sayyid ridiculed the Bengali leaders of the Congress, saying "How can a Bengali, who never saw the face of a gun and never participated in a battle, advise the Gov-ernment?"[58]

Sir Sayyid also opposed the Congress' demands for the in-troduction of an election in the Viceroy's Legislative Council, and a competitive examination for the covenanted services to be held in India. Examined from the Hindu viewpoint, these two positions appear unprogressive, but Sir Sayyid viewed them from the angle of a Muslim nationalist—whether or not the Con-gress' demands were conducive to furthering Muslim nationalist interests. Relatively backward in acquiring English education, Muslim youth were not yet prepared during the last two decades of the nineteenth century to compete with the Hindus. For a country like India, where cultural and religious heterogeneity was the rule, competitive examination, Sir Sayyid believed, would introduce elements of tension in the administration. Com-petition would open the doors to "low-class" men to achieve high positions. This would be resented by the Indian upper classes. Neither did he believe that "low-class" English bureau-crats were useful to India and her Government. "Only the high-class Englishmen establish the prestige of the British people and their government in the hearts of [the Indians]; they also treat the Indian landlords courteously and maintain gentle relations with them."[59] In his class consciousness Sir Sayyid was a typical Vic-torian Moghul, and in soliciting the help of the traditional Mus-lim bourgeoisie he used arguments which he thought were most appropriate. However, the crux of his argument, was that com-petition could be recommended in a binational state, if relative equality of education and culture was available, but that was not so in India.

On substantially similar ground Sir Sayyid opposed in December 1887 the one-man one-vote principle of election for the Viceroy's Legislative Council. He said:

The demand of the National Congress is that the people should elect a section of the Viceroy's Council. They want to copy the English House of Lords and House of Commons. Now let us suppose that we have universal suffrage, as in America, and that all have votes. And let us first suppose that all Muslim voters vote for a Muslim member and that all Hindu voters for a Hindu member and now count how many votes the Muslim member will have and how many the Hindu. We can prove by simple arithmetic that there will be four votes for the Hindu to every one for the Muslim. Now how can the Muslim guard his interests? It will be like a game of dice in which one man had four dice and the other only one.[60]

Instead of joint election on the principle of one-man one-vote, Sir Sayyid favoured proportional representation of both the Hindus and the Muslim. "In direct proportion to census, Muslim and Hindu members should be appointed; consequently, we will have one vote and [the Hindus] will have four. There is no other method of equitable representation."[61] After Sir Sayyid's death Muslim leaders succeeded in obtaining a guarantee from the British Government of separate or national representation, which is generally called by the Indian nationalists "communal representation."

The fundamental questions are: were separate electorates the sole cause of the evolution of a separate Muslim nationalism; was the principle of separate electorates discreetly created by the British for their own purposes or was it an independent demand of a nationality apprehensive of its own political future? The habit of Indian nationalists to view the history of the last one hundred years in the light of the divide and rule policy of the British, has led them to a blind alley, where frustration abounds and the issues of Hindu-Muslim relations are further obfuscated. Sir Sayyid was unquestionably pro-British, but he was by no means a British tool who would betray the interests of his own nation to please the ruler. Neither was he completely an autocrat. Theoretically he remained a democrat,[62] although political issues at times placed him in seemingly undemocratic positions. In judging his policies one must constantly remind oneself that Sir Sayyid was a Muslim nationalist first, and an Indian second, and he saw no contradiction between these two orientations.

7

Religious Modernism

INDIC ISLAMIC CULTURE, despite some violent reactions against the infusion of certain modern elements within its fold, continuously accommodated itself to the introduction of modern education, and a rational approach towards the Islamic convictions and social reforms. Regarding the latter, however, the *'ulamā'* made their contributions within the framework of traditional Islam and were not at all influenced by Western rationalism. The movement for the Islamic reformation was undertaken by Shah Waliy Allah (1703–1762), and developed by his followers, including Shah 'Abdul Aziz (1746–1831), Sayyid Ahmad Shahīd (1786–1831), and Mawlana Isma'īl Shahīd (d. 1831). Sir Sayyid, while he was deeply influenced by Shah Waliy Allah, and knew intimately the last three, adopted their rational approach to Islam; and particularly their view of the Muslims' social reforms.

Framework of Social Reforms

Muslim leadership in India, traditional as well as modern, has always been called upon to define Islamic culture and the limits of its interaction with Hindu culture. While Hindu culture has always been assimilative, Islam in the Indian cultural environment had to face the problem of preserving its distinct identity, which greater cultural relations with the Hindu society would progressively erode. Striking a balance between the two processes (i.e., cultural identity vs. cultural synthesis) has not been easy; and despite the creation of Pakistan in 1947 the problem for the Indic Muslims has remained unsolved.

To Shah Waliy Allah and his followers, Islamic culture was described in a simple paradigm: *sunna plus shari'a minus bida'a.* *Sunna* literally means "trodden path," and was understood by the pre-Islamic Arabs as the model behavior established by the founders of a tribe (*sunna al-umma*). Also, the term was later applied to the normative conduct (*sunna al-Nabiy*) of the Prophet Muhammad. The prophet's normative conduct, which reflected some of the pre-Islamic customs, established the primary norm of Islamic culture. The term *Shari'a,* literally the path to be followed, applied to the Canon law of Islam—the totality of Allah's commandments—and embraced all individual as well as social actions. Broadly speaking the *Shari'a* defined injunctions of five kinds. "Those strictly forbidden are *harām.* Between them are two middle categories, namely, things which you are advised to do (*mandūb*), and things about which religion is indifferent (*ja'iz*). . . . Thus the *Shari'a* is totalitarian; all human activity is embraced in its sovereign domain." *Bid'a,* or impious innovation, "is that which contravenes the Prophetic model [*sunna*]".[1]

This paradigm of Islamic culture is essentially ideal; the real culture of all Muslim societies including those of the Middle East falls short of this ideal considerably. Pre-Islamic cultural patterns have survived, although the traditional social reformers have attacked them as *bid'a* and urged the Muslims (both Arab and non-Arab) to discard them in favor of the *sunna.* In the Indian environment *bid'a* became a synonym for the Hindu folkways and mores which were retained by the converts, and because of them were diffused into Indic Muslim society. Consequently, for Shah Waliy Allah and his followers, Muslim social reforms led to the greater Islamization of the society. Islamization, as a sociological term, implied eschewing Hindu cultural patterns (the converse of which would lead to cultural assimilation with the Hindus) and adhering to those cultural values of the Arabs which were accepted and exemplified by the Prophet Muhammad as his *sunna*. Traditions and customs analogous to those of the Muslims in the Middle East were desired and valued, while customs reflecting a Hindu coloring were positively discouraged and disdained. Islamization as a process of Muslim social reform was always the obverse side of Muslim politics in India.

In his well-known last testament,[2] *Al-Maqālah al-Wadīya Fī al-Nasīhah Wa al-Wasīya*, Shah Waliy Allah established the guidelines for the process of Islamization in the Hindu cultural milieu of India. In the seventh precept, he said:

(a) Muslims should not "abandon the customs and mores of the early Arabs, because they were the immediate followers of the Prophet Muhammad."

(b) Muslims "must not adopt the mores of the Hindus, or those of the people of *ajam*"—countries beyond Arabia.

He also highlighted the Muslims' marriage and funeral customs, which come under the category of *bid'a*. (1) "One of the reprehensible mores of the Hindus is their prohibition of a second marriage for widows. This was not a tradition among the Arabs, neither during the *jahiliyah* (pre-Islamic) period nor after the advent of the Prophet Muhammad. May God bless him who would put an end to this [Hindu custom]." (2) Regarding the Muslim marriage, he stated: "One of the reprehensible habits of our people is that in the marriage contract an excessive dower is fixed. The Prophet Muhammad, on account of whom we are honored in religion and in this world, fixed for his spouses a dower, the value of which amounted to 500 dirhams." (3) "Another undesirable custom among our people is the incurring of unnecessary and exhorbitant expense on occasions of happiness. The Prophet fixed only two ceremonies [on the occasions of marriage and birth], that of *Walīyma*[3] and *'Aqīqah;*[4] only these two should be observed, and all others should be discarded."

Shah Waliy Allah also criticized Muslims' funeral ceremonies. (4) "We are also spendthrifts about funeral ceremonies. We have invented *Saywam* (third day), *Chelum* (fortieth day), *Shash Mahiy* (six monthly), and then *Salana* (annual) days of mourning, and the offering of prayers for the deceased. None of these customs existed among the ancient Arabs. The messages of condolence should be extended in the first three days and the family of the deceased should be treated to only three dinners. No other custom should be followed. After three days the women of the clan should get together and apply perfume to the garments of the deceased's female heirs. If the widow is involved then she should observe mourning during the *'iddā* [i.e., the waiting period of four months and ten days, or if the widow is pregnant, till delivery, whichever is longer]; after this period she should wear mourning dress no more."

Shah Waliy Allah also extended the concept of *bid'a* to the mystical practices of the Indian Sufis (mystics). (5) "One should not become a disciple of contemporary Sufis, because they are engaged in varieties of *bid'a* (impious innovations)." He described them as miracle-mongers, who preached "annihilation in God" and considered the injunctions of *Shari'a* merely as a man's confession of his inability "to pursue annihilation in and eternity with God." This preoccupation of some Muslims "in the domains of annihilation and eternity, and the mystical practices" appeared to Shah Waliy Allah as causing a deep malaise among the Indic Muslims.[5]

Sayyid Ahmad Shahīd and his followers produced a prodigious amount of literature on Muslim social reforms both in prose and verse. Their simple and direct style of Urdu prose deviated for the first time in the history of Urdu literature from the formal and verbose model of Abul Fadl's Persian prose. This style was cultivated by Sir Sayyid, and it also became the accepted model of Urdu journalism during the nineteenth century. The traditional social reformers' works can be divided into two categories: (a) the works of Shahīd and that of his close associates, which were designed mainly for the literate stratum of the Muslim society; and (b) the tracts which were written either in prose or verse by Shahīd's itinerant preachers. They explained social reforms in simplistic terms appealing more to emotions than to reason. They attacked *bid'a,* which Muslims innovated themselves, and the ones they adopted or retained from the Hindu culture. Some of the more popular tracts were: *Nasīyhat al-Muslimīyn* (advice to Muslims) by Khurram Ali; *Hidayat al-Muminiyn wa Sawalat Asharat al-Muharram* (guidance for believers and questions about the ten days of Muharram) by Hasan Qanawji; *Manajīy al-Muslimīyn* (deliverer of the Muslims) by Qadi Muhammad Husain; and *Hujjat-i Qati'h* (cutting proof) by Karamat Ali Jawnpuriy. Written primarily from 1854 to 1868, they were published in Lahore, Delhi, Lucknow, and Calcutta.

Rigidly sectarian in their approach, the traditional social reformers attacked the *Shi'ite* traditions as vehemently as they attacked the Hindu customs. To Hasan Qanawjiy, Islam was corrupted by *bid'a* during the Umayyad Caliphate (661–749) because the converts who secretly cherished their pre-Islamic customs diffused them into Muslim society. This process ultimately weakened Islam, especially in India where "Muslims profess the faith, and also worship idols. They adorn the tombs with Lingams upon them. Pirzadahs and Majawers (spiritual guides and tombs' custodians), while receiving offerings from their followers, shout: *Gangaji key jay* or *Rama Mahadev.* These 'Muslims' visit Mathura, Benares, Ajmer, and Makanpur as if they are on a pilgrimate [to Mecca]. They observe a thousand other idolatrous customs." Also, *shi'a* ceremonies on Muharram celebrating the martyrdom of al-Husain (October 10, 680), the grandson of the Prophet Muhammad, were described as impious innovations. "In what place God or the Prophet stated that after Imam Husain was martyred a mourning procession or *ta'zīyah* should be taken out annually?" The usage, according to Qanawjiy was neither sanctioned by the Qur'ān nor by common sense; the Muharram passion play was merely a show, which unfortunately terminated fatally especially in Lucknow, and other cities of India. Khurram Ali, Qadi Muhammad Husain, and Karamat Ali Jawnpuriy covered much the same ground with varying emphasis on different un-Islamic customs, while Jawnpuriy lamented the fate of Islam

in Bengal where even books on Islam were not available except
in large towns.

The poems on social reforms were simple and provocative,
and equally offensive to the Shi'ites. *Mazhar al-Haq,* a Persian
poem composed during Emperor Aurangzeb 'Alamgīr's reign
(1658–1707), was popularized by Shahīd's itinerant reformers.
Qadi Muhammad Husain published it as an appendix to his tract,
Manajīy al-Muslimīyn, published in 1877 in Lahore with a prefatory remark that the poem was designed to expose superstitions
and corrupt practices of the Muslims during 'Alamgīr's time, but
that they have survived and deserve to be condemned again:

> For their child parents become infidels;
> To preserve him from the small-pox they worship idols.
> Scholars too are profligate, encumbering weddings with expenses
> and impious innovations.

The poem *Rah-i Sunnat* (the way of the sunna) by Mawlavi
Awlād Hasan, first published in 1868 in Bombay, attacked the
ceremonies on the Prophet's birthday, the mourning of al-Husain
in Muharram, and condemned overt loyalty to the British Government. Consisting of 256 quatrains, and written diagonally in
frames with a horizontal line under each, an Urdu poem, *Haraq
al-Ashrār* (burner of the wicked), delivered stern warnings of
divine wrath against the worshippers of adorned sepulchres, the
deceits of *pīrs,* and the adoption of Hindu cultural patterns. Finally, *Risalah Radd-i Shirk* (elimination of idolatry) and *Risalah
Jihādiyah* (treatise on war) invoked Allah's aid against superstitious and deviant Muslims, whose "idolatry cannot be removed
except by the sword."

> Religion of Islam is on the decline
> Domination of infidelity is ruining Islam.
> Had our forefathers not waged jihad,
> India would have not flourished with Islam.
> The power of sword ensured the domination of Muslims,
> Had our forefathers been idle, what would have happened to
> Islam.

Shahīd did not write any book himself, but his *malfūzat* (epistles) dealing with religious and social reforms were collected by Mawlana Isma'īl Shahīd and Mawlana 'Abd al-Haīy in *Sirāt al-Mustaqīym* (The Straight Path) and further amplified by Isma'īl Shahīd in *Taqīya al-Iman Wa Tadhkīyr al-Akhwān* (Strengthening of the Faith & Admonition to the Brothers). *Sirat al-Mustaqīym* divided *bid'a* into three categories: (a) the innovations which sprung from Muslims' association with the *mushrikīyn*, those who identify any animate or inanimate object with God, but appeared like genuine sufis; (b) those innovations which have developed by association with the Sh'ites; (c) and those corrupt and impious innovations which spread among the common people by virtue of their contacts with the Hindus. Under these categories Shahīd and his followers not only reiterated five kinds of impious innovations, which Shah Waliy Allah had enumerated, but added quite a few of their own determination. Shahīd's message was summed up in a comprehensive exhortation: "Follow the example of Muhammad of Arabia and relinquish all the customs of India, Iran and Rome." [6]

Sir Sayyid had accepted Shah Waliy Allah, and Sayyid Ahmad Shahīd and his associates' framework of Muslim social reforms. However, he added a new dimension to the concept of *bid'a* in urging Muslims that in secular matters where Islam was "indifferent," modern Western ways could be legitimately adopted; while he continued to highlight the imperative of eliminating Hindu customs from the Muslim culture. In his general approach to maintaining the Muslims' solidarity, Sir Sayyid deemphasized shi'a-sunni differences and appealed to both sects to reform their cultural patterns. While Shahīd's polemics with the shi'ites had sharpened antagonism, and weakened his movement considerably, Sir Sayyid's liberal approach forged cohesiveness among the shi'a and the sunni, making them effective partners in their cultural and political struggles. In a nutshell, Sir Sayyid's paradigm of the Muslim social reforms included: Islamization plus modernization. (The repercussions of this dynamic process are visible today in Pakistan as well as among the Muslims in India.)

Paradigm of Social Reforms

Sir Sayyid owed his social reforms paradigm partly to Mill, Addison, and Steele. On the *Tatler* and the *Spectator* was modelled his monthly journal, *Tahdhīb al-Akhlāq*. First issued in 1870, the *Tahdhīb al Akhlāq*'s publication was suspended in 1876 for two years, only to reappear on the public's insistent demand in 1878. Surviving for two years and five months during his second phase of its life, the *Tahdhīb* appeared the third time in 1893, and finally disappeared after three years.[7] What were the aims and objects of the *Tahdhīb al-Akhlāq?* An article in the first issue of December 24, 1870, with this rhetorical question as its title enumerated the aims: (1) inducing the Muslims to accept modern civilization; (2) presenting Islam as a stimulus to civilization's progress; (3) popularizing natural sciences among the Muslims, (4) eliminating from Muslim society the un-Islamic folkways and mores of the Hindus and the religious superstitions of the Jews and the Roman Catholics, and (5) reforming the Muslims' manners and Urdu literature, especially poetry, in Steele and Addison's tradition.[8]

To achieve these goals, Sir Sayyid developed in 1870 an elaborate paradigm of cultural change for the Muslims. He recommended that some of their mores which had been influenced by contact with the Hindus be replaced by the Middle Eastern Islamic customs and selective Western manners. Also he urged the Muslims to adopt a Western orientation stressing science and secular education.

Paradigm for Social and Cultural Change:[9]
    (I) *Family and Social Customs*
        1. Elimination of polygamy.
        2. Removal of Hindu influences from funeral and marriage ceremonies.
        3. Emancipation of women.
        4. Adoption of European table manners.
        5. Cultivation of polite manners—in the Western sense.
    (II) *Improving the image of the Muslim Nation*
        1. Efficient utilization of time.
        2. Elimination of lavish conspicuous consumption on social occasions.

     3. Promotion of a national—instead of an individual and selfish—outlook among the Muslims.

(III) *Property*
     1. Introduction of modern techniques of cultivation among Muslim peasants.
     2. Promotion of trade among Muslims.
     3. Utilization of Western technology.

(IV) *Education*
     1. Harmonization of religious and secular training.
     2. Propagation of Western science and technology.
     3. Traditional education in home economics for women.

(V) *Religion*
     1. Reformation of rituals.
     2. Discarding of irrational dogmas.
     3. Codification of definitive beliefs.

This paradigm for social and cultural change revealed Sir Sayyid's concern for a comprehensive transformation of the Muslim society. Utilizing the concept of diffusion (see chapter 5) he developed a theory of progress in which the salient strands of this paradigm occupied well-defined places. Initially the All-India Muhammadan Educational Congress adopted several resolutions at its annual meetings, which related to each strand of his social reform paradigm. However, in 1901 (three years after Sir Sayyid's death) the Educational Congress established a separate department to deal with social reform issues.[10] Consequently, this newly created Social Reforms Department's Secretary, Khawja Ghulam al-Thaqlain published several anthologies, by Sir Sayyid and his associates, of articles on social reforms, and established in 1903 a monthly journal, 'Aser-i Jadīd, to propagate Sir Sayyid's doctrines on social reform.[11]

Among the family and social customs, Sir Sayyid condemned polygamy the most, while he admitted that it was not too widespread among the Muslims. He believed that the Prophet Muhammad intended to gradually elminate it, but as a realist he did not ban it outright since the institution could be defended in terms of natural and social laws, and also as an established practice in Judaism and Christianity. Finally, Sir Sayyid relied on the *Qur'ān* to deduce his conclusion that the Prophet's real intent was to establish monogamous marriage among Muslims:

> If ye fear that ye shall not
> Be able to deal justly
> With the orphans,
> Marry women of your choice,
> Two, or three, or four;
> But if ye fear that ye shall not
> Be able to deal justly [with them],
> Then only one, of [a captive]
> That your right hands possess.
> That will be more suitable,
> To prevent you
> From doing injustice (IV:3)

Since the Qur'ān demands the impossible condition of showing equality in "material things as well as in affection and immaterial things" only monogamy was the real matrimonial option.[12]

Europeans, Sir Sayyid believed, had a very distorted view of Muslim women's status, but he conceded that their conditions could still be improved. Women could help improve the table manners, because when the more civilized people observed "our eating habits they were inclined to vomit with disgust." To civilize the Muslim's eating style, Sir Sayyid suggested that to eat with knives and forks would amount to emulating the prophetic *sunna,* since the Prophet Muhammad was known to have cut meat with a knife. To sit at the dinner table was an "acceptable innovation," amounting by no means to a *bid'a,* because the Muslims have adopted the practice of using pottery and eating from china dishes—a possibility unknown to the Prophet.[13]

Sir Sayyid acknowledged Mawlana Isma'īl Shahīd's pioneering reform movement which had very nearly succeeded in eliminating Hindu social influence from the Muslims' funeral and marriage ceremonies, but he lamented that some had remained. On occasions of happiness, Muslims squandered their meager resources most thoughtlessly. To demonstrate that family spending for prestige could be converted to national uplift, Sir Sayyid solemnized his grandson Ross Mas'ūd's (later the Vice-Chancellor of the Aligarh Muslim University) bi-ism Allah (confirmation) ceremony at the eighth annual session (1893) of the All-India Muhammadan Educational Congress. Instead of spending money lavishly to entertain his friends and relatives he offered Rs. 500 to the MAO College Fund, while his two devoted friends—Sayyid Mahdi Ali Khan and Raja Jaikishan Das—emulating him, pledged Rs.500 each to the College fund. To drive home the lesson he asked his audience a rhetorical question: "What would have been better—an expensive feast or donations to a national cause?" [14]

Sir Sayyid thought that the Muslim national dress could be improved by adopting the Western style. To encourage others by his personal "innovation" Sir Sayyid himself started wearing English trousers, a Turkish long-fitting coat, and a fez, and made this dress mandatory for the students at the Aligarh College. Between the East and the West the Turkish dress was a happy compromise, since he saw the Turks as the most westernized and advanced of all Muslim nations.

Muslims wasted their time to their collective detriment, and thus lost valuable hours which could be utilized for economic production. Sir Sayyid lamented especially the forced idleness of the landed aristocracy, whose members spent their time gambling, smoking, and drinking. The Muslim middle classes frittered their energy in jealousy and enmity which were generated largely by competition over women or agricultural land. Finally, Muslims, because of their bigoted attitudes, cheated themselves out of the potential benefits of learning from more advanced Western nations.

Generally, Muslims mismanaged their property. Farmers did not know the modern techniques of fertilizing and agricultural production, and they formed the most backward stratum of the society. Gentlemen farmers and peasants often sold or mortgaged their property to pay for the extravagantly celebrated marriages of their children or their parents' death ceremonies. At Lahore, the third annual session (1888) of the Educational Congress adopted a resolution providing for "a fraternal-punitive cess" against spendthrift farmers. Money thus recovered was to be spent on their children's education.[15] Trade, an index of national progress and civilization, was completely out of the Muslims' control. Muslims needed to learn the modern techniques of trade and business management. In fact, Sir Sayyid realized that cooperative national efforts were needed to encourage the Muslims' participation in trade and commerce.

To round off his paradigm, it might be added that he never intended to subordinate religious to secular education. To him, science and technology strengthened Islamic convictions since Islam was not dialectically opposed to reason. In fact, he expected modern education to be an ally of Islam—sustaining it with rationalist underpinning. However, Islam needed to be reinterpreted and updated in order to remove irrational accretions added by the Muslim theologians. Consequently, for analysis, Sir Sayyid's modernistic interpretations can be divided into three broad categories: (1) the Qur'ān and the Apostolic Traditions; (2) the demythologizing of Islam; and finally the emergence of (3) a modern orientation for Islam.

The Qur'ān and the Apostolic Traditions

Sir Sayyid was keenly aware of the need for *ijtihād* (the right of interpreting Islam) in modern times. On this subject he was deeply influenced by Shah Waliy Allah, who lived in Delhi during the decadent period of the Mogul Empire. Dr. Muhammad Iqbal rightly pointed out that the first Muslim in India to feel the "urge of a new spirit in him" was Shah Waliy Allah. He was convinced that Islam and the Muslims of India were entering upon a new and critical era in the eighteenth century. The spirit of Islam which had animated their forefathers was moribund. Muslims had generally accepted the concepts of the four schools of *fiqh* as final. Consequently, the circumstances under which these schools were founded had changed, but the laws remained the same. Shah Waliy Allah went back to the original sources of Islamic law, the *Qur'an* and *hadith*. He stressed a rational reinterpretation of Islamic thought to make it acceptable to the new age. He pointed out that Islam would not be understood by Muslims nor appreciated by others unless it was presented in a rational way.

This rational approach to religion which was so ardently advocated by Shah Waliy Allah won over Sir Sayyid. In his efforts to harmonize the laws of nature with Islam, he acquired the sobriquet of *Nechari* (naturist), but in his outlook he was no more of a naturist than the great *mujtahid* of India—Shah Waliy Allah.

Utilizing Shah Waliy Allah's approach to the Qur'ān's interpretation, Sir Sayyid differed with him only occasionally, and on matters of detail. For the study of the Qur'ān, Sir Sayyid adopted a rational approach, and then concluded: "I found that if the principles yielded by the Qur'ān were adopted there remained no opposition between the modern sciences and Islam." [16] Fifteen principles of the Qur'ānic exegesis established by him thus stood as a landmark, dividing the traditional from modern and rational Islam: (1) God is the creator of all, omnipresent and omnipotent; (2) He sent Apostles, including Muhammed, for man's guidance; (3) the Qur'ān is a divine speech; (4) which was conveyed to Muhammad's mind by a process of revelation, whether the revelation was literal or otherwise or conveyed by Angel Gabriel was of no consequence.

However, Shah Waliy Allah believed that "the words of the Qur'ān are only in Arabic, which was familiar to Muhammad and in which he could think, while the ideas flowed from the unseen. . . ." [17] Sir Sayyid rejected the distinction between the ideas and the language, saying "no idea divested of words can come to mind." (Iqbal, following Sir Sayyid, accepted this interpretation). (5) the Qur'ān is true, containing nothing antihistorical or incorrect; (6) God's positive and negative attributes, which are mentioned in the Qur'ān, are true; (7) God's attributes "are the essence itself," having no limitations. The dialectical theologians, however, believed that "the attributes of the Creator are neither the essence itself nor other than the essence." But the mystics regarded them "as the essence itself and declare their manifestation to be necessarily demanded by the essence." [18] Citing Shah Waliy Allah in his support Sir Sayyid described these subtle distinctions as a syntactic quibbling, producing no light.

Sir Sayyid described (8) God's attributes as infinite and absolute. "He does what He wills and decides what He wills." By that law of nature, so long as that law existed is impossible." The Qur'ān has said: "*Verily everything have we created by measure*" (IV:49), and in another Surah it has stated: "*There is no changing the words of God*" (X:65). Sir Sayyid thus concluded: "The 'words of God' and the 'creation of God' are two synonyms, which mean that no change can occur in nature." (9) the Qur'ān contains nothing which is contrary to the laws of nature. As for the miracles, Sir Sayyid cited Shah Wally Allah's *Al-Tafhīm al-Ilahīyyah:* "God the glorious has not mentioned anything of miracles in His Book, and never referred to them"; (10) the existing Qur'ānic text is complete and final without any additions or interpolations; (11) citing this time Shah Waliy Allah's *al-Fawz al-Kabīr:* "In the Prophet's time every *Surah* was preserved and recorded," Sir Sayyid stated that the Qur'ān's chapters follow a chronological sequence. (12) The doctrine of *al-Nāsikh wa al-Mansūkh* (the abrogating and abrogated verses of the Qur'ān) must be rejected. Surah ii:106:

> None of our [*ayah*] revelation
> Do we abrogate or cause to be forgotten. But we
> Substitute
> Something better or Similar:
> Knowest thou not that God Hath power over all things?

To Sir Sayyid the abrogation in this verse related to the pre-Islamic religious laws and not the Qur'ānic verses. (The term *ayah* referred to pre-Islamic religions.)

Again following Shah Waliy Allah, Sir Sayyid believed: (13) that the Qur'ān was revealed to the Prophet piecemeal according to the requirements of a situation. (14) The revelation cannot be opposed to scientific actuality. An agreement between God's *word* and *work* is essential. (15) Finally, sufficient linguistic ability in Arabic must be developed to appreciate subtle expressions of the Qur'ān.

Summing up these fifteen principles, Sir Sayyid concluded rather boldly that revelation and natural law are identical. Similarly, Sir Sayyid applied Shah Waliy Allah's[19] rational approach to highlight the relative importance of *hadith* (the Prophetic Tradition) for the modernization of Islam. Sir Sayyid believed that notwithstanding the care exercised by classical traditionists, a sizable number of traditions[20] contained in the "six sound works" of *hadith* are false, even though the common people insist upon their authenticity. His grievance against the *ahl al-hadith* was that they too have been blinded by *taqlīd* (following the precedents). The time has come, he reasoned, when the traditions should be tested on the touchstone of rationality. The fact that a tradition is included in one of the "six sound works" of tradition is no guarantee of its soundness. Sir Sayyid completely relied on the guideposts of Shah Waliy Allah for the analysis of *Hadith* literature.[21] According to Shah Waliy Allah, as Sir Sayyid pointed out, the works of Tradition stand or fall on the basis of their *soundness, reputation,* and *acceptance*[22] by the *'ulamā.'*

After establishing a hierarchy of reliable *hadith* literature, of which four categories were mentioned,[23] Sir Sayyid argued that each tradition should be accepted only after testing its rationality. Although he was dedicated to independent thinking in matters of theology, he did not establish a personal criterion for checking the authenticity of traditions. If he did not find a definitive rule in the words of his mentor, he referred to his son, Shah 'Abdūl Azīz (1746–1823), who had succeeded his father in the Madrasa Rahīmīya in the old city of Delhi.

Sir Sayyid says: According to Shah 'Abdūl Azīz, unsound and fabricated traditions can be detected if tested by the following standard: a tradition is, no doubt, false if it is contrary to established historical facts, or narrated by an enemy [of the Prophet Muhammad or Islam], or deals with such religious obligations which should be known and discharged by all, but is narrated only by one individual, or contravenes the *Shari'a,* defies human intelligence and is contrary to contemporary standards of comprehension. A tradition is false if it describes an event which in the case of its occurrence should have been witnessed by thousands of persons, but is narrated by only one individual. Often unidiomatic expressions and unsuitable subject matter of a tradition betray its spuriousness. A tradition indicating punishment or reward completely out of proportion to the corresponding acts of sin or merit, or promising a reward for a pilgrimage to be obtained for insignificant deeds cannot be sound. Similarly no sound and authentic tradition can bestow upon ordinary individuals extraordinary and significant blessings of God which are granted only to Prophets. Lastly, should the narrator admit the false nature of a tradition, then naturally it should be rejected.[24]

Why did the Muslims fabricate numerous traditions? Again, relying upon the explanations of Shah 'Abdūl Azīz, Sir Sayyid pointed out that

in order to spur enthusiasm for the study of the Qur'ān some zealots fabricated traditions, indicating the superiority of one passage [of the Qur'ān] over the other. Infidels popularized irrational and false traditions in order to ridicule Islam. At least 14,000 traditions were invented by the Zindīqs. In a similar vein bigots of different shades of opinion invented traditions to strengthen their pet prejudices and to humiliate their opponents. Polemicists also fabricated traditions; occasionally even the saints became unconscious victims of the practice of hadith-making. For example, if a saint saw the Prophet in his dream and conversed with him, he conveyed the Prophet's utterances to his disciples as if they were authentic traditions. Uninformed but well-meaning individuals, however, considered any pious statement of the 'ulamā' as a saying of the Prophet Muhammed.[25]

Sir Sayyid cautioned his coreligionists, saying that senseless statements attributed to the Prophet and all kinds of fantastic stories about his life only expose Islam to contempt and ridicule. In one of the issues of the Tahdhīb al-Akhlāq he published the following so-called traditions, describing them as utterly false and fabricated by partisans of vested interest.[26]

1. The saying that imān (faith) is a reflection of an individual's deeds and speech and that it can fluctuate is only a statement which can be attributed to the Companions and the Companions' Companions.

2. There is no sound tradition indicating that the word of God [*Kalam Allah,* i.e. the Qur'ān] is the eternal and uncreated word of God. They are only statements of the Companions and their Companions.

3. Traditions about Murji'ah, Qadariyyah, and Asharīyah:[27] all current traditions are false.

4. Traditions about the birth of the angels and drops of water falling off the wings of Gabriel causing the birth of angels are false.

5. There is no authentic tradition indicating the naming of children [after the Prophet] as Muhammad or Ahmad as a meritorious and a pious act.

6. All traditions discussing the nature of wisdom and its superiority are flase.

7. Traditions describing the long life of Elias and Khudr are baseless.

8. Traditions regarding knowledge and saying that a search for knowledge is every Muslim's obligation are not authentic.

9. Traditions condemning the concealing of knowledge are not authentic.

10. Traditions assigning special eminence to some *Suras* of the Qur'ān over others are, with the exception of a few, baseless.

11. Traditions describing the preeminence of Caliph Abu Bakr are mere inventions.

12. With the exception of one, all traditions eulogizing the qualities of Caliph Mu'awīyah (661–679 A.D.) are fabrications.

13. Traditions either condemning or describing the superior qualities of Imam Abu Hanīfah (d.767 A.D.) and al-Shafi'i (767–820) are sheer fabrications.

14. Traditions indicating the superiority of the cities of Qazvin, Asqalon, Sakhrah, and Bait al-Maqdas are mere inventions.

15. Traditions disallowing the use of water heated by the sun are not sound.

16. After performing ablution, the drying of hands and feet is not prescribed by any tradition.

17. Scratching of beard and cleaning of ears and neck is not prescribed in any sound tradition.

18. The mandatory performing of ablution after touching a woman is not based on sound tradition.

19. Obligatory bathing of oneself after washing a corpse is not a sound tradition.

20. There is no authentic tradition forbidding entrance into a public bath.

21. The teaching that *Bism Allah* (in the name of Allah) is the introductory verse of each chapter, and that it should be recited aloud during prayers is not a sound tradition.

22. Obligatory prayers in a mosque, if a mosque is in the neighborhood, and the leading of congregational prayers by a pious Muslim are not sound traditions.

23. The belief that an individual must repeat missed prayers before he can hope to have his current prayer accepted is also a baseless tradition.

24. Mandatory prayers and fasting during travel is not a sound tradition.

25. The prohibition of funeral services in Mosques is also an unsound tradition.

26. Expectation of compassion only for the compassionate is an unsound tradition.

27. If the wealthy shirk the responsibility of helping the needy, the statement that they thereby diminish their own divine blessings is not based upon any sound tradition.

28. No sound tradition requires that *zakā* be paid on honey, vegetables, and ornaments.

29. Traditions indicating that dyeing grey hair and applying collyrium are meritorious actions are sheer inventions of later times.

30. The statement that a Muslim who can afford to go on a pilgrimage to Mecca and refuses to do so dies only the death of a Jew or Christian is a mere fabrication.

31. The statement that a fast is broken if one bleeds is an unsound tradition.

32. The statement that interest on loans amounts to usury is not a sound tradition.

33. The statement that the cutting of meat (for eating) with a knife is prohibited is a mere fabrication.

34. The statement attributed to the Prophet that a knowledge of Persian or conversation in that language is not meritorious is also based on unsound tradition.

35. The rubbing of hands over one's face after prayers is similarly an unsound tradition.

36. There is no sound tradition indicating the superiority of a white rooster or *henna* powder.

37. The statement that an illegitimate child is condemned to hell is not based on any sound tradition.

38. The statement that the signs of the day of judgement will appear in particular months is not based on sound tradition.[28]

Despite Sir Sayyid's admission that he merely selected these generally known traditions out of a total of 99 from Alama Majd al-Din Firozabadiy's *Safar al-Sa'dat,* he had taken the first step in demythologizing Islam.

Demythologizing of Islam

Essentially Islamic mythology had developed through the *hadith* (the Prophetic Traditions) literature and the Prophet's biographies. Twisting any Qur'ānic statement regarding the Prophet, the traditionists and biographers often allowed their imaginations to take irrational flights. To the believer these stories became a source of delight, but in the age of reason they embarrassed the educated. Sir Sayyid experienced both sentiments in his intellectual development. As a traditional believer from 1842 to 1868, Sir Sayyid wrote in 1842 the Prophet's profile, *Jilā al-Qulūb bi Dhikr al-Mahbūb* (delight of the hearts in remembering the beloved), and reproduced all traditionally accepted miracles, and described some of the most known ones in some detail: (1) on the night of Muhammad's birth Kesra's palace was shaken and fourteen pinnacles were thrown down; (2) at age 12 Muhammad accompanied his uncle, Abū Tālib, for trade to Syria, where at Busra a Christian monk, Bahira, stated that all trees and stones prostrated themselves in front of Muhammad, and two angels sheltered him from the scorching sun; (3) when 41 years and 9 months old the Prophet ascended to the heavens, stopping on his way in Jerusalem; riding on burāq (a mythical winged animal) he visited the seven heavens separately and then communicated with God; (4) at the Prophet's death the angel of death, disguised as a bedouin, appeared to "snatch" his soul.[29]

Proudly but indiscriminately, Sir Sayyid admitted that his sources were Shah Waliy Allah's Surūr al-Mahzūn and an unnamed author's Madarij al-Nabūwwat. Mawalana Muhammad Nūr al-Hasan polished the style and checked the facts. A rationalist 36 years later, Sir Sayyid was embarrassed by his early credulity. Reviewing his Jilā al-Qulūb, Sir Sayyid commented: Madarij al-Nabūwwat contained numerous apocryphal stories and I incorporated some of them in my book. Then I was proud of authoring this tract, but now I am astounded after reading it."[30]

After his return from Europe Sir Sayyid graduated to the Newtonian view of nature. Consequently, he adopted a rational approach towards fundamental Islamic convictions including the role of the Prophet, revelation and the "proofs" of prophecy— the miracles. This intellectual transformation earned him the sobriquet of Nechari, the naturist.

The Newtonian philosophy of nature postulated that it was enough to define mathematically the action of the forces of nature, such as gravity. Was it possible to say what the causes of natural forces are? Newton himself did not succeed in this, and it is not clear that he believed the attempt to find such causes could be fruitful. In one of his letters, Newton stated: "it is inconceivable, that brute matter should, without the mediation of something else, which is not material, operate upon, and affect other matter without mutual contact."[31] Newton meant that neither gravity nor matter were independent of God. The divine purpose willed the cause of all fundamental properties, and laws of nature. Newton came close to saying God is nature, though not nature alone. Given this attitude, it was but a short step to the conclusion that

the man of science, in examining the physical world and reveal-
ing its hidden patterns, was engaged in a task that would bring
him closer to a comprehension of God.

In discussing the various categories of scientists, Sir Sayyid
stated that one category "believed in a world that is ruled by
laws, and God is the creator of these natural laws. These men are
true Muslims, and follow truthfully the principles of Islam." The
second category held the world to be composed of matter, and
God to be irrelevant; consequently, "they considered faith in
God to be utterly useless." They are the atheists. The third category asserted that "reality existed only in the empirically verifiable phenomena. Maybe God exists, maybe he doesn't. These
scientists are skeptics."[32]

In the first instance of scientific approach Sir Sayyid saw an
alliance between science and religion. Like Victorian theologians
he argued that whatever science one chose, it disclosed the
power, wisdom, and goodness of God. Moreover, science and
religion had two different sets of concerns, but they were not
dialectically opposed to each other. While religion dealt with the
ultimate cause, the scientists carried out observations and experiments to search for networks of connections among data; i.e.,
how is water made, and how are clouds formed. He saw nature
as "the work of God," and defined religion as "the word of
God," and maintained that Islam as a natural religion contained
no dichotomy between the "word" and the "work" of God.[33]
Consequently, Sir Sayyid dismissed the traditionally accepted
miracles of the Prophet Muhammad as the fabrications of zealous
Muslims, who sought to match Muhammad's "miracles" with
those of Moses and Christ.

In order to illustrate this point one might describe Sir
Sayyid's explanation of the *Isrā'* (the nocturnal journey of the
Prophet Mohammad to heaven). The traditionalists believed that
the Prophet was instantly transported from al-Ka'bah to Jerusalem before his *mi'rāj* (ascent) to *Sadrat al-Muntahāh,* the boundary
tree beyond the seventh Heaven, where the abode of the Almighty begins. The reference to *Isrā'* is made in *Surah Bani Israel*
of the Qur'ān:

Glory to God
Who did take His Servant
For a Journey by night
From the sacred Mosque
To the Farthest Mosque (*Masjid al-Aqsa*) [34]
Whose precincts we did
Bless,—in order that we
Might show him some
Of our signs: For He
Is the One Who heareth
And seeth (all things) [35]

Sir Sayyid maintained that the traditional commentators interpreted these verses literally and contended that the *Isrā'* was a physical experience. "For this assumption they possessed no authority from the Qur'ān, but merely asserted it after a philological and somewhat heated discussion upon the meaning of certain words. Thus the word *Isra* (nocturnal journey), they say, cannot be applied to a dream or vision, because it means 'travelling by night' and therefore, it must signify an actual journey. Similarly, they assert, the words *ba-abdehe* used in the verse to mean 'his servant,' are applicable to the soul and body combined since man is composed of both. The word *rowyā,* they assert (which simply means 'to see'), although generally understood to signify the seeing with the eye. Therefore, they conclude that in the Qur'ān the latter interpretation might have been intended." [36]

In dismissing this strictly literal interpretation, Sir Sayyid finally offered a simple but rational explanation of this well-known but controversial "miracle." "All that Muslims must believe respecting the ascension is this: the Prophet saw himself in a vision transported from Mecca to Jerusalem, and in this vision he actually saw some of the greatest signs of the Lord." [37]

Another British scientist who revolutionized Sir Sayyid's philosophy of nature was Charles Darwin, whose *The Origin of Species* was published in 1859, exactly ten years before Sir Sayyid's visit to Britain. Unlike the naturalists as well as the theologians, who believed that species were immutable productions, and had been separately created, Darwin convincingly demonstrated the fact of evolution. He indicated that: (1) existing animals and plants could have been separately created in their present forms, but must have evolved from earlier forms by slow transformation; (2) the theory of natural selection provided a mechanism by which such transformation could and would automatically be produced. Natural selection, Darwin deduced, must inevitably bring about the improvement of organisms, always in relation to the conditions of life. Once the fact of evolution was established it became clear that man had spans of time ahead of him as vast as those he had enjoyed for his entire evolution from his first submicroscopic ancestor. Thus evolution was viewed as a process of realization of new possibilities, involving an element of progress. Also, it emerged that man constituted the latest dominant group, capable of achieving major advances in the future.[38]

Darwin's book completely reopened the debate on the nature of the relationship between scientific and religious truths. Science and religion could no longer remain partners in an intellectual alliance when the scientists began to claim, under the impact of Darwinian theories, that the religious realm was ultimately reducible to the scientific. This meant that science was supreme, and it was the final arbiter of knowledge.

Sir Sayyid accepted the Darwinian theory of evolution as a scientific and rational explanation of the descent of man, but refused to accept the alleged superiority of scientific knowledge over the Qur'ān. He continued to assert that the scientists interrogated nature objectively in order to yield certain knowledge. This accurate scientific knowledge only served to establish the existence of God, and His rational religion—Islam. In Sir Sayyid's eyes, man could scarcely expect to go beyond that level of comprehension. Thus, the theory of evolution was yoked, by Sir Sayyid, to the service of Islam.

"If we accept that man evolved from an ape, it does not vitiate our religious principles which are derived from the Qur'ān," declared Sir Sayyid, "because the Qur'ān has addressed itself only to that animal which appeared (in the world) as homo-sapiens." Man was thus God's best of the creations, although in

TABLE 7.1. TRADITIONAL RELIGIOUS ORIENTATIONS JUXTAPOSED TO
SIR SAYYID'S MODERN ORIENTATIONS

Traditional Orientations	*Modern Orientations*
1. The old religious principle stressed that man was created for religion.	1. The new religious principle emphasized that religion was created for man.
2. Man should engage in self denial by eliminating his desire and appetite.	2. Man should keep his desire and appetite alive, and gratify them in accordance with the designated principles of the Creator.
3. In eliminating the carnal urge man purifies his personality.	3. The carnal urge is "pure" in itself, and should be applied for its proper purpose.
4. Man should eat and sleep less; live ascetically and in constant worship in order to attune his heart to God so that he annihilates himself in God.	4. These ascetic practices create in man melancholia; heart should be kept healthy for its proper biological functions.
5. The worldly relationships should be renounced and only contact with God should be maintained.	5. In renouncing the world man negates God's will. The universe was created for man's benefit.
6. One should be content with a limited portion of material goods which enable him to survive.	6. All of material goods can be utilized as God's blessings to man.
7. Man should trust his fate, and be thankful for it.	7. Fate is an occurrence and to await it is to vitiate God's will, which urges prudence, and caution.
8. Man should search God with eyes completely closed.	8. With eyes wide open man should investigate the phenomena of nature in order to comprehend God.
9. God's greatness can make water act like fire, and *vice versa*.	9. This unnatural view detracts from God's greatness, and the grand design of His Creation.
10. The recitation of the Qur'ān assures healing of the sick.	10. The Qur'ānic understanding uplifts man spiritually.
11. One can achieve God's blessings for another person, especially after his death, by acts of charity in the deceased's name.	11. "One cannot eat for someone else's stomach," it is simple as that.
12. Miracles establish the Prophets' claims in their prophethood.	12. The prophetic claims are established only by nature.
13. Religion is equally applicable to secular and religious affairs.	13. Religion deals only with spiritual matters.
14. Scientific knowledge suppresses religion.	14. Scientific knowledge reveals "the truthfulness of a true religion."

his earlier stages of development man was a savage animal. God willed in him the faculty of improvement, and eventually he assumed his present developed position. "God only knows, how much progress man has yet to make. From Adam to Noah, when did man learn to build an ark? The Old Testament measures this span of time by 1,657 years. This is amusing!"[39]

To harmonize Darwinian ideas with Islam, Sir Sayyid wrote several articles in the *Tahdhīb al-Akhlāq* which unjustifiably earned him the wrath of the Orthodox, who branded him an "infidel."[40]

Modern Religious Orientations

As a consequence of his intellectual exposure to western sciences Sir Sayyid developed an entirely new set of religious orientations. To the orthodoxy this was not only an affront to Islam, but also a challenge to the socio-political position of the *'ulamā'*, traditional religious scholars. Gradually, however, the modern Muslim youth internalized these new religious values and orientations, and discarded the old ones. This was Sir Sayyid's greatest achievement (see Table 7.1).[41]

Remaining steadfast in his liberal approach to Islam, Sir Sayyid finally transcended religious parochialism and graduated to a larger concept of religious pluralism. During the time of our species, Sir Sayyid asserted, "God sent his prophets for their moral improvements. It is absurd to believe that the prophets appeared only in Arabia and Palestine to reform a handful of Arabs and Jews, and that God condemned the peoples of Africa, America, and Asia to ignorance." Surely whoever followed God's prophets achieved salvation; "it was immaterial whether the prophet was from China, America, Mongolia, Africa, India, or Iran, or if he preached God's message to savages or civilized man."[42]

Epilogue

IT IS NOT farfetched to state that Muslim national theory in India after 1857 was the child of Sir Sayyid's Aligarh Movement. This is, however, not to say that the Muslim nation was born with the theory and policies of Sir Sayyad Ahmad Khan. Political theory and, for that matter, the theoretical framework of any discipline must follow the existence of facts. If the primary function of theory is to offer a conceptual scheme by which the relevant data are systemized, classified, and interrelated, then it is obvious that without the facts of Muslim national life the Aligarh Movement could have developed no political theory. The facts of Muslim national culture—the development of Urdu, the extra-territorial allegiance expressed through the institution of the Caliphate, the thousand year rule in India, etc.—had separated the Muslims from the Hindus before the advent of the British Raj. Muslim national life was never called into question under the Mughals and the British before 1857. With the political philosophy of the Congress, aiming at the creation of a joint Hindu-Muslim Indian nationality, the need for a Muslim national theory was crystallized.

I

The Aligarh movement became the catalyst for the general diffusion of cultural and educational modernization among the Muslims. In some provinces, either inspired by its example or advice, the Muslims established local organizations, including Anjuman Mufiyd-i Islam in Madras, the Central Muhammadan Association in Bengal, which was established by Justice Sayyid Amir Ali in 1877, and Anjuman-i Islam in Bombay, which was headed by Justice Badr-ud-Din Tayyabji. However, the Punjab was most receptive to the challenge of modernity, and proved to be an ally of the Aligarh movement in the realization of its mission. The Anjuman Himayat-i Islam in Lahore (1884), and 53 other anjumans in the Punjab were established to spread modern education among the Muslims. After Sir Sayyid's death in 1898 the Punjab enthusiastically participated in the movement for the establishment of Aligarh Muslim University, which came into being in 1920. In Bengal, Sir Sayyid's younger contemporary, Nawab Abdul Latif (1828–1893) established the Muhammadan Literary Society (1863–1889) to popularize "general and scientific education." Sir Sayyid delivered a lecture at this society on October 6, 1863, to posit his theory of patriotism, and to highlight the necessity of promoting modern education among the Muslims. Cooperation between the two leaders continued throughout their lives.

Secularism vs. Modernity: In the post-Sir Sayyid period (1898–1947) the concept of secularism became the big divide among the modernists. Should Muslims accept a United India in which the state would be neutral in religious and cultural matters? Until the freedom of India is achieved, would the political and economic interests of the Muslims be best served if they joined the All-India National Congress, and refrained from creating a political party of their own? Lastly, what role and significance would the *shari'a* (Islamic laws) have in a secular India if its application is essential to preserving the culture and personality of the Muslims? During this crucial period conflicting answers were provided to these questions.

II

Following Sir Sayyid's orientations, and his theory of Muslim nationalism, an overwhelming majority of the modernists, led particularly by the Muslim League, which had come into being in 1906, rejected secularism. Formulating a two-nation theory, they adopted the so-called "Pakistan Resolution" in 1940 at Lahore, which paved the way for the creation of Pakistan in 1947. The poet-philosopher, Dr. Muhammad Iqbal (1877–1938), and the founder of Pakistan, Muhammad Ali Jinnah (1876–1948), were the stalwarts of modernists, who are now generally known as Muslim nationalists. Their philosophical and political orientations are well-known, and they need not be discussed here.

Paradoxically, almost all the traditional Islam-oriented political parties, including the Jami'at ūlamā'-i Hind, Jama't-i Islami, and Majlis-Ahrār, opted for a united and secular India. (The Ahrars were active primarily in the Punjab, and thus exercised only limited influence.) Often motivated by their conflicting orientations, only a handful of the modernists supported democratic and secular, and territorially united, India. In this category the most outstanding leaders were Badr-ud-Din Tayyabji (1844–1906), Abul Kalam Azad (1888–1958), Dr. Zakir Husain (1897–1969), and his associates at the Jamia Millia Islamia of New Delhi. A brief analysis of their theoretical formulations might be illuminating.

Badr-ud-Din Tayyabji: To Tayyabji, as much as to Sir Sayyid, the issue of the partition of India into two or three states was irrelevant. A territorially united India under the British Raj was an immutable historical fact in their assumptions. How should the Muslims articulate their demands, in cooperation with the All-India National Congress or the British? Basically, on this issue, they differed. Like Sir Sayyid, Tayyabji did not consider "the whole of India as one nation." [1] In his presidential address to the Madras Congress in 1887, and then in a personal letter of February 18, 1888, to Sir Sayyid, he reiterated that "there are numerous communities or nations which had peculiar problems of their own to solve." [2] To solve their common problems, the

National Congress was the most appropriate institution. Sir Sayyid had urged the British that in order to ensure adequate Muslim representation in the provincial and municipal legislative councils the principle of separate electorates should be adopted. This policy was not unacceptable to Tayyabji; only the method of articulation was. He informed Sir Sayyid forthrightly: "My policy, therefore, would be to act from within rather than from without [the Congress]."³ In other words, the Congress should play the major role in aggregating the Muslims' articulated interests, and finally present them to the British government for its acceptance. Tayyabji also tried to assure Sir Sayyid and other Muslim leaders that the Congress would not allow the discussion of any issue which was opposed by a majority of the Muslim leaders.⁴ But he failed to eliminate their misgivings. Tayyabji insinuated that Sir Sayyid, Amir Ali, Nawab Abdul Latif, and their associates had spurned the Congress in order "to stand well with the Government."

Frustrated in his ambitions to be a bridge of understanding between the Muslims and the Congress, Tayyabji began to realize that "an overwhelming majority of Mohammadans is against the [Congress] movement"; and thus inferred that it "ceases to be a general or national Congress." In a confidential letter of October 27, 1888, Tayyabji confided in the founder of the Congress, Allan Octavian Hume (1829–1912), that "the prime object of the Congress was to unite the different communities and provinces into one and thereby promote harmony, . . . not only have the Mohammadans been divided from the Indus [northwest] in a manner they never were before, but the Mohammadans themselves have been split into two factions."⁵ Consequently, Tayyabji advised Hume not to convene the Congress for five years; and to decide the future of the Congress after this moratorium. If the Muslims did not join the Congress then "we can drop it with dignity . . . conscious of having done our utmost for the progress of India, and the fusion of the different races into one."⁶ In Badr-ud-Din Tayyabji's personal papers, preserved in the National Archive of India, Hume's response to his suggestions is not available. However, Hume's life-long colleague in the Indian Civil Service (ICS) and associate in initiating the Congress, Sir William Wedderburn, has stated that Hume "believed that within three years the anti-Congress party would collapse." Derisively, Hume described this party consisting of "a few Indian fossils, honest, but wanting in understanding."[7]

It is unlikely that Tayyabji's strategy would have worked; nor for that matter had Hume's prediction come true. A Scotch "radical," Hume had been forced to retire from the ICS in 1882. Unhappy with the English imperious style, Hume "had identified himself with the Indian people." By 1887 Hume had initiated an "aggressive propaganda campaign" on the model "of the Anti-Corn Law League in England" in order to politicize the Indians. He distributed half a million pamphlets, translated into twelve Indian languages. More than one thousand meetings were held, where thousands of persons listened to the Congress leaders. The British government was urged (1) to: create legislative councils in the provinces; (2) to refer all budgets to these councils for their approval; (3) to create a standing committee of the House of Commons to aggregate the grievances of these councils; (4) not to undertake military expeditions against Burma and Afghanistan; and (5) to arrange competitive examinations for the ICS in India, with the minimum age of the competitors fixed at 23. Outraged, the British bureaucracy urged the Viceroy to deport Hume to Britain.

The Governor of the Northwest Provinces, Sir Auckland Calvin, whose territory had been the scene of the 1857 rebellion, criticized Hume in his private correspondence for the Congress "agitation." This correspondence was subsequently published by Hume in a pamphlet, *Audi Alteram Partem*. Their arguments reflected different orientations. Calvin, haunted by the 1857 rebellion like Sir Sayyid, considered the Congress' leadership unrepresentative, and its activities premature and at worst disruptive of the British empire. To Hume "no more efficacious safety-valve than our Congress movement could possibly be devised."[8] In Bombay, far away from the Delhi tragedy of 1857, Tayyabji could easily empathize with Hume, while Sir Sayyid could only appreciate Governor Calvin's forebodings so forcefully expressed publicly, as well as privately, in his correspondence with Hume. Sir Sayyid's traumatic reactions drew him closer to those English bureaucrats who were opposed to the Congress; thus, a psychological wedge drawn between the Congress and the Muslim leadership spawned political policies which were diametrically opposed.

Abul Kalam Azad: A maverick among the secularists, a progressive theologian among the traditionalists, and stoically impervious to popular opinions, Azad's tragedy was that of an arrogant but brilliant intellect, which failed to lead, and failed to be led by other Muslim leaders. Despite his failures, Azad managed to retain his influence among the traditionalists. In utter desperation they looked up to him, in order to find justification for the Indian secularism within the framework of Islamic traditions, since the challenge of the Muslim modernists put them on the defensive.

Azad did not acquire a modern English education, although he had achieved a working knowledge of English and could read English studies. His close association with Jawaharlal Nehru and other Western-educated Congress leaders also enabled him to grasp the spirit of modernity. His formal education, however, was strictly traditional, and he outgrew it as years wore on. Consequently, during the earliest phase of his life (1912–20), Azad was a fundamentalist, and political traditionalism was the ideology which he expounded in his weekly journal, *Al-Hilal,* which he had established in 1912. His theoretical formulations in this period bear a striking similarity to those of Abul ala Maududi's (1903–79). (Maududi established the Jama't-i Islami in India in 1941, and then in 1947 he migrated along with his movement to Pakistan.) For this unexplained "parallelism" critics have alleged that Maududi's current crusade for fundamentalism in Pakistan is essentially a continuation of Azad's early doctrinal position. Azad's followers, however, continued to hold the views which he had between 1912 and 1920, but failed to detect the metamorphosis in Azad's thinking, which was caused by his reaction to the Caliphate debacle in the 1920s.

Analysis of Azad's fundamentalism not only is intellectually rewarding, but also contradicts his later claims made in *India Wins Freedom* (1958) that during this period (1912–20) he was associated with Shyam Sunder Chakravarty and other revolutionaries of Bengal, who were then described as "anarchists." A Muslim correspondent asked Azad what political policy he favored: (a) should Muslims continue to follow the established policy (presumably pro-British); (b) should they adopt the ways of moderate Hindu leaders who demanded more political rights within the framework of the British Empire; or (c) should they emulate the Hindu anarchists of Bengal. The correspondent also asked Azad to distinguish between his political views and religious convictions.

On September 8, 1912, Azad answered these questions in an article, *"Al-Hilal Kā Maqsid Awr Political Ta'līym"* (Al-Hilal's Aims and Political Education). It was doubtful, Azad indicated, if he could separate religion from politics. "According to our belief," he wrote, "any ideas not derived from the Qur'ān are tantamount to sheer infidelity and political views are not an exception to this rule." He believed that Islam brought an exalted and comprehensive social order for mankind and that there was not a single social problem for which Islam did not provide a solution. "It is regrettable," said Azad, "that the Muslims have not examined Islam at its zenith. If they did, they would not be bowing their heads in subjection to the Hindus." He declared that *Al-Hilal's* aim was to invite Muslims to follow the book of Allah [the Qur'ān] and the *Shari'a* of His Prophet." [9]

In discussing the policies of the two Hindu political groups—the moderates and the anarchists—Azad stated that he did not follow either of these. "Islam is so exalted a religion," he declared, "that its followers are not constricted to ape the Hindus for the formulation of their political policy. Muslims need not join any political party. They were the leaders of the world. If they would submit to God, the entire world would submit to them." *Al-Hilal's* policy for the Muslims was distrust of the British Government and noncooperation with the Hindus. He wanted the Muslims to follow "the straight path of Islam." As far as concrete political aims were concerned, "Hindus can, like

other nations, revive their self-awareness and national consciousness on the basis of secular nationalism but it is indeed not possible for the Muslims. Their nationality is not inspired by racial or
geographic exclusivity; it transcends all man-made barriers. Until
they are inspired by Islam the spirit of self-awareness will not be
inbued in the Muslims." [10]

Azad exhorted the Muslims to strive for political liberty
with a responsible parliamentary system. This was, according to
him, a religious injunction for the Muslims. "Has not the Qur'ān
said: do not cause strife on earth after the establishment of
peace?" Azad appreciated the *pax Britannica* which made freedom
of conscience and worship possible for the Muslims. Therefore
"any rebellious activity, breach of peace and law would be tantamount to an offense against God." This was indeed a moderate
political program, not very different from that of the Muslim
League. In fact, Azad blessed and approved the League's goal of
political leadership.

In the 1920s, Azad completely but silently repudiated these
views; the political developments in the Middle East were responsible for this change in his orientations. After the war Ata-
turk abolished the Caliphate, which had demanded the allegiance
of the Muslims of all nationalities as a matter of religious obligation. Simultaneously, however, Arab nationalism, appealing to
all Arabs on the basis of language and common history regardless
of religious affiliation, asserted itself. Impressed by these developments, Azad ceased to be a Muslim nationalist and instead became a secular modernist. He accepted the secular and territorial
principles of Arab and Turkish nationalisms, and applied them
rather rigidly to the political situation in India. He maintained
that following the pattern of Arab nationalism, Hindus and Muslims could create a united and secular Indian nationality. Had not
the Prophet of Islam done more or less the same thing? Addressing a provincial assembly of the Caliphate Movement in Agra on
October 25, 1921, he referred to the Prophet Muhammad's Covenant between the Muslim inhabitants of Medina and the Jews,
which was negotiated after the Prophet's entrance (622 A.D.) into
Medina. Its purpose was to establish a common defense against

the hostile Quraysh who had persecuted the Prophet in Mecca and forced him to migrate to Medina. The preamble of the covenant stated:[11] *Bism Allah Al-Rahmān al-Rahīm. Hadha kitāb min Muhammad al-nabīy bayn al-miminīn wa-almuslimīn min Quraysh wa-yathrib wa-man tab'hum falhaq bham wa-jahad ma'ham al-naham ummat wahidat min dūn al-nās.* "In the name of God the Compassionate, the Merciful. This is a document from Muhammad the Prophet [governing the relations] between the believers and Muslims of Quraysh and Yathrib [Medina], and those who followed them and joined them and labored with them. They are one community (*Ummat wahidat*), to the exclusion of all men."[12]

Azad's rendition of the key phrase—*Ummat Wahidat*—gives it a connotation that is different from any of those which are generally accepted. He renders the translation thus: "We enter into an agreement and a truce with all the tribes inhabiting the suburbs of Medina and we together want to constitute a nation."[13] If the Prophet Muhammad's followers could visualize a nation in an alliance with the Jews of Medina, then why couldn't Muslims create an Indian nation in cooperation with the Hindus? Azad's interpretation of this covenant provided a theoretical framework both for territorial nationalism and a secular India: that this was not an adequate base for evolving a joint Hindu–Muslim nation in India remained beyond his intellectual horizon.

Dr. Zakir Husain and the Jamia Millia Islamia, New Delhi: National Muslim University, now located in Delhi, was born (1920) at Aligarh in a fit of anger and protest by the alumni of Aligarh Muslim University. The anger was caused because the Aligarh Muslim University's administration refused to liquidate itself by allowing its faculty and the students to participate in Mahatma Gandhi's noncooperation movement. Also, Aligarh Muslim University prevented them from migrating to Afghanistan in deference to the decrees of *hijrat* (migration) issued by Mawlana 'Abdūl Barī, and Abul Kalam Azad[14] in support of the Turkish Caliphate. Their protest was directed against Sir Sayyid's political legacy, which continued to urge the Muslims to cooperate with the British Government.

In defiance of Aligarh Muslim University's policy the

leaders of the Alumni (including Mawlana Muhammad Ali, Mawlana Shawkat Ali, Hakīm Ajmal Khan, and Mawlana Hasrat Mūhanī) seized a university building. After their eviction they declared the creation of Jamia Millia Islamia on October 29, 1920, and initiated their classes in hurriedly constructed tents pitched not very far away from the campus of Aligarh Muslim University. Some radically inclined young faculty and some advanced graduate students (including the late Dr. Zakir Husain, who became the President of India) constituted the faculty of the new university. Finally, in March 1925 Jamia was transferred to Delhi, where it started to shed its agitational role and seriously started to develop into an institution of advanced learning.[15]

In 1926 a trio of dedicated scholars came to Jamia, including doctors Zakir Husain, Abid Husain, and Professor M. Mujeeb, who had completed their graduate work in European universities. Under their guidance Jamia became what it is today: a modernist university dedicated to training the youth with a secular nationalist ideology. Since its advent Jamia has flourished under the wings of the Congress party, and has tried to translate its ideology into educational terms. What are the educational goals? Dr. Zakir Husain has explained:

(a) Jamia's aim is to prepare an outline for the Indian Muslims' collective life, where Islam is the focal point, and contains also those elements of India's national culture which are in harmony with the general civilization of man; (b) Jamia is based upon a conviction that the true education of religion would inculcate among Indian Muslims patriotism and national unity and enable them to participate in India's progress; (c) Jamia neither subscribes to the traditional view that knowledge should be acquired for knowledge's sake nor to the contemporary view that education is a means to earn a livelihood. Jamia, on the contrary, believes in the principle of knowledge for the broad scope of life inclusive of religion, philosophy, politics, economics, and industrial manufacturing. Students should develop a sensitivity to the needs of the country, and the willingness to subordinate their careers to the collective interests of the national culture.[16]

The extent to which the Jamia has been successful in the realization of its goals remains to be assessed. However, it stands as a symbol of Muslim modernists' dedication to the ideal of a secular and territorially united India.

III

Looking upon diffusion as the key to progress the Aligarh Movement exposed the Muslim culture to the dynamic culture of the West. The Muslim culture not only underwent changes in material traits, but also adopted modern political orientations. This process created a strand of liberal and "secular" thought in the mainstream of Muslim national theory. For the first time attempts were made to draw a line between matters distinctly religious and "functionally secular." This dichotomy reflected itself vividly in the Muslim League policies. The Muslim League created the Pakistani state in which the Muslim national culture would develop without the fear of it being Hinduized. Within this conceptual framework should be examined the statement of the founder of Pakistan, Muhammad Ali Jinnah, exhorting the Constituent Assembly of Pakistan in August 1947 to adopt a functionally secular attitude in lawmaking:

We are starting the State with no discrimination, no distinction between one community and another, between the caste or creed. We are starting with the fundamental principle that we are citizens of one state. We should keep that in front of us as our ideal and you will find that in the course of time Hindus would cease to be Hindus and Muslims, not in the religious sense because that is the personal faith of an individual, but in the political sense as the citizens of one nation.[17]

Since Jinnah's statement of August 1947 the pendulum of political orientations in Pakistan has swung from Islamic modernism to Islamic fundamentalism. Jinnah's "functional secularism" has not been taken very seriously. During this period (1947–1979) and in the name of these orientations several sets of elites in Pakistan merely replaced one another, providing an illustration of Vilfredo Pareto's theory of social elites and their circulation. Three distinct types of elites appeared on the political spectrum: (I) the *governing elites,* consisting of (1) military officers; (2) higher echelons of the civil service; (3) landed aristocracy; (4) capitalists, and (5) politicians. (II) The *non-governing elites:* this second collectivity consisted mainly of the regional elites from the smaller provinces of Pakistan and East Bengalis. However, since 1971, Pakistan's regional elites have been endeavoring to have not only parity of esteem for their regional languages and cultural traditions, but also parity of participation in the political processes of the state. (III) Denied any share in power, the *counterelites* consisted of the fundamentalist religious scholars and Islamic political parties (i.e., the Jama't-i Islami, Jami'at'ulamā'-i Islam, and its rival Jami'at'ulamā'-i Pakistan, etc.). They have endeavored to exercise political power with or without the cooperation of the governing elites, while pressuring the latter to reorganize the polity in their conception of Islamic fundamentalism.

Trained in the modernizing tradition of the Aligarh Movement the governing elites managed the problems of (a) constitution-making, (b) organizing the mode of economy, and (c) the social reforms in the light of modernist Islam rather than the Islamic fundamentalism of the counterelite. During a period of 32 years the various combinations of the governing elites ruled by four different constitutions, each reflecting the initiators' orientations. The British constitutional reforms of 1935, with appropriate amendments, enabled the modernized politicians, bureaucrats, and landed aristocracy (with the Military's support) to rule the country until 1956. No determined attempt was made to draft a new Islamic constitution; only the Objectives Resolution was adopted, stating that "sovereignty over the entire universe belongs to God Almighty . . . the [sovereign] state exercises its power and authority through the chosen representatives of the people" with adequate protection "for the minorities to practice and profess their religion and develop their cultures," and "the independence of the Judiciary shall be fully secured." While the counterelite believed that it scored a victory, the government's policies remained functionally secular.

Theoretically, however, the constitution of 1956 was con-

EPILOGUE   293

strued to be a substantial gain by the fundamentalist elite. The
country was now called the Islamic Republic of Pakistan, the
president was to be a Muslim, and the legislation enacted by the
parliament could not be "repugnant to the Qur'ān and sunnah."
This constitution of the Islamic Republic lasted only for 18
months and 15 days. In 1958, the military elite subordinated the
politicians, and in cooperation with the landlords and the bureaucracy initiated the third constitution in 1962, naming Pakistan
simply a republic. From 1958 to 1970 the counterelite of Islamic
fundamentalists supported the governing elite with Islamic justifications, to develop and expand the capitalist mode of economy. Thus, the capitalist collectively emerged as a recognized
member of the governing elite.[18] The concept of distributive justice, which had been so vigorously propounded by Iqbal, was
relegated to the background. Instead, the regime initiated reforms to ameliorate women's social status with the Muslim Family Laws Ordinance of 1961. Multiple marriages were discouraged, and family courts were established to effect reconciliation
between estranged couples. Additionally, vigorous measures
were adopted for birth control and family planning. To update
Islamic laws, the Institute of Islamic Research was established to
compete with the fundamentalist interpretations of the counterelite.

The fourth constitution was adopted in 1973 by the political
elite, replacing the military which had lost prestige in 1971 as a
consequence of a major defeat in Bangladesh. Z. A. Bhutto of
the Pakistan Peoples Party had established electoral alliance with
the nonelites (i.e., masses) of Pakistan, promising them "bread,
shelter, and clothing." However, an attempt was made to concil-
iate the fundamentalist elite in making Pakistan an Islamic republic. All existing laws were to be "brought in conformity with the
injunctions of Islam as laid down in the Holy Qur'ān and Sunnah." A Council of Islamic Ideology was established to recommend "the ways and means" of Islamizing the individual and
collective lives of Pakistani Muslims. To women, full participation "in all spheres of national life" was guaranteed. Finally,
the elimination of exploitation was mandated with "the gradual

fulfilment of the fundamental principle, from each according to his ability to each according to his work." Nationalization of the industries delivered a heavy blow to the upper stratum of the capitalist elite, and the land reforms created the middle-sized farmers who developed agriculture on capitalist lines. Thus, the governing elite alienated the capitalists and some members of the landed aristocracy, and the slogans of Islamic socialism earned the enmity of the Islamic fundamentalists.

The military elite staged yet another coup d'etat in July 1977, following the widespread agitation against the Bhutto regime. Organized by the Islamic fundamentalists and some modernists, this agitation was in protest against the "rigged" general elections which had taken place in March 1977. Consequently, the military elite and the opposition parties went into an alliance after establishing "a doctrine of necessity" in the Supreme Court of Pakistan. This doctrine legitimized the waltzing circle of the military to power, while enabling it to selectively abrogate the 1973 constitution. This was an alliance of the right with the right in which the fundamentalist interpretations of the Jama't-i Islami and Jami'at ūlamā'-i Islam prevailed. Partly out of conviction, and partly designed to sedate the masses, General Zia Ul-Haq, head of the military government, issued martial law ordinances of three distinct types to establish the shari'a (the Islamic laws) as the law of the land: (1) The 1973 Constitution was amended in February 1979 to empower the High and Supreme Courts to decide if any law was repugnant to the shari'a. Simultaneously, shari'a benches of the High Courts, and the shari'a appellate bench of the Supreme Court, were constituted to exercise Islamic judicial review. However, the shari'a benches would not entertain petitions challenging personal and procedural laws— laws relating to revenue, banking, and taxation. (2) To provide guaranteed funds for social welfare, zaka (welfare tax) and 'ushr (tithe on agriculture) were established in July–October 1979. A zaka fund with an initial investment of Rs.2,250 million—contributed mainly by Saudi Arabia and the United Arab Emirates— has already been created. The zaka tax would be voluntary on "invisible assets," and compulsory on "visible assets," enabling the state to collect 2 ½ percent on savings accounts (estimated in 1979 to exceed Rs.25,000 million), and none on current accounts. Also, an ordinance was issued to initiate interest-less banking. (3) Maximum penalties for drinking, adultery and defamation, and theft were provided. (General Zia admitted that for two habitual thieves the amputation of left hands was provided, but no surgeon in Pakistan was forthcoming to mutilate the culprits.) At least, maximum penalties of flogging and stoning to death for defamation and adultery, and amputation of hands for theft, became a legal possibility.

It is doubtful if the modernists Sir Sayyid, Iqbal, or Jinnah would have approved of the application of these draconian measures to "eliminate" drinking of alcoholic beverages, theft, or adultery. They would have supported the levy of *zaka* and *'ushr,* and would have heartily applauded the *shari'a*'s supremacy over all other laws. To all three the military dictatorship of 1958, 1969, and 1977 would have appeared un-Islamic. Despite his elitist orientations, Sir Sayyid was truly a social democrat. Even today, he would have reiterated with confidence his democratic philosophy, which he had described to an English friend with pride during his stay in Britain from 1869 to 1870:

Arab blood runs through my veins. My religion is Islam, and I believe in it firmly. Islam stands for some radical principles in as much as it is not in harmony with one-man rule. Islam does not approve of limited monarchy or hereditary kingship. A president, elected by the people, is preferred by Islam. Islam does not stand for the concentration of wealth in fewer hands. In light of this principle, Islam's founder established the rule that the deceased's property should be distributed among the heirs. No matter how vast an individually owned property there might be, after two generations it would split into many shares. Thus, religiously and in terms of my heritage, I am a radical.[19]

Appendix A

Civil List of the Provinces Including Burma, October 1893

Province	Numbers			Percentages	
	Muslim	*Hindus*	*Total*	*Muslim*	*Hindus*
(1) The Punjab	162	312	474	34.2	65.8
(2) Sindh	114	206	320	35.6	64.4
(3) Bengal	127	1,190	1,317	9.6	90.4
(4) Northwestern and the Awadh	439	660	1,099	39.9	60.1
(5) Central Province	225	496	721	31.2	68.8
(6) Bombay	62	938	1,000	6.2	93.8
(7) Madras	38	590	628	6.5	93.95
(8) Assam	16	199	215	7.5	92.5
(9) Burma	18	425	443	4.1	95.9
Grand Total	1,201	5,016	6,217	19.3	80.7

Appendix B

The Punjab Civil List, October 1893

Department	Rank	Numbers			Percentages	
		Muslim	*Hindu*	*Total*	*Muslim*	*Hindu*
Civil Service	Divisional Judges	1	1	2	50	50
	Assistant Commissioners	3	1	4	75	25
	Extra Assistant Commissioners	5	6	11	45.5	54.5
Provincial Civil Service	District Judges	0	1	1	0	100
	Extra Judicial Assistant Commissioners	4	5	9	44.4	55.6
	Extra Assistant Commissioners	31	47	78	39.8	60.2
	Tehsildars	49	76	125	39.2	60.2
Forestry	Extra Assistant Conservators	2	4	6	33.3	66.4
Salt	Superintendents	1	0	1	100	0

| Department | Rank | Numbers | | Total | Percentages | |
		Muslim	Hindu		Muslim	Hindu
Post Office	Superintendents	0	5	5	0	100
	Examiners	1	2	3	33.3	66.7
	Postmasters	3	19	22	13.6	86.4
	Inspectors	4	6	10	40	60
Telegraph	Telegraph Masters	1	3	4	25	75
Finance	Assistant Accountant Generals	0	1	1	0	100
Paper	U.C.S.	0	1	1	0	100
Judiciary	Judges Small Cause Court	1	2	3	33.3	66.7
	Munsifs	15	68	83	18.1	81.9
Jail	Superintendents	0	7	7	0	100
Registration	Subregistrars	36	40	76	47.4	52.6
Police	Assistant District Superintendents	4	3	7	57.1	42.9
Education	Inspectors	0	3	3	0	100
	Gazetted Subordinate Service (Officers)	1	11	12	8.3	91.7
Grand Total		162	312	474	34.2	65.8

Notes

Introduction

1. Steven Runciman, *A History of the Crusades* (New York: Harper & Row, 1964) Vol. I, p. 108.

2. V. I. Lenin, "Imperialism, The Highest Stage of Capitalism," *Selected Works* (Moscow: Foreign Languages Publishing House, 1952), p. 525.

3. Leopold von Ranke, *Serbien Und Die Turkei Im Neunzehnten Jahrhundert,* in *Sammtliche Werke* (Leipzig: 1879), Vols. 43–44, pp. 518–19; translated in Hajo Holbern, *The Political Collapse of Europe* (New York: Alfred A. Knopf, 1959), p. 7.

4. Stanford Jay Shaw, "Some Aspects of the Aims and Achievements of the Nineteenth Century Ottoman Reformers," in *Beginnings of Modernization in the Middle East,* William R. Polk and Richard L. Chambers, eds. (Chicago: University of Chicago Press, 1968), pp. 30–31.

5. Fritz Steppart, "National Education Projects in Egypt Before the British Occupation," in *Beginnings of Modernization,* pp. 292–93.

6. Hafez Farman Farmayan, "The Forces of Modernization in Nineteenth Century Iran: A Historical Survey," in *Beginnings of Modernization,* pp. 128–29.

7. Nikki R. Keddie, *An Islamic Response to Imperialism* (Berkeley: University of California Press, 1968), pp. 27, 42–45.

8. Alexandre A. Bennigsen and S. Enders Wimbush, *Muslim National Communism in the Soviet Union* (Chicago: University of Chicago Press, 1979), p. 193.

9. *Ibid.,* pp. 58–68.

10. Guenter Lewy, *Religion and Revolution* (New York: Oxford University Press, 1974), p. 191.

11. Howard M. Federspiel, *Persatuan Islam: Islamic Reform in Twentieth Century Indonesia* (Ithaca: Cornell University Mongraph Series, 1970), pp. 4–9.

12. Hafeez Malik, *Muslim Nationalism in India and Pakistan* (Washington, D.C.: Public Affairs Press, 1963), Chapter 5.

13. Talat Sait Halman, "Islam Tomorrow," *The New York Times,* January 15, 1980, is an excellent restatement of the secularist view in Islam.

14. Hafeez Malik, "Abul Kalam Azad's Theory of Nationalism," *The Muslim World* (Hartford: January 1963); *Five Tracts of Hasan Al-Banna* (1906–1949), *Majmū'āt Rasā' il al-Imam al-Shahīd Hasan al-Bannā'*, Charles Wendell, trans. (Berkeley: University of California Press, 1978); Ishak Musa Husaini, *The Moslem Brethren* (Lebanon: Khayat, 1956); Franz Rosenthal, "The Muslim Brethren in Egypt," *The Muslim World* (Hartford: October 1947); R. Bayly Winder, "Islam as the State Religion: A Muslim Brotherhood View in Syria," *The Muslim World* (Hartford: July–October 1954).

15. For the draft of the new Iranian constitution, see "Matan-i Kāmil Qanūn Asasīy Iran," *Ittila'āt* (Tehran: 1358/1979, no. 16007). The Constitution follows closely Khomeini's *Islamic Government* (1971). In this study he attacked monarchy and dynastic succession as alien to Islam. He developed a Shi'a fundamentalist paradigm of an Islamic state, where sovereignty belongs to God, and the Government is headed by a *faqih* (*Waliyat-i faqīh*), the jurist who exercises political power in the absence of al-Mahdi, the hidden *imam*. The parliament is not to *legislate,* "but will be an *agenda-setting* institution to clarify for the ministers the best means for administering social services." See an excellent study on the role of clergy in Iran by Shahrough Akhavi, *Religion and Politics in Contemporary Iran: Clergy-State Relations in the Pahlavi Period* (Albany: State University of New York Press, 1980), Chapter 6. See also, Amin Saikal, *The Rise and Fall of the Shah* (Princeton: Princeton University Press), pp. 193–94, 196.

16. Chaudhari Muhammad Ali, "How to Release the Spirit of the East," *The Civil and Military Gazette* (Lahore: April 21, 1962); Misbah-ul-Haq Siddiqui, *Iqbal: A Critical Study* (Lahore: Farhan Publishers, 1977), pp. 67–86.

17. The most notorious Kelsen cases of Pakistan's Supreme Court are: (1) Federation of Pakistan vs. Moulvi Tamizzudin Khan (1955); (2) The State vs. Dosso (1958); (3) Begum Nusrat Bhutto vs. The Chief of the Army Staff (1977). In an equally important case (Miss Asma Jilani vs. The Government of the Punjab, [1972]) the Supreme Court had rejected the Kelsen doctrine, only to reaffirm it in 1977 in the Begum Bhutto case.

18. Justice Munir has explained his views very thoroughly in Nazir Husain Chaudhari, *Chief Justice Muhammad Munir: His Life, Writings, and Judgements* (Lahore: Research Society of Pakistan, 1973), pp. 519–51.

19. For a comparative study of Kelsenian theory of revolutionary legality and its extensive impact on the courts of British Commonwealth countries, see Leslie Wolf-Phillips, *Constitutional Legitimacy: A Study of the Doctrine of Necessity* (London: Third World Foundation, 1980?), pp. 1–24, 27–39nn. For Kelsen's doctrines, see Hans Kelsen, *Principles of International Law,* ed. Robert W. Tucker (New York: Holt, Rinehart and Winston, 1966), pp. 381–87.

1. *The Framework of Modernity*

1. Arnold Toynbee, *A Study of History,* abridged by D. C. Somervell (Oxford: Oxford University Press, 1957), Vol. II, p. 148; see also C. E. Black, *The Dynamics of Modernization: A Study in Comparative History* (New York: Harper and Row, 1967), p. 6.

2. David Apter, *The Politics of Modernization* (Chicago: University of Chicago Press, 1966), p. 43.

3. W. Wilson Hunter to Miss Murray, December 17, 1862, in Francis Henry Skrine, *Life of William Wilson Hunter* (London: Longmans, Green, 1901), p. 70.

4. Lucian W. Pye, *Aspects of Political Development* (Boston: Little, Brown, 1965), p. 8.

5. Sayyid Ahmad Dehlawī, *Rasūm-i Dehli* (Delhi: Mukhzan Press, 1905), pp. 37–41.

6. Thomas William Beale, *Miftah al-Tawarīkh* (Lucknow: Matba' Nawel Kishawr, n.d.), pp. 234, 297, 327, 340, 343; see also Beale's *An Oriental Biographical Dictionary* (London: W. H. Allen, 1894), pp. 42, 95, 201, 308.

7. Sayyid Yusuf Bukhari, *Yeh Dīllī Hai* (Delhi: Maktaba-i-Jahan-Numa, 1944, pp. 14–15 ff.

8. *Ibid.*, pp. 99 ff.

9. *Ibid.*, pp. 9 ff, especially the chapter on *Dīllī Kīy Gallīyān* (Streets of Delhi); see also Sayyid Yusuf Bukharīy, *Baz Gasht* (Delhi: Maktaba-i-Jahan-Numa, 1944), p. 67 ff.

10. Muhammad Zahīr-ud-Din Mirza Aali Bakht Azfarī, *Waqiat-i Azfarī* (Rampur Ms; 1806), p. 3a; see also, Imtiyaz Ali Khan 'Arashī, "Deybachech," *Nadarāt-i Shahī* by Shah 'Alam (Rampur; Hindustan Press, 1944), p. 27.

11. Beale, *Miftah al-Tawarīkh,* pp. 360–61; Azfarī, p. 3a gave *'Alam Ka Gham* (1202 A.H./1788) as the chronogram of this tragic incident.

12. For the full text of the Persian letter and its English translation, see William Francklin, *The History of the Reign of Shah-Aulum* (London: Cooper and Graham, 1798), pp. 242–49.

13. Percival Spear, *Twilight of the Mughals* (Cambridge: Cambridge University Press, 1951), p. 34.

14. India Office Misc. [whereafter abbreviated I.O.] Vol. 492, pp. 251–52. Wellesley to Shah Alam, July 27, 1803.

15. *Ibid.*, Vol. 485, pp. 196–98. Lake to Shah Alam, August 8, 1803.

16. I do not agree with Spear's (p. 35) contention that Lake "went beyond his superior's intentions and unintentionally played into Shah Alam's hands." Lake wrote to Shah 'Alam under no pressure whatever, and carried out the Governor-General's policy of establishing an ambiguous legal relationship with the Emperor.

17. Spear, *Twilight,* p. 38.

18. For the detailed elaboration of the concept of "affective orientation," see Gabriel A. Almond and Sidney Verba, *The Civic Culture* (Princeton: Princeton University Press, 1963), pp. 13–15 ff.

19. Spear, *Twilight,* pp. 39, 62.

20. I. O. Home Misc., Vol. 708, p. 28.

21. Muhammad Husain Azad, *Ab-i Hayat* (Lahore: Shaikh Ghulam Ali and Sons, 1957) p. 149. Sawda also composed a *Shaher Ashawb* (Lament of the City), mourning the vanished glory of the Mughal rule, and the humiliations to which the citizens of Delhi had been subjected.

22. For the text of Shah Alam's elegy, see Francklin, *History,* pp. 251–54; Beale, *Miftah al-Tawarīkh,* pp. 361–62; Hakīm Sayyid Abd al-Hayyī, *Gul-i Ra'nā* (Azamgarh: Matba-i-Ma'ārif, 1950), pp. 259–60.

23. Muhammad Husain Azad, *Ab-i Hayat,* p. 261.

24. Faiz-ud-Din, *Bazm-i Akher* (Delhi: Dānish Mahal, 1945), pp. 27–46.

25. Mirza Farhat Allah Beg, *Bahadur Shah Awr Phul Wallun Key Seyr* (Delhi: Kutab Khana 'ilam Wa Adab, n.d.), pp. 7 ff; Khawjah Sayyid Nāsir Nazīr Firāq, *Mudamīyn-i Firāq* (Delhi: Mahbub al-Mataba', n.d.), see his essay "Jahan Abad," pp 149–60; see also Agha Shā'ir Qizilbash, *Khumaristan: Mudamiyn Ka Majmu'ah* (Delhi: Kitāb Gher, 1943), pp. 78–84.

26. William Francklin, *The History of the Reign of Shah-Aulum,* see Appendix I, pp. 202, 210.

27. Sir Sayyid Ahmad Khan, *Athar al-Şanadīd* (Delhi: Central Book Depot Urdu Jama'a Masjid, 1965), pp. 459–701.

28. *Ibid.,* p. 459.

29. Lucian W. Pye and Sidney Verba, *Political Culture and Political Development* (Princeton University Press, 1965), p. 21.

30. For the definitions see Fazlur Rahman, *Islam* (New York: Doubleday, 1969), pp. 60–62; Asaf A. A. Fyzee, *Outlines of Muhammadan Law* (Oxford: Oxford University Press, 1964), pp. 15–16.

31. Shah Walīy Allah, *Al-Maqalah al-Wadīya fi al-Nasihah Wa al-Wasīyah* (Hyderabad: Shah Walīy Allah Akademiy, 1964), pp. 50–53.

32. *Walīyma* is a wedding feast intended to solemnize and publicize the event of marriage. Cf. Shah Walīy Allah, *Hujjat Allah al-Balighah,* trans. Mawlana 'Abdūl Rahīm (Lahore, Qawmi Kutab Khana, 1962), Vol. 2, pp. 544–45.

33. *'Aqīqah* are the ceremonies performed on the birth of a male or female child; usually a lamb (two for a male child, one for a female) or sheep is slaughtered and the *āzan* is said in the ear of the newlyborn child. The Prophet Muhammad performed these ceremonies for his children and grandchildren. Shah Mu'īn-ud-Din Ahmad Nadwi, *Siyār al-Sahabah* (Azamgarh Dar al-Musenafin, 1956), Vol. 6, pp. 2, 142; see *Mustadark Hakim,* Vol. 3, p. 76.

34. Walīy Allah, *Al-Maqalah,* pp. 47–48.

35. *Sirat al-Mustaqīym* (Lahore: Shaikh Muhammad Ashraf, n.d.), p. 156.

36. Karl W. Deutsch, "Social Mobilization and Political Development," *The American Political Science Review,* 4, no. 3 (Washington, D.C., September 1961), p. 494.

37. S. C. Sanial, "The Itimad-ud-Daulah Institution at Delhi," *Islamic Culture,* 4, no. 2 (Hyderabad, April 1930), pp. 310–311.

38. Charles F. Andrews, *Zaka Ullah of Delhi* (Cambridge: W. Heffer & Sons, 1929), pp. 36, 39–40, 42–43.

39. Lucian W. Pye, *Communications & Political Development* (Princeton: Princeton University Press, 1963), p. 150.

40. Altaf Husain Hali, Hali Key Kahaniy Khud Unkey Zabanīy," in *Mataliah-i Halī,* ed. Shujā'at Ali Sandaylvi and Nazir Kakawrawīy (Lucknow: Farogh-i Urdu, 1956), p. 9; see also Shaikh Muhammad Isma'īl, *Tadhkirah-i Halī* (Dehli: Mercantile Press, 1935), p. 38. Andrews was misinformed when he stated that Hali was one of the alumni of the Delhi College. See *Zaka Ullah of Delhi,* p. 38.

41. Mawlavi 'Abd al-Haq, *Merhūm Delhi Kālij* (Delhi: Anjuman Traqi-i-Urdu, 1945), pp. 96–97; for the syllabi of Western and Oriental Departments, see pp. 78–94.

42. *Ibid.,* pp. 107–10.

43. *Ibid.,* pp. 139–45.

44. D.R.R. Political & Miscellaneous, Case 1, no. 3; Spear, *Twilight,* p. 65.

45. Spear, p. 68.

46. Ghulam Rasūl Mehr, *Ghālib* (Lahore: Shaikh Ghulam Ali, 1946), p. 69*n*1.

47. Muhammad Walīy al-Haq Ansarīy "Akbar Abad (Agra): Shammaliy Hindustan ka Ayk 'Ilmīy wa Adabīy Markaz," *Fiker Wa Nazer* (Aligarh: April 1965), p. 106.
48. *Malfūzat Shah 'Abdūl 'Azīz* (Delhi: Mutba-i Mujtabaī, 1314 A.H.), p. 117; also its Urdu trans. by Mawlavi Muhammad Ali Lutfiy and Mufti Intizam Allah Shahabīy (Karachi: Pakistan Educational Publishers, 1960), pp. 214–16; see also an excellent article by Muhammad 'Azd-ud-Din Khan, "Khanwadah-i Shah Walīy Allah Muhadith Dehlawiy say Muta 'laq Dow Rawayatun Key Tahqiq Wa Tanqīd," *Burhān* (Delhi: May 1967), pp. 261–73.
49. For Ghalib's contact with the British society and officialdom and his visit to Calcutta, see Altaf Husain Halī, *Yadgar-i Ghālib* (Lahore: Majlis Traqi-Adab, 1963), pp. 24–37.
50. *Naqsh-i Azad,* ed. Ghulam Rasūl Mehr (Lahore: Kitāb Manzil, ३४x४), pp. 274–78.
51. Asad Allah Khan Ghālib, *Kuliyāt-i Ghālib Farsī* (Lahore: Shaikh Mubarak Ali, 1965), pp. 144–46.

2. Sir Sayyid's Political Socialization and Orientations

1. Sir Sayyid Ahmad Khan, *Sīrat-i Farīdīyah* (Karachi: Pakistan Akademiy, 1964), p. 80.
2. Altaf Husain Halī, *Hayat-i Javid* (Lahore: Akademiy Punjab Trust, 1957), p. 80.
3. W. W. Hunter to Miss Murray, December 6, 1862 in Skrine, p. 63.
4. Sir Sayyid, *Sīrat-i Farīdīyah,* p. 81.
5. Khawjah Farīd-al-Din Ahmad, *Fawā'id al-Afkar fi A'mal al-Farja* (Delhi, n.d.), see Deybacheh.
6. Sir Sayyid, *Sīrat-i Farīdīyah,* p. 100.
7. For Akbar Shah's dealings with the company on the subject of royal pensions see Spear, *Twilight,* pp. 38–40.
8. Sir Sayyid, *Sīrat-i Farīdīyah,* p. 106.
9. *Ibid.,* pp. 110–111; Halī, *Hayat-i Javid,* p. 87.
10. *Ibid.,* p. 91.
11. *Ibid.,* p. 108.
12. A thirteenth-century Arabic manuscript with miniatures contains stories on morals; it was composed by al-Harīry.
13. Among the ancient Arabic odes the so-called "Seven Mu'llaqāt" (suspended) hold first place. Legend has it that each of these odes was awarded the annual prize at the fair of Ukaz, and was inscribed in golden letters and suspended on the walls of the Ka'bah. Hammad al-Rawīyah, the famous rhapsodist who flourished in the middle of the eighth century, chose the seven odes from among many others, and compiled them into a separate group. Ahmad Hasan Ziyāt, *Tarīkh Adab-i 'Arabi,* trans. 'Abd al-Rahmān Tāhir Suratī (Lahore: Shaikh Ghulam Ali, 1961), p. 71.
14. The author of the book is 'Ubaiyd Allah bin Mas'ūd bin Sadr al-Shari'at al-Thani al-Mahbūbi (d. 1346).
15. The author's name is Burhan al-Din Abū al-Hasan Ali bin Abi Bakr bin 'Abd al-Jalīl al-Marghinanī 16. A well-known commentary on Hanafi jurisprudence.
17. It is a commentary on Siraj al-Din Abū al-Sana Muhammad bin Abi al-'Urmavī's (d. 1283) work, *Matali'al-Anwār.*

18. A collection of the Prophet Muhammad's Traditions; *Mishkat*'s author was Walīy Al-Din Abu 'Abdūllah Muhammad bin 'Abdūllah al-Khatīb al-Tabrizī. It was completed in 1336.

19. The collector of the Prophet's traditions, *Sahīhy Muslim*, was Muslim ibn al-Hajjaj (d. 875) of Naysabur.

20. "He is very timid, but clever. Named Syed Ahmad." Sir Robert Hamilton to Colin Lindsay, n.d., probably written before 1846, in G.F.I. Graham, *The Life and Work of Sir Syed Ahmad Khan* (London: Hodder & Stroughton, 1909), p. 6.

21. See the "Preface" by an anonymous British writer in Sayyid Ahmad Khan, *Asaroos- Sunnadeed* (Delhi: printed at the Indian Standard Press by William Demonte, 1854).

22. *Ibid.*, "Preface."

23. Halī, *Hayat-i-Javid*, p. 116.

24. *Ibid.*, p. 117.

25. Sir Sayyid Ahmad Khan, *Tarīkhanā Halat Awr Jadīd Waq'iāt* (Agra: Matb'a Mufiyd-i'Aām, n.d.), p. 3. The lecture was delivered by Sir Sayyid on December 30, 1889, at the Fourth Annual Session of Muhammadan Educational Conference, Aligarh. See also, *Mukamal Majmū'ah Lecktures Wa Spiches Sir Sayyid Ahmad Khan*, ed. Imam al-Dīn (Lahore: Mustafahiy Press), pp. 398–437.

26. Graham, *The Life and Work*, p. 21; Hali, *Hayat-i Javid*, 134.

27. Asad Allah Khan Ghālib, *Dastanbū* in *Urdu-i Mu'allā: Ghalib Number* (New Delhi: Vol. V, no. 2–3), p. 27.

28. *Ibid.*, p. 219; Ghalib to Mir Mahdīy Majrūh, February 2, 1859, in *Khatūt-i Ghālib*, ed. Ghulam Rasūl Mehr (Lahore: Shaikh Ghulam Ali, 1962), pp. 280–81.

29. Spear, *Twilight*, p. 219.

30. Ghālib to Alā al-Din Khan, *Urdu-i Mu'alā* p. 318.

31. Ghālib, *Dastanbū*, pp. 124–26, 183; The ode contained sixty Persian verses.

32. For Ghālib's view of 1857 see an excellent article by G. C. Narang, "Ghalib and the Rebellion of 1857," *Mahfil*, Vol. 5, no. 4 (East Lansing, 1968–69), pp. 45–57; Mehr, *Ghālib*, p. 303.

33. Sir Sayyid, *Tarīkhanā Halat Awr Jadīd Waq'iat*, p. 4.

34. Sayyid Ahmad Khan, *Shukriyah Jow Moradabad Kay Musalmanūn Nay July 28, 1859 Kaw Kiyā* (Meerut: Mofussilite Press, n.d.), pp. 1, 3–4; also its English translation in the same volume, pp. 1–5; this author has cited the English text with some modifications in translation. The English is not always accurate since it is a free translation.

35. Halī, *Hayat-i Javid*, p. 161.

36. *Ibid.*, 175.

37. From A. Shakespeare, Collector and Magistrate, Bijnore, to R. Alexander, Commissioner, Rohilkhand Dicision, Breilly, June 5, 1858, Sir Sayyid Ahmad Khan, *Risālah Khair Khawahān Musalmanan: Hissa Awwal* (Meerut: Mofussilite Press, 1860), p. 25.

38. From G. Edmonstone, Secretary to the Government of India, to William Muir, Secretary to the Government of N.W.P., no. 346, July 29, 1858.

39. Halī, p. 139 *n1*.

40. Sir Sayyid, *Risālah*, p. 3.

41. *The Seventh Discourse of Sir Syed Ahmad: Reprint From the Mohamedan Commentary on the Holy Bible* (London: The Christian Literature Society, 1910), p. 38. In order to benefit from Hebrew Sources Sir Sayyid learned Hebrew and hired Salem, a Yemenite Jew as a tutor.

42. *Proceedings of the First Meeting of the Scientific Society*, Ghazeepur, January 9, 1864, *Fiker Wa Nazar* (Aligarh: April 1963), p. 8.

43. *Ibid.*, pp. 10–11.

44. *Ibid.*, p. 16.

45. "Extract from the speech of Syed Ahmad Khan: Appendix to Letter No. 13," *Fiker Wa Nazer*, April 1963, pp. 42–45.

46. *Ibid.*, p. 10.

47. *Ibid.*, p. 14; see also, *Aligarh Institute Gazette*, July 21, 1876, pp. 1–8.

48. For the titles of at least thirty books see, 'Abd al-Haq, *Sir Sayyid Ahmad Khan; Halāt Wa Afkār* (Delhi: Urdu Markaz, 1960), pp. 151–53.

49. Syed Ahmad Khan to H. J. Prinsep, September 15, 1864, *Fiker Wa Nazer* (April 1963), pp. 48–50.

50. "Memo about the Government Garden prepared by Syed Ahmad Khan," May 24, 1877, Aligarh, *Fiker Wa Nazer*, October 1963, pp. 120–23.

51. "Syed Ahmad to J. H. Prinsep, Collector of Aligarh, December 30, 1865," *Fiker Wa Nazer*, July 1963, p. 71.

52. See, "From Collector of Aligarh [J. c. colvin] to the Secretary, Scientific Society, Aligarh, August 19, 1875, no. 320 of 1876"; and "Officiating Secretary to Government [A. Colvin], N.W. Provinces to the Commissioner of Meerut Division, Allahabad, March 20, 1876, and May 1876, No. 276A of 1876, No. 710A of 1876," *Fiker Wa Nazer*, October 1963, pp. 117–19.

53. "Memo about the Government Garden prepared by Syed Ahmad Khan," p. 123.

54. 'Al-Haq, p. 146–47; *Proceedings of the first meeting of the Scientific Society* (January 9, 1864), p. 14.

55. *Hayat-i Javid*, pp. 181–82.

56. Sayyid Mahmood to the Under Secretary of State, June 9, 1869, in Public Department, Home Correspondence, Secretary of State for India, no. 5/48 indicated arrival date, May 4, 1869.

57. Sayyid Ahmad Khan to Mahdī Ali Khan, July 9, 1869 in *Maktūbāt-i Sir Sayyid*, ed. Isma'īl Panīpatī (Lahore: Majlis Traqi-i Adab, 1959), p. 51.

58. Minutes of the Council of India, India Office (hereafter abbreviated I.O.) July to December, 1869, Vol. 23, p. 145; On August 7, 1869, M. G. Grant Duff, Under Secretary of State for India, Communicated the decision to Sir Sayyid.

59. Sir William Muir to Lord Mayo, May 11, 1869, in *Order of the Star of India, Dispatches & Recommendations From Institutions of Order Till 1870 (1860–1870)*, Vol. 3, pp. 917–20, I.O.

60. *Ibid.*, p. 879. Sir John Lawrence had recommended for 1869 some 77 individuals (1 for Class I, 24 for Class II, and 52 for Class III) for the Order of the Star of India award, but the Secretary of State selected only 24 individuals (1 for Class I, 3 for Class II, and 20 for Class III). The Class I Star was awarded to the Rana of Dholepore, Class II to the Raja of Cochin and two British officials, and Class III to 17 Britons, one Parsee businessman (Cowasjee Jehanghier), Sir Sayyid Ahmad Khan, and another Muslim (whom history has already forgotten), Mir Akbar Ali.

61. Currently a lower-middle-class rooming house, called Grenville House (Room and Breakfast). Its building, according to the present (1969) owner, is 150 years old. Describing the social position of the owner of this house, Sir Sayyid wrote in his letter of October 15, 1869:" those who let out a portion of their houses in London are poor; and so they are, but they are, at the same time, of respectable family." Graham, p. 127.

62. Graham, *The Life and Work*, p. 125; Sir Sayyid Ahmed Khan, *Musafirān-i Landon*, ed. Shaikh Muhammad Isma'īl Panīpatī (Lahore: Majlis Traqi-i Adab, 1961), pp. 182–83.

63. *Ibid.*, pp. 185–86; Graham, p. 127.

64. *Musafirān-i London*, p. 184; Graham, p. 126.

65. Sir Sayyid, *Musafirān-i London*, p. 173.

66. *Ibid.*, pp. 172–74; figures for the funds were provided by Sir Sayyid in rupees, not knowing the rates of exchange of that period I have not tried to give either dollars or pounds sterling.

67. Sayyid Ahmad Khan to Mahdī Ali Khan, September 10, 1869, in *Maktūbat-i Sir Sayyid*, p. 66.

68. *Ibid.*, p. 124; Sayyid Ahmad Khan to Mahdī Ali Khan, June 28, 1870.

69. "Ayk Mu'azez angrayz kay nām," *Maktūbāt-i Sir Sayyid*, pp. 187–88.

70. Sayyid Ahmad to Mahdī Ali Khan, August 20, 1869, *Maktūbāt*, p. 62.

71. *Ibid.*

72. Sir Sayyid, *Musafirā-i London*, pp. 253–66.

3. Perceptions of 1857 and the Theory of Participatory Rule

1. Sir Sayyid Ahmad Khan, *Sarkashīy-i Dhilā Bijnor* (Delhi: Nadwah al-Mussennefin, 1964), p. 91; see also Hafeez Malik and Morris Dembo, *Sir Sayyid's History of the Bijnor Rebellion* (East Lansing, Michigan: State University Asian Studies Center, 1971), p. 1.

2. H. R. Neville, *Bijnor: A Gazetteer* (Allahabad: Government Press, 1928), Vol. 14, p. 1.

3. Sir Sayyid Ahmad Khan, *Maqālāt-i Sir Sayyid: Tarīkhy Mudamīyn Wā Tarıkh Sarkashiy Dhillā Bijnor*, ed. Mawlana Muhammad Isma'īl Panīpatī (Lahore: Majlis Traqi-i Adab, 1962), p. 302.

4. *Ibid.*, p. 307.

5. *Ibid.*, p. 300.

6. *Ibid.*, pp. 309–10.

7. *Ibid.*, p. 327.

8. *Ibid.*, p. 337.

9. *Ibid.*, p. 352.

10. *Hayat-i Javid*, pp. 136–37.

11. Sir Sayyid Ahmad Khan, *Asbāb-i Baghāwat-i Hind* (Aligarh: Aligarh Muslim University Press, 1858), p. 30; *The Causes for the Indian Revolt by Syed Ahmad Khan Bahadur, C.S.I.*, trans. Ma. Gen. G. F. I. Graham and Sir Auckland Colvin, (Benares: Medical Hall Press, 1873), p. 2.

12. Sir Sayyid, *Asbāb*, p. 42.

13. Sir Sayyid, *The Causes for the Indian Revolt*, p. 24.

14. Following the publication of Eshwar Chandra Vidyasagar's book, *Marriage of Hindu Widows* (Calcutta: 1856), Vol. 5, p. 191, Bengalis petitioned the Legislative Council to pass the Hindu Widows' Remarriage Act, while 55,746 Hindus opposed it in a signed petition. Government of India, Legislative Council, *Proceedings, from January to December, 1856*, Vol. 2, pp. 436–38.

15. B. H. Baden-Powell, *Land Revenue & Its Administration in British India* (Oxford: Clarendon Press, 1913), p. 54.

16. *Ibid.*, p. 55.

17. William Wilson Hunter, *The Indian Musalmans* (London: Trubner, 1871), pp. 183–85.

18. Sir Sayyid, *Asbāb*, p. 26.

19. Sir Sayyid called the first category of land Pulich, but *A'in-i Akbari* described it Polaj, and further subdivided it into the three categories of good, middling, and bad. (I have used the latter spelling.) Cf. Abul Fadl, *A'in-i Akbari*, trans. H. S. Jarrett (Calcutta; royal Asiatic Society of Bengal, 1949), Vol. 2, A in XI. It gives in detail the statistical data regarding the revenue of each category of land, and the method of its computation.

20. Sir Sayyid, *Asbāb*, p. 55.

21. The Shah Jahani *bigha*, which was adopted by the British, is the square of a linear unit, which is 60 gaz (each gaz, or Indian yard, being 33 inches in length). The *bigha* is thus 3,025 sq. yards = ⅝ of an acre. See Baden-Powell, *Land Revenue*, p. 12.

22. In 1876, their breakdown was as follows. British army: officers, 2,986; men 60,224; total 63,210. Indian army: British officers and staff corps, 3,398; Indian noncommissioned officers and men, 123,479; total 126,877. The forces were distributed in the presidencies of Bengal, Madras, and Bombay. Emory Upton, *Armies of Asia & Europe* (New York: D. Appleton, 1878), pp. 33–87. Currently, both India and Pakistan maintain armies consisting of one and a half million men.

23. Sir Sayyid, *Asbāb*, p. 72–73.

24. *Ibid.*, p. 74.

25. Gabriel A. Almond and Sidney Verba, *The Civic Culture* (Princeton: Princeton University Press, 1963), pp. 24–25.

26. Sir Sayyid, *Asbāb*, p. 15.

27. *Ibid.*, p. 13.

28. Sir Sayyid has used the word *intakhāb*, which is currently translated as election, but in 1858 when the memorandum was written, election in India was unknown. Therefore, he probably used the word *intakhāb* for selection or nomination.

29. A. L. Lowell, *The Government of England*. See also Theodore F. T. Plucknett, *English Constitutional History* (Boston: Houghton Mifflin, 1960), pp. 572–75.

30. Sir Sayyid, *The Causes*, p. 41.

31. *Ibid.*, p. 40.

32. *Ibid.*

33. *Ibid.*

34. *Ibid.*, pp. 42–43.

35. Sahibzada Aftab Ahmad Khan, Vice-Chancellor of Aligarh University (1923–26), is known to have stated to Hume when he visited him in Britain: "Sir Sayyid's memorandum, *The Causes for the Revolt of India*, inspired me to initiate a movement like the National Congress," *Aligarh Institute Gazette*, December 12, 1887; Tufaiyl Ahmad Mangloriy, *Musalman Ka Roshan Mustiqbal* (Delhi: Matba-i 'Alīmi, 1945), p. 286; see also, Harun Khan Sherwaniy, "Sir Sayyid Ahmad Khan Awr Hindu-Muslim Ittahad," *Aligarh Tahrīyk: Aghaz Ṭā Imroz*, eds. Professor Rashid Siddiqi and Professor Āl Ahmad Sarūr (Aligarh: Muslim University, 1960), p. 195.

4. Muslim Reaction to Modern Education

1. Sayyid Ahmad Khan to C. A. Elliot, Secretary to Government, N.W. Provinces, dated Banares, 14 June 1872, in *Fiker wa nazer* (Aligarh: January 1964), p. 149.

2. Hali, *Hayat-i Javid*, p. 224.

3. The Select Committee consisted of the following members: (1) Mawlavi Sayyid Farid-ud Din Ahmad, (2) Muhammad Sami'y Allah Khan, (3) Mawlavi 'Abd al-Rahmān, (4) Munshi Yār Muhammad Khan, (5) Muhammad Qutb-ud-Din, (6) Mawlavi Sayyid 'Abd Allah, (7) Mawlavi Muhammad 'Arif, (8) Mirza Rahmat Allah Beg, (9) Mawlavi Ashraf Husain Khan, (10) Mawlavi Hafiz-ud-Din Ahmad, (11) Munshi Akbar Husain. Sir Sayyid Ahmad Khan, "Tariyqah Ta'liym Musalmanan," *Tahdhibal-Akhlāq* (Aligarh: 10 Rabi I, 1289 AH./1872).

4. Sayyid Ahmad Khan, *Report of the Members of the Select Committee for the Better Diffusion and Advancement of Learning among Muhammadans of India* (Banares: Medical Hall Press, 1872), pp. 4–5 (henceforward called *Report of the Select Committee*).

5. William Wilson Hunter, *Indian Musalmans* (London: 1871), p. 184.

6. Sir Sayyid, *Report of the Select Committee*, pp. 16–27.

7. Director of Public Instruction, N.W. Provinces, *Educational Report: 1867–68*, p. 10.

8. For the nature of "Islamic Science," and the Muslim contribution to the progress of science see an excellent study, Seyyed Hossein Nasr, *Science and Civilization in Islam* (Cambridge: Harvard University Press, 1968), p. 27 ff.

9. Qadi Muhammad bin Ali, *Al-Durr al-Mukhtār* (Meerut: Matba Hashmiy, 1277 A.H./.1860), p. 5; see also its Urdu translation by Khuram Ali, *Ghayāt al-Wattar* (Brailey: matba Siddiqiy, 1288 A.H./1871), Vol. I, p. 11.

10. *Mujam al-Matbū'at* (Cairo: 1928), Vol. I, p. 778.

11. Sir Sayyid, *Report of the Select Committee*, p. 49.

12. These four schools, named after their founders, are: (1) Hanfi, (2) Shafi'ī, (3) Maliki, and (4) Hanbali. The founder of the Hanfi school, Abū Hanīfah al-Nu'mān bin Thabit (700–767) was born in Kufa, and died in Baghdad. Muhammad bin Idris al-Shafi'ī (767–819), the founder of the Shafi'ī School, was born in Askalon (Palestine), and died in Cairo. The Maliki School was founded by Abū 'Abd Allah Mālik bin Ans (716–795), who was born in Madina and died there. The Hanabali School was established by 'Abd Allah bin Hanbal, who was born in Baghdad in 780 and died in 855. Muhammad al-Khudariy, *Tarikh al-Tashri'al-Islami* (Cairo: 1348 A.H./1930), 3d edition; see also its Urdu trans. by 'Abhūs Salām Nadviy, *Tarikh Fiqh-i Islami* (Azamgarh: Dar al-Musennefiyn, 1381 A.H./1961), 2d edition.

13. Sir Sayyid, *Report of the Select Committee*, p. 50.

14. *Ibid.*, p. 51.

15. *Ibid.*, p. 52.

16. Department of Education, *Report on the Progress of Education in the Northwestern Province During 1890–91;* Memorandum from M. Kempson to C. A. Elliot, Secretary to the Government of the N.W. Provinces, No. 1728, dated Naynee Tal, 28 August 1872; the Government of India, *Home Department Proceedings: Education*, September 1873, no. 48, p. 699 I.O.L.

17. *Ibid.*, fn. 1.

18. *Ibid.*, p. 694.

19. From A. C. Colvin, Secretary to the Government of the Northwestern Provinces, dated Allahabad, 18 April 1873, no. 263 A, to A. C. Lyall, Secretary to the Government of India, *ibid.*, p. 686.

20. From Sir James Fitz-James Stephen to W. W. Hunter, September 8, 1871, in *Francis Henry Skrine, Life of Sir William Wilson Hunter* (London: Longmans, Green, 1901), p. 200.

21. William Wilson Hunter, *The Indian Musalmans* (London: Trubner, 1871), p. 160.

22. *Ibid.*, pp. 159–71.

23. The Government of India, *Home Department Proceedings: Education, 1873,* p. 524, I.O.L.

24. *Ibid.*, pp. 574–75.

25. Syud Ameer Hossein, *A Pamphlet on Muhammadan Education in Bengal* (Calcutta: Bose Press, 1880), p. 20.

26. *Ibid.*, p. 21.

27. The Government of India, *Home Department Proceedings: Education, 1873.*

28. *Ibid.*, pp. 473–74.

29. *Ibid.*, p. 471.

30. *Ibid.*, p. 477.

31. *Ibid.*, p. 478.

32. From C. A. R. Browning, Director of Public Instruction, Oudh, to the Officiating Secretary to Chief Commissioner of Oudh, no. 1840, dated Lucknow, 6 September 1871; the Government of India, *Home Department Proceedings: Education, 1873,* p. 540. I.O.L.

33. *Ibid.*, p. 541.

34. *Ibid.*, p. 542.

35. From J. W. Neill, Assistant Secretary to the Chief Commissioner of the Central Provinces, no. 1502–81, dated Nagpore, 23 April 1872, to E. C. Bayley, Secretary to the Government of India, the Government of India, *Home Department Proceedings: Education, 1873,* p. 549, I.O.L.

36. From Captain T. G. Clark, Officiating Secretary to the Chief Commissioner of Mysore, no. 3314–16G, dated Banglore, 4 October 1871, to the Secretary to the Government of India, Home Department, the Government of India, *Home Department Proceedings: Education, 1873,* p. 537. I.O.L.

37. From Lt. Col. J. Puckle, Officiating Secretary to the Chief Commissioner of Coorg, no. 82–6, dated Nandidroog, 30 April 1872, to E. C. Bayley, Secretary to the Government of India, the Government of India, *Home Department Proceedings: Education, 1873,* p. 555, I.O.L.

38. From Major W. Tweedie, First Assistant Resident, Hyderabad, No. 10, dated Hyderabad, 16 April 1872, to E. C. Bayley, Secretary to the Government of India. The Government of India, *Home Department Proceedings: Education, 1873,* pp. 556–57 I.O.L.

39. T. W. Arnold, *The Preaching of Islam* (London: Constable, 1913), p. 255.

40. For points of similarity between Islam and Sikhism, see Hafeez Malik, "An Appreciation of Gurū Nānak in Iqbal's Poetry," *Studies in Islam,* 6, nos. 2–3, (New Delhi: April–July 1968), pp. 146–60

41. Percival Spear, *A History of India* (Baltimore: Penguin Books, 1965), Vol. 2, p. 135.

42. For the roles of Sayyid Ahmad Shahīd and Mawlana Ismaʿīl Shahīd in the Muslims' struggle for independence, and the overthrow of Sikh rule in the Punjab, see Hafeez Malik, *Muslim Nationalism in India and Pakistan* (Washington; D.C.: Public Affairs Press, 1963), Ch. 6.

43. "Agarcheh Punjabi būd bisyar faḍīylat ba istiʿdād dāsht" (although a Punjabi, he [Saʿd Allah Khan] was a profound scholar, in addition to being resourceful). Sadr al-Dīn Muhammad, *Irshād al-wuzarā,* Ms. or 233, fs. 64–5 Br. Mus.; see also, Khafi Khan, *Muntakhab al-Lubāb* (Calcutta: College Press, 1869), Vol. 2, pp. 291–95.

44. Sayyid Sulaiman Nadvīy, "Taj Mahal Awr Lal Qila Kay Maʿmār", *Maʿrif*

(Azamgarh: March–April 1936); see also, *Maqālāt-i Sulaiman*, ed. Sayyid Sbah al-Din 'Abd al-Rahmān (Azamgarh: Ma'rif Press, 1966), Vol. 1, pp. 239–345.

45. Muhammad Basheer Ahmad, *The Administration of Justice in Medieval India* (Aligarh: Historical Research Society, 1941), p. 42.

46. 'Abd al-Haq, *Urdu Key Nashav wa numā mein sufiyā Karām Kā Hisa* (Delhi: Anjuman Taraqi-i Urdu, 1939), pp. 7–9.

47. "Note on the State of Education in India During 1866–67," *Parliamentary Papers* (London: 1870), p. 25, I.O.L.

48. *Ibid.*, p. 26.

49. From Captain W. R. M. Holroyd, Officiating Director of Public Instruction, Punjab, no. 7, dated Lahore, 9 January *1868*, to C. U. Aitchison, Officiating Secretary to the Punjab Government, *Parliamentary Papers, 1870*, p. 322, I.O.L.

50. *Ibid.*, p. 26.

51. *Ibid.*, p. 23.

52. From Lapel Griffin, Officiating Secretary to the Government of the Punjab, no. 683, dated Lahore, 21 February 1873, to H. L. Dampier, Officiating Secretary to the Government of India. The Government of India, *Home Department Proceedings: Education, 1873*, p. 521, I.O.L.

53. *Ibid.*, p. 536.

54. *Parliamentary Papers, 1870*, p. 313.

55. From T. H. Thornton, Secretary to the Punjab Government, dated Lahore, 27 May 1868, no. 235, to E. C. Bayley, Secretary to the Government of India, *Parliamentary Papers, 1870*, p. 312.

56. *Ibid.*, pp. 356–57.

57. Halī, *Hayat-i Javid*, p. 667.

58. From A. Colvin, Secretary to the Government of the Northwestern Provinces, dated Allahabad, 18 April 1873, no. 263A, to A. C. Lyall, Secretary to the Government of India, the Government of India, *Home Department Proceedings: Education, 1873*, p. 688.

5. Mobilization of National Will for Modern Education

1. Talcott Parsons, *Essays in Sociological Theory* (Glencoe: The Free Press, 1954), p. 21; Talcott Parsons, *The Social System* (Glencoe: The Free Press, 1951), pp. 328–66; for the refinement of some related ideas see also, "Applications of Parsonian Theory," *Sociological Inquiry*, 28, no. 2 (1968).

2. The concept of diffusion was discussed towards the end of the nineteenth century, although it has been since refined. See Clarke Wissler, *Man and Culture* (New York: Thomas Y. Crowell, Co., 1938), pp. 128–72; Roland B. Dixon, *The Building of Cultures* (New York, 1928), pp. 59–106; Ralph Linton, *The Study of Man* (New York: Appleton-Century-Crofts, 1936), p. 324.

3. Sayyid Ahmad Khan, "Ta'assub," *Tahdhīb al-Akhlāq*, I Shawwal 287/1870, pp. 1–2; Sir Sayyid Ahmad Khan, *Maqālāt-i Sir Sayyid: Akhlaqī awr Islāhī Muḍamin*, ed. Mawlana Muhammad Isma'ī (Lahore: Majlis Traqqi-i Adab, 1962), pp. 351–52.

4. Sayyid Ahmad Khan, *Maqālāt-i Sir Sayyid: Ilmi wa Tahqīqī Madamin* (Lahore: Majlis Traqqi-i Adab, 1962), p. 340.

5. *Ibid.*, p. 347.

6. Sayyid Ahmad Khan, *Maqālāt-i Sir Sayyid: Ilmi wa Tahqīqī Maḍamīn* (Lahore: Majlis Traqqi-i Adab, 1962), p. 348.

7. Sir Sayyid mentions the following first contenders: (1) Imam 'Abd al-Mālik b. 'Abd al-'Azīz (d. 772); (2) Abū Nasr Sa'īd b. Arūba (d. 773); and (3) Rabi' b. Sabbīh (d. 777).

8. Sayyid Ahmad Khan, *Tahdhīb al-Akhlāq*, 15 Dhul-Qa'da 1288/1871. *Maqālāt-i Sir Sayyid: Maḍamīn muta'alliq Sawanih wa Siīyar*, ed. Mawlana Muhammad Isma'ī (Lahore: Majlis Traqqi-i Adab, 1962), p. 213.

9. *Ibid.*, p. 124.

10. See also, Philip K. Hitti, *History of the Arabs* (London: Macmillan & Co., 1956), p. 311; 'Abd al-Salam Nadwī, *Hukma-i-Islam* (Azambarh; Ma'rif Press, 1953), pp. 75, 79.

11. Hitti, *History*, p. 310.

12. *Ibid.*, p. 307; De Lacy O'Leary, *Arabic Thought and Its Place in History* (London: Routledge and Kegan Paul, 1958), p. 295.

13. Sayyid Ahmad Khan, *Maqālāt-i Sir Sayyid: Ilmi wa Tahqīqī Maḍamīn*, p. 347.

14. *Ibid.*, p. 350.

15. *Ibid.*, pp. 351–52.

16. *Ibid.*, p. 356.

17. Eduard Heinmann, *History of Economic Doctrines* (New York: W. W. Norton, 1945), pp. 75–76.

18. Adam Smith, *The Wealth of Nations* (New York: Appleton-Century Crofts, 1937), p. 80.

19. Sayyid Ahmad Khan, *Maqālāt-i Sir Sayyid: Maḍhhabi wa Islami Maḍamīn*, pp. 277–78.

20. *Ibid.*, p. 260.

21. See Heinmann, *History*, pp. 73–74.

22. *Holy Qur'ān*, trans. 'Abad Allah Yusūf Ali (Lahore, n.d.), XXVI, 221–26.

23. See footnote, 19, p. 262.

24. *Ibid.*, p. 269.

25. See footnote.

26. Sir Sayyid, *Maqālāt-i Sir Sayyid: Maḍhhabi wa Islami Madamīn*, p. 274.

27. *Kayfīyat Imtihān Panchayatīy Madressa Muraadabad, Babat Imtihān Awwal, January 1, 1960* (Meerut: Mofussilite Press, n.d.), p. 10.

28. *Ibid.*, p. 11.

29. *Ibid.*, p. 12.

30. Sir Sayyid Ahmad Khan, *Leckchurran Ka Majmū'ah Ma Mukhtsar Swaneh 'Umrīy*, ed. Munshiy Siraj al-Din (Lahore: Ismlamīyah Press, 1890), pp. 9, 14, 16.

31. "The British India Association, North West Provinces, to H.E. the Viceroy and Governor General of India in Council, August 1, 1867," *Parliamentary Papers 1870: Note on the State of Education in India, 1866–67*, p. 320, I.O.L.

32. From E. C. Bayley, Secretary to the Government of India to the President and Members of the British Indian Association, N.W. Provinces, no. 4217, 5 September 1867, *Parliamentary Papers, 1870*, p. 316, I.O.L.

33. Syed Ahmad Khan, *Strictures upon the Present Educational System in India*, Public Education & Ecclesiastical Department. Home Correspondence, No. 5/55, Letter no. 2583, I.O.L.

34. Syed Ahmad Khan, *Strictures*, pp. 5–6.

35. *Ibid.*, p. 12.

36. *Ibid.*, pp. 17–18.

37. Sir Sayyid, "Tariyqah Ta'liym Musalmanan," *Tahdhīb al-Akhlāq*, Aligarh, Rabi al-Awwal 10, 1289 A.H./1872.

38. *Ibid.*

39. Sayyid Ahmad Khan, "Maddrassah al-'Ulūm Musalmanan Kaisa Ho Gā," *Tahdhīb al-Akhlāq*, Aligarh, Rajb 1, 1289 A.H./1872.

40. Sir Sayyid Ahmad Khan, *Musalmanan Key Qismat Kā Faysalāh: "Qudrat ka fatwā hai kah agr qawm mutfiq ho ker qawm key Ala darjeh key Ta'līym wa Tarbiyat ka Saman mohhayyā nehyn kartiy to qawm key traqqī say mayusiy hai,"* (Agra: Matba'a-i Mufiyd 'Ām, 1894), pp. 13–14.

41. Circular from the Muhammadan Anglo-Oriental College Fund Committee, Benares, N.W.P., India, pp. 2, 3. Received in I.O.L. on October 27, 1869. For the Urdu text of this appeal see "Chandāh Maddrassah al-'Ulūm Musalmanan," *Tahdhīb al-Akhlāq*, Jamadi I, 15, 1290 A.H./1873. From London Sir Sayyid sent several copies of this appeal to Sayyid Mahdī Ali Khan (Mohsin al-Mulk) who was then a *tehsīldar* (revenue collector) in Mirzapur. Considering this appeal an exercise in futility, Mahdī Ali Khan locked them in a box until Sir Sayyid's return from Europe. "Not every man is a Sayyid Ahmad Khan equipped to do this kind of work," commented Khan, who then returned the copies to Sir Sayyid. Halī, *Hayat-i Javid*, p. 223.

42. Sir Sayyid estimated the total value of Nawab Kalb-i Ali's donations at Rs. 50,000. Sayyid Ahmad Khan, "Madrassah al-'Ulūm Musalmanan Key Roudadiyn Tahdhīb al-Akhlāq Mein Nah Chapiyn," *Tahdhīb al-Akhlāq*, Rabi II, 1, 1291 A.H./1874.

43. *The Aligarh Institute Gazette*, March 1874.

44. *Tahdhīb al-Akhlāq*, Jamadi II, 15, 1290 A.H./1873.

45. *The Aligarh Institute Gazette*, May 28, 1875.

46. Sayyid Ahmad Khan to C. A. Elliot, Secretary to N.W. Provinces Government, Naynee Tal, dated Benares, 14 June 1872, *Fiker Wa Nazer* (Aligarh: January 1964), pp. 149–51.

47. Sayyid Ahmad Khan to C. A. Elliot, dated Benares 24 July 1873; C. A. Elliot to A. C. Lyall, Secretary to the Government of India, dated Naynce Tal, 25 August 1873, Government of India, *Home Department Proceedings: Education*, October 1873, p. 703, I.O.L.

48. C. A. Elliot, Secretary to the N.W. Provinces Government, to Sayyid Ahmad Khan, dated Naynee Tal, 28 January 1875, *The Aligarh Institute Gazette*, March 5, 1875.

49. Sayyid Ahmad Khan, "Dar al-'Ulūm Musalmanan Kay Makhalifin," *Tahdhīb al-Akhlāq*, Safar 10, 1290 A.H./1873.

50. *Ibid.*

51. For the text of Sir Sayyid's opponents' interrogatory see "Naqal Istaftā Matbū'ha Akhbar Kanpur," Sayyid Ahmad Khan, *Maqālāt-i Sir Sayyid*, ed. Muhammad Isma'īl Panīpatiī (Lahore: Majlis Traqqi-i Adab, 1962), Vol. 10, p. 203.

52. Cf. Halī, *Hayat-i Javid*, p. 632–33.

53. Sayyid Mahmud, *A History of English Education in India* (Aligarh: 1895), p. 90; Mawlavi Anwar Ahmad Zubairy, *Khutbāt-i 'Alīyā* (Aligarh: Muslim University Press, 1927), Vol. 1, p. 33; Halī, pp. 246, 685.

54. Sayyid Iqbal Ali, *Sayyid Ahmad Ka Safar Namah-i Punjab* (Aligarh, n.d.). Scattered all over the pages of this volume, the donations can be classified as follows. Punjab's Donations to the MAO College: Lahore, 3,954; Amristar, 1,590; Gurdaspur, 2,319; Jallandher, 394; Ludhana, 1,584; Patiala, 295; Total, Rs. 9,742.

55. Sayyid Ahmad Khan, "Hamariy Qawm," *Maqālāt-i Sir Sayyid,* ed. Muhammad Isma'il Panipati (Lahore: Majlis Traqqi-i Adab, 1962), Vol. 10, pp. 191–92.

56. Sayyid Ahmad Khan to Nawab Muhammad Mudzamal Allah Khan, 10 September 1889, Aligarh, *Makatiyb-i Sir Sayyid Ahmad Khan,* ed. Mushtaq Husain (Aligarh: Friends Book House, 1960), p. 212.

57. Sayyid Ahmad Khan to Secretary, Government of N.W. Provinces, 12 October 1878, *Makatiyb Sir Sayyid Ahmad Khan,* ed. Mustaq Husain, pp. 123–25.

58. Sayyid Ahmad Khan to the Registrar of Allahabad University, 31 October 1888, *Makatiyb-i Sir Sayyid Ahmad Khan,* ed. Mushtaq Husain, pp. 202–4.

59. Mohsin al-Mulk, *Note on the Progress of the Muhammadan Anglo-Oriental College Aligarh Before the Trustee, August 4, 1903, comparing 1894–1898 period to 1899–1903.* (I.O.L.: March 24, 1906), statement no. 4.

60. *Ibid.,* statement no. 5.

61. *Ibid.,* p. 2; Hali, *Hayat-i Javid,* pp. 337; his total figures are inaccurate, although Hali's detailed description of Lal's methods of embezzlement is reliable.

62. *Ibid.,* See the Statistics of Statements no. 4 and 5.

63. Sir Sayyid Ahmad Khan, *Majmū'ah Rayzolūshan-hay Dah Salah:* 1886–1895 (Agra: Matba'a Mafiyd 'Ām, 1896), p. 37. This resolution (no. 5) was seconded by Muhammad Hashmat Allah, M.A., and was most vigorously defended by Sir Sayyid.

64. See *Institute Gazette,* Aligarh, February 19, 1898.

65. Sir Sayyid, *Report Select Committee for the British Diffusion,* p. 66; Sir Sayyid, *Musalmānū key Qismat ka Faysalāh,* pp. 31–33; 'Abd al-Haq, *Sir Sayyid Ahmad Khan* (Delhi: Urdu Markaz, 1960), p. 85; Ali, *Sayyid Ahmad Khan Ka Safar Namah-i Punjab,* pp. 256–66.

66. Sir Sayyid Ahmad Khan, *Majmū'ah Resolūshan-hay Dah Salah* (1886–1895) (Agra: Matba Mufiyd-i 'Ām, 1896), p. 35; see also Anwar Ahmad Marherwy, ed., *Murraqa-i Conference* (Aligarh: Muslim University Press, 1935) pp. 36–37.

67. Khalid B. Sayeed, *Pakistan: The Formativve Phase* (New York: Oxford University Press, 1968), p. 31; Abdul Hamid, *Muslim Separatism in India* (Lahore: Oxford University Press, 1967), pp. 40–41.

68. Muhammad Habīb-ur-Rahman, "Deybacheh Jild Soyem," *Khutbāt-i-'Āliyā* (1917–27), Vol. 3 (Aligarh: Muslim University Press, 1927), p. 22.

69. Sir Sayyid, *Majmū'ah Resolushon-hay,* pp. 9–12.

70. Two factors were mainly responsible for the decline of Sir Sayyid's popularity. First, Sham Bihari Lal, a Hindu Treasurer of the MAO College embezzled Rs.105,409, bringing the College Corporation to virtual bankruptcy. The Trustees attributed this development to Sir Sayyid's mismanagement. Secondly, Sir Sayyid insisted in 1897 that his son, Justice Sayyid Mahmud, be elected by the Trustees as the new Secretary to succeed him, and that he should occupy this position for the rest of his life. The Trustees were appalled by this "demand" because Sayyid Mahmud, though a brilliant Judge of the Allahabad High Court, had been "persuaded" to resign this prestigious position as a consequence of his addiction to alcohol. As an alcoholic, Sayyid Mahmud had become a *persona non grata* to his father's traditional supporters, who rightly believed that Sayyid Mahmud had lost mental equilibrium. Unable to live with his son, Sir Sayyid moved out of his residence during the last year of his life, and died a heart-broken man. Hali, *Hayat-i Javid,* pp. 330–34; "Hali to Shibli Nu'mani, September 18, 1899," *Makatiyb-i Hali,* ed. Shaikh Muhammad Isma'il Panipati (Karachi: Urdu Academy Sindh, 1950), p. 37; Muhammad Amin Zubairy, *Tadhkirā-i Waqar* (Aligarh: Aligarh Muslim University Press, 1938), pp.

151–60; Zubairy, *Hayat-i Muhsin* (Aligarh: Muslim University Press, 1934), pp. 77–80.

71. Anwar Ahmad Marherwy, *Murraqa Conference* (Aligarh: Muslim University Press, 1935), pp. 44, 50.

72. *Khutbāt-i Sadarat Panjah Sala Jubhīy All-India Muslim Educational Conference, 1886–1934* (Aligarh: Muslim University Press, 1938), pp. 163–66.

73. *Ibid.*, pp. 44, 74, 80, 249, 261, 288–303.

74. The Anjuman was staffed by well-known Urdu historians, writers, and poets, including Moulavi Nazīr Ahmad, Zaka Allah, Khawja Altaf Husain Halī, and Shibli Num'anī. Professor T. W. Arnold was its first President. Ghulam Rabbani, *Anjuman Traqqi-i Urdu key Kahanī* (Delhi: Anjuman Traqqi-i Urdu, 1939), p. 6.

75. Marherwy, *Murraqa Conference,* p. 131.

76. Any language is identified by the following critera: (1) grammar, (2) script, (3) vocabulary, and (4) literary forms. Urdu and Hindi share a common grammar, but radically differ in other aspects. Urdu's script is Arabic-Persian; vocabulary is derived from Arabic, Persian, Turkish, more recently from English, and to a much lesser extent from Hindi; its prose and poetic forms are based on Arabic and Persian models. Urdu writers looked to the Middle East for spiritual inspiration rather than to India and Sanskrit, the focal sources of enrichment for Hindi.

77. Rabbani, *Anjuman Traqqi-i Urdu,* p. 43.

78. For the text of this agreement see Sayyid Hashmī Farīdabadī, *Panjah Salā Tarīkh Anjuman Traqqi-i Urdu* (Karachi: Anjuman Traqqi-Urdu Pakistan, 1953), pp. 77–78.

6. *Theory of Muslim Nationalism*

1. Hans Kohn, *The Idea of Nationalism* (New York: Macmillan, 1944).

2. For the impact of Sir Sayyid's European tour on his religious ideas, see also Hafeez Malik, "The Religious Liberalism of Sir Sayyid Ahmad Khan," *The Muslim World* (July 1964).

3. Sir Sayyid Ahmad Khan, 'Insān Wa Haywān,' *Tahdhīb al-Akhlāq,* Jamadi al-Thani, 1297 A.H./1879; also *Maqālāt-i Sir Sayyid,* ed. Muhammad Isma'īl (Lahore: Majlis Traqqi-i Adab, 1962), pp. 144–46.

4. *The Holy Qur'ān,* trans. Abd Allah Yusuf Ali (Lahore: Shaikh Muhammad Ashraf, 1938), p. 1405.

5. Sir Sayyid Ahmad Khan, "Qawmi ta'līym, qawmi hamdardī awr bahami itifāq," *Tahdhīb al-Akhlāq* (23 January 1884).

6. Sir Sayyid Ahmad Khan, "Hubb-i Watan," *Tahdhīb al-Akhlāq,* 1 Rabi II, 1294/1877, pp. 98–101.

7. Sir Sayyid, "Intikhāb-i-Alfaz i-Motto barai Tahdhīb al-Akhlāq," 15th Rabi I. See also *Maqālāt-i-Sir Sayyid: Maḍamīn muta'alliqāh Tahdhīb al-Akhlāq* (Lahore: Majlis-i Taraqqi-i-Adab, 1962), pp. 52–59.

8. Sir Sayyid, "Insān wa haywān," *Tahdhīb al-Akhlāq,* 5th Jumadi, II, 1279/1862, p. 25; see also *Akhlāqī awr Islāhī Maḍamin,* ed. Mawlana Muhammad Isma'īl (Lahore: Majlis-i-Taraqqi-i-Adab, 1962), pp. 144–46.

9. Sir Sayyid, *Akhlāqī awr Islāhī Madamin,* p. 172.

10. Sir Sayyid Ahmad Khan, "Apnī madad Āp: Khuda unki madad kartā hai jo ap apni madad Kartay hain," *Tahdhīb al-Akhlāq,* Aligarh, Vol. 6, Sha'ban I, 1292 A.H./1875, pp. 113–26. See also *Maqālāt-i Sir Sayyid,* Vol. 5, p. 79.

11. Sir Sayyid Ahmad Khan, "Hindustan Kay Mu'azez Khandān," *Akhbār Scientific Society* (7 April 1876).

12. *Ibid.*, pp. 79–80.

13. Sayyid Sulaiman Nadwī, "Khilafat awr Hindustan," *Ma'arif* (Azamgarh, October 1921), pp. 133–99; 'Abdūl Halīm Sharar, *Tarīkh-i-Khilafat* (Lucknow: Dilgudāz Press, 1928), pp. 15–19; Abul Kalam Azad, *Mas'alah-i-Khilafat* (Lahore: Maktabah-i-Ahbab, Wasanpura, n.d.), pp. 10–15; T. A. Arnold, *The Caliphate* (Oxford: Clarendon Press, 1924), pp. 60–77.

14. For a brief biographical sketch of Taj Rezah see the scholarly article of Agha Abdus Sattar Khan, "Taj Rezah," *The Islamic Culture* (Hyderabad–Deccan, July 1940), pp. 359–66.

15. Sayyid Sabah-ud-Din, 'Abdūr Rahmān, *Bazm-i-Mamlūkiyah* (Azamgarh: Dar al-Musannifin, 1955), pp. 101–9 and 141–43.

16. For the development of secular Muslim nationalism, as the aftermath of the Caliphate, see also Hafeez Malik, *Muslim Nationalism in India and Pakistan* (Washington, D.C.: Public Affairs Press, 1963), Ch. 9.

17. *Letters of Iqbal to Jinnah,* ed. M. A. Jinnah (Lahore: Shaikh Muhammad Ashraf, 1956), pp. 18–20; 'Ashiq Husain Batalwi, *Iqbal kay Akhirī Do Sāl* (Karachi: Iqbal Academy 1961), p. 521 ff; *Iqbal: Poet-Philosopher of Pakistan,* ed. Hafeez Malik (New York: Columbia University Press, 1971), Ch. 4.

18. Rahmat Ali, *What Does the Pakistan National Movement Stand For* (Cambridge, 1933).

19. Ibn Khaldun, *The Muqaddima,* trans. Franz Rosenthal (New York: Pantheon Books, 1958), p. 393 and n.225.

20. Sir Sayyid Ahmad Khan, "Khilafat awr Khalifah," *Madhhabī wa Islami Maḍamīn* (Lahore: Majlis-i-Taraqqi-i-Adab, 1962), pp. 164–68. Before Sir Sayyid, the historian al-Maqrizi (d.1441) had revived the doctrine that with the rise of the Umayyads the Caliphate had become a Kingdom of violence and tyranny; Taki-Eddin Ahmad al-Makrizi, *Histoire des Sultans Mamlouks de l'Egypte,* trans. M. Quatremere (Paris: Benjamin Dupart, 1837), Vol. 1, p. 76.

21. Sir Sayyid Ahmad Khan, *Madhhabī wa Islami Maḍamīn,* pp. 157–58.

22. *Ibid.,* p. 161.

23. Muzaffar Ahmad, *The Communist Party of India and Its Formation Abroad* (Calcutta: National Book Agency, 1962), pp. 11–97.

24. Abul Kalam Azad (1888–1958), who was the leader of the Nationalist Muslims, had accepted the political philosophy of the Congress. For his role in the Khilafat Movement see Hafeez Malik, "Abdul Kalam Azad's Theory of Nationalism," *The Muslim World* (January 1963).

25. Sir Sayyid Ahmad Khan, "Ek Mu'azzaz Angrez ke Nām," *Maktūbāt-i-Sir Sayyid* (Lahore: Majlis-i-Taraqqi-i-Adab, 1959), p. 187.

26. Sir Sayyid, *Musafiran-i-London,* ed. Shaikh Muhammad Isma'īl (Lahore: Majlis-i-Taraqqi-i-Adab, 1961), pp. 132–42.

27. *Akhbār Scientific Society,* Aligarh (5 May 1876), p. 1.

28. *Ibid.,* pp. 1–2.

29. Sir Sayyid, "Nā-Muhadhab Government," *Tahdhīb, al-Akhlāq,* 1st Ramadan, 1292 A.H./1875, p. 145; see also *Maqālāt-i-Sir Sayyid; Mulkī wa Siyāsī Maḍamīn* (Lahore: Majlis-i-Taraqqu-i-Adab, 1962), pp. 1–2.

30. *Ibid.,* p. 10 ff.

31. Sir Sayyid Ahmad Khan, "Hindustan Kay Mu'azaz Khandān," *Akhbār Scientific Society* (7 April 1876).

32. A great Urdu poet and satirist, Inshā Allah Khan, was born in Murshidabad between 1756 and 1758. His father, Mir Mashā Allah Khan, was a courtier of Nawab Siraj-ud-Daulah. When sixteen, Insha left Murshidabad for Lucknow, where for some time he was connected with the court of Shuja-ud-Daulah. On the latter's death he came to Delhi, where he was received kindly by Emperor Shah Alam. See Muhammad Sadiq, *A History of Urdu Literature* (Oxford: Oxford University Press, 1964), p. 125; for a critique of his poetry see Sayyid 'Abdūl Hayī, *Gul-i-Ra'nā* (Azamgarh: Ma'rif Press, 1949), Vol. 2, p. 257; Muhammad Husain Azad, *Aab-i-Hayat* (Lahore: Shaikh Mubarek Ali, 1957), pp. 254 ff.

33. Sir Sayyid, "Hindustan Kay Mu'azaz Khandān," p. 95.

34. Sir Sayyid, "Ayk tadbir: Musalmanun kay khandan ko Tabahīy awr Barbadī Say bachanay key," *Tahdhīb al-Akhlāq*, (Aligarh: Zil Qa dah, 1296 A.H./1878); *Maqālāt-i Sir Sayyid*, Vol. 5, pp. 97–138.

35. This referred to the efforts of some Bengali landlords who had petitioned the British Government to open an agricultural school. See Sir Sayyid Ahmad Khan, "Hamary Raū'sā Awr Qawmi Bhala'īy," *Akhbār Scientific Society* (13 July 1866).

36. *Ibid.*

37. Sir Sayyid, "Ta'līm Awr Atfaq," *Maqālāt-i Sir Sayyid: Taqrīri Maqālāt* (Lahore: Majlis Traqqi-i Adab, 1963), p. 160.

38. Iqbal Ali, *Sir Sayyid Ka Safer-i Punjab,* pp. 140, 167.

39. *Ibid.,* p. 161.

40. Sir Sayyid, "Madresseh al-'Ulūm Key Darūrat," *Taqrīri Maqālāt,* p. 120.

41. To counteract the territorial and secular nationalism of the All-India National Congress, Sir Sayyid established the Patriotic Association in August 1888. Under its influence regional Islamic associations protested against the political policy of the Congress throughout India. The Patriotic Association made it clear to the British that more than one nationality existed in India and that the yoking of Hindus and Muslims under a parliamentary system would work only to the detriment of the minority.

42. Sayyid Ahmad Khan to Mahdī Ali Khan Muhsin al-Mulk, 29 April 1870, in *Maktūbat-i Sir Sayyid,* ed. Shaikh Muhammad Isma'īl Panīpatī (Lahore: Majlis Traqqi-i Adab, 1959), p. 103.

43. *Ibid.,* p. 104.

44. *Musalmanun Key Quismat Kā Faysalāh* (Agra, 1894), p. 72, contains speeches of Sir Sayyid and other leaders of the Aligarh Movement, which were delivered at the 6th Session of the Muhammadan Educational Conference at Aligarh.

45. In order to gain a view of the Muslims' share in the administration of the British-Indian Government, see Appendices A and B.

46. See Iqbal Ali, *Sir Sayyid Ka Safer-i Punjab,* pp. 144–46.

47. See Sir Sayyid Ahmad Khan, *Majmū'ah Resolūshon-hay Deh Salah: Muhammadan Anglo-Oriental Educational Conference* (Agra: Matba' a Mufīd-i 'Āam, 1896), pp. 9, 35.

48. This obviously refers to the Western-educated Bengali elite, which collaborated with Allen Octavian Hume in establishing the All-India National Congress in 1885.

49. Sayyid Tufayl Ahmad Manglorī, *Musalamanun Ka Roshan Mustaqbil* (Delhi: Matba' 'Ilīmi, 1945), p. 279. In the later years of Sir Sayyid's life Mawlavi Sami'y Allah was his major opponent.

7. RELIGIOUS MODERNISM 319

50. Mir Waliyat Husain "Madmūn," *Conference Gazette*, Aligarh (8 November, 1935), as cited in Manglori, *Musalmanun ka Roshan Mastaqbil*, p. 280.

51. The Muhammadan Defense Association was founded by Sir Sayyid to create a political platform for the Muslims' views, and it opposed the politics of the Congress. See Halī, *Hayat-i Javid*, pp. 318–20.

52. S. Abid Husain, *The Destiny of Indian Muslims* (New York, 1965), p. 39. During his visit in May 1967 to Hafeez Malik (at Villanova University, Pennsylvania), Dr. Husain admitted that no authentic evidence was available supporting the contention that Sir Sayyid was thoroughly dominated by Beck, and that he formulated his policies on Beck's suggestion. Dr. Husain also regretted the fact that instead of doing his own independent research on this issue, he relied excessively upon Manglorī's assertions.

53. "Pas lazim ata hai keh Hindustan kay āmān kay laiy awr mulk mein her chīyz key traqqi kay laiy English Government of bahut dinun tak balkeh hameshah kay laiy rahna ẓarūrī hai." *Sir Sayyid Ahmad Khan Kay Lekcharun Ka Majmū'ah Ma'a Mukhtaser Sawaneh 'Umrīy*, ed. Munshi Muhammad Siraj-ud-Din (Lahore: Fadl-ud-Dīn, 1890), p. 367.

54. Mohandas K. Gandhi, *An Autobiography: The Story of My Experience with Truth* (Boston: Beacon Hill, 1957), p. 214.

55. *Ibid.*, p. 449.

56. Sir Sayyid Ahmad Khan, *Mukammal Majmū'ah Lekchers Wa Spiches* (Lahore, 1891), p. 367.

57. *Ibid.*, pp. 348–49.

58. *Ibid.*, p. 357.

59. *Ibid.*, pp. 351–52.

60. *Ibid.*, p. 353.

61. *Ibid.*, p. 354; see also Halī, *Hayat-i Javid*, pp. 316–17.

62. For Sir Sayyid's view of democracy, the concept of Muslim nationalism and national progress, see also Hafeez Malik, "Sir Sayyid Ahmad Khan's Role in the Development of Muslim Nationalism in the Indo-Pakistan Sub-Continent," *Islamic Studies*, Rawalpindi, 5, no. 4 (December 1966); and "Sir Sayyid Ahmad Khan's Theories of Muslim National Progress," *Modern Asian Studies* (July 1968).

7. Religious Modernism

1. For the definitions of *sunna*, *Shari'ā*, and *Bid'ā* see Fazlur Rahman, *Islam* (New York: Doubleday, 1969), pp. 60–62; Asaf A. A. Gyzee, *Outlines of Muhammadan Law* (Oxford: Oxford University Press, 1964), pp. 15–16.

2. Shah Walīy Allah, *Al-Maqālāh al-Wadīya fi al-Nashīhya wa al-Wasīyah* (Hyderabad: Shah Waliy Allah Akademiy, 1964), pp. 50–53; for an English translation, see Hafeez Malik, "Shah Waliy Allah's Last Testament," *The Muslim World* (Hartford, Connecticut, April 1973) pp. 105–18.

3. *Walīma* is a wedding feast intended to selemnize and publicize the event of marriage. Shah Waliy Allah, *Hujjat Allah al-Balighah*, trans. Mawlana 'Abd al-Rahīm (Lahore: Qawmi Kutab Khanā, 1962), Vol. 2, pp. 544–45.

4. *'Aqīqah* are the ceremonies performed on a male or female child's birth; usually a lamb or sheep is slaughtered and the *āzān* is said in the ear of the newly born child. The

Prophet Muhammad performed these ceremonies for his children and grandchildren. Shah Mu'īn-ud-Din Ahmad Nadwīy, *Sīyar al-Sahabah* (Azamgarh: 1965), Vol. 6, pp. 2 and 142; see also *Mustaḍark Hākim*, Vol. 3, p. 76.

   5. Shah Walīy Allah, *Al-Maqālāh*, pp. 47–48.
   6. *Sīrat al-Mustaqīm* (Lahore: n.d.), p. 156.
   7. Sir Sayyid's personal contributions to the *Tahdhīb al-Akhlāq* were as follows:

Years	Total No. of Articles	No. of Guest Columns	Sir Sayyid's Articles
1870–76	226	8	112
1878–81	67	8	23
1893–96	(Sir Sayyid wrote almost all the articles during this period.)		

SOURCE: Halī, *Hayat-i Javid*, pp. 222–23.

   8. Sir Sayyid, "Parchah Tahdhīb al-Akhlāq Awr Us Kay Aghrād wa Maqāsid," *Tahdhīb al-Akhāq*, Aligarh: Shawwal 1, 1287/December 24, 1870; also Muharram 1, 1289 A.H./1872.
   9. Sir Sayyid, "Kin kin chizon mein tahdhīb chahiye," *Tahdhīb al-Akhlāq*, Dhu-l Hijja 1, 1287 A.H./1870.
   10. See for instance, *Risalah Conference Mut'laq Tamaddan wa M'ashirat* (Lahore: Hamīdīyah Stiym Press, n.d.)
   11. Anwar Ahmad Marherwiy, *Muraqqā-i Conference: All-India Muslim Educational Kānfrans Kay Paintalīys Salah Ijlasawn Key Kaiyfiyat* (Aligarh: Mataba-i Aligarh Muslim University, 1935), pp. 24–25.
   12. Sir Sayyid, *Khutbāt-i Ahmadīya* (Agra: 1870); pp. 238–40; *Sirat-i Tayyabah Kay Mut'laq Barah Tahqīqīy Awr Tanqīydīy Maqālāt*, ed. Mawlana Muhammad Isma'īl Panipatī (Lahore: majlis Traqqi-i Adab, 1963), pp. 280–92; *Essays on the Life of Muhammad* (London: Trubner, 1870), see "Essay on the Question Whether Islam Has Been Beneficial or Injurious to Human Society in General", pp. 8–12.
   13. *Sir Sayyid kay Mudamīyn Tahdhīb al-Aklāq*, ed. Malik Fadl al-Dīn (Lahore: n.d.), p. 72.
   14. Marherwiy, *Murraqa Conference*, pp. 51–52.
   15. *Ibid.*, pp. 23–24.
   16. Sir Sayyid, *Al-Tahrīr Fī 'Usūl al-Tafsīr* (Aligarh: 1892), p. 33.
   17. Shah Walīy Allah, *Al-Tafhīmat al-Ilahīyyah*, p. 581.
   18. Muhammad Daud Rahbar, "Sir Sayyid Ahmad Khan's Principles of Exegesis: Al-Tahrīr fī 'Usūal al-Tafsīr," *The Muslim World* 46, no. 2 (April 1956), p. 108.
   19. Hafeez Malik, *Muslim Nationalism in India and Pakistan* (Washington, D.C.: Public Affairs Press, 1961), pp. 125–40.
   20. "The two words *hadith* and *sunna*, either of which might with some justification be translated tradition, are commonly used but differ in their significance. *Hadith* really means a story or a report, and so represents an account of what happened, whereas *sunna* means a practice or custom. . . . Briefly, the *sunna* is what was practiced and the *hadith* is the record of what was practiced by the Prophet Muhammad." *Mishkat al-Masabih*, trans. James Robson (Lahore: Shaikh Muhammad Ashraf 1960), p. 1.

21. Sir Sayyid Ahmad Khan, "Kutub-i Ahadith," *Tahdhīb al-Akhlāq*, 1288 A.H./1871; see also under the same title *Maqālāt-i Sir Sayyid: Madhhabī wa Islami*, pp. 60–64.

In his essay, *Kutub-i-Ahadith*, Sir Sayyid does not document the statements of Shah Walīy Allah, but they are from *Hujjat Allah-al-Baligha*, Vol. 1. This author has documented Shah Walīy Allah's passages from an Urdu translation of *Hujjatallah al-Baligha*, available in the Library of Congress, Washington, D.C.

22. "*Soundness means that the author recorded only correct traditions; if he added less reliable traditions then he simultaneously indicated their weakness (naqs).* Reputation implies that throughout generations the traditionists not only studied them but also taught them to laymen. *Acceptance* connotes that the specialists never questioned their reliability and correctness." Shah Waliy Allah has added a supplementary condition, which Sir Sayyid did not include in his essay. The former pointed out that "it was necessary that the '*ulamā*' of Mecca should have accepted a tradition, applying its substance to their conduct." Shah Walīy Allah, *Hujjatallah al-Baligha*, Urdu trans. Mawlana 'Abdūr Rahīm (Lahore: Qawmi Kutab Khana, 1953), Vol. 1, pp. 620–21.

23. Sir Sayyid does not mention this in his article, but Shah Walīy Allah established a fifth category of *hadith* books, including only "those traditions which did not appear in the first four categories, but remained throughout on the tip of the tongues of jurists, theologians, and Sufis." *Ibid.*, pp. 627–28. Why leading traditionists fail to note such well-known traditions is not explained by Shah Walīy Allah.

24. Sir Sayyid does not always document the statements of Shah 'Abdūl 'Azīz. This author has attempted to identify Shah 'Abdūl 'Azīz's works wherever possible. Sir Sayyid Ahmad Khan, *Kutub-i-Ahadith*, p. 62; Sir Sayyid cited for it Shah 'Abdūl 'Azīz's, *Ijalāh al-Nafīha* in his article, "Ahadit," *Tahadhīb al-Akhlāq*, Zilqadah 1, 1312 A.H., Vol. 2. no. 2, pp. 23–24.

25. *Ibid.*, p. 63.

26. Sir Sayyid Ahmad Khan, "Ahadith Ghayr M'utamad," *Tahdhib al-Akhlaq*, 1288 A.H./1871. Sir Sayyid indicated that he did not originally select these traditions, but found them in Alama Majd-ud-Din Firozabadi's work, *Safar al-Sa'dāt*; see *Maqālāt-i Sir Sayyid: Madhhabī wa Islami*, pp. 78–83.

27. The Murji'ite sect (Murj'iah) arose in the Umayyad age. The fundamental article of faith of this sect consisted in the suspension ('*irja*) of judgement against believers who commit sin and in not declaring them infidels. "To the followers of this doctrine," says Professor Hitti, "the fact that the Umayyads were nominally Muslims" sufficed. The most illustrious representative of the moderate wing of this school was the great divine Abū Hanīfah (c. 767 A.D.). Hitti, *History*, p. 247.

The Qadarites (Qadariyyah) were really the earliest school of philosophy in Islam, achieving their greatest popularity during the Umayyad period. Two of the Umayyad Caliphs, Mu'awiyah II and Yazid II, were Qadarites. They were advocates of free will (from *qadar*-power) as opposed to the Jabrites (from *Jabr*-compulsion). The doctrine of free will was first enunciated by Ma'bad al-Juhani (d. 80 A.H.), who taught mainly in Damascus. See De Lacy O'Leary, *Arabic Thought and Its Place in History* (London: Routledge & Kegan Paul, 1958), p. 85. The Ash'arite system of theology adopts its name from Abu l-Hasan Al-Ash'ari of Baghdad (d. 330 or 340 A.H./935); he is credited with exploding the Mu'tazilite theories, i.e. (1) that the Qur'ān was created; (2) the denial of the beatific vision; and (3) the freedom of will and reestablishing the orthodox creed of Islam. It was, however, Abū Hamid al-Ghazalī (1058–1111) who fixed the ultimate form of the Ash'ariya creed. *Ibid.*, pp. 212, 213; Hitti, *History*, pp. 430–31.

28. Hafeez Malik, "The Religious Liberalism of Sir Sayyid Ahmad Khan," *The Muslim World*, 54, no. 3 (1964), pp. 160–69.

29. Sir Sayyid, *Jila al Qulūb bi Dhiker al-Mahbūb*, see in, *Maqālāt-i Sir Sayyid*, ed. Mawlana Muhammad Isma'īl Panīpatī (Lahore: Majlis Traqqi-i Adab., 1962), Vol. 7, pp. 6–22, 22–23.

30. Sir Sayyid, *Jila al-Qulūb* Per Review, June 1878," *Tasanīf-i Ahmadiya* (Aligarh: 1883), Vol. 1.

31. A. Rupert Hall, *From Gallileo to Newton* (New York: Harper & Row, 1963), p. 316.

32. Sayyid Ahmad Khan, "Tabiy'ūn ya nacharīyūn ya Fitratīyun," *Tahdhīb al-Akhlāq*, Vol. 1, no. 5; Safer 1, 1312/1894.

33. Sayyid Ahmad Khan, "al-Islam haw al-fitrat wā al-fitrat hiy al-Islam," *Maqālāt-i Sir Sayyid: Falsafīyanah Mudamīn* (Lahore: Majlis Traqqi-i Adab, 1961), pp. 16–22.

34. The farthest mosque refers to the site of the Temple of Solomon in Jerusalem on the hill of Moriah, at or near which stands the Dome of the Rock, also called the Mosque of Caliph Umar. This and the mosque known as the Farthest Mosque (Masjid al-Aqsa) were completed by 'Adb al-Mālik in 68 A.H./687. See *The Holy Qur'an*, trans. Abd Allah Yusuf Ali (Lahore: Shaikh Ashraf, 1938), p. 693.

35. *Ibid., XVII*: 1.

36. Sayyid Ahmad Khan, *Al-Khutbāt-i Ahmadiya* (Lahore: Traqqi-i Adab, 1963), pp. 721–22.

37. *Ibid.*, p. 764.

38. See Charles Darwin, *The Origin of Species* (1859), and *The Descent of Man* (1871).

39. Sayyid Ahmad Khan, "Adna halat say 'alā halet per insān key traqqī," *Tahdhib al-Akhlaq*, Vol. 2, no.,; Sh'ban', 1313/1895; also *Maqālāt-i Sir Sayyid: Ilmī Wa Tahqīqi Muḍamin* (Lahore: Majlis Traqqi-i Abad, 1962), Vol. 4, pp. 41–47.

40. Some of Sir Sayyid's detractors composed poems to call him a new prophet of naturism:

> *Yahī Dīn-i nature kay hain khās mursal*
> *Yah nature anihyn ka hai wahi manzal*
> *Yahī jāntay hain kitāb-i mufaṣal*
> *Anīhy per khulā hai har ik rāz mujmal*
> *'Ayān hain nubuwat kay miṣdāq un-kay*
> *Sahīfay hain Tahdhīb al-Akhlāq un-kay*

He [Sir Sayyid] is the messenger of "Natural religion"
This natural religion was indeed "revealed" to him.
He alone knows the secrets of the Book, because
All the esoteric knowledge has been vouchsafed to him.
The evidence of his prophethood is visible to all,
It is visible in the pages of his *Tahdhīb al-Akhlāq*.

For the collection of these derogatory poems see Mawlana Abul Biyān Muhammad Salīm al-Din Taslīym, *Hadīqat al-Madhab* (Rajalwer: Matbā'-i yūsufīy, 1305 A.H./1887), p. 164.

41. Sayyid Ahmad Khan, "Madhabīy khayāl zamana qadīym awr zamanā jadīd kā, *Maqālāt-i Sir Sayyid: Falsafīyanā Mudamīyn* (Lahore: Majlis Traqqi-i Adab, 1961), Vol. 3, pp. 24–27.

42. Sayyid Ahmad Khan, "Mudhab insan ka Amer-i tabiy'y hai", *Maqālāt-i Sir Sayyid: Ilmī wa tahqīqy mudamīn* (Lahore: Majlis Traqqi-i Adab, 1962), Vol. 4, pp. 260–71.

Epilogue

1. Badr-ud-Din Tayyabji to Sir Sayyid Ahmad Khan, 18 February 1888, Papers of Badr-ud-Din Tayabji, Microfilmed, National Archives of India, New Delhi, 1965.

2. *Ibid.*

3. *Ibid.*

4. Cf. Badr-ud-Din Tayabji's published letter to the *Pioneer* (Allahabad), *Sir Syed Ahmad on the Present State of Indian Politics* (Allahabad: The Pioneer Press, 1888), p. 54.

5. Badr-ud-Din Tayyabji to Allan Octavian Hume, 27 October 1888, papers of Tayyabji, 1965.

6. *Ibid.*

7. Sir William Wedderburn, *Allan Octavian Hume: Father of the Indian National Congress* (London: T. Fisher Unwin, 1913), pp. 71–72.

8. *Ibid.,* p. 77.

9. Abul Kalam Azad, *Mudamin-i Abul Kalam Azad* (Delhi: Hindustani Publishing House, 1944), pp. 14–22.

10. *Ibid.,* pp. 25–29, 87.

11. Adb al-Malik Ibn Hisham, *Kitāb Sīrat Rasūl Allah,* ed. Dr. F. Wustenfeld (Gottingen: Dieterichsche Universitats-Buchhandlung, 1858), p. 341.

12. Aflred Guillaume, *The Life of Muhammad,* a trans. of Ibn Hisham's *Kitāb Sirat Rasūl Allah* (London: Oxford University Press, 1955), p. 232. Muir, however, translates it thus: "The Jewish clans in allegiance with the several tribes of Medina are one people with the believers." Sir William Muir, *The Life of Muhammad* (Edinburg: John Grant, 1912), p. 184.

13. Abul Kalam Azad, *Khutbāt-i Abul Kalam Azad* (Lahore: Al-Minara Academy, n.d.), p. 42; see Hafeez Malik, "Abul Kalam Azad's Theory of Nationalism," *The Muslim World* (January 1963), pp. 33–40.

14. For the text of Abul Kalam Azad's decree see "Hijrat Kā Fatwā," *Daily Ahl-i Hadīth* (Amritsar: July 30, 1920), as reproduced in Ghulum Rasul Marh, *Tabarkāt-i Azad* (Lahore: Kitāb Manzil, 1959), pp. 203–6. For its English translation see Hafeez Malik, *Moslem Nationalism in India and Pakistan,* pp. 343–44.

15. 'Abd al-Ghaffār Madhawli, *Jamiā' Key Kahānī* (Delhi: Koh-i Nur Press, 1965), pp. 19, 26, 70.

16. *Ibid.,* pp. 390–92.

17. *The Pakistan Times,* August 13, 1947.

18. Hafeez Malik, "The Spirit of Capitalism and Pakistani Islam," *Contributions to Asian Studies,* ed. Aziz Ahmad (Leiden: E. J. Brill, 1971), pp. 59–78.

19. "Ayk mu' azaz angrez kāy nām," *Maktūbāt-i Sir Sayyid,* ed. Shaikh Muhammad Isma'īl (Lahore: Majlis Traqqi-i Adab, 1959), pp. 186–87.

Bibliography

I. Sir Sayyid Ahmad Khan's Works

Asbab-i Baghawat-i Hind (Causes for the Revolt of India). 1858.

A Speech by Sayyid Ahmad Khan on the Institution of the British Indian Association, N.W. Provinces, with the By-Laws of the Association. No. 1 (Aligarh: Sayyid Ahmad Khan's Private Press, 1867).

Āthar al-Sandadīd. Delhi: Central Book Depot, Urdu Bazaar, 1965.

British Indian Association, N.W.F.P. (No. II, A Petition from the landlords of Aligarh to the Government of N.W.F.P. praying for the establishment of an Educational Committee in that District; No. IV, A Memorial to the British Government soliciting a reduction in the book postage, with the Government's Reply; Nos. V & VI, Article on the Public Education of India & correspondence with the British Government concerning the education of the natives of India through the vernaculars. Aligarh: Institute Press, 1869.

Circular From the Muhammadan Anglo-Oriental College Fund Committee (Registered Under Act, XXI, 1860. Benares, N.W.P. India) London: Henry S. King & Company. Received in India on October 27, 1869.

[English] Translation of the Report of the Members of the Select Committee For the Better Diffusion & Advancement of Learning Among Muhammadans of India. Benares: Medical Hall Press, 1872.

Intikhāb al-Akhawayn (Civil Law Digest). 1841.

Jalā'al-Qulūb Bi-Dhiker al-Mahbūb (The Prophet's Life). 1843.

Jam-i Jam (History of the Mughal Emperors of India). 1840.

Lektur: Mut'liq Yazdaham Muhammadan Anglo-Oriental Educational Conference. Agra: Matb'a Mufīd-i 'Āam, 1896.

Maḍmūn: Nibbat Tannazul ulum Dinya Wa Arabiya Wa Falsafah-i Yunaniyah. Agra: Matb'a Mufīd-i 'Āam, 1897.

Maqalat-i Sir Sayyid: Akhbarāt Per Tanqīdiy Muḍamīn. Ed. Mawlana Muhammad Isma'īl. Lahore: Majlis Traqqu-i Adab, 1962.

Maqalat-i Sir Sayyid: Akhlaqī Awr Islahīy Muḍamīn. Ed. Mawlana Muhammad Isma'īl. Lahore: Majlis Traqqi-i Adab, 1962.

Maqalat-i Sir Sayyid: Dhatīy 'Aqā'id Kay Mut'laq Muḍamīn. Ed. Mawlana Muhammad Isma'īl. Lahore: Majlis Traqqi-i Adab, 1962.

Maqalat-i Sir Sayyid: Falsafayanā Muḍamīn. Ed. Mawlana Muhammad Isma'īl. Lahore: Majlis Traqqi-i Adab, 1962.

Maqalat-i Sir Sayyid: Ilmi Wa Tahqīqiy Muḍamīn. Ed. Mawlana Muhammad Isma'īl. Lahore: Majlis Traqqi-i Adab, 1962.

Maqālati-i Sir Sayyid: Muḍamīn Mut'laq Swaneh Wa Siyar, Adabīy, Tanqīyd Wa Tabserah. Ed. Mawlana Muhammad Isma'īl. Lahore: Majlis Traqqi-i Adab, 1962.

Maqālat-i Sir Sayyid: Madhabīy Wa Islami. Ed. Mawlana Muhammad Isma'īl. Lahore: Majlis-i Traqqi-i Adab, 1962.

Maqālat-i Sir Sayyid: Muḍamīn Muta'lliqah Tahdhīb al-Akhlāq. Ed. Mawlana Muhammad Isma'īl. Lahore: Majlis-i Traqqi-Adab, 1962.

Maqālat-i Sir Sayyid: Mulkīy Wa Siyāsīy Muḍamīn. Ed. Mawlana Muhammad Isma'īl. Lahore: Majlis-i Traqqi Adab, 1962.

Maqālat-i Sir Sayyid: Mushtamal Ber Qur'āni Qisās. Ed. Mawlana Muhammad Isma'īl. Lahore: Majlis Traqqi-i Adab, 1965.

Maqālat-i Sir Sayyid: Mutfaraq Muḍamīn. Ed. Mawlana Muhammad Isma'īl. Lahore: Majlis Traqqi-i Adab, 1963.

Maqālat-i Sir Sayyid: Sirat-i Tayyabah Say Mut'alaq Barah Tahqiqīy Muḍamīn. Ed. Mawlana Muhammad Isma'īl. Lahore: Majlis-i Traqqi-i Adab, 1963.

Maqālat-i Sir Sayyid: Ta'līmy, Tarbi'yatīy Awr Ma'shrity Muḍamīn. Ed. Mawlana Muhammad Isma'īl. Lahore: Majlis Traqqi-i Adab, 1962.

Maqālat-i Sir Sayyid: Taqrīrīy Maqālat. Ed. Mawlana Muhammad Isma'īl. Lahore: Majlis Traqqi-i Adab, 1963.

Maqālat-i Sir Sayyid Tafsīry Muḍamīn. Ed. Mawlana Muhammad Isma'īl. Lahore: Majlis Traqqi-i Adab, 1961.

Musaferan-i London. Ed. Shaikh Muhammad Isma'īl. Lahore: Majlis Traqqi-i Adab, 1961.

Report of the Primary Examination of the Moradabad Maddrissa, Held on January 1, 1860. Meerut: Mofussilite Press, 1860.

Review on Dr. Hunter's Indian Musalmans: Are They Bound in Conscience to Rebel Against the Queen? Benares: Medical Hall Press, 1872.

Risālah Rah-i Sunnat Wa Radd-i Bid'at (A Polemic Supporting the Wahhabi Doctrines), 1850.

Silsilat al-Mulūk (Chronology of the Delhi Rajas and Muslim Kings). 1852.

Sirat-i Farīdiyah. Karachi: Pak Academy, 1964.

Strictures Upon the Present Educational System in India. London: Printed for private circulation, by Henry S. King & Company, 1869.

Supplement to By-Laws of the British Indian Association. Aligarh: Institute Press, 1869.

Tabīyn al-Kalām Fi Tafsīr al-Turāt Wa al-Injīl: The Muhammadan Commentary on the Holy Bible, Part I & II. Aligarh: Sir Sayyid's Private Press, 1865.

Tahdhīb al-Akhlāq. Vol. II, Shawwal I, 1312—Ramadan 30, 1313 A.H. Aligarh: Institute Press, 1896.

Tarīkh-i Dhilla Bijnor (History of the Bijnor District). 1857.

Tarīkh Sarkashīy-i Dhilla Bijnor. 1858.

Tarjamah Faysalajat Sadr-i Sharqi Wa Sadr-i Maghrībī (Trans. of the Civil Court's Judgements of the Eastern and Western Provinces). 1849.

Tarjamah-i Kimya-i Sa'dat (Urdu trans. of al-Ghazzali's Persian work on ethics). 1853.

Tarqīm Fī Qissā ashāb al-Kahf War-Raqīm. Agra: Matb'a Mufid 'Āam, 1307 A.H.

Tashīl fi Jarr al-Thaqīl (Urdu trans. of a Persian treatise on mechanics). 1844.

The Present State of Indian Politics: Speeches & Letters. Allahabad: Pioneer Press, 1888.

The Seventh Discourse of Sir Sayed Ahmad. London: Christian Literature Society, 1910.

Tuhfah-i Hasan (Urdu trans. of Shah 'Abdūl Azīz's Persian treatise on Shi'a-Sunni polemics, *Tuhfah Ithna Ashariyah*). 1844.

WORKS BY SIR SAYYID IN THE BRITISH MUSEUM, GENERAL CATALOGUE OF PRINTED BOOKS, LONDON

An Account of the Loyal Mahomedans of India. Meerut, 1860.

An Essay on the Causes of the Indian Revolt. Agra, 1859.

Review of Hunter's Indian Musalmans. English pp. 53. Benares, 1872. Reprinted from the *Pioneer,* pp. 11,71. viii. Pioneer Press, Allahabad, 1888.

Thanksgiving Offered up by the Mahomedans of Moradabad on the 28th July, 1859. J. A. Gibbons, Meerut [1859].

The Truth About the Khilafat Compiled by Kazi Sirajud-Din Ahmad; pp. IV. 65. Lahore, 1916.

The Seventh Discourse of Sir Syed Ahmad. Reprinted from *The Mohomedan* [sic] *Commentary* on the Holy Bible [with note by Joseph Passmore] pp. 36. Christian Literature Society for India: London; Madras [printed], 1910.

II. Parliamentary Papers of the British Government, India Office Library

PRIVATE PAPERS

Elgin Collection (1894–98) [*Mss. F-84, 152, 53, 54, 55, 56*]
(1) Correspondence with Persons in India, July to December 1897, original mss. [Letter 332, Viceroy's visit 317, 318a, 332, 359a].
(2) Home Miscellaneous, Vol. 725, Mutiny Papers [original mss.]. of Sir J.W. Kaye, Narratives, Dians, Memoranda (pp. 1011–16).
(3) Lyttan papers. Eur. Mass.
(4) 8th Duke of Arygll Papers (Private letters from the Earl of Mayo to the Duke of Argyll, with Enclosures; 1869–1870)

OFFICIAL PROCEEDINGS

(1) Public Letters received from India (Home Department [Public]) Vol. 22, 1878.
(2) Home Correspondence, Public, Educational and Ecclesiastical Department, Vol. 3, January 1868 to December 1870.
(3) Collections to Educational Despatches, India, Home Department, Vol. II, 1865–67; Vol. XII, 1868–69; Vol. XIII, 1870–71; Vol. XIV, 1872–76.
(4) *Abstracts of the Proceedings of the Legislative Council of the Governor-General of India:* Vol. XVIII, 1879; Vol. XIX, 1880; Vol. XXX, 1881; Vol. XXI, 1882; Vol. XXII, 1883.
(5) Proceedings of the Government of India (Home Department), Proceedings Vol. 520, Education Branch, March–April 1873.
(6) Selections from the Records of the Government of India, Home Department (Serial No. 2).
(7) Despatch to the Government of India on the Subject of General Education in India, Return to an Order of the House of Commons, July 18, 1854, *Department of Education,* India.
(8) Proceedings of the Government of the North Western Provinces, General and Education Departments, 1870–98.
(9) Proceedings of the Government of Eastern Bengal and Assam, April 1906, Home Department, Education.
(10) Statements of Sayyid Mahmud & Beck, *Proceedings of the Public Service Commission,* Vol. II, pp. 132–33.

PARLIAMENTARY PAPERS

(1) Parliamentary papers 1857–58, Vol. 33.
(2) Parliamentary papers 1869, Vol. 8.
(3) Parliamentary papers 1870, Vol. 52, Session of February 8–August 10,

1870; entirely devoted to Education in India. *Accounts & Papers: East India (Education)*, Vol. LIII, Sess. 1870.

(4) Parliamentary papers 1893–94, Vol. 63. *Note on the State of Education in India During 1866–67* by A. P. Powell, Esq., Under Secretary to the Government of India.

LEGISLATIVE ENACTMENTS

(1) A Collection of the Public General Statutes passed in the Third & Fourth Year of the Reign of His Majesty King William IV, London, 1833.

(2) The Acts of the Legislative Council of India, 1834–67, Vol. 4, Calcutta, 1868.

CONFIDENTIAL FILES

(1) Confidential Annual File #20010½, Criminal Home Department, Government of India.

(2) Reference to Sir Syed in Lytton Papers, European Ms., Vol 518/6.

(3) Selections from Government of Punjab Record: Confidential Series, No. A-XXI, Lahore, 1884.

(4) MacDonnell Papers, May 7, 1897; Ms. Eight History C-353.

GOVERNMENT CORRESPONDENCE

Home Correspondence, Political Department, Vol. 69, 1870–1878.

Home Department, Selections from the Records of the Government of India. Serial No. II, No. CCV.

Index. Public & Home Correspondence, Vol. III.

Public Home Correspondence, Government of India. Vol. 37; 1858–1829.

Punjab Notes & Queries, Government of India. Vols. 1–4; 1883–88.

Register, Political Department, House Correspondence, Vol. 89; 1866–1869.

Aligarh. Bharat-Varshiya National Association and the Lyall Library, Annual Report 1903. Allahabad, 1904.

—— Muhomedan Anglo-Oriental College. Note on the progress of MA-O.C. August 4, 1903 period of 1889–1903 compared with the previous 5 yrs., 1894–1898.

—— *The N.W.P. British Indian Association* By-Laws & Publications of the Association, Nos. 1–7 (1867–69).

—— *Muslim University*, Rahman. (Abdur, Syed) Round the new Aligarh World, the cradle of Muslim Hope and the flower of Muslim Intelligentsia, 1932 28 C.14. (h)

—— *British Indian Association*, Report of writing on the Subject of the Founding of a British Indian University. Calcutta, 1868 (p. 26) 41.v.34.

III. Works on Sir Sayyid Admad Khan and His Movement

'Abd Allah, Doctor Sayyid. *Sir Sayyid Ahmad Khan Awr Unkay Namwar Rufqā Key Urdu Nather Kā Fannī Awr Fikerī Jā'izah.* Lahore: Maktaba-i Karwan, 1960.

—— *The Spirit and Substance of Urdu Prose Under the Influence of Sir Sayyid Ahmad Khan.* Lahore: Shaikh Muhammad Ashraf, 1940.

Abd ul-Haq, Mawlavi, Merhum Dehliy Kalij. Delhi: Anjuman Traqqi-i Urdu, 1945.

—— *Sir Sayyid Ahmad Khan.* Delhi: Urdu Markaz, 1960.

Ali, Sayyid Iqbal. *Sayyid Ahmad Khan Kā Safar Nameh-i Punjab.* Aligarh, 1885?

Baljon, J. M. S. *The Reforms and Religious Ideas of Sir Sayyid Ahmad Khan.* Lahore: Orientalia, 1958.

Dar, Bashir Ahmad. *Religious Thought of Sayyid Ahmad Khan.* Lahore: Institute of Islamic Culture, 1957.

Graham, George F. Irving. *The Life & Work of Sir Syed Ahmad Khan.* London: Hodder & Stroughton, 1909.

Hali, Altaf Husain. *Hayat-i Javid.* Lahore: Punjab Academy Trust, 1957.

Husain, Mushtaq. *Makatīyb-i Sir Sayyid Ahmad Khan.* Vols. I, II. Delhi: Union Printing Press, 1960.

Khan, Doctor Yusuf Husain. "Scientific Society Kay Mut'laq Ghair Matbū'ah Khatūt Angrazīy." *Fiker Wa Nazar.* Aligarh: Muslim University, April, July, Oct., 1963; January, 1964.

—— "MAO College, Say Mut'laq Ghair Matbū'ah Khatūt." *Fiker Wa Nazar.* April 1963.

Mangloriy, Sayyid Tufyl Ahmad. *Musalmanuñ Kā Roshan Mustaqbil.* Delhi: Matb'a'Alīmi, 1945.

Mohsin-ul-Mulk. *Note on the Progress of the Mahomedan Anglo-Oriental College Aligarh.* Aligarh: Institute Press, 1903.

Noorani, A. Gafoor. *Badruddin Tyabi.* New Delhi: Ministry of Information, 1969.

Panipati, Shaikh Muhammad Isma'īl. *Maktūbat-i Sir Sayyid.* Lahore: Majlis Traqqi-i Adab, 1959.

Panipati, Sayyid Wahidud Din Saleem. *Lektur: Musulmanun Key Mawjūda Ta'limīy Halet Per.* Agra: Matb'a Mufid-i 'Aam, 1895.

Qureshīy, Naseem. *Aligarh Tahrīk: Aghaz tā Imroze.* Lucknow: Muslim Press, 1960.

Rahman, Nur al. *Tadhkirā Sir Sayyid Ahmad Khan.* Agra: Shamsīy Machine Press, 1925.

Razaqqiy, Shahid Husain. *Sir Sayyid Awr Islah-i Mu'āshirah.* Lahore: Adarah Thaqatat-i Islamiya, 1963.

Sadiqiy, Rashid Ahmad. "Sir Sayyid Kā Maghribiy Ta'līm Ka Tassawar Awr Us Ka Nifaḍ Aligarh Mein," *Fiker Wa Nazar. Aligarh: Muslim University,*

April, July, October, 1965; October, 1966; April, October, 1967; January, 1968.

Salimīy, Safdar. *Sir Sayyid: Pakistan Ka Maʿmār-i Awwal.* Lahore: Adarah Talūʿa-i Islam, 1967.

Sana-Allah, Muhammad. *Risalah Conference Mutʿaliq Tamadan Wa MaʿShirat.* Lahore: Hamidiyah Steam Press, n.d.

Sherwanīy, Mawlana Muhammad Habīb ur-Rahman. *Waqār-i Hayat.* Aligarh: Muslim University Press, 1925.

Shirwānīy, Muhammad Muqtada Khan. *Khutbāt-i Sadarat: Panjah Sala Jublīy Munʿaqidah, March 1937.* Aligarh: Shirwānīy Printing Press, 1938.

Sivaprasad, Raja, C.S.I. *Strictures Upon The Strictures of Sayyid Ahmad Khan Bahadur C.S.I.* Benares: Medical Hall Press, 1870.

Wedderburn, Sir William. *Allan Octavian Hume.* London: T. Fisher Urwin, 1913.

Zaka-Allah, Mawlavi Muhammed. *Makāram al-Akhlāq.* Delhi: Mataʿba Murtadwi, 1891.

Zubairīy, Mawlavi Anwar Ahmad. *Khutbāt-i ʿAāliya: All-India Muslim Educational Conference Kay Chehl Salah Khutbāt-i Sadarat Ka Majmūʿa.* Vol. 1 (1886–1906); Vol. 2 (1907–1916); Vol. 3 (1917–1927). Aligarh: Muslim University Press, 1927, 1928.

—— *Muraqqʿā-i Conference: All-India Muslim Educational Conference Kay Pantiyalīs-Sala Ijlāsawn Key Kayfīyat (1886–1834) Wa Pass-Shūdah Resolutionun Key Fahrist.* Aligarh: Muslim University Press, 1935.

Zubairīy, Muhammad Amīn. *Hayat-i Mohsin.* Aligarh: Muslim University Press, 1934.

—— *Tadhkīra-i Waqār.* Aligarh: Muslim University Press, 1938.

Index

Abbasid Caliphate (750-1258), 3, 10, 23, 59, 86, 235

Abid, Kalb-i, 163

'Abd al-Wahhāb, Muhammad (1703-87), 11

'Abdūl Azīz, Shah (d.1823), 8, 41, 57, 71, 74, 111, 135, 255, 269

Abdullah, Muhammad bin, 201

Abū Bakr (632-34), 12, 178

Ackland, Lord, 122

Afghanistan, 15, 18, 19, 60, 116, 154, 285

Agricultural experiments, 88-89

Ahmad, Farīd al-Din, 60-61, 63, 64-65, 67-69

Ahmad, Muhammad (1844-85), founder of the mehdiyya movement in the Sudan, 11

Ahmad, Nazir, 50, 53

Aimak, 18

Akbar, Emperor (1556-1605), 25, 114

Akbar Shah II (1806-37), 28, 34, 64, 65

Akhbar Institute Gazette, 89

Al-'Abbas, Ibn abd al-Muttalib, 59

Al-Afghani, Sayyid Jamal-al-Din, 6, 9, 237

Al-Din, Shah Kabir, 91

Alexander, C. W. W., 163

Ali, al-, Imdād, 201

Al, Chaudhary Rahmat, 236

Ali, ibn Abi Tālib (656-61), 12, 59, 236

Ali, Justice Amir, 170-71, 282

Ali, Khurram, 44, 45, 259

Ali, Mawlana Muhammad, 290

Ali, Mawlana Shawkat, 290

Ali, Mawlavi Nawazish, 72

Ali, Qadi Muhammad bin (Ala al-Din al-Haskafiy), 134

Ali, Sayyid Turab, 106

Aligarh Educational Committee, 92-93

Aligarh graduates in government service, 216

Aligarh Movement, 38, 101, 281, 291, 292

Aligarh Muslim University, 101, 222, 265, 282, 289

Allah, Mawlana Makhsūs, 72

Allah, Zaka, 49-50, 53

All-India Muslim League, 218, 221, 238, 291

All-India National Congress, 84, 123, 229, 238, 246, 248, 250, 252, 282, 284-85

Andrews, Charles F., 49

Angad, Guru, 157

Anjuman Himayat-i Islam, Lahore, 282

Anjuman Mufiynd-i Islam, Madras, 282
Anjuman Traqqi-i Urdu, 227
Anjuman-i Islamia Punjab, 202
Anjuman-i Punjab, 163-67, 201
Apostolic traditions, 266-73
Apter, David, 22
'Aqīqah (ritual sacrifice at child's birth), 43
'Arabi, al-, Muhiy al-Din ibn, 60
'Araf, Zaiyn al-'Abidīyn, 57
Argyll, Duke of (George Douglas Campbell), 88, 94, 95, 123
Aristocratic nationalism, 241-44
Arnold, T. W., 155
'Arshīy, Imtiaz Ali Khan, 33
Arya Samaj, 245-47
Asaf-al-Daulah, Nawab, 62
Aurangzeb, Emperor, 25, 28, 36, 38, 45, 61, 121, 139, 157, 239, 260
Awliya, Nizām al-Din, 78
Azad, Abul Kalam (1888-1958), 11, 38, 57, 283, 286-88, 289
Azerbaijanis, 18
Azurdah, Mufti Sadr-ud-Din, 34

Bahadur Shah I, 25
Bahadur Shah II (1837-58), 25, 28, 31, 33, 34, 38, 73, 78
Bakht, Prince Jawan, 29
Bakhtiar, Yahya, 16
Bakhtiaris, 18
Baluch, 18
Barī, Mawlana 'Abdūl, 289
Bayt al-Hikmah, 179
Beck, Theodore, 248
Bedan, Cecil, 83
Beg, Mirza Khuda Dad, 94
Begum, Husan Jahan, 57
Begum, Nawab Sikander, 90
Bharata Warsha National Association, 245
Bharatiya Sahitya Prishad, 227
Bhutto, Z. A., 16, 293, 294
Bid'a (impious innovation), 41, 42, 256-57, 258-59, 261-62
Bigi, Mūsa Jarallah (1875-1949), 6
Bijnor Rebellion, 104-10
Blockmann, H., 76, 140
British East India Company, 21, 30, 32, 36, 39, 49, 57, 61, 74, 83, 91, 105, 108, 111

British-Egyptian condominium over the Sudan, 7
British Indian Association, 189-90, 191, 193
Britton, John Elliot, 97
Brohi, A. K., 16
Boer War, 249
Bolingbroke, Henry St. John, 244
Bubi, Abdullah, 6
Buddhism, 181

Calcutta Madressah (Madressah Aliyah), 63
Caliphate, 1, 9-11, 235, 238, 281
Canning, Lord, 83
Capitalism, 97-98
Central Asian Muslim states, 6
Chakravarty, Shyam Sunder, 287
Chand, Lala Malūk, 68-69
Chander, Babu Noveen, 164
Chandra, Ram, 52
Christendom, 2
Christianity, 2, 50, 181
Colvin, Sir Auckland, 83, 84, 285
Colvin, B. W., 89
Colvin, J. C., 89
Committee for the Better Diffusion and Advancement of Learning among Muhammadans of India, 126-36, 194
Congress of Berlin, 4
Council of Islamic ideology, 293
Counter-jihād, 3
Crusades, the, 3-4
Cultural identity, 256; vs. cultural assimilation, 41-46
Cunningham, Major George, 32

Dagh, Nawab Mirza Khan, 56
Dampier, H. L., 162
Dar al-Islam (land of Islam), 1
Dar-al-Harb (the land of war), 8
Dars-i Nizamiyya, 72
Darwin, Charles, 175, 275-76; theory of evolution, 276-77
Das, Raja Jaikishan, 88, 265
Dassi, Shriniti Rasmure, 91
Dehlawi, Sayyid Ahmad, 25
Delhi College, 24, 48-50, 52-60, 71, 159
Delhi Sultanate, 250

Democracy, Image of, 238
Deoband Dar al-'ulūm, 10, 223-24
De Tassy, Garcin, 76, 88
Deutsch, Karl W., 47, 48
Devonport, John, 100
Doctrine of necessity, 15-17
Doctrine of original intention, 10-11

Education Commission, 92
Educational Conference: annual sessions, 220; total resolutions, 221-28
Educational Congress' latent political functions, 219
Educational experiments, 187-91
Egalitarian mass education, 101
Egypt, 15
Elitist education, 101
Ellenborough, Lord, 122
Ethnic communities, 18-19
Ethnic tensions, 17-18
Exposure to the West, 94-100

Faḍl, Abul, 44, 76, 258
Fard (obligation), 42
Fitrat, Abdur Rauf, 6
Fort William College, 58
Francklin, William, 37
Frazer, William, 57
Functional secularism, 291

Galiev, Mīr Sa'īd Sultan (1880-1939), 7
Gandhi, Mahatma, 249
Ganj-i Shakar, Shaikh Farīd al-Din Mas'ūd, 157
Gasprinski, Isma'īl Bey (1851-1914), 6
Ghālib, Asad Allah Khan, 34, 57-58, 78-79
Ghayba, the doctrine of (Imam Muhammad Hujattallah, al-Mehdi's "hidden presence"), 13
Ghazzali, al-, Abu Hamid, 179
Ghuzzīy, al-, Shams al-Din Muhammad Abdullah, 134
Gilchrist, Dr. John, 58
God's word and work, 275
Graham, Col. George F. Irving, 85-87, 95
Griffin, Lepel, 162
Gurmukhi, 157

Haderly, Captain Alexander, 57
Haiy, al-, 'Abd, 46, 261

Hakīm, al-, Allamah 'Abd, 156
Hali, Altaf Husain, 51, 82, 171
Hamid, Sayyid, 81, 94
Hamilton, Sir Robert, 73
Hanafi, al-, Jamal Ibn al-Abd Allah Umar, 84
Hanīfah, Abū, 271
Haq, al-, Shaikh 'Abd, 135
Harbans, Raja, 163
Hasan, al-, Mawlavi Faiz, 71
Hasan al-Bannā' (1906-49), 11
Hasan, Mawlavi Awlād, 260
Hatta, Muhammad, 99
Hindu-Muslim cultural synthesis, 25-26
Hindu-Muslim struggle for power, 250
Hindu Widows' Remarriage Act XV (1856), 112
Hazara, 18
Hume, A. O., 84, 123, 284-85
Hunter, W. W., 62, 128, 140, 142
Husain, Dr. Abid, 248, 290
Husain, al-, Imam, 35, 45, 59, 259
Husain, Mir Waliyat, 248
Husain, Qadi Muhammad, 44, 45, 259
Husain, Dr. Zakir, 289-290

Ibn al-Saud, House of, 7
Ibn Khaldun (1332-1406), 15, 16, 236
Ibn Tamiya (1263-1328), 15, 16
Ibrahimov, Abdur Rashid, 6
'Iddā (waiting period for a widow), 43
Ijma' (consensus), 201
Ijtihād (the right of interpreting the Qur'ān and the sunna or of forming a new opinion by applying analogy), 6-7, 171, 185, 241
Ikhwān al-Muslimīn (Muslim Brotherhood of Egypt and Syria), 11
Imam (the shi'ite term for caliph), 12; Ja'fer al-Sādiq (d.765), 13; Mūsa al-Kazim, 13; Isma'īl, 13; Muhammad Hujjat Allah, surnamed al-Mehdi (the guide), 13; hidden, 14
Imperialism, 4, 9
Inam Commission, 113
Indian Civil Service (ICS), 22, 36, 247, 287
Indian Councils Act (1861), 123
Indic Islamic Culture, 41
Institute Gazette, 248

Interest articulation and aggregation, 219-20

Iqbal, Dr. Muhammad, 99, 236, 266, 267, 283, 295

Iran, 18, 19, 60

Iranian constitution (1979), 13-14

Iranian ruling elite, 5-6

Iraq, 17, 18, 19

Ishaq, Hunayn b., 178

Islam, 1-2; confrontation with the west, 2-5; fundamentalist, 9-10, 11, 12, 19; shi'īte fundamentalism, 12, 15; secularist, 10, 20; modernist, 14-15, 17, 19, 20; Islamic system, 9-10, 15, 20; fiscal system, 20; demythologizing of, 273-77

Islamic civilization and Greek sciences, 23

Islamic culture paradigm, 10-13, 41-42

Islamic fundamentalism, 7-8, 10-13, 19, 292-93, 294

Islamic militancy, ix

Islamic obscurantism, 23

Islamic state, 8, 10-11, 12, 20, 201

Islamization, 256-57, 261

Isrā (Prophet's ascension), 275-76

Jahangir, Emperor, 25

Jahiliyah (pre-Islamic ignorance), 43, 257, 260

Jama't-i Islami, 10-11, 283

Jami'at'ulamā'-i Hind, 10, 283

Jami'at'ulamā'-i Islam, 292

Jamia Millia Islamia, New Delhi, 289-90

Jan, Muhammad, 163

Jang, Nawab Ghazi-ud-Din Firuz, 48

Jang, Sir Salar, 55

Jawnpurīy, Karamat Ali, 44, 45, 259

Jerusalem, Conquest of, 2

Jinnah, Muhammad Ali, 283, 291, 294

Jizya (poll-tax on non-Muslims), 11

Kalash, 18

Karkhanadar (worker) culture, 26-28

Kashmiri Muslim, 18

Kay, Sir John William, 95

Kazim, al-, Mūsa, 13

Kelsen, Hans, 15

Kempson, M., 125, 132, 137-40

Khan, Ali Bakhsh, 201

Khan, Ali Mardan, 37

Khan, Allama Taffadal Husain, 62

Khan, Ambassador Haji Muhammad Khalīl, 63

Khan, Amir Kabir Taqi, 6

Khan, Barkat Ali, 202

Khan, Hakīm Ahsan Allah, 74

Khan, Hakīm Ajnal, 290

Khan, Hashim Ali, 78

Khan, Inshā Allah, 34, 242

Khan, Itimad-ud-Daulah Sayyid Fadl Ali, 49

Khan, Khalīl Allah, 73

Khan, Khan Bahadur Rahīm, 163

Khan, Khawjah Zayn al- 'Abidīyn, 71

Khan, Mahdi Ali, 100, 246, 265

Khan, Mawlavi 'Abd al-Latīf, 87, 170, 171, 231, 282

Khan, Muhammad Nabīy, 63

Khan, Muhammad Sam'īy Allah, 202, 203, 214, 248

Khan, Nawab 'Abdūl Majid, 163

Khan, Nawab Ghazi-ud-Din, 37

Khan, Nawab Kalbi Ali, 90

Khan, Nawab Mahmūd Khan, 105-108

Khan, Nawab Sa'd Allah, 156

Khan, Rahmat, 108, 109

Khan, Sa'dat, 37

Khan, Sa'dat Ali, 63

Khan, Sir Sayyid Ahmad, x, 8-9, 20; framework of modernity, 21-58; political socialization, 59-66; 82-84; Muslim nationalist, 77; remorse for collaboration with British, 80-83; scientific society, 84-94; agricultural experiments, 88-90; British Indian Association, 91-93; exposure to the west, 94-100; perceptions of 1857, 103-4; revolt in Bijnor, 104-9; causes for India's revolt, 110-18; theory of Participatory rule, 118-23; Muslim reaction to modern education, 125-72; national will for modern education, 173-74; theory of national progress, 175-86; educational experiments, 187-93; stratified education for differentiated social system, 194-197; MAO College, 198-217; Muhammadan Educational

Conference, 174-228; role of Urdu, 226-28; theory of Muslim nationalism, 229-53; image of democracy, 238-40; aristocratic nationalism, 241-43; relations with Congress, 248-52; religious modernism, 255-79; social reforms, 258-65; paradigm for cultural change, 262-63
Khan, Wahīd al-Din, 78
Khedive Ismaʿīl, 5
Khomeini, Ayatollah, 13
Kurd, 18
Kurghiz, 18

Laissez-faire, role of government, 182-86
Lake, Lord, 30, 64
Lal, Chaman, 52
Lal, Raja Sohan, 73
Lal, Sham Bihari, 204
Lawrence, Sir John, 94-95
Leitner, G. W., 163
Lenin, V. I., 4
Liberal nationalism, 81
Lindsay, C. R., 163
Lurs, 18
Lyall, A. C., 139, 172
Lytton, Lord, 123, 203

Maclagan, Col. R., 163
Madni, Maulana Husain Ahmad, 223-24
Madressah-i Frangīy Mahal, 72
Madressah-i Ghazi-ud-Din (Delhi College), 48
Mahmud, Sayyid, 81, 94, 95, 96, 198
Majid, Sultan ʿAbdūl, 237
Majlis-i Ahrar, 10, 283
Makiyn, Mirza Muhammad Fakher, 33
Makrūh (undesirable), 42
Maʿmar, Ustad Ahmad, 156
Mandūb (desirable), 42
Manglori, Sayyid Tufayle Ahmad, 248
Mansurov, Burhan (d.1937), 7
MAO College: allocation of resources to, 198-206; religious composition, 211-12; graduates compared to other universities' Muslim graduates, 215
Marathas, 29, 30, 61, 62, 65, 66
Marjani, Shihab-ud-Din (1818-99), 6
Marriage and funeral customs, 257-58

Marx, Karl, 96, 182
Marxist nationalism, 7
Masjid al-Aqsa, 276
Masʿūd, Ross, 265
Maudūdi, Abul Ala (1903-79), 11, 286
Mayo, Lord, 125, 140
McLeod, Sir Donald, 164
Mehdi of Sudan, 7, 11
Mehdiyya movement (1881-99), 7, 11
Metcalf, Sir Charles, 49
Mirza, Iskander (Pakistan's former President), 16
Modernist Muslims, 5, 6, 286, 291, 295
Modernization, ix, x, 19-20, 21-24, 40, 261, 269, 282
Momin, Hakim Momin Khan, 34
Mughal, 30, 66
Mughal Empire, 2, 74
Mughal mansabdars, 36-37
Mughal royalty, 28-30, 36
Muhammad, Ghulam (Pakistan's former Governor General), 16
Muhammad, the Prophet (571-632), 10-11, 19, 35, 42, 45, 59, 74, 100, 183, 273-75
Muhammad Shah, Emperor, 37
Muhammadan Anglo-Oriental College, 101, 127, 167, 172, 174, 198-217, 247, 248
Muhammadan Civil Service Fund Association, 247
Muhammadan Defense Association, 248-49
Muhammadan Educational Conference, 174-228, 248, 263, 265
Muhammadan Literary Society, Calcutta, 87, 282
Muhani, Mawlana Hasrat, 290
Muhsin al-Mulk, 207
Muir, Sir William, 94, 100, 139, 199
Mumtaz Mahal, 35
Munir, Chief Justice Muhammad, 16
Muslim contribution to Punjab University, 163-67
Muslim education (Punjab), 152-58; Central Provinces (Mysore, Coorg, and Berar), 150-51; Awadh, 148-49; Bombay and Sindh, 146-48; Madras, 145-46; Bengal, 143-44; Muslim reaction to

Muslim education (*Continued*)
  modern education, 125-72; Muslim reaction to scientific education, 133-35; Muslim student population in government institutions, 137
Muslim elites, 36-40; traditional elites, 39
Muslim-English intermarriage, 56-57
Muslim nationalism, 77, 82, 174, 229-53; and the Caliphate, 235-38
Muttaqīy, Sayyid Muhammad, 60-62, 64-65, 74

Najib-ud-Daulah, 29, 105
Nanak, Guru, 155, 157
Nasir-ud-Din, Shah, 6
Nath, Raja Kaydar, 66
Nation, conception of, 244-45
National Communism, 7
National Muhammadan Association, 247
Nationalism: definition, 230-32; aristocratic, 241
Natural selection, 277-78
Nechari (naturist), 267
Nehru, Jawaharlal, 38, 286
Newtonian view of nature, 274-75
Nisa, al-, 'Azīz, 61, 67, 69-71
Nizam, Shaikh, 156
Nizam-ul-Mulk, 48
Normatively oriented action, 186-87
Nu'mani, Shibli, 171
Nuristani, 18

Ochterlony, Sir David, 56-57, 63
Ottoman empire, 3-5

Pakistan, 12, 286, 291, 293, 295; political development, 15
Pakistan Resolution, 238
Pan-Islamism, 9-10
Pareto's theory of social elites, 291
Pashtun, 18
Pax Britannia, 31
Permanent Settlement Act (1793), 141
Pfander, Rev. C. G., 100
Phūl Wallūñ key seyr (a promenade of the flower gatherers), 35
Pirzada, Sharifuddin, 16
Pope Urban, 3

Post Office Act (1866), 92
Pre-Islamic customs, 259
Princep, James, 54
Proletarian nations, 7
Prophet Muhammad's Medina Covenant, 288-89
Punjab University, 163-67, 170
Punjabi, 155-57
Punjabi Muslim, 18
Pye, Lucian W., 23, 40

Qanawjī, Hasan, 44, 259
Qashqais, 18
Qur'ānic interpretations, 266-69
Qutb, Sayyid, 11

Radhakishan, Pandit, 106
Rahbar: and the constitutional position of Ayatollah Kohmeini, 13-14
Rahman, al-, Shaikh 'Abd, 201
Rai, Nobina Chandra, 163
Ram, Bakhshi, 106
Ranke, Leopold von, 4
Ray, Raja Sukh, 66
Razi, al-, Fakher al-Din, 185
Red Fort, Delhi, 25, 29-30, 31-32, 34, 37, 56, 65, 78, 156
Religious Disabilities Act XXI (1850), 112
Religious pluralism, 278
Representative government, 250
Revelation and natural law, 268-69
Revenue settlements, 114-15
Revolt in Bijnor, 104-10
Revolutionary legality, Hans Kelsen's doctrine of, 15-16
Rewanshaw, E. C., 55
Rezah, Taj, 235
Ripon, Lord, 123, 247
Roberts, A. A., 75, 76
Roberts, Sir Abraham, 97
Rohila, Ghulam Qadir, 29
Russian empire, 6
Rylan, Sir Edward, 55

Sadiq, al-, Ja'fer, 13
Sahbai'y, Imam Bakhsh, 34
Sales Laws or Regulation VII, 114

Sapte, B., 87
Saudi Arabia, 12; Saudi fundamentalists, 19
Sawda, Mirza Muhammad Rafī', 33
Scientific Society, 84-90
Secularism vs. modernity, 282
Seton, Charles, 57
Shah Alam (1759-1806), 28, 29, 30, 31, 33, 34, 57
Shah, Emperor Fateh Ali, 63
Shah Jahan, Mughal Emperor (1628-58), 24, 25, 60, 61, 116, 139, 156
Shah, Muhammad, 163
Shahīd, Isma'īl (1879-31), 8, 11, 41, 46-47, 75, 156, 255, 264
Shahīd, Sayyid Ahmad (1786-1831), 8, 11, 41, 44, 46-47, 75, 156, 255, 258, 261
Shaiftah, Nawab Ghulam Mustafa Khan, 34
Shakespeare, Alexander, 106
Shams-ud-Din, Faqīr, 163
Shari'a (Islamic Canon Laws), 8, 11, 12, 15, 31, 41, 224, 236, 239, 282, 287, 295
Sharīf (superior) culture, 26-28, 38; society, 38
Shi'a, 44-45, 47, 74, 105, 259, 261
Shi'ite fundamentalism, 12-14
Shirk (identifying anything with God), 46
Shivaji festivals, 245
Shukoh, Prince Dara, 37, 61
Siba'i, al-,Shaikh Mustafa, 11
Sindhi Muslim, 18
Singh, Guru Gobind, 155
Singh, Maharaja Ranjit, 67, 117, 156
Singh, Rai Mul, 163
Singh, Sardar Dayal, 244
Sipahsalar, Mirza Husain Khan, 6
Smith, Adam, 182-83
Social radicalism, 99
Social reforms, 259-66
Socialist Muslims, 7
Sovereignty, a gift of God, 249
Soviet Union, 18, 238
Stanley of Alderly, Lord, 95
Stephen, Sir J. Fitz-James, 140
Strachey, Sir Edward, 97
Subject political culture, 31
Sukarno, Ahmed, 99

Sultan Mahmud Ghaznavi, 1, 155
Sultan Salim I, 3
Sunna, 7, 11, 41, 256-57, 265, 293
Sunna al-umma (tribal model behavior), 41
Sunni, 10-11, 105
Syria, 17

Tabīyn al-Kalam, 90
Tagore, Dawarka Nath, 55
Tahdhīb al-Akhlāq, 194, 200, 232, 242, 270, 279
Tajik, 18
Tanzīmāt (Reorganization), 5
Taqlīd (submission to traditional authority), 7, 185, 269
Tayabji, Justice Bader-ud-Din, 170, 171, 282-85
Ta'zīyah (mourning procession), 259
Thabit, Zayd Ibn, 178
Thaqlain, al-, Khawja Ghulam, 263
Thomas, Edward, 75
Tilak, 245
Toynbee, Arnold, 21-22
Transnational orientations, 19
Treveleyan, Sir Charles, 86
Turkey, 5, 9, 10, 20
Turkish Caliphate, 237-38
Turkish Republic, 238
Turkoman, 18

'Umar ibn al-Khattāb, 2
Umayyad Calipate (661-749), 1, 44, 59, 86, 235, 259
Urdu, 26, 28, 33, 34, 37, 49, 54-55, 57, 75, 89, 93, 131, 152, 154, 158, 160, 162, 165, 189, 190, 221; the role of, 226-28, 245, 281
Urdu-Hindi conflicts, 93, 133, 245-46
'Usher (tithe), 11, 295
Usurpation of power, 15-16
Uthman (644-56), 12
Uzbek, 18

Vahitov, Mulla-Nur (1885-1918), 7
Vernacular University, 93
Viceroy's Legislative Council, 251

Wahdat al-Wujūd (unitarian monism), 60
Wahhabism, 7; Wahhabi doctrines, 75
Wakf l-awalad (Islamic family endowment),
  243
Walīy Allah, Shah (1703-63), 8, 41, 42, 44,
  47, 73, 179, 255-58, 261-62, 266-69
Walīyma (wedding feast), 43
Wedderburn, Sir William, 84, 285

Wellesley, Lord, 30, 63
Wilson, Crecraft, 109

Zaiyn, Ahmad bin, 201
Zaka (mandatory charity), 11, 295
Zawq, Ibrahim, 34
Zia-ul-Haq, Chief of Army Staff, 16, 17,
  295

Translations from the Oriental Classics

Major Plays of Chikamatsu, tr. Donald Keene   1961

Four Major Plays of Chikamatsu, tr. Donald Keene. Paperback text edition.   1961

Records of the Grand Historian of China, translated from the Shih chi of Ssu-ma Ch'ien, tr. Burton Watson, 2 vols.   1961

Instructions for Practical Living and Other Neo-Confucian Writings by Wang Yang-ming tr. Wing-tsit Chan   1963

Chuang Tzu: Basic Writings, tr. Burton Watson, paperback ed. only   1964

The Mahābhārata, tr. Chakravarthi V. Narasimhan. Also in paperback ed.   1965

The Manyōshū, Nippon Gakujutsu Shinkōkai edition   1965

Su Tung-p'o: Selections from a Sung Dynasty Poet, tr. Burton Watson. Also in paperback ed.   1965

Bhartrihari: Poems, tr. Barbara Stoler Miller. Also in paperback ed.   1967

Basic Writings of Mo Tzu, Hsün Tzu, and Han Fei Tzu, tr. Burton Watson. Also in separate paperback eds.   1967

The Wakening of Faith, Attributed to Aśvaghosha, tr. Yoshito S. Hakeda. Also in paperback ed.   1967

Reflections on Things at Hand: The Neo-Confucian Anthology, comp. Chu Hsi and Lü Tsu-ch'ien, tr. Wing-tsit Chan   1967

The Platform Sutra of the Sixth Patriarch, tr. Philip B. Yampolsky. Also in paperback ed.   1967

Essays in Idleness: the Tsurezuregusa of Kenkō, tr. Donald Keene. Also in paperback ed.   1967

The Pillow Book of Sei Shōnagon, tr. Ivan Morris, 2 vols. 1967

Two Plays of Ancient India: The Little Clay Cart and the Minister's Seal, tr. J. A. B van Buitenen 1968

The Complete Works of Chuang Tzu, tr. Burton Watson 1968

The Romance of the Western Chamber (Hsi Hsiang chi), tr. S. I. Hsiung. Also in paperback ed. 1968

The Manyōshū, Nippon Gakujutsu Shinkōkai edition. Paperback text edition. 1969

Records of B. Historian: Chapters from the Shih chi of Ssu-ma Ch'ien. Paperback text edition, tr. Burton Watson 1969

Cold Mountain: 100 Poems by the T'ang Poet Han-shan, tr. Burton Watson. Also in paperback ed. 1970

Twenty Plays of the No Theatre, ed. Donald Keene. Also in paperback ed. 1970

Chūshingura: The Treasury of Loyal Retainers, tr. Donald Keene. Also in paperback ed. 1971

The Zen Master Hakuin: Selected Writings, tr. Philip B. Yampolsky 1971

Chinese Rhyme-Prose: Poems in the Fu Form from the Han and Six Dynasties Periods, tr. Burton Watson. Also in paperback ed. 1971

Kūkai: Major Works, tr. Yoshito S. Hakeda 1972

The Old Man Who Does as He Pleases: Selections from the Poetry and Prose of Lu Yu, tr. Burton Watson 1973

The Lion's Roar of Queen Śrīmālā, tr. Alex and Hideko Wayman 1974

Courtier and Commoner in Ancient China: Selections from the History of The Former Han by Pan Ku, tr. Burton Watson. Also in paperback ed. 1974

Japanese Literature in Chinese. Vol. I: Poetry and Prose in Chinese by Japanese Writers of the Early Period, tr. Burton Watson 1975

Japanese Literature in Chinese. Vol. II: Poetry and Prose in Chinese by Japanese Writers of the Later Period, tr. Burton Watson 1976

Scripture of the Lotus Blossom of the Fine Dharma, tr. Leon Hurvitz. Also in paperback ed. 1976

Love Song of the Dark Lord: Jayadeva's Gītagovinda, tr. Barbara Stoler Miller. Also in paperback ed. Cloth ed. includes critical text of the Sanskrit. 1977

Ryōkan: Zen Monk-Poet of Japan, tr. Burton Watson 1977

Calming the Mind and Discerning the Real: From the Lam rim chen mo of
Tsoṅ-kha-pa, tr. Alex Wayman   1978

The Hermit and the Love-Thief: Sanskrit Poems of Bhartrihari and Bilhaṇa,
tr. Barbara Stoler Miller. Also in paperback ed.   1978

The Lute: Kao Ming's P'i-p'a chi, tr. Jean Mulligan. Also in paperback
ed.   1980

Modern Asian Literature

Modern Japanese Drama: An Anthology, ed. and tr. Ted T. Takaya   1979

Nepali Visions, Nepali Dreams: Selections from the Poetry of Laxmiprasad
Devkota, tr. David Rubin   1980

Mask and Sword: Two Plays for the Comtemporary Japanese Theater, by
Yamazaki Masakazu, tr. J. Thomas Rimer   1980

Yokomitsu Riichi, Modernist, by Dennis Keene   1980

Studies in Oriental Culture

1. The Ōnin War: History of Its Origins and Background, with a Selective
   Translation of the Chronicle of Ōnin, by H. Paul Varley   1967

2. Chinese Government in Ming Times: Seven Studies, ed. Charles O.
   Hucker   1969

3. The Actors' Analects (Yakusha Rongo), ed. and tr. by Charles J.
   Dunn and Bunzō Torigoe   1969

4. Self and Society in Ming Thought, by Wm. Theodore de Bary and
   the Conference on Ming Thought. Also in paperback ed.   1970

5. A History of Islamic Philosophy, by Majid Fakhry   1970

6. Phantasies of a Love Thief: The Caurapañcāśikā Attributed to Bilhaṇa,
   by Barbara Stoler Miller   1971

7. Iqbal: Poet-Philosopher of Pakistan, ed. Hafeez Malik   1971

8. The Golden Tradition: An Anthology of Urdu Poetry, by Ahmed Ali.
   Also in paperback ed.   1973

9. Conquerors and Confucians: Aspects of Political Change in Late Yüan
   China, by Jorn W. Dardess   1973

10. The Unfolding of Neo-Confucianism, by Wm. Theodore de Bary and
    the Conference on Seventeenth-Century Chinese Thought. Also
    in paperback ed.   1975

11. *To Acquire Wisdom: The Way of Wang Yang-ming,* by Julia Chiang   1976

12. *Gods, Priests, and Warriors: The Bhṛgus of the Mahābhārata,* by Robert P. Goldman   1977

13. *Mei Yao-ch'en and the Development of Early Sung Poetry,* by Jonathan Chaves   1976

14. *The Legend of Seminaru, Blind Musician of Japan,* by Susan Matisoff   1977

15. *Sir Sayyid Ahmad Khan and Muslim Modernization in India and Pakistan,* by Hafeez Malik   1980

Neo-Confucian Studies

Instructions for Practical Living and Other Neo-Confucian Writings by Wang Yang-ming, tr. Wing-tsit Chan   1963

Reflections on Things at Hand: The Neo-Confucian Anthology, comp. Chu Hsi and Lü Tsu-ch'ien, tr. Wing-tsit Chan   1967

Self and Society in Ming Thought, by Wm. Theodore de Bary and the Conference on Ming Thought. Also in paperback ed.   1970

The Unfolding of Neo-Confucianism, by Wm. Theodore de Bary and the Conference on Seventeenth-Century Chinese Thought. Also in paperback ed.   1975

Principle and Practicality: Essays in Neo-Confucianism and Practical Learning, ed. Wm. Theodore de Bary and Irene Bloom. Also in paperback ed.   1979

The Syncretic Religions of Lin Chao-en, by Judith A. Berling   1980

Companions to Asian Studies

Approaches to the Oriental Classics, ed. Wm. Theodore de Bary   1959

Early Chinese Literature, by Burton Watson. Also in paperback ed.   1962

Approaches to Asian Civilizations, ed. Wm. Theodore de Bary and Ainslie T. Embree   1964

The Classic Chinese Novel: A Critical Introduction, by C. T. Hsia. Also in paperback ed.   1968

Chinese Lyricism: Shih Poetry from the Second to the Twelfth Century, tr. Burton Watson. Also in paperback ed.   1971

A Syllabus of Indian Civilization, by Leonard A. Gordon and Barbara Stoler Miller   1971

Twentieth-Century Chinese Stories, ed. C. T. Hsia and Joseph S. M. Lau. Also in paperback ed.   1971

A Syllabus of Chinese Civilization, by J. Mason Gentzler, 2d ed.   1972

A Syllabus of Japanese Civilization, by H. Paul Varley, 2d ed.   1972

An Introduction to Chinese Civilization, ed. John Meskill, with the assistance of J. Mason Gentzler   1973

An Introduction to Japanese Civilization, ed. Arthur E. Tiedemann   1974

A Guide to Oriental Classics, ed. Wm. Theodore de Bary and Ainslie T. Embree, 2d ed. Also in paperback ed.   1975

Introduction to Oriental Civilizations
Wm. Theodore de Bary, *Editor*

Sources of Japanese Tradition 1958   Paperback ed., 2 vols. 1964
Sources of Indian Tradition   1958   Paperback ed., 2 vols. 1964
Sources of Chinese Tradition 1960   Paperback ed., 2 vols. 1964